Disclaimer

The publisher of this book is by no way associated with the National Institute of Standards and Technology (NIST). The NIST did not publish this book. It was published by 50 page publications under the public domain license.

50 Page Publications.

Book Title: Committee Reports for the 90th National Conference on Weights and Measures, July 10-14, 2005, Orlando, FL (SP1037)

Book Author: Linda D. Crown; L T. Sebring

Book Abstract: The 90th Annual Meeting of the National Conference on Weights and Measures was held in Orlando, FL, July 10-14, 2005. The theme of the conference was 100 Years of Equity in the Marketplace. The NCWM develops and recommends laws and regulations, technical codes for weighing and measuring devices used in commerce, tests methods, enforcement procedures, and administrative guidelines for adoption by regulatory agencies in the interest of promoting uniformity of requirements and methods in state and local jurisdictions. The annual meeting brings together government officials and representatives of business, industry, trade associations, and consumer organizations for the purpose of hearing and discussing subjects that relate to the field of weights and measures technology.

Citation:

Keyword:

REPORT OF THE 90TH NATIONAL CONFERENCE ON WEIGHTS AND MEASURES

NIST
United States
Department of
Commerce

Technology
Administration

National
Institute of
Standards and
Technology

as adopted by
the 90th
National
Conference on
Weights and
Measures 2005

National Conference on Weights and Measures
100 YEARS of EQUITY IN THE MARKETPLACE

NIST
Special
Publication **1037**
2005

Report of the 90th National Conference on Weights and Measures

Orlando, FL – July 10 through 14, 2005
as adopted by the 90th National Conference on Weights and Measures 2005

Editors:
Kenneth Butcher
Linda Crown
Lynn Sebring
Technical Advisors to the Standing Committees

National Institute of Standards and Technology
Weights and Measures Division
Gaithersburg, MD 20899-2600

U.S. Department of Commerce
Carlos M. Gutierrez, Secretary

Technology Administration
Michelle O'Neill, Acting Under Secretary of Commerce for Technology

National Institute of Standards and Technology
William Jeffrey, Director

NIST Special Publication **1037**

November 2005

The National Conference on Weights and Measures is supported by the National Institute of Standards and Technology and is attended by officials from various States, counties, cities, as well as representatives from U.S. Government, other nations, industry, and consumer organizations.

Abstract

The 90th Annual Meeting of the National Conference on Weights and Measures (NCWM) was held July 10 - 14, 2005, at the Hilton in Walt Disney World, Orlando, Florida. The theme of the meeting was, "100 Years of Equity in the Marketplace."

Reports by the NCWM Board of Directors, Standing Committees, and Special Purpose Committees constitute the major portion of this publication, along with the addresses delivered by Conference officials and other authorities from government and industry.

Special meetings included those of the Scale Manufacturers Association, Meter Manufacturers Association, Gasoline Pump Manufacturers Association, American Petroleum Institute, National Association of State Departments of Agriculture, the Industry Committee on Packaging and Labeling, and Associate Membership Committee.

Key words: laws and regulations; legal metrology; meters; scales; specifications and tolerances; training; type evaluation; uniform laws; weights and measures.

Library of Congress Catalog Card Number 26-27766.

Note: The policy of the National Institute of Standards and Technology is to use metric units of measurement in all of its publications. In this publication, however, recommendations received by the NCWM technical committees have been printed as they were submitted and, therefore, may contain references to inch-pound units where such units are commonly used in industry practice. Opinions expressed in non-NIST papers are those of the authors and not necessarily those of the National Institute of Standards and Technology. Non-NIST speakers are solely responsible for the content and quality of their material.

Natl. Inst. Stand. Technol. Spec. Pub. 1037, 264 Pages (November 2005) CODEN: NSPUE2

U.S. GOVERNMENT PRINTING OFFICE
WASHINGTON: 2005

For sale by the Superintendent of Documents, U.S. Government Printing Office
Internet: bookstore.gpo.gov – Phone: (202) 512-1800 – Fax: (202) 512-2104
Mail: Stop SSPO, Washington, DC 20402-0001

Table of Contents

Page

Abstract..ii
Past Chairmen of the Conference iv
Organization Chart v

General Session

President's Address – Dr. Hratch Semerjian, National Institute of Standards and Technology..........GS - 1
Chairman's Address – G. Weston Diggs, Virginia Product and Industry Standards...........................GS - 7
New Chairman's Address – Don Onwiler, Nebraska Department of Agriculture/Weights & Measures.............GS - 9
2005 Annual Meeting Honor Award Recipients...GS - 13

Standing Committee Reports

Report of the Board of Directors (BOD)..BOD - 1
    Appendix A. Report on the Activities of the International Organization of Legal Metrology (OIML)
        and Regional Legal Metrology Organizations...BOD - A1
    Appendix B. Associate Membership Committee Annual Meeting Minutes and Summary Report........BOD - B1
        Appendix B1. AMC Funds Allocation...BOD - B5
    Appendix C. NTEP Conformity Assessment Program Update...BOD - C1
        Appendix C1. Initial Verification...BOD - C3
        Appendix C2. Administrative Review of Certificates of Conformance........................BOD - C11
        Appendix C3. Verified Conformity Assessment Program (VCAP) ....BOD - C17

Report of the Committee on Laws and Regulations (L&R)..L&R - 1
    Appendix A. Item 221-1: Documentary Standards..L&R - A1

Report of the Committee on Specifications and Tolerances (S&T) ....S&T - 1
    Appendix A. Item 360-1: Proposed Section 5.59..S&T - A1
    Appendix B. Item 360-2: Appendix A Fundamental Considerations...................................S&T - B1
    Appendix C. Item 360-5: Developing Issues..S&T - C1

Report of the Professional Development Committee (PDC)..PDC - 1
    Appendix A. Strategic Direction for the PDC..PDC - A1

Report of the National Type Evaluation Program (NTEP) Committee..NTEP - 1
    Appendix A. NTEP Participating Laboratories and Evaluations Report.............................NTEP - A1
    Appendix B. NTETC - GMM and NIR Sector Annual Meetings, Summary of Decisions...................NTEP - B1
    Appendix C. NTETC - Measuring Sector Annual Meeting, Summary of Decisions........................NTEP - C1
    Appendix D. NTETC - Weighing Sector Annual Meeting, Summary of Decisions.........................NTEP - D1
    Appendix E. Provisional Committee on Participation Review (CPR) Meeting Summary..................NTEP - E1

2005 Annual Meeting Attendees ....ATTEND - 1

Past Chairmen of the Conference

Conference Year Chairman

Conference	Year	Chairman
43rd	1958	J. P. McBride, MA
44th	1959	C. M. Fuller, CA
45th	1960	H. E. Crawford, FL
46th	1961	R. E. Meek, IN
47th	1962	Robert Williams, NY
48th	1963	C. H. Stender, SC
49th	1964	D. M. Turnbull, WA
50th	1965	V. D. Campbell, OH
51st	1966	J. F. True, KS
52nd	1967	J. E. Bowen, MA
53rd	1968	C. C. Morgan, IN
54th	1969	S. H. Christie, NJ
55th	1970	R. W. Searles, OH
56th	1971	M. Jennings, TN
57th	1972	E. H. Black, CA
58th	1973	George L. Johnson, KY
59th	1974	John H. Lewis, WA
60th	1975	Sydney D. Andrews, FL
61st	1976	Richard L. Thompson, MD
62nd	1977	Earl Prideaux, CO
63rd	1978	James F. Lyles, VA
64th	1979	Kendrick J. Simila, OR
65th	1980	Charles H. Vincent, TX
66th	1981	Edward H. Stadolnik, MA
67th	1982	Edward C. Heffron, MI
68th	1983	Charles H. Greene, NM
69th	1984	Sam F. Hindsman, AR
70th	1985	Ezio F. Delfino, CA
71st	1986	George E. Mattimoe, HI
72nd	1987	Frank C. Nagele, MI
73rd	1988	Darrell A. Guensler, CA
74th	1989	John J. Bartfai, NY
75th	1990	Fred A. Gerk, NM
76th	1991	N. David Smith, NC
77th	1992	Sidney A. Colbrook, IL
78th	1993	Allan M. Nelson, CT
79th	1994	Thomas F. Geiler, MA
80th	1995	James C. Truex, OH
81st	1996	Charles A. Gardner, NY
82nd	1997	Barbara J. Bloch, CA
83rd	1998	Steven A. Malone, NE
84th	1999	Aves D. Thompson, AK
85th	2000	G. Wes Diggs, VA
86th	2001	L. Straub, MD
87th	2002	Ron Murdock, NC
88th	2003	Ross J. Andersen, NY
89th	2004	Dennis Ehrhart, AZ

National Conference on Weights and Measures, Inc.
Organization Chart
2004/2005

Board of Directors		
Office Representation	**Name/Affiliation**	**Term Expires**
Chairman:	G.W. Diggs, VA*	2005
Chairman-Elect:	D. Onwiler, NE*	2005
NTEP Committee Chair:	J. Truex, OH*	2006
Treasurer:	T. Geiler, MA	2005
Active Membership/Northeastern:	C. Carroll, MA*	2009
Active Membership/Central:	J. Cardin, WI	2005
Active Membership/Southern:	S. Pahl, TX*	2008
Active Membership/Western:	M. Cleary, CA	2007
At-Large:	C. Guay, Proctor & Gamble	2008
At-Large:	M. Pinagel, MI	2006
Associate Membership:	D. Flocken, Mettler-Toledo	2007
*National Type Evaluation Program (NTEP) Committee Member		
Honorary NCWM President:	H. Semerjian, Acting NIST Director	
NCWM Executive Secretary:	H. Oppermann, NIST W&M Division	
NCWM Executive Director:	B. Palys, CAE, NCWM Headquarters	
BOD Advisor:	G. Vinet, Measurement Canada	
NTEP Director:	S. Patoray, NCWM Headquarters	
NTEP Committee Technical Advisor:	S. Cook, NIST W&M Division	

Committees			
Laws & Regulations Committee		**Specifications & Tolerances Committee**	
Position Name/Affiliation	**(Term Expires)**	**Position Name/Affiliation**	**(Term Expires)**
Chair:	J. Gomez, (2005)	Chair:	J. Kane, MT (2005)
Members:	J. Benavides, TX (2006)	Members:	C. Cooney, OR (2006)
	J. Cassidy, MA (2007)		M. Sikula, NY (2007)
	V. Dempsey, OH (2008)		Carol Fulmer, SC (2008)
	D. Johannes, CA (2009)		Todd Lucas, OH (2009)
Associate Member Rep:	V. Orr, ConAgra Foods	Associate Member Rep:	TBD
Canadian Tech Advisors:	D. Hutchinson B. Lemon	Canadian Tech Advisor:	T. Kingsbury
NIST Tech Advisors:	T. Coleman K. Dresser S. Cook	NIST Tech Advisors:	R. Suiter J. Williams

Org Chart

Committees (continued)	
Professional Development Committee	**Metrology Committee**
Chair: K. Deitzler, PA (2006) Members: C. Bennett, MI (2006) A. Shields, OH (2008) J. Buendel, WA (2009) W. Wotthlie, MD (2009) S. Strnad, TX (2009) Safety Liaison: C. Gardner, NY Staff Liaison: B. Levy, NCWM Associate Member Rep: TBD	Chair: TBD Co-Chair: TBD Members: TBD NIST Tech Advisor: V. Miller
Nominating Committee	**Legislative Liaison**
Chair: R. Andersen, NY Members: W. Diggs, VA D. Onwiler, NE A. Thompson, AK D. Flocken, Mettler-Toledo G. Prince, Kroger Company L. Straub, Fairbanks Scales	Chair: TBD Members: TBD
Credentials Committee	**Appointed Officers**
Chair: R. Johnson, NM (2006) Members: T. McBride, TN (2005) W. Cobb, WV (2007) Coordinator: NCWM Staff	Parliamentarian: A. Thompson, AK Chaplain: M. Belue, Belue Associates Sergeants-At-Arms: E. Payne, MD M. Quisenberry, CA G. W. Diggs, VA Presiding Officers: L. Stump, IN V. Massey, TN R. Hayes, MI J. Flanders, GA
Associate Membership Committee	
Chair: Vice Chair: Secretary/Treasurer: S. Members:	M. Galletta, CA, Nestlé USA (2006) G. Lameris, Hobart Corporation (2007) Langford, Cardinal Scale (2008) R. Murnane, Jr., Seraphin Test Measures (2006) W. Sveum, Kraft Foods (2007) D. Flocken, Mettler-Toledo (2008) C. Frye, International Dairy Foods Association (2008) V. Orr, ConAgra Foods (2009) P. Lewis, Rice Lake Weighing Systems (2009) M. Gaspers, Farmland Foods, Inc. (2009)

Regional Weights and Measures Association Contacts	
Northeastern Weights and Measures Assn. (NEWMA): Annual Meeting: May 16-19, 2005 Best Western Airport Inn - Albany, NY	William J. Wilson Clinton County, New York, Weights & Measures (518) 565-4681 clinton.wts@yahoo.com
Southern Weights and Measures Assn. (SWMA): Annual Meeting: October 23-26, 2005 Hotel: TBD - Memphis, TN	Randy F. Jennings Tennessee Dept. of Agriculture (615) 837-5747 randy.jennings@state.tn.us
Central Weights and Measures Assn. (CWMA): Annual Meeting: September 18-20, 2005 The Lodge, Bettendorf, Iowa Annual Meeting 2006: April 30-May 3, 2006 Holiday Inn – Dayton Mall, Miamisburg	Vicky Dempsey Montgomery County, Ohio, Weights &Measures (937) 225-6309 DempseyV@mcohio.org
Western Weights and Measures Assn. (WWMA): Annual Meeting: September 11-15, 2005 Ritz-Carlton - Phoenix, Arizona	Debra E. Rader Arizona Dept. of Weight & Measures (623) 463-9955 drader@azdwm.gov

Org Chart

National Type Evaluation Technical Committees (NTETC)			
Weighing Sector		**Measuring Sector**	
Chair:	D. Flocken, Mettler-Toledo	Chair:	M. Keilty, Endress & Hauser Flowtec AG
Tech Advisor:	S. Cook, NIST/WMD	Tech Advisor:	R. Suiter, NIST/WMD
Public Sector Members:	C. Ainsworth, GIPSA R. Andersen, NY W. Bates, GIPSA L. Burtini, Measurement Canada A. Buie, MD C. Carter, OK G. Castro, CA T. Davis, KS G. W. Diggs, VA J. Kane, MT D. Onwiler, NE D. Parks, CA J. Truex, OH J. Vanderwielen, GIPSA W. West, OH R. Wyckoff, OR	Public Sector Members:	R. Andersen, NY J. Butler, NC G. Castro, CA S. Hadder, FL T. Kingsbury, Measurement Canada J. Makin, Measurement Canada S. Malone, NE C. Nelson, CA W. West, OH R. Wotthlie, MD
Private Sector Members:	D. Biette, Sartorius North America J. Elengo, Contractor R. Feezor, Norfolk Southern Corp. W. GeMeiner, Union Pacific RR D. Hawkins, Thurman Scale Co. J. Hughes, Avery Weigh-Tronix, Inc. R. Jimenez, Association of American Railroads G. Lameris, Hobart Corp. S. Langford, Cardinal Scale Mfg. P. Lewis, Rice Lake Weighing Systems L. E. Luthy, Brechbuhler Scales, Inc. N. Puri, NMB Technologies, Inc. D. Quinn, ISWM Consultant L. Straub, Fairbanks Scales, Inc. J. Wang, A&D Engineering, Inc. O. Warnlof, Consultant W. Young, Emery Winslow Scale	Private Sector Members:	F. M. Belue, Belue Associates J. Beyer, Liquid Controls M. Buttler, Emerson Process Management - Micro Motion J. Buxton, Daniel Measurement & Control R. Cooper, Actaris Neptune M. Forkert, Tuthill Transfer Systems M. Gallo, Clean Fueling Technologies P. Glowacki, Murray Equipment M. Hankel, MCH Engineering Assoc. D. Hoffman, TopTech Systems G. Johnson, Gilbarco, Inc. Y. Katselnik, Dresser Wayne, Inc. R. Kretzler, Dresser Wayne, Inc. D. Long, RDM Industrial Electronics W. Mattar, Invensys/Foxboro R. Miller, FMC Measurement Solution R. Murnane, Jr., Seraphin Test Measure A. Noel, Neptune Technology J. Parrish, Brodie Meter Company, LLC D. Rajala, Veeder-Root Company O. Warnlof, Consultant

National Type Evaluation Technical Committees (NTETC) (cont'd)	
Belt Conveyor Scales Sector	**Grain Analyzer Sector**
Chair: TBD	Chair: C. Eigenmann-Pierson, DICKEY-john Corp.
Tech Advisor: S. Cook, NIST/WMD	Tech Advisors: G. Diane. Lee, NIST/WMD J. W. Barber, J. B. Associates
Public Sector Members: A. Buie, MD	Public Sector Members: R. Burns, AR T. Butcher, NIST A. Gruneisen, CA D. Onwiler, NE R. Pierce, GIPSA E. Szesnat, Jr., NY C. Tew, NC R. Wittenberger, MO
Private Sector Members: R. Jimenez, Association of American Railroads L. Marmsater, Merrick Industries B. Ripka, Thermo Electron P. Sirrico, Thayer Scale - Hyer Industries, Inc. T. Vormittag, Sr., SGS Minerals Services O. Warnlof, Consultant	Private Sector Members: J. Bair, NA Miller's Association H. Biermann, Bizerba GmbH & Co KG M. Clements, The Steinlite Corp. V. Gates, Shore Sales Company A. Gell, Foss North America C. Hurburgh, Jr., Iowa State University D. Krejci, Grain Elevator & Processing Society T. O'Connor, National Grain & Feed Assn. T. Runyon, Seedboro Equipment

Org Chart

THIS PAGE LEFT INTENTIONALLY BLANK.

President's Address
National Conference on Weights and Measures
Orlando, FL
July 12, 2005

Dr. Hratch Semerjian
Acting NIST Director

Thank you for that fine introduction. I welcome this opportunity to address the National Conference on Weights and Measures' 90th Annual Meeting, a meeting that celebrates the NCWM's 100th anniversary.

It's an honor to be part of this centennial celebration. I feel right at home. At home—not only because I am, as the Acting NIST Director, the Honorary President of the National Conference on Weights and Measures—but also because everyone in this room, including this speaker, shares the same vision.

The theme of our conference is "100 Years of Equity in the Marketplace." Certainly, the quest for honest weights and measures and all that this entails for competitiveness, commercialization, innovation and open markets are the heart and soul of both our organizations. It is our way of life. It is our mission. It is the way we serve our nation, its people and, increasingly, the world.

It is a pleasure to recognize at the outset of my remarks one very special person — Henry Oppermann. Henry was, until his retirement two weeks ago, chief of NIST's Weights and Measures Division. He is, in a very real sense, one of the authors of this feast, a weights and measures person who has devoted 30 years to nurturing the NCWM-NIST bond. Henry is a long-time friend and tireless champion of our work and has had a hand in virtually all the joint programs I will talk about today. His technical expertise and vision are without compare, and he is widely respected in all arenas of the weights and measures community. His contributions have spanned the spectrum of the legal metrology system, from laboratory metrology to type evaluation to field inspection to weights and measures administration.

Thank you, Henry, for a lifetime of service and contributions to the people and the nation. We are grateful for your promise to be available for consultations and advice to both NIST and the NCWM.

Weights and measures have been a national concern from the birth of our republic. Article I, Section 8 of the Constitution declares, "The Congress shall have the power to …fix the standard of weights and measures." In 1901 the federal government established the National Bureau of Standards (now NIST). Within four years – 1905 – Samuel Stratton, NBS's first director, and Louis Fischer, the Bureau's chief of weights and measures, convened a meeting of state sealers of weights and measures. That meeting of officials from eight states and the District of Columbia marked the birth of this great organization.

We were born in an era when good men and women first understood the dangers of adulterated products as well as the need to enact reforms such as the pure food and drug laws. We opened up shop as America moved on to the world stage as an industrial power. With each passing year, advances in science and technology have expanded our means of serving the nation.

Together, NIST and the Conference helped shape a new age, fostering—with honest weights, sure measures, and common national standards—the economic miracle that has brought a good, decent life to millions.

Now some, especially people outside this room, might be tempted to ask what am I talking about! That's understandable.

I once saw a *New Yorker* magazine cartoon that captured a more stereotypical view of our work. It portrayed a group of glum, mustached bureaucrats sitting around a conference table. A bespectacled, middle-aged man at the head of the table is saying, "I'm afraid, Gentlemen, we must learn to live with the hard truth. The Office of Weights and Measures is, by its very nature, colorless, non-controversial, scandal-free, and likely to remain so forever."

Well–let's face it–as a bureaucrat, I have to admit—colorless is fine… non-controversial is desirable…and scandal-free is more than good. It is absolutely necessary.

As weights and measures officials, state laboratory metrologists, and industry leaders in weighing and measuring devices, however, we know one very important truth–we have laid the groundwork for today's fair, competitive and equitable marketplace benefiting the citizenry and business.

As Massachusetts Governor Curtis Guild told the Conference in 1908, "Some reforms only touch the average citizen once in a lifetime; but the enforcement of honest weights and measures touches every human being at every moment of every day."

Our collaboration is symbolized by this commemorative reprint of the NBS 1915 publication on the tolerances and specifications for weighing and measuring devices. This publication was the forerunner of NIST Handbook 44, which has been adopted by all 50 states, the District of Columbia, and the Territories as their standard for commercial weighing and measuring devices. It is used in everything from gas pumps to grain moisture meters.

Handbook 44 paved the way for other weights and measures handbooks including Handbooks 112, 130, 133, 105, 143, and 145. They cover model laws for states, standardized field test procedures, and ways to check the net contents of packaged goods–from corn flakes to cooking oils. They save us immense time and expense and promote uniformity in weights and measures requirements and practices.

Our collective efforts have resulted in documents used by an estimated 3,200 state and local weights and measures officials across the United States and 50,000 private-sector representatives.

It is a fact that weights and measures rules, regulations, and standards annually affect about $4.5 trillion transactions, representing over half of the U.S. gross domestic product (GDP).

Yet another fact, one that grows in importance every day, is that while we have accomplished much in the last 100 years, we now must do even better.

It's the 21st Century. We are beginning to recognize that the system created in 1905 is less and less suited for the needs of the marketplace in 2005, let alone 10 years from now. The marketplace is changing–and significantly today's environment is faster paced. Weighing and measuring equipment grows ever more diverse and complex. Administrators must tackle high turnover and lengthy training periods for the staff. Manufacturers, competing in a global marketplace, must continually be on guard for international standards that are at variance with national standards. Businesses must comply with a daunting network of regulations, many overlapping and sometimes conflicting. Consumers' needs have changed, with a strong focus on convenience and timeliness.

Clearly we need continually to reassess how we do business with regard to standards development. Technical topics are so diverse and technology so rapidly changing that the current system cannot provide the technical expertise needed to address the wide range of topics. Affected parties aren't effectively informed about impending changes. Limited budgets prevent participation in many of the technical discussions. Decisions are often made without adequate information or understanding. Too often, for instance, NCWM committees neither have sufficient time to adequately review and make decisions about technical issues nor do they have access to the technical resources they need.

And on top of all that, our weights and measures budgets have shrunk. At both the federal and state level, weights and measures jurisdictions compete for funding with other functions, such as homeland security, health, education and welfare.

So, what needs to change? What are the most significant influences we face? How can we be most expedient? How can we ensure input and involvement from all parties? How can we ensure sound technical decisions? And how can we be most cost-effective as resources grow increasingly scarce?

NIST has begun a long, hard look at these challenges. We have gone to our customers and asked, "What needs to be changed?" We have asked that question not just in technical meetings and through correspondence but also in focus groups, including meetings with many of the manufacturers and weights and measures officials here today.

We are learning a great deal. We have ideas for a new template for legal metrology standard development, a way to better organize this effort, and even a national plan to roadmap America's measurement needs for a stronger innovation infrastructure.

Our conversations convince us that it is critical to expand participation in the development process for legal metrology standards.

Again and again we have heard calls for more **transparency** in the process with an end to hidden agendas or behind-the-scenes actions. Many parties stress the need for **openness, impartiality, due process, balance** and **consensus** with information freely shared and readily available to all impacted by the prospective standard …decisions based on the national interest ... the views of all duly considered. ...results generally agreed to and accepted by all participants.

Others call for more **relevance,** in which standards are championed that have real benefit and impact on products. And for **performance orientation,** in which actions take into account the impact of potential standards and their cost benefit to products. As well as **timeliness,** in which actions reflect priority needs of manufacturers distributing goods and services, as well as regulatory officials faced with ensuring an environment for fair competition among businesses.

People want **flexibility** that allows a standard to survive changing needs of parties due to changing technology, changing global influences, changing market practices and changes in related regulations. And, of course, there is a plea for more **technical literacy** and **coherence**—in other words, a standards development process that avails itself of technical expertise and produces results that are clear and understandable.

Few of us would disagree with the desirability of a legal metrology standards development process that is characterized by all these elements or virtues, from **transparency** and **openness to coherence** and **technical literacy.**

It's a bit like being in favor of motherhood and apple pie. But the big question is how do we do it? How do we make the ideal that we all strive for, the norm for all of us?

NIST and the NCWM Board of Directors are engaged in a joint effort to consider alternatives for improving and enhancing the current system. This partnership is lighting the way to a more productive future.

Recently, we met to discuss an approach, which would expand upon a "work group" model that NIST uses to develop U.S. comments on International Organization of Legal Metrology (OIML) documents, as well as for the development of technical requirements and test procedures for specialized technical topics such as belt-conveyor scales.

You may have already heard of this proposal through presentations given at the Spring 2005 regional weights and measures association meetings by your incoming NCWM Chairman, Don Onwiler.

Under this model, work groups consisting of technical experts from industry and the regulatory community would be used to develop and address technical issues such as those currently considered by NCWM standing committees.

Recommendations of the work groups would feed into the existing NCWM process, thereby providing additional technical resources to the standing committees and enhancing the efficiency of the process.

These work groups may draw upon the expertise of existing technical committees, such as the National Type Evaluation Technical Sectors.

Both NIST and the NCWM Board of Directors are optimistic that such an approach could, if properly implemented, address many of the key issues and concerns about the current process.

NIST is excited by the prospect of **partnering** with the NCWM to implement such a model to facilitate the development of legal metrology standards in the U.S.

We look forward to working with the NCWM leadership in the coming months to develop the details of this effort.

I also look forward to NCWM participation in the initiative we recently launched to take the pulse of U.S. measurement capabilities and infrastructure. NCWM is a logical partner in this effort. Its work to set legal metrology standards—combined with NIST services—is central to the national measurement system.

In 2004 NCWM-member state metrology laboratories provided more than 360,000 calibrations to regulatory agencies, research institutes and manufacturers and scale and meter service companies. This year the 16th state laboratory received its accreditation under NIST's National Voluntary Laboratory Accreditation Program (NVLAP)! That's a great accomplishment! Mass calibrations concerns will be a major concern of the initiative and NCWM can make a fine contribution to this effort.

This strong private-public sector partnership called "Roadmapping America's Measurement Needs for a Strong Innovation Infrastructure" will make the first-ever evaluation of the breadth, depth and overall health of the U.S. measurement system.

The final report, expected in early 2007, will identify priority measurement infrastructure needs across industry and the economy, recommend steps to address them, and point out the consequences of inaction.

To kick off this process, NIST is reaching out to top customers and stakeholders in the United States Measurement System, such as NCWM. We are collecting and reviewing previously published roadmaps and workshop reports focused on future science and technology challenges and opportunities, and we are planning an initial set of focused workshops in key technology areas.

Business, trade and professional associations are encouraged to identify and advise NIST of pressing measurement needs and gaps in their particular areas.

Together we will document America's priority measurement needs and their economic implications. We anticipate that our findings will motivate interested and affected parties to take action and ultimately ensure that our national measurement system is healthy and capable of serving U.S. institutions and citizens in the 21st Century.

Meanwhile, we will continue efforts to document best practices, harmonize national standards with international standards, and prepare for a new metrics-only ruling that could affect U.S. exports.

Thanks to the input received from the weights and measures community, as well as industrial partners, NIST recently completed a two-year benchmarking and needs assessment study. This limited look at the effectiveness of the national weights and measures infrastructure identified some of the challenges facing regulators and industry. With this kind of information plus your feedback on the study and with the help of experts in the field, we hope to begin identifying "best practices" and components, starting with the area of retail motor-fuel dispensing inspections.

Efforts in this field could be the prototype of more efforts in other weights and measures inspection areas.

As we work together to enhance our national system, we are also confronted with the need to think more globally. To keep markets open to American manufacturers of goods and services, our national system must strive to establish national standards that are harmonized with (or at least equivalent to) standards adopted by other nations.

NCWM efforts complement NIST efforts in this field. NCWM committees routinely consider international documents when considering proposed changes to U.S. standards. In addition, NCWM participation in the International Organization of Legal Metrology (OIML) meetings helps to raise the visibility of U.S. standards and eliminate differences. NCWM is considering participation in an OIML Mutual Acceptance Arrangement (MAA), which would greatly facilitate the type approval process for device manufacturers. And that would be very good for us all.

I cannot close my remarks without mentioning the metric system. We are very conscious of the fact that the European Union has set January 1, 2010, as the deadline for implementation of a Metric Directive that requires only metric units to be used on products, including packaged commodities. This deadline is of significant concern to U.S. exporters. With others, we are exploring the possibility of changing the U.S. Federal Fair Packaging and Labeling Act to allow consumer packaging companies to continue labeling the net contents of packages in both inch-pound and metric units as they do now or to label, on a purely voluntary basis, the net contents in only metric units.

Today 45 states allow metric only labeling for products. I strongly encourage the remaining states to move forward with the adoption of NIST Handbook 130, which permits metric-only packaging.

And now, my friends, I congratulate you once more and wish you well as you begin your second century of service to the nation. I am confident that with imagination, creativity, cooperation and hard work we—together—will build a better future for our nation and our people. Thank you.

THIS PAGE LEFT INTENTIONALLY BLANK.

Chairman's Address
National Conference on Weights and Measures
Orlando, Florida
July 12, 2005

G. Weston Diggs
Virginia Office of Product and Industry Standards

It is my pleasure to welcome you to the 90th Annual Meeting of the National Conference on Weights and Measures. It has been an honor to serve a second term as Chairman of this Conference. We are here to conduct important business that relates to weights and measures issues that will affect us nationally and internationally. At the same time, we are celebrating 100 years of providing equity in the marketplace. In this celebration, we recognize our relationship with the National Institute of Standards and Technology (NIST). In 1905 the Department of Commerce, in its mission to establish uniformity in weights and measures, created the National Conference on Weights and Measures. To a great extent, we owe our success to our partners at NIST. Although, like in any relationship, we have had our differences; the leadership and support provided by people like Mac Jensen, Carol Brickenkamp, Henry Oppermann and their staff have been invaluable.

I would like to take some time to discuss a few of our accomplishments that occurred this year, as well as some of what I believe to be challenges for the future.

The National Conference is gaining international recognition. We have, to some extent, always been involved in the international world of legal metrology. For the most part this was accomplished through the sponsorship of NIST at meetings of the International Organization of Legal Metrology (OIML) where NIST represented the United States. This year, Steve Patoray, our NTEP Director, was invited to speak at a Japanese Forum on legal metrology. He was asked to discuss the U.S. system of weights and measures and our National Type Evaluation Program. Partly as a result of Steve's visit, a delegation from Japan visited California, Maryland, and NIST and met with me representing the National Conference before going to Canada. Japan is in the process of modifying its legal metrology system. This delegation was looking for ideas they could incorporate into their new system. In support of our members that export weighing and measuring devices, the Conference is participating in OIML's Committee on Participation Review. The long-range goal is to become an "issuing authority" under the Mutual Acceptance Agreement. This would mean we could issue OIML certificates in the same manner we now issue NTEP certificates. We will not sign any agreement until we have reached the status of an "issuing authority." The reality of our international involvement is that it is very expensive, in terms of money and time for meetings and travel. I believe it is important, as we develop international relations, to identify a single person to represent the National Conference. For the sake of consistency, I believe Steve Patoray needs to be that person. That lends itself to another problem—Steve has enough to do with his current workload in NTEP. We are adding international travel and the possibility of a new NTEP Software Sector. Even with the capable assistance of Linda Bernetich and Steve Cook, Steve Patoray's workload is reaching the crisis point. Next year the Board of Directors will have to make some tough choices in this area.

The Conference must do more to make the public aware of the importance of its work. Over the years we have made attempts in this area with very limited success. The last effort I can remember was in the mid-nineties when we considered having Popeye, the cartoon caricature, as the NCWM spokesman. With the addition of Judy Markoe to the Management Solution's staff, we have a resource that could develop a plan for marketing, not only the importance of the Conference activities, but weights and measures in general.

On June 30 our new website was activated. Based on the initial feedback, this new site is a vast improvement over what we had in the past. A lot of money and time has been expended to make this site a reality. It is our hope the new site is more user-friendly and helpful to those interested in the National Conference's activities. We would like to express our appreciation to the AMC Committee for its support of this effort. I would also like to acknowledge the hard work of Linda Bernetich, Steve Patoray and Judy Markoe of our management staff.

I was your chairman in 2000 when we were experiencing a low point in the Conference's relationship with our partners at NIST. I am happy to report that since that time, with Henry Oppermann's leadership and the support of NIST upper-management, our relationship has continued to improve. Henry cannot be replaced but we look forward to working with whomever follows in his place.

With our partners at the Weights and Measures Division, the Board of Directors is planning to initiate an improved method of managing conference issues. On the surface this may seem to be adding another level of bureaucracy to the process. We need to realize we have many new officials on committees who are learning about the conference process. This process is designed to help direct issues coming from the sectors and regional associations to the appropriate committee or work group. In some cases a special work group may have to be created to develop the issue or, if the issue lacks adequate information, it may be returned to its source. Don Onwiler and Henry Oppermann will go into more detail on this plan later during the Conference.

The system of weights and measures in our country is unique in that there is no federal weights and measures law. Although federal agencies preempt us in certain areas, the enforcement is the responsibility of state and local officials, which is particularly true at the retail level. In recent years, the Conference, as well as the weights and measures community as a whole, has been frustrated because of dwindling resources. Weights and measures jurisdictions continue to be asked to do more with fewer resources, not only in terms of dollars but in terms of people. Both conditions are having an adverse effect on the Conference and its ability to operate. The money is no doubt important. Besides running our respective programs, it also allows us to attend the meetings and be involved in development of the issues. However, even now the lack of people with weights and measures experience is affecting our ability to operate as effectively as we would like. The lack of experienced people is not only on the regulatory side but on the industry side as well. No one is questioning the dedication to our profession by our new officials and industry members. It takes time to gain the knowledge to understand the wide range of issues that come before our Conference. While knowledge is necessary, it has been my experience this Conference operates to a great extent on a person's credibility. Whether it is desirable or not, issues are often decided by the position a person with credibility takes on an issue. My point to this is credibility doesn't come by registering and getting a name tag. In this organization it takes both time and participation to gain credibility.

Most of us in government, and perhaps the industry members as well, have to justify travel to meetings and conferences to a higher authority within our agencies. If you are a weights and measures official, you probably justify attendance at conference meetings by saying it is important because this is where the requirements relating to weights and measures are developed that affect the citizens in your jurisdiction. I believe this a true statement, but it goes beyond that. You are to be complimented by your attendance and participation because in doing so you are supporting our system of weights and measures in the United States. Without your continued participation our system would surely fail.

Before I close, I would be remiss if I did not touch on two other topics. You have heard this from me before so I will keep it short. First, the Conference must do something to correct its current voting requirements for getting issues passed. It is ridiculous that because of low attendance three or four members can cause an issue to fail. Those not in attendance have in effect voted "NO" on all the issues. In many cases these jurisdictions may not be members of the Conference. It is not equitable to those who invest their time and resources developing issues and have them fail because of a relatively few "No" votes at the Annual Meeting and the "NO" votes by those who do not attend. Second, I believe NIST Handbook 44 needs to be brought inline with today's technology and written so its intended users can effectively use it in the field. I would like to believe I am wrong concerning both of these issues, but only time will tell.

In closing, I would like to thank the Board of Directors and all of the Conference membership for their support during this past year. I would especially like to express my thanks to Beth Palys and the staff at the NCWM Headquarters. Until you are chairman of this Conference, you have no conception of the amount of work turned out by our management group or how much is done without the knowledge of the general membership. I also would like to thank the staff at home for their support.

As I close out my career in weights and measures, I hope you will remember me as someone who was not always right but someone who would always listen and you always knew where he stood.

I thank you very much, and it has been an honor to serve as your Chairman.

New Chairman's Address
National Conference on Weights and Measures
Orlando, Florida
July 14, 2005

"Back to the Basics as Stepping Stones to the Future"

Don Onwiler

Nebraska Department of Agriculture/Weights & Measures

As I was preparing for this, I took the time to review remarks of previous chairmen in the Annual Reports. Several talked about "change." It's not one of our favorite subjects. The NCWM, it's members and partners have all seen many changes in recent years. We have been through some challenging times in terms of defending our programs, protecting our budgets, and focusing on "maintaining" when we would prefer to focus on "improving."

Difficult times are also times of opportunity. Willingness to adapt is how we grow. Should we simply concentrate on doing those things that have worked for us in the past, or should we be looking for a fresh approach to those difficulties we face? In our program back home, we emphasize both. There I have learned the importance of researching and understanding our history while maintaining an eye on the horizon. This is the foundation for this year's theme, *"Back to Basics as the Stepping Stones to Our Future."*

So what did get us where we are? In his speech on Tuesday, Dr. Semerjian reflected on that first meeting in 1905. The subsequent success of NCWM is based on recognition that attendance, thoughtful participation, inclusion of our stakeholders, and tireless volunteer effort are critical to meeting our goals. The success of both NCWM and NIST Weights and Measures Division has hinged historically on a spirit of cooperation toward that end.

Concern for a healthy system of measurement goes back farther than that meeting of state officials in 1905. In his first message to Congress in 1790, George Washington said, "...uniformity in the currency, weights and measures of the United States is an objective of great importance, and will, I am persuaded, be duly attended to."

Unfortunately, there is no longer strong recognition or acknowledgement from our leaders in Washington of the importance of weights and measures. Many state and local governments are also overlooking this fundamental ingredient to a fair business environment. One reason for this is that we have done such a tremendous job of instilling confidence into the marketplace. We should take pride in that. But, as former Chairman Dennis Ehrhart pointed out, we need to be in the public eye. We need an identity.

Creating awareness of weights and measures activities is not our specialty, but we're working on it. We have revamped our website to be more interesting and informative to first-time visitors. In the process, we have made it more functional to our members. We will also draw on the expertise of Judy Markoe, a new member of the Management Solutions team. She will help us develop a plan to elevate the NCWM to a higher level of public awareness.

The NCWM has also struggled recently with reduced attendance. The effects of this are tremendous. Valuable input has been lost. We have a smaller pool of volunteers to serve on committees and work groups. We are doing less mentoring in the organization because we can't afford to get new people to the meetings. Go back and read those reports from the early 1900's. Do you think it was easy getting to meetings then? It was a challenge, but they persevered. When we do get new attendees, we sometimes overlook them. When we get new volunteers, we tend to overwhelm them. Sure, as the economy improves membership and attendance will rebound, and attendance is also issue driven to some degree, but there are things we can do to help—basic things.

As an example, I'll take you back to my first National Conference in 1993. I did not know anyone at that meeting, not even the other representatives from my state, so Tina Butcher of NIST took the time to tutor me on the process of the Annual Meeting. Darryl Brown of Iowa and Will Wotthlie of Maryland told me my input was important and I should speak up. Others, like Steve Malone of Nebraska and Sid Colbrook of Illinois, asked me my opinions and, Heaven help them, they even listened to me. David McKay from Utah and his wife Carolyn saw a newcomer from Nebraska who looked lost. Now, David was a quiet man, but he promoted the NCWM by doing what came naturally to him. He extended friendship and offered support. And, lastly, I was asked to serve.

Now I ask you, aren't all these basic things that we can be doing? How often have we all overlooked them? No doubt, some of you wish I had been ignored in 1993 so that, just maybe, I would have gone away. Had I been ignored, I would have.

Once we gain awareness and get new people involved, they must find value in our organization or we will lose them. The efforts of the Professional Development Committee and NIST to improve training and create a certification program will provide part of that value. The value will also come from our proactive approach to standards development. A process that is responsive to the needs of our stakeholders will provide benefit in participation. We will continue working to develop and implement the plan Henry Oppermann and I presented to you this week to improve our standards development process. I like this plan because it does not replace what we do. It enhances what we do. I also like it because it is something the NCWM and NIST are developing together. As we move forward, it will continue to require a strong partnership of our organizations.

The relationship between the NCWM and NIST has been a concern. Both organizations have had to redefine themselves to some degree. There may have been occasions where we have duplicated efforts or neglected needs. There may have been occasions when some of our membership has been compelled to "choose sides." I am asking you now to let that go. Both organizations remain committed to our respective charges. Both continue to share common goals. We will continue to have agreements and disagreements along the way, but we are finding ways to move forward together, rebuilding the partnership that has served us so well in the past. I thank Henry Oppermann and Wes Diggs for the role they have played in that effort.

Another thing I remember from my first meeting was how much I admired the people who served on Standing Committees. They worked long hours, often into the evenings. They understood the need to put forward a quality agenda for the voting session. I noticed they included very difficult, sometimes political or emotional issues on the agenda. They welcomed stakeholders with specific agendas and members with unpopular opinions to the microphone. The Committee members demonstrated dedication, intelligence, patience, and a desire to get it right. They knew the tough issues were also important issues.

It was all so glamorous from the outside looking in but any of us who have been there know it is difficult to listen to disagreements among membership, sorting through the opinions and facts to work toward the best solution. It is difficult to generate quality final reports to serve as an historical record of the NCWM. But it's worth it. I commend all of you who give so much of yourselves to be part of that process.

Over the years, we have endured many discussions regarding harmonization with OIML standards. Do you know that one of the early roadblocks to developing our system in the U.S. was the lack of a uniform measurement system internationally? Efforts toward harmonization are similar to our struggle for uniformity among the 50 states. We will never fully achieve it, but working toward the goal is a necessity if we want to improve the measurement system in the U.S. We will continue to strive for harmonization by considering proposals to amend our standards and making recommendations to modify international standards. We will continue to consider our options in the world arena as we participate in the development process for the Mutual Acceptance Arrangements.

So you see, I'm not suggesting change after all. I'm not advancing a new agenda as your Chairman. My agenda dates back to 1905. If we look back at our successes and our failures, learn from those experiences what works and what doesn't, we can apply that knowledge, and we will be successful. Let's get back to the basics, be innovative in our approaches, and keep our eye on the horizon.

What do you see when you look forward? Where do you think we need to be in terms of technology, training, and field enforcement? How well we predict these things and respond to them will determine the effectiveness of the NCWM and our level of importance in United States legal metrology.

Part of the equation lies in computer technology. I appreciate the Board of Directors' decision this week to address software in a comprehensive manner. Once again we are leaving our comfort zone. The Software Sector will draw new experts into our organization, increasing our abilities and broadening our resources. These particular experts are the future of our business and we will surely welcome them in.

The Board of Directors and NIST WMD have committed to performing market surveys in the next year. We will follow the protocol established by the NCWM in 1999. Our first task will be to identify the scope of the survey. We have a team established per NCWM protocol and the team will proceed, reporting to the Board of Directors. Market surveys may be conducted for devices, for packaged commodities, or any area of weights and measures enforcement activity.

The Board of Directors has heard criticism occasionally because our revolving door of leadership can easily create a change of priorities. This can cause issues or pet projects to go unfinished as new projects are introduced. Some might guess software to be my pet project. It's not. My pet project is doing what we can to get this organization hitting on all cylinders. Having a group of experts assembled to assist us on software issues is part of that effort. If we can do that, we will succeed as a multi-functional organization and projects won't fall through the cracks.

Temperature compensation, stored vehicle tare weights, software-based devices... there is no lack of difficult issues, but think about the marketplace in 1905. Think about the technology or, if you prefer, lack of technology that existed at that time. Keeping up with new technology and marketing practices is our business. It's not getting harder. We just struggle sometimes to fully implement the system we have. We face the same obstacles that have been there from the beginning, and we honor those who are committed to helping this organization overcome those obstacles.

Let's recognize those who attend, participate, and contribute their talents. Let's be proactive in promoting our meetings and our agendas. Lets instill pride, the kind of pride so many of us have, into every new member who walks into the room. Let's not be afraid to take on tough issues. Let's talk to the political leaders and invite them to participate. Let's work with our partners to achieve good things.

Now, with our eyes on the horizon, I make the following appointments:

Laws and Regulations Committee:
    Stephen Benjamin, North Carolina (5)

Specifications and Tolerances Committee:
    Brett Saum, San Luis Obispo County, California (5)

Professional Development Committee:
    There are no vacancies on this committee this year. The committee has requested a reassignment of terms of its current members to provide for the traditional staggered terms for standing committee members. In response to that request, I am extending the following terms:
        Ken Deitzler of Pennsylvania to 2007
        Will Wotthlie of Maryland to 2010.
    By recommendation of the Associate Membership Committee, Gary Lameris will serve as the Associate Member to the Professional Development Committee.

Nominating Committee:
    Ross Andersen, New York
    Tom Geiler, Barnstable, Massachusetts
    Max Gray, Florida
    Steve Malone, Nebraska
    Aves Thompson, Alaska
    Jim Truex, Ohio

Credentials Committee:
    Mark Buccelli, Minnesota (3)

> Presiding Officers:
>> Kristin Young, Colorado
>> Bill Timmons, Massachusetts
>> Steve Pedersen, Iowa
>> John Junkins, West Virginia
>
> Parliamentarian:
>> Aves Thompson, Alaska
>
> Chaplain:
>> Mike Belue, Belue Associates
>
> Sergeants-at-Arms:
>> To be provided by the City of Chicago, Dept. of Consumer Services
>
> Board of Directors to complete Mike Cleary's term:
>> Joe Gomez, New Mexico (2)
>> Jim Truex, Ohio, will continue as NTEP Committee Chairman to fill the vacancy resulting from Wes Diggs' retirement. Thank you, Jim, for your continued service. We are fortunate to have you.

Thank you, each of you, who have accepted appointments for offering your time and talents to the NCWM.

Now some personal remarks if I may: To my wife, Peggy, and our children, Phil, Mark, Tim, and Janessa, who are here this morning, thank you for your tolerance, thank you for being here this week, and most of all thanks for not changing the locks when I'm away.

To Steve Malone and our staff back home, thank you for giving me your support to dedicate so much time to the NCWM. Steve, you have always seen more in me than I could see in myself. Thank you for giving me the confidence to stand here today and thank you for allowing me to make my own mistakes.

It will be my honor to serve the NCWM this year. Chairman-Elect Mike Cleary and I look forward to seeing all of you again throughout the year as we visit the regions and continue the work of the National Conference on Weights and Measures.

Thank you.

NCWM 2005 Annual Meeting Honor Award Recipients

Full Name	Organization	State	No. of Years
Steven B. Steinborn	Hogan & Hartson	DC	5
Brett Gurney	Utah Department of Agriculture & Food	UT	5
Steven Beitzel	Systems Associates, Inc.	IL	5
Kenneth Deitzler	Bureau of Ride & Measurement Standards	PA	5
Stephen Casto	West Virginia Weights & Measures	WV	5
William Cobb	West Virginia Weights & Measures	WV	5
Robert McGrath	Boston ISD Weights & Measures	MA	10
O.R. "Pete" O'Bryan	Foster Farms	CA	10
Jack Kane	Montana Bureau of Weights & Measures	MT	10
Gordon W. Johnson	Gilbarco, Inc.	NC	15
Gilles Vinet	Measurement Canada	Ontario	15
Robert A. Reinfried	Scale Manufacturers Association	FL	20
Robert G. Williams	Tennessee Dept. of Agriculture W&M	TN	25
Richard L. Davis	Georgia-Pacific	WI	25
Henry Oppermann	NIST	MD	25
Steven Malone	Nebraska Division of Weights & Measures	NE	30

THIS PAGE LEFT INTENTIONALLY BLANK.

Report of the Board of Directors
G. Weston Diggs
Virginia Product and Industry Standards

Introduction

The Board held its quarterly Board of Directors meeting on Saturday, July 9, 2005, and continued that meeting during work sessions throughout the remainder of the Annual Meeting. The Board of Directors and the NTEP Committee invited members to dialogue with the Board on the following issues: Conformity Assessment, NCWM Organizational Structure, the National Training Program, Voting Procedures, Public Relations campaign and participation internationally, i.e., OIML, CFTM, APLMF, and USNWG.

Table A
Table of Contents

Subject Page

Introduction..1
1. NTEP Chair Position...2
2. The Use of Work Groups..2
3. National Training Program Curriculum..2
4. Voting Procedures..2
5. Marketplace Surveys..2
6. Meetings..3
7. Conformity Assessment..3
8. Electronic Copies of Pub 14..3
9. Website Revamp...3
10. Participation in International Standards Setting...3
11. Nominating Committee..3
12. Future Meetings...3

Table B
Appendices

Appendix Title Page

A Report on the Activities of the International Organization of Legal Metrology (OIML) and
   Regional Legal Metrology Organizations...A1
B Minutes,   NCWM Associate Membership Committee...B1
   B-1 AMC Funds Allocations...B5
C Conformity   Assessment Program Update..C1
   C1 Initial   Verification..C3
   C2   Administrative Review of Certificates of Conformance..C11
   C3   Verified Conformity Assessment Program (VCAP)...C17

1. NTEP Chair Position

The Board discussed the feedback received from the membership regarding a longer term for the NTEP Chair position. They did not get a sense of urgency from comments heard on this item. As a result, a decision was made to not move forward with this issue at this time.

2. The Use of Work Groups

Some members of the Board and NIST WMD senior staff met in May to discuss how to identify the need for and fund work groups. The consensus was to form a Review Panel made up of a member of the NCWM Board of Directors, representatives from NIST WMD, the appropriate NCWM Standing Committee chairpersons, and designated representatives from the Associate Membership Committee. This panel will assess all new proposals to NCWM standing committees put forward from the regional associations and other sources, and make recommendations to the standing committees regarding the best method to develop each proposal. This Review Panel will operate on a trial basis for all new proposals coming forward from the regions in the fall of 2005 for the NCWM Interim Meeting in January 2006. Recommendations may include:

1. Assigning the proposal to an existing work group of experts for proper development,
2. Creating a new work group of experts to develop the proposal,
3. Returning the proposal to the source region for further development, or
4. Completing the development of the proposal within the standing committee.

The Board and NIST WMD will jointly address funding for work groups and recognize that some work groups may be able to accomplish their work through alternative means including email, telephone, web or video conferencing, or meeting in conjunction with other meetings. When funding is requested, there should be an identified product outcome and a timeline for achieving that outcome. The outcome should, at the completion of the committee's work, be reported to the appropriate standing committee for action on the item by the NCWM.

3. National Training Program Curriculum

The Board has turned over the National Training Program Curriculum to the Professional Development Committee and issues will now revert to the Professional Development Committee agenda items and report. This issue will no longer be on the BOD's agenda.

4. Voting Procedures

Reduced attendance at NCWM annual meetings in recent years due to budget constraints has caused difficulty for standing committees to move forward on some difficult voting issues. This prompted proposals to the Board to amend the voting procedures in the bylaws. The Board has heard testimony in past meetings both supporting and opposing such changes. The historical perspective for the current bylaws indicates that the goal is to get support for or against an item from a majority of the states and territories prior to adopting or rejecting a voting item.

Hearing no feedback on this issue at the 2005 Interim Meeting, the Board withdrew the proposal.

5. Marketplace Surveys

There was positive feedback and interest in conducting marketplace surveys. NCWM will refer to the product survey protocol adopted in 1999 for the coordination of any product surveys it conducts. The Board formed a team in accordance with the protocol and will plan a market survey in the next year as a joint effort with NIST WMD.

The Board believes marketplace surveys can be a useful tool for weights and measures jurisdictions. Based on comparisons with other jurisdictions, the data may be useful in protecting or increasing funding to a particular program and may be valuable in generating visibility for the value of weights and measures programs.

6. Meetings

Some of the constraints that had been in place for the selection of meeting sites and facilities have been removed. The Board indicated that the regional rotation does not necessarily need to continue nor does the mandatory Federal per diem room rate.

7. Conformity Assessment

The work groups are continuing work on their particular charges. A presentation by each of the three task forces was made during the Board's open hearings. Good progress has been made, and the Board asked the task forces to continue to move forward with developing the model. The current plan is to focus a pilot program on one device type for Initial Verification and Certificate Administrative Review. See Appendix C for complete Conformity Assessment update and presentations by the three task forces.

8. Electronic Copies of Pub 14

Some of our membership had requested the opportunity to purchase electronic copies of Pub 14 instead of the traditional hard copy. The Board recognized the added value electronic copies would provide our membership and gave staff direction to move forward with the creation of electronic copies of Pub 14. Staff completed the project and copies were available for sale at the Annual Meeting. Print copies will still be offered.

9. Website Revamp

The website revamp has been completed. The new website provides improved navigation to popular pages and more tools to benefit members. The regional associations were offered the opportunity to place their content as a section on the NCWM website, and the Central Weights and Measures Association has taken advantage of that opportunity.

10. Participation in International Standards Setting

The Board unanimously agreed to participate on the Committee on Participation Review, but NCWM will not sign the Declaration of Mutual Confidence document until it is ready to sign as a Country A with regard to R76 and R60. However in light of the decision by the NIST Force Group not to participate in OIML R60 testing of load cells, the Board is being asked to reconsider its position regarding R60. Specifically, the Board is being asked to consider being a "utilizing country" for R60 data since it may not be possible for a U.S. laboratory to conduct such evaluations. The Board has designated representatives for the Committee on Participation Review for R60 and R76. The Board recognized the need to involve the brick and mortar labs in the process.

11. Nominating Committee

The Nominating Committee submitted the following report to the NCWM Board of Directors:

- Chairman Elect: Mike Cleary, California
- Treasurer (one-year term): Tom Geiler, Town of Barnstable, Massachusetts
- Active Membership/Central (five-year term): Judy Cardin, Wisconsin

12. Future Meetings

NCWM Annual Meetings

Year	Dates	Location
2006	July 9 - 13	Chicago Marriott, Chicago, IL
2007	July 8 - 12	Snowbird Resort, Salt Lake City, UT

BOD 2005 Final Report

NCWM Interim Meetings

2006 January 22 - 25 Omni Jacksonville, Jacksonville, FL
2007 January 21 - 24 Omni Jacksonville, Jacksonville, FL
2008 January 13 - 16 Marriott Convention Center Hotel, New Orleans, LA

NTEP Lab & Sector Meetings

GMM/NIR Sector Meeting: August 24 - 25, 2005, Kansas City, MO
Weighing Sector Meeting: September 25 - 27, 2005, Columbus, OH
Measuring Sector Meeting: October 21 - 22, 2005, Memphis, TN

1. Membership Report

The total NCWM membership, as of July 10, 2005, is 2510. The membership breakdown by category is:

State Government	849
Local Government	492
U.S. Government	27
Foreign Government	31
Associate Members	844
Foreign Associate	42
Retirees	225

2. Financial Report

The Board reviewed the 2003-04 year-end audited financial report.

	Statement of Activities ending September 30, 2004	2004 Budget
Revenue & Support		
Government Dues	$ 93,220	$ 97,500
Associate Dues	$ 58,055	$ 61,750
National Type Evaluation Program	$435,397	$432,025
Interim Meeting Fees	$ 27,580	$ 21,750
Annual Meeting Fees	$ 68,822	$ 80,900
Publications	$ 20,274	$ 18,850
Advertising	$ 775	$ 975
Investment Return	$ 8,287	$ 7,500
Total revenue & support	$712,410	$721,250
Expenses		
Programs		
Membership	$ 12,749	$ 10,814
National Type Evaluation Program	$428,538	$431,662
Interim Meeting	$ 47,227	$ 51,056
Annual Meeting	$ 81,356	$ 95,545
Publications	$ 11,265	$ 15,601
Newsletter	$ 15,753	$ 15,315
Total Programs	$596,888	$619,993

BOD 2005 Final Report

Management & General
Management Fees	$ 48,655	$ 48,655
Board of Directors	$ 42,075	$ 25,000
Bank Fees	$ 11,697	$ 6,400
Website	$ 10,317	$ 11,635
Legal & Accounting	$ 5,479	$ 7,225
FMA Expense	$ 4,380	$ 0
Committee Travel	$ 1,972	$ 2,500
Insurance	$ 1,854	$ 2,700
Office Supplies	$ 1,495	$ 1,200
Telephone	$ 1,246	$ 2,000
Storage Fees	$ 960	$ 960
Printing & Duplicating	$ 932	$ 1,000
Miscellaneous	$ 168	$ 0
Postage	$ 47	$ 100
Total Management & General	$131,277	$109,375
Total Expenses	$728,165	$729,368
Change in net assets	($15,755)	

Net assets, beginning of year — **$622,387**
Net assets, end of year — **$606,632**

Assets

Current Assets
Cash & Cash Equivalents	$197,396
Certificates of Deposit	$551,267
Accounts Receivable	$ 299
Prepaid expenses	$ 2,506
Interest Receivable	$ 5,099
Total Assets	$756,567

Liabilities & Net Assets
Accounts payable	$ 626
Deferred Dues Revenue	$133,280
Total Liabilities	$133,906

Net Assets
Unrestricted $622,661
Total liabilities and net assets	$756,567

G. Weston Diggs, Virginia, NCWM Chairman
Don Onwiler, Nebraska, NCWM Chairman-Elect
Judy Cardin, Wisconsin
Charles Carroll, Massachusetts
Michael Cleary, California
Tom Geiler, Town of Barnstable, Massachusetts
Stephen Pahl, Texas
Michael Pinagel, Michigan
Christopher B. Guay, Procter & Gamble Co.
Darrell Flocken, Mettler-Toledo, Inc.
NCWM Staff: Beth W. Palys, CAE
NIST: Henry Oppermann

Board of Directors

THIS PAGE LEFT INTENTIONALLY BLANK.

Appendix A

Report on the Activities of the
International Organization of Legal Metrology (OIML)
And Regional Legal Metrology Organizations

International Legal Metrology Group
Weights and Measures Division, NIST

The International Legal Metrology Group (ILMG) of the Weights and Measures Division (WMD) of the National Institute of Standards and Technology (NIST) is responsible for coordinating U.S. participation in OIML and other international legal metrology organizations. Learn more about OIML at the OIML website at   http://www.oiml.org and the WMD website at   http://www.nist.gov/owm on the Internet. Dr. Charles Ehrlich, Group Leader of the ILMG, can be contacted at charles.ehrlich@nist.gov or at 301-975-4834 or by fax at 301-926-0647.

Please note: OIML publications are now available without cost at http://www.oiml.org

Table A
Table of Contents

I.   Report on the Activities of the OIML Technical Committees..A1
II. Mutual Acceptance Arrangement (MAA) on OIML Type Evaluations...A4
III. Report on the 39th Meeting of the International Committee of Legal Metrology (CIML)...............................A5
IV. Report on the 12th International Legal Metrology Conference..A5
V. Report on the 40th Meeting of the International Committee of Legal Metrology (CIML) A6
VI. 11th Annual Asia-Pacific Legal Metrology Forum (APLMF)...A7

I. Report on the Activities of the OIML Technical Committees

This section reports on recent activities and the status of work in OIML Technical Committees (TCs) and Technical Subcommittees (SCs) of specific interest to members of the NCWM. Also included are schedules of future planned activities of the Secretariats, the U.S. National Work Groups (USNWGs), and the International Work Groups (IWGs) of the Committees and Subcommittees. The name in *italics* after the Committee or Subcommittee is the country responsible for secretariat activities.

TC3 Metrological Control (United States)
A joint work group of the OIML, the International Bureau of Weights and Measures (BIPM), and the International Laboratory Accreditation Cooperation (ILAC) developed a draft revision of OIML D1 "Elements for a Law on Metrology." In early 2004, the NIST WMD reviewed the document for consistency with NIST Handbook 130. The revision of D1 presents the various elements that should be considered when preparing laws related to metrology. This document gives advice on general laws covering all the aspects of legal metrology, as well as specific laws related to some distinct aspects of metrology, such as legal units and traceability. OIML D1 was approved by the CIML in October 2004, has been published, and is available for free on the OIML website.

TC3/SC1 "Pattern Approval and Evaluation" (United States)
The OIML documents D19 "Pattern evaluation and pattern approval" and D20 "Initial and subsequent verification of measuring instruments and processes" have not been revised in over fifteen years. The subcommittee has approved the U.S. proposal for a combined revision of OIML D19 and D20 into a single document "Principles of metrological control of measuring instruments: type approval and verification." Key elements of OIML D3 "Legal Qualification of Measuring Instruments," R34 "Accuracy Classes of Measuring Instruments," and R42 "Metal Stamps for Verification Officers" will also be incorporated into the combined revision of OIML D19 and D20.

BOD 2005 Final Report
Appendix A - Report on Activities of OIML

The revised documents will incorporate recent developments such as the OIML certificate system, D27 "Initial verification of measuring instruments utilizing the manufacturer's quality management system," and the "Framework for a mutual acceptance arrangement (MAA) on OIML type evaluations." Consideration will be given to the appropriate conformity assessment options developed by the International Organization for Standardization (ISO) Council Committee on Conformity Assessment (ISO CASCO), including quality systems, product certification, and accreditation. Consideration needs to be given as well to information technology and statistical methods to increase or decrease verification intervals based upon proven instrument performance. For more information on this activity, contact Dr. Ambler Thompson at 301-975-2333 or at ambler@nist.gov.

TC5/SC1 Electronic Instruments (Netherlands)
The final Draft Document of D11 "General Requirements for Electronic Measuring Instruments" was approved by CIML postal ballot in 2004 and has been published. This is an especially important document in the OIML system because its testing requirements will become general guidance for all OIML Recommendations for electronic measuring instruments.

TC5/SC2 Software (Germany and France)
In May 2004, all OIML TCs and SCs that are currently revising an OIML Recommendation were contacted to ensure that software aspects are considered in revised Recommendations. All OIML Documents and Recommendations published since 1990 are being reviewed for terms and requirements related to software. A pre-draft of the document "Software in Legal Metrology" was circulated in October 2004 by the Secretariat. When complete, the document will serve as guidance for technical committees addressing software requirements in Recommendations for software-controlled instruments. The ILMG submitted U.S. comments on the pre-draft in February 2005, and the next draft is expected late in 2005. Please contact Wayne Stiefel at 301-975-4011 or by email at stiefel@nist.gov if you would like to participate in this project. Please see http://ts.nist.gov/ts/htdocs/230/235/TC5-SC2.htm to review the documents.

TC8/SC1 "Static Volume Measurement" (Austria)
The Secretariat submitted 1st CD revisions in January 2005 for OIML R71 "Fixed Storage Tanks," R80 "Road and Rail Tankers," and R85 "Automatic Level Gages for Measuring the Level of Liquid in Fixed Storage Tanks." U.S. comments, including those of the American Petroleum Institute, on all three of these documents were sent in April 2005. The Secretariat held a subcommittee meeting in April 2005 in Vienna, Austria. Another meeting of the subcommittee is scheduled for October 2005. Please contact Wayne Stiefel at 301-975-4011 or at stiefel@nist.gov if you would like copies of the documents or to participate in these projects.

TC8/SC3 "Measuring Instruments for Liquids other than Water." (Germany) and TC8/SC4 "Dynamic Mass Measurements (Liquids other than Water)" (United States)
OIML R117 "Measuring Instruments for Liquids other than Water" is undergoing an extensive revision, incorporating new instrument technologies and merging the document with OIML Recommendations R86 "Drum Meters" and R105 "Mass Flowmeters." This is a high priority project for OIML. ILMG is working with the U.S. National Work Group on flowmeters, Germany, and the Netherlands on this effort. Meetings of the U.S. National Work Group on flowmeters were held during the NCWM Annual Meeting in July 2004 in Pittsburgh, the NCWM Interim Meeting in January 2005 in Santa Monica, and the NCWM Annual Meeting in July 2005 in Orlando. Measurement Canada has been a strong contributor to this effort. A 2nd CD of R117 was circulated to the two international subcommittees and received over 90 % international "yes" votes in July 2004. The Draft Recommendation (DR) will be circulated to OIML member nations in the late summer of 2005 with an objective of receiving full CIML approval on R117 in 2006. If you have questions or would like to become involved in this effort, please contact Mr. Ralph Richter by email at ralph.richter@nist.gov or at 301-975-4025.

TC8/SC7 "Gas Metering" (Belgium and France)
The Secretariat circulated a 3rd CD of the Recommendation "Measuring Systems for Compressed Natural Gas (CNG) for Vehicles" and annexes covering performance tests for electronic devices and basic test procedures. In April 2003 the United States cast a negative ballot on the 3rd CD because the testing requirements were unrealistic. A 4th CD is being prepared by the Secretariat.

A ballot was circulated on the 3rd CD "Measuring Systems for Gaseous Fuel" in March 2004. This Recommendation is intended for large pipelines with large flow rates and high operating pressures, or systems not fitted with diaphragm gas meters. Different types of measuring systems are covered by the Recommendation: measuring systems providing indications of volume at base conditions or mass converted from a volume of gas determined at metering conditions, measuring systems providing directly the mass of gas, and measuring systems providing indication of energy corresponding to a volume at base conditions or a mass of gas. Based on a review of the 3rd CD and its requirements, the United States voted "no" in June 2004; comments were sent to the Secretariat recommending that several sections needed clarification, that the test report procedure be improved to better define flow conditions for improved meter measurement, and that severity levels be changed in the electrostatic discharge test. A 4th CD was received from the Secretariat and comments are due in November 2005. Please contact Wayne Stiefel at 301-975-4011 or at stiefel@nist.gov if you would like to obtain a copy of these documents or to participate in these projects.

TC8/SC8 "Gas Meters" (Netherlands)
Based on a poll of subcommittee members, R6 "General provisions for gas volume meters," R31 "Diaphragm Gas Meters", and R32 "Rotary Piston Gas Meters and Turbine Gas Meters" have been revised and combined into a single Recommendation. The Secretariat circulated a 2nd CD of this document, and U.S. comments were returned in March 2005. A subcommittee meeting to discuss the document was held in June 2005 in the Netherlands. Please contact Wayne Stiefel at 301-975-4011 or at stiefel@nist.gov if you would like to participate in this project.

TC9/SC1 "Nonautomatic Weighing Instruments" (Germany and France)
The current review cycle of R76 "Non-automatic Weighing Instruments" is of major importance to U.S. interests because the Recommendation serves as the foundation for a majority of the laws and regulations that governs weighing instruments around the world. This review is significant for U.S. weighing instrument manufacturers because international harmonization of requirements would eliminate technical barriers to trade and reduce the delays and the cost of getting new weighing instruments into the global marketplace. It is also important for legal metrology officials since it is taking place when the NCWM is considering its participation in the OIML Mutual Acceptance Arrangement (MAA) for type evaluations with other countries. The United States returned comments on the first working draft of the revised R76 in April 2004. This draft included new language addressing metrological controls for type evaluations, conformity, and initial and subsequent inspections. A first committee draft was circulated to the USNWG, and a U.S. response with comments was sent to the Secretariat in April 2005. The USNWG held a meeting in July 2005 and is being consulted concerning proposals to harmonize Handbook 44 and R76. If you would like to participate in this effort, please contact Steve Cook at 301-975-4003 or steven.cook@nist.gov.

TC9/SC2 "Automatic Weighing Instruments" (United Kingdom)
The Recommendation R134-1 "Automatic Instruments for Weighing Road Vehicles in Motion – Total Load and Axle Weighing" is out for final vote. If approved, the document should be published in early 2006. If you would like to receive a copy of this document, please contact Richard Harshman at 301-975-8107 or harshman@nist.gov.

TC17/SC1 "Humidity" (China)
The Secretariat is working closely with the United States and a small international work group (IWG) to revise OIML R59 "Moisture Meters for Cereal Grains and Oilseeds." The Secretariat distributed a first committee draft to the IWG in May 2003. All drafts have been distributed to the U.S. National Work Group, which for the most part is a subset of the NTEP Grain Sector. In October 2003 China hosted a meeting of the TC17/SC1 subcommittee in Beijing to review and discuss this revised document. A second committee draft that incorporated U.S. comments was circulated in May 2004 by the Secretariat. A meeting of the IWG was held in Paris in September 2004 to resolve conflicts on the document. U.S. comments on the 3rd CD of R59 were returned to the Secretariat in July 2005. Please contact Diane Lee at 301-975-4405 or at diane.lee@nist.gov if you would like to participate in this work group.

TC17/SC8 "Quality Analysis of Agricultural Products" (Australia)
A new subcommittee has been formed to study the issues and write a working draft document "Measuring Instruments for Protein Determination in Grains." Australia is the Secretariat for this new subcommittee. A work group meeting was held in May 2004 in Sydney. A second working draft of this document was received in August 2004, and a third working draft was received in May 2005. A work group meeting was held in June 2005 in Berlin

to discuss the latest round of comments on the third working draft. Please contact Diane Lee at 301-975-4405 or at diane.lee@nist.gov if you would like to participate in this working group.

II. Mutual Acceptance Arrangement (MAA) on OIML Type Evaluations

The OIML MAA has now entered the implementation phase. The first "provisional" Committee on Participation Review (CPR) has been established for OIML R60 (Load Cells) and R76 (Non-automatic Weighing Instruments). The CPR is being called 'provisional' to reflect the fact that the participants are under no obligation to sign either of the Declarations of Mutual Confidence (DoMCs) that are expected to result.

The first meeting of the CPR was held June 15 and 16, 2005, in Lyon, France, in conjunction with the 40th CIML Meeting and the 50th Anniversary Celebration of OIML. Mr. Stephen Patoray represented the NCWM, Mr. Steve Cook represented the Secretariat of OIML TC9 responsible for OIML R60, and Dr. Charles Ehrlich represented the Secretariat for OIML TC3/SC5 responsible for the MAA. Twenty-one countries had representatives at the meeting, with nine of the countries indicating interest in participating as an 'Issuing Participant' for at least one of the two DoMCs. (An 'Issuing Participant' is one that performs tests and issues certificates under the DoMC.) The CPR reviewed the application files of the nine countries wishing to be Issuing Participants and decided that two of the countries needed to have peer reviews conducted. (For reasons of confidentiality, no countries are being identified by name until the DoMC is signed.) A training course for peer review auditors will be held in September 2005 in Paris, and the peer reviews are expected to be completed by January 2006. Signing of the DoMCs for R60 and R76 is tentatively set for early 2006, shortly after the second CPR meeting to be held in February 2006. At that time countries who do not sign at least one of the DoMCs will no longer be members of the CPR (the CPR will then no longer be 'provisional'). It was proposed that countries may subsequently apply to join the CPR during two specified periods per year. (The CIML will be voting on this.).

Also at the first CPR meeting a draft 'Operating Rules for CPRs' was discussed, and it was agreed among CPR members that an 80 % voting rule would apply, with no more than one negative vote from an 'Issuing Participant'. The 'Operating Rules', containing this proposal and others, will be put forward to the CIML for postal vote. A draft implementation document on using ISO/IEC 17025 (requirements for testing laboratories), to be used for conducting the legal metrology audits, was also discussed. Another implementation document on ISO Guide 65 (requirements for issuing authorities) was circulated to the CPR for comment after the meeting. These implementation documents will ultimately be distributed as Working Drafts to OIML TC3/SC5 to be developed as OIML Documents.

The NCWM Board of Directors (BOD) had indicated to the BIML its desire to participate on the CPR, primarily to help answer many of the NCWM's questions and concerns, and realized that many details regarding the implementation of the MAA will be developed through discussions of the CPR. The NCWM also indicated to the BIML that the NCWM anticipates it will sign a DoMC only when it is prepared to do so as an OIML Issuing Authority that issues test data and OIML Certificates under the MAA (i.e., as an Issuing Participant). The BIML allowed the NCWM to participate on the provisional CPR under this arrangement. The United States is for now considered by the BIML as a country that will not issue OIML Certificates under the MAA but rather might in the future utilize those issued by other countries (a 'Utilizing Participant'). This arrangement could change as negotiations continue and the CPR discussions advance. At their July 2005 Annual Meeting in Orlando, the Board began considering whether NCWM should be a Utilizing Participant for R60 since all of the necessary load cell testing capability in the United States is not available. A final decision is anticipated at the January 2006 Interim Meeting in Jacksonville.

At their meeting in Berlin in 2004, the CIML instructed OIML TC3/SC5 to start revising both publication B10-1 (*MAA*) and publication B3, "OIML Certificate System for Measuring Instruments" after some experience with the MAA has been gained. Further implementation of the MAA may require that other detailed regulations be developed.

For further information on the MAA and its implementation, please contact Dr. Charles Ehrlich at charles.ehrlich@nist.gov or at 301-975-4834 or by fax at 301- 975-5414.

III. Report on the 39th Meeting of the International Committee of Legal Metrology (CIML) (held October 2004)

Representatives from 54 of the 59 member nations participated in the 39th Annual Meeting of the CIML in November 2004 in Berlin. Dr. Charles Ehrlich, the CIML Member for the United States, led the U.S. delegation. The delegation also included Dr. Richard Kayser, NIST Acting Deputy Director; Mr. Henry Oppermann, Chief of the NIST Weights and Measures Division; Dr. Claire Saundry, Chief of the NIST International Affairs Office; Mr. Stephen Patoray, Director of the U.S. National Type Evaluation Program (NTEP) of the National Conference on Weights and Measures (NCWM); and Dr. Jane Cowley, Office of Technical Specialized Agencies, Bureau for International Organization Affairs, U.S. Department of State.

Work of the TCs/SCs

The CIML approved the following International Documents and one International Recommendation:

- Revision of D1 Elements for a law on metrology;
- Revision of D9 Principles of metrological supervision;
- Revision of D11 General requirements for electronic measuring instruments;
- Revision of D14 Training of legal metrology personnel - Qualification - Training programs;
- Combined Revision of D6/D8 Measurement Standards - Requirements and Documentation;
- New D28 Conventional value of the result of weighing in air (reclassification of R 33); and
- R111-2 Weights of classes E1, E2, F1, F2, M1, M1-2, M2, M2-3 and M3. Part 2: Test Report Format (Edition 2004).

The Committee approved the assignment of the Secretariat of TC6 "Prepackaged products" to South Africa and the Secretariat of TC9/SC3 "Weights" to Germany. It was noted that Germany wishes to relinquish the Secretariat of TC12 "Instruments for measuring electrical quantities."

The Committee approved two new working projects:

- Revision of R99/ISO 3930 *Instruments for measuring vehicle exhaust emissions* as jointly proposed by TC16/SC1 and ISO TC22/SC5;
- New Recommendation on *Clinical infrared ear thermometers* as proposed by TC 18/SC2.

CIML Presidency

The Committee elected Mr. Alan E. Johnston (CIML Member for Canada) as its President for the next six years, effective at the opening of the 40th CIML Meeting in June 2005. The Committee was unable to elect a First Vice President because the required majority of votes was not obtained. Prof. Kochsiek (of Germany) agreed to continue his role as CIML First Vice President until the election of a new First Vice President at the 40th CIML Meeting.

IV. Report on the 12th International Legal Metrology Conference

Representatives from 54 of the 59 member nations participated in the 12th International Legal Metrology Conference from October 26-29, 2004, in Berlin. This Conference is held only once every four years. Members of the U.S. delegation to the Conference are listed in the CIML section (above) in this report.

Work of the TCs/SCs

The Conference formally sanctioned those new or revised Recommendations already approved by the CIML since the 11th Conference in 2000.

Recommendations approved in 2001:

- R16-1 Mechanical non-invasive sphygmomanometers (Edition 2002)
- R16-2 Non-invasive automated sphygmomanometers (Edition 2002)

BOD 2005 Final Report
Appendix A - Report on Activities of OIML

- R75-1 Heat meters. Part 1: General requirements (Edition 2002)
- R75-2 Heat meters. Part 2: Type approval tests (Edition 2002)
- R133 Liquid-in-glass thermometers (Edition 2002)

Recommendations approved in 2002:

- R84 Platinum, copper, and nickel resistance thermometers (for industrial and commercial use)(Edition 2003)
- R134-1 Automatic instruments for weighing road vehicles in motion. Total vehicle weighing (Edition 2003)

Recommendations approved in 2003:

- R48 Tungsten ribbon lamps for the calibration of radiation thermometers (Edition 2004)
- R49-1 Water meters intended for the metering of cold potable water. Part 1: Metrological and technical requirements (Edition 2003)
- R49-2 Water meters intended for the metering of cold potable water. Part 2: Test methods (Edition 2004)
- R52 Hexagonal weights - Metrological and technical requirements (Edition 2004)
- R61-1 Automatic gravimetric filling instruments. Part 1: Metrological and technical requirements – Tests (Edition 2004)
- R87 Quantity of product in prepackages (Edition 2004)
- R135 Spectrophotometers for medical laboratories (Edition 2004) Recommendation approved in 2004 by CIML postal approval
- R111-1 Weights of classes E1, E2, F1, F2, M1, M1-2, M2, M2-3 and M3 Part 1: Metrological and technical requirements (Edition 2004)

One Draft Recommendation, R136 *Instruments for measuring the area of leathers,* was directly sanctioned by the Conference.

OIML Recommendations R33 *Conventional value of the result of weighing in air* (Revised as D28) and R62 *Performance characteristics of metallic resistance strain gauges* were withdrawn. The Conference decided that OIML Test Report Formats, which are of an informative nature and concern the implementation of the Recommendation in national regulations, shall be approved by the CIML according to the rules applicable to International Documents without having to be sanctioned by the Conference.

OIML Publications – Now Available Without Cost

The conference approved a proposal to make all OIML publications, except those which are published jointly with other organizations, available free of charge in electronic format on the OIML website and to cease publishing Recommendations in paper format.

Administrative and Financial Matters

The conference adopted the *Budget for the Financial Period 2005-2008*; it represents a zero-real-growth increase (2 %) over the previous financial period. No Member State offered to host the 13th International Legal Metrology Conference (to be held in 2008). It was decided that the BIML will 'host' the 13th Conference in France if no other country steps forward.

V. Report on the 40th Meeting of the International Committee of Legal Metrology (CIML) (held June 2005)

The 40th CIML meeting was held in conjunction with the 12th International Metrology Congress, June 18 - 20, 2005, in Lyon, France. Representatives from 52 OIML member states participated in the meeting that also included a celebration of the 50th Anniversary of OIML.

BOD 2005 Final Report
Appendix A - Report on Activities of OIML

Opening addresses at the meeting were given by both the (outgoing) Acting CIML President Manfred Kochsiek (Germany) and the recently-elected CIML President Alan Johnston (Canada). Discussions at the meeting included concerns on implementing new financial regulations at the BIML, activities of the Presidential Council, and the OIML long-term strategy and action plan. A report was given on the activities of the Permanent Work Group on Developing Countries. Dr. Steven Carpenter, Director of the NIST Office of International and Academic Affairs, represented the United States on the work group. Reports were also given by representatives of several liaison organizations (such as BIPM and ISO) and several Regional Legal Metrology Organizations (such as SIM and APLMF).

The BIML Director gave a presentation on the organization and activities of the Bureau. Another presentation concerned efforts of the BIML to improve communication, coordinate the production of OIML publications, and improve the OIML web site.

Technical Activities:
The Committee decided:
- to disband and discontinue the work of TC 10/SC 6 Strain gauges,
- to merge TC8/SC1 Static volume measurement and TC8/SC2 Static mass measurement under the Co-secretariat of Austria and Germany with title TC8/SC1 Static volume and mass measurement, (disbanding the old TC8/SC2),
- to allocate the Secretariat of TC10/SC3 Barometers to China,
- to withdraw the following work projects:
  - TC7/SC1: p 1 revision R 30 *End standards of length (gauge blocks)*,
  - TC10/SC4: p 2 *Requirements for force measuring instruments for verifying material testing machines* in favor of the utilization of ISO 376,
  - TC17/SC6: p 1 *Calibration procedure for mine methanometers* and p 2 *Procedure for calibration of alarms of combustible gazes and vapors*.

The Committee approved the proposal from TC3/SC5 to use the Guides for the application of ISO 17025 and Guide 65 drawn up by the CPR on R60 and R76 as a first Working Draft and to proceed following the Directives for Technical Work. The Committee authorized the Bureau, together with the TC4 Secretariat (Slovakia), to decide together with ILAC on the best way of publishing the revised D10 *Recalibration intervals for measuring equipment used in testing laboratories*. The Committee instructed the Bureau to organize a meeting with the Secretariats of TC8/SC7 and TC8/SC8 (*Gas Meters*) and to redefine the scope of these Subcommittees' projects so as to avoid unnecessary discrepancies and the duplication of work.

The Committee took note of a report presented by Mrs. Gaucher, MAA Project Leader at the BIML, showing the progress in the implementation of the MAA and the outcome of the first CPR Meeting. *[Details on the MAA and the CPR are given in the MAA section of this report.]*

The Committee elected Mr. Stuart Carstens (South Africa) for a six-year term as First Vice President. He will take over his duties immediately. Prof. Kochsiek (Germany) will remain Vice President until the 41st CIML Meeting in 2006. The Committee approved the renewal of the contract of Mr. Magaña as BIML Director from January 1, 2006, to December 31, 2010. A new Assistant Director will be appointed in 2007, and a selection committee for that position was chosen; Dr. Ehrlich is on the selection committee.

Future CIML Meetings
The 41st CIML Meeting will be hosted by South Africa in Capetown in October 2006. The Committee noted that the People's Republic of China was considering inviting the CIML to hold its 42nd Meeting in China in October 2007. A decision on this will be made at the 41st CIML Meeting.

VI. 11th Annual Asia-Pacific Legal Metrology Forum (APLMF)

The 11th Annual Meeting and Work Group meetings of the Asia-Pacific Legal Metrology Forum (APLMF) were held October 6 - 8, 2004, in San Diego, CA. As host, the United States was represented by Dr. Charles Ehrlich, Mr. Henry Oppermann, and Mr. Wayne Stiefel of NIST, Mr. Michael Cleary, California Division of Measurement

BOD 2005 Final Report
Appendix A - Report on Activities of OIML

Standards, Mr. Chris Guay, Procter and Gamble Company, and Ms. Kathleen Thuner, Commissioner and Sealer of Weights and Measures for San Diego County. Ms. Thuner's staff graciously provided logistical support. The meetings were attended by more than 50 delegates from 18 member countries. There are presently 26 member economies, 20 full members and 6 corresponding members in the Forum.

Mr. Guay provided a special host economy presentation on "International and Regional Labeling Requirements: Local Control at what Local Cost" that explored the difficulties encountered by consumer product packagers when exporting into multiple countries. Issues discussed included different consumer product regulations, units of measure, expression of units, language requirements, regulated package sizes vs. unit pricing, and enforcement policies and practices. The need to reduce barriers through use of international guidelines and standards, harmonization of requirements, and mutual recognition of capabilities was emphasized.

The President of APLMF is Dr. Akira Ooiwa, who is Director of the Mechanical Metrology Division at the National Metrology Institute of Japan. Japan has agreed to continue serving as Secretariat until next year, but a new Secretariat is being sought. The Forum currently has seven active work groups: (1) Training chaired by Australia, (2) Prepackaged Goods chaired by New Zealand, (3) Mutual Acceptance Arrangements chaired by United States, (4) Utility Meters chaired by Canada, (5) Medical Measurements chaired by Chinese Taipei, and (6) Rice Moisture Measurements chaired by Japan. A new work group (7) on Traceability in Legal Metrology is being started by Japan. All of these work groups held meetings in San Diego.

The main activity of the APLMF has been to conduct regional training. Training on developing legislation for the implementation of OIML R87 (Prepackages) was held in Malaysia in July 2004. The training was conducted by New Zealand. A Seminar on Sphygmomanometers was held in Chinese Taipei from August 30 - September 5, 2004. Guest speakers from the United States and Germany provided most of the training. A training session on the verification of non-automatic weighing instruments is planned for November 2004 in Shanghai with trainers from the Peoples Republic of China and Australia. Training on electricity meters is scheduled for late 2004 in Vietnam, with Canada to provide the training. Mr. Cleary indicated that California might be able to provide training on CNG. The U.S. Food and Drug Administration has been asked to provide a training session on medical thermometers.

Malaysia will host the 2005 APLMF meeting in Kuala, Lampur, November 23 - 25, 2005. Please contact Dr. Ehrlich for details at charles.ehrlich@nist.gov or at 301-975-4834 or by fax at 301-926-0647.

BOD 2005 Final Report
Appendix B – AMC Minutes

Appendix B

NCWM Associate Membership Committee Minutes

July 11, 2005

The following individuals were in attendance:

Mark Galletta	Nestlé USA	mark.galletta@us.nestle.com
Gary Lameris	Hobart	gary.lameris@hobartcorp.com
Stephen Langford	Cardinal Scale	slangford@cardet.com
Paul Lewis	Rice Lake	paulew@rlws.com
Vince Orr	ConAgra Foods	vince.orr@conagrafoods.com
Chris Guay	Procter & Gamble	guay.cb@pg.com
Bill Sveum	Kraft Foods	wsveum@kraft.com
Gale Prince	Kroger	gale.prince@kroger.com
Krister Hardaf Segerstad	IKEA	krister@memo.ikea.com
Zina Juroch	Pier 1 Imports	zmjuroch@pier1.com
Richard Davis	Georgia Pacific	richard.davis@gapac.com
Darrell Flocken	Mettler-Toledo	darrell.flocken@mt.com
Pete O'Bryan	Foster Farms	obryanp@fosterfarms.com
Steve Steinborn	Hogan & Hartson	sbsteinborn@hhlaw.com
Carolyn Hall	Foster Farms	hallcd@fosterfarms.com
Michael Kelley	Wal-Mart Stores, Inc.	mkelly1@wal-mart.com
Bob Murnane	Seraphin Test Measures	rmurnane@pemfab.com
Louis Straub	Fairbanks Scales	lou.e.straub@fancor.com
Beth Palys	NCWM Headquarters	

Chairman Galletta called the meeting to order at 12:05 pm.

The minutes from the January 23, 2005, meeting, included as Appendix B in the NCWM Board of Directors report in NCWM Publication 16, were reviewed. Gary Lameris asked that the spreadsheet referred to in the minutes be included as part of the minutes. With this addition, the minutes were approved.

Financial Condition

Chairman Galletta reviewed the financial condition of the AMC stating that nine thousand dollars had been used to aid in the development of the NCWM website and that ten thousand dollars was reserved for support of the special event. Payment of the training requests for Washington and Arizona Weights and Measures had been made. The fund had a balance of $18,810.47 as of June 30, 2005, before any deduction for the special event.

Board of Directors Report

Darrell Flocken, the AMC representative on the NCWM Board of Directors, gave a report about Board activities:

- The Board of Directors is developing a Review Panel. This panel will act as a support group to the conference standing committees by reviewing new items. Don Onweiler and Henry Oppermann will make a presentation during this meeting to review the goals of this panel. The panel is made up of one Board of Directors member, a technical advisor from NIST WMD, the chair of the standing committees and industry experts in the field of scales, LMD, and packaging. The Board of Directors requests the AMC provide names for the three industry experts. The panel may also call upon other industry experts as the need arises.

- The AMC needs to recommend an associate member representative for the Professional Development Committee.

- Henry Oppermann, Chief of NIST WMD, retired effective July 1st of this year. NIST is planning on seeking a replacement for him and will be posting the position both internally and externally. NIST management hopes to name Henry's replacement by January 2006, but is not certain that this can be accomplished in this relatively short period of time. In the meantime, NIST will use department leaders on a rotating basis to perform Henry's duties. Tina Butcher will perform this role during July, Georgia Harris will do it in August, Chuck Erlich in September, and Ken Butcher in October. Four NCWM Board of Directors met with Belinda Collins of NIST to provide information on what characteristics Henry's replacement should have in order to ensure that the NCWM/NIST relationship continues to develop.

- The Board of Directors is reviewing a new NCWM budget for the next fiscal year. This budget includes an increase in NTEP Certificate of Conformance maintenance fees of ten dollars (from $145 to $155 per certificate), an increase of $10 in membership dues (from $65 to $75) and an increase in annual meeting registration of $50 (from $250 to $300). Chair-elect Don Onweiler stated that the conference has operated in the red for the last three years and that these increases will result in a projected profit of $7,648.

- Management Solutions has added Judy Markoe to their staff to work on public relation efforts to increase the membership of the NCWM. There will be no addition to management fees for this work.

- There have been additional discussions regarding changing the voting policy of the conference but there is no support for these changes from the Board of Directors at this time. This item will be dropped from the Board's agenda.

- The Board of Directors extends its thanks and appreciation to the AMC for the funds allocated to the new website. This new website is up and running with some cleanup and tweaking remaining to be completed. (There have been reports of large white areas in the screens when viewing the site. If you experience this, you should advise Management Solutions and include your hardware type, browser type and revision so that the problem may be resolved.)

- The 2007 annual meeting will take place on July 8 - 12 at Snowbird Resort in Salt Lake City, Utah. The 2008 Interim Meeting of the NCWM will be held in New Orleans from January 13 - 16.

- The NCWM and NIST WMD are developing the next steps in a market survey plan. Don Onweiler will speak on this topic on Tuesday and may appoint a team to develop a plan for the survey.

- There has been a small decrease in some segments of NCWM membership but the Board feels that this is close to a turnaround in membership and that they expect it to grow in the future.

NCWM Website

Beth Palys of Management Solutions reported that the new NCWM website came online last week and that they are accepting feedback about the site content and operation. The site will undergo further development and refinement. The AMC listserve will be activated at the conclusion of this meeting. If you experience problems with the operation of the site, please report your problem to Management Solutions personnel.

Elections and Appointments

- Vince Orr was elected as the new Secretary for the AMC
- Gary Lameris was elected as the recommended associate member representative on the Professional Development Committee
- Lou Straub was appointed as the scale expert to the new Review Panel
- Gordon Johnson was appointed as the LMD expert to the new Review Panel
- Mark Galletta was appointed as the packaging expert to the new Review Panel

Training Requests

Mark Galletta will draft a new procedure for reviewing training requests and forward it to committee members for review and comment.

New Business

Vince Orr proposed a technical roundtable discussion for next year's meeting. He suggested a topic on Net Content Control to provide specific information to NCWM membership in this area. He indicated that he will ask the Professional Development Committee to help sponsor it. The panel will consist of at least three industry representatives, one legal representative, and two weights and measures representatives. The discussion should take about 2 hours. This should be more fully developed by the NCWM Interim Meeting.

Adjournment

The meeting was adjourned at 12:55 pm.

Respectfully submitted,
Stephen Langford
Secretary/Treasurer, AMC

THIS PAGE LEFT INTENTIONALLY BLANK.

Appendix B1

AMC Funds Allocations

AMC Fund Allocations				
AMC Fiscal Report as of 12/30/04		**Amount**	**Current AMC Balance**	**28,245**
Fund Balance on 9/30/04		16,030	Allocations:	Reserved
Revenue this Fiscal YTD		12,215	Special Event	10,000
Amount Paid Out		---	AMC "reserve"	500
Current AMC Balance		28,245	Available for Website & Training	17,745

	Jurisdiction	Contact	Category	Purpose	Requested	Approved
1	NCWM	Board of Directors	Website	NCWM website revamp	29,000	9,000
2	CO Dept of Ag	Kristin Young (A)	Attend Meetings	T&E for 1 representative at 2 meetings (NCWM & NTEP)	2,200	0
3	NH	Richard Cote	Attend Meetings	T&E for 1 representative at 2 meetings (NCWM & NEWMA)	1,000	0
4	AK	Ed Comiskey	Attend Training	T&E for 1 person at NIST Basic Metrology Seminar	3,260	0
5	CO Dept of Ag	Kristin Young (B)	Attend Training	T&E for several inspectors at H44 training	1,300	1,300
6	CO Dept Labor	Mahesh Albuquerque	Attend Training	Field inspector training (1 person)	1,500	0
7	CT	Frank Greene	Attend Training	Fees for 9 inspectors (statistical sampling)	500	500
8	HI	Michael Tang	Attend Training	T&E for 1 person NIST Advanced Metrology Seminar	1,500	0
9	SD	David Phahler	Attend Training	T&E for 3 inspectors at H44 training	2,085	2,085
10	Spokane	Steve Parker	Attend Training	T&E for 2 inspectors (scale certification & commodity inspection	1,000	1,000
11	WA	Gerald Buendel	Attend Training	Fees for 14 inspectors (retail computing scales)	500	500
12	AZ	Dennis Ehrhart	Conduct Training	Facilitator fee for HB 44 training offered to W&M program members	700	700
13	MA	Charles Carroll	Conduct Training	Room rental, equipment rental, printing costs & related expenses	2,000	1,710
14	OH	Kenneth Wheeler	Conduct Training	Purchase training materials for Training Assistants Program	450	450
15	PA	Ken Deitzler	Conduct Training	Purchase PowerPoint projector	4,000	0
16	WA	Gerald Buendel	Conduct Training	Expenses for 2 programs (random pack & market survey)	500	500
	Totals				51,485	17,745
				Still Available:		0

AMC approved $1,710 for now – and up to $2,000 if approved training funds from other jurisdictions are not spent by end of August '05.

THIS PAGE LEFT INTENTIONALLY BLANK.

Appendix C

NTEP - Conformity Assessment Program (CAP) Update

During the NCWM Annual Meeting held July 9 - 14, 2005, in Orlando, FL, the chairs of the three work groups for the Conformity Assessment Program (CAP) gave a presentation to the NCWM Board during their work session and again to the NCWM membership during the open hearings. Presenting were: Don Onwiler, Administrative Review of NTEP CC's; Lou Straub, Initial Verification (IV); and Mark Knowles, Verified Conformity Assessment Program (VCAP). Each chairman used a prepared PowerPoint presentation while narrating the details related to each slide. The presentations were well received by both the Board and general membership. After the presentation, questions from the floor were answered by the respective chairs.

The presentations as they were given at the meeting are included in this Appendix. It was evident after the presentation that additional work is still needed to answer all of the remaining questions regarding the details needed to implement each of these sections of the overall program. In some cases the work groups will meet in an attempt to answer these questions. In the case of the IV work group, a pilot of the IV Program on small-capacity computing scales is planned in order to gain insight where additional information may be needed and how data may best be handled.

Once these questions have been answered by the work groups, the NCWM Board and NTEP Committee may also have additional work to address any changes or clarifications to the exiting policy before the full program is implemented.

THIS PAGE LEFT INTENTIONALLY BLANK.

Appendix C1

Initial Verification

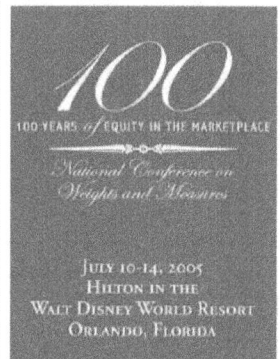

NTEP Administrative Policy

- Conformity Assessment Process: Three Steps

- Initial Verification
- Administrative Review of CC
- Verified Conformity Assessment Program

Initial Verification

- Initial Verification Work Group Established

- Weights and Measures Officials
- NIST
- Scale Manufacturers
- Meter Manufacturers

Initial Verification Work Group

- First Meeting: May, 2004

- Work Group identified three areas to be addressed in their initial meeting

Initial Verification Work Group

1. What are the areas of concern that an initial verification should cover?

BOD 2005 Final Report
Appendix C1 – Initial Verification

Initial Verification Work Group

2. What is needed to conduct an Initial Verification Test and who is able to perform the Initial Verification Test?

Initial Verification Work Group

3. What is done with the information collected?

BOD 2005 Final Report
Appendix C1 – Initial Verification

Initial Verification Work Group

- Second Meeting: May, 2005

- Established a Pilot Program

- Developed a Test Procedure and Report Form

Initial Verification Pilot Program

- Selected one device type for a Pilot Program

- Small Capacity Scales (less than or = to 100 lbs)

- 58 Active CC's for Computing Scales

Initial Verification Test Procedures

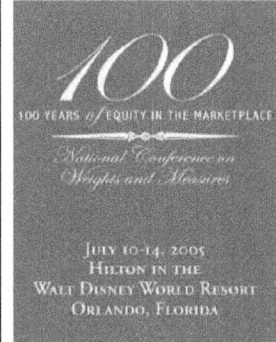

- NIST Handbook 44

- Established EPO's found in NIST Handbook 112

EPO No. 1
Retail Computing Scales

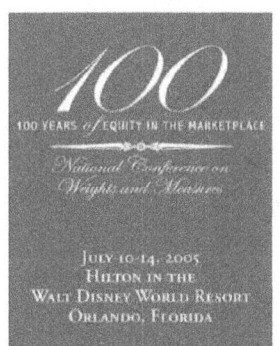

1. Zero-load balance as found. For pre-packaging scale,
   check to determine if tare is being taken........................S.1.1., UR.4.1., S.2.1.1., S.2.1.2.,G-S.5.2.2.(d) (1/1/86)
2. General Considerations
   Selection........................G-UR.1.1.
   Installation   G-UR.2.1.,G-UR.2.2., UR.2.2.
   Supports and clearance........................UR.2.1., UR.2.4.

   Check to be sure the scale supports are adequate to support the scale and test weights equal to the capacity of the scale !

   Accessibility for inspection, testing, and sealing........................G-UR.2.3.
   Testing devices at a central location........................G-UR.4.6.
   Assistance........................G-UR.4.4.
   Position, customer readability........................G-UR.3.3., S.1.8.3.
   Level indicating means and condition........................S.2.4., UR.4.2.
   Maintenance, use, and environmental factors
                   (cleanliness, obstructions, modifications, etc.)G-S.2.,G-UR.1.2., G-UR.3.1.,
   G-UR.3.2.,   UR.3.5.,G-UR.4., UR.2.3., UR.4.3.

3. Marking........................S.6.3.,G-S.5.24, S.5.1., S.6.2
   a. Marking requirements - all devices
      Identification........................G-S.1.
      Name or ID of manufacturer........................Retroactive
      Model designation........................Retroactive
      Model prefix........................(1/1/03)
      Nonrepetitive serial number........................(1/1/68)

BOD 2005 Final Report
Appendix C1 – Initial Verification

Initial Verification Test Report Form

- The NCWM Voluntary Program Assessment Work Group developed an evaluation checklist

- Inspector Evaluation Checklist for Small Capacity Scales used as a model Test Report Form

Scale Capacity Scale Inspection Checklist

2. Inspection and Marking Requirements
The Initial verification inspection must verify the device complies with marking requirements in NIST HB 44 Scales Code, Table S.6.3.a. and Table S.6.3.b.

2.1	Zero load balance as found	Yes No
2.2	Zero indication [S.1.1.(c),S.1.1.1.(b)]	Yes No NA PMT
2.3	Level indicating means	Yes No NA PMT
2.4	The name, initials, or trademark of the manufacturer._____	Yes No PMT
2.5	The model designation (model, type or pattern)_____	Yes No PMT
2.6	NTEP Certificate of Conformance number_____	Yes No PMT
2.7	A non-repetitive serial number._____	Yes No PMT
2.8	The marked accuracy class. NIST HB 44 Scales Code, Table 3 _____	Yes No PMT
2.9	The nominal capacity by minimum scale division. (on both the customer and operator sides of the scale) _____	Yes No PMT
2.10	Does the scale verification scale division, e, equal the displayed scale division, d?	Yes No NA PMT
2.11	If no, than e must be marked on the scale. _____	Yes No NA PMT

Initial Verification Pilot Program

- We need volunteers to test the Pilot Program!
- Not every State will have to participate.
- Will some minimal training be necessary?

Initial Verification Pilot Program

- Administrative review of CC's will assist the Initial Verification process
- Other device types can be added by following the established EPO's in NIST HB 112

NTEP Conformity Assessment

- Any Questions for the Initial Verification Work Group?

Appendix C2

Administrative Review of Certificates of Conformance

The Goals of Administrative Review

- Uniform application of NTEP by weights and measures officials is dependent on good Certificates.
- We are focusing on;
  - **Content**,
  - **Format**, and
  - **Accuracy of Information**.

BOD 2005 Final Report
Appendix C2 – Administrative Review of CCs

Certificate Content

Images such as photos or drawings my be beneficial in many cases to assist in field verification.

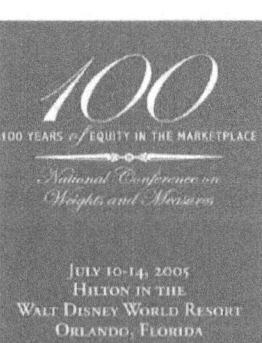
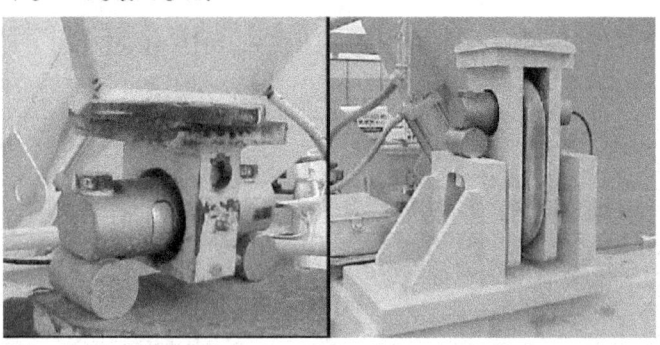

Unapproved | Approved

Certificate Format

- Relatively simple to address.
- Format has evolved over time.
- The template labs use can be modified to assist in this effort.
- The new template would apply to all certificates as they are reviewed and updated.

Accuracy of Information on Certificates

- Some certificates allow parameters beyond those allowed by Pub 14.
- If the manufacturer has not taken full advantage of incorrect parameters, resolution may be relatively easy.
- In those cases where manufacturers have taken advantage of the wider parameter, additional NTEP policy may be warranted to gain a resolution.

BOD 2005 Final Report
Appendix C2 – Administrative Review of CCs

Accuracy of Information on Certificates

- Have there been changes in manufacturing that would;
    - Require additional evaluation?
    - Require amendment of the Certificate?
- Assistance from manufacturers and NTEP laboratories may be necessary.

Who will perform the Certificate Review?

- We're not sure at this point.
    - Manufacturer?
    - NTEP Laboratory?
    - NTEP Director?
- May need a cooperative effort of all three.
- May be handled on a case-by-case basis.

How do we proceed?

- Work in conjunction with the Initial Verification pilot program for computing scales.
- Use feedback from that project to define content and format.

How Do We Pay For It?

- If labs assist, they will want fees.
- If NTEP Director Assists, NTEP will want fees.
    - Will the NTEP Director have time, or will additional staff be required?
- Manufacturers may be able to simplify process and reduce costs.
- NTEP Committee may need to address through policy.

THIS PAGE LEFT INTENTIONALLY BLANK

Appendix C3

Verified Conformity Assessment Program (VCAP)

Verified Conformity Assessment Program

VCAP
By: Mark Knowles
Carla Nagel

NCWM Annual Meeting
July 2005
Orlando, FL

Core Members

- Mark Knowles –   HBM Inc. – Chair
- Carla Nagel –   Avery Weigh-Tronix – Co Chair
- Darrell Flocken – Mettler-Toledo
- Frank Rusk –   Coti Inc.
- Gary Lameris – Hobart
- Jesus Zapien – A+D Engineering Inc.
- Link Yeager –   Cardinal Scale Manufacturing
- Paul Lewis Sr. – Rice Lake Weighing
- Mark McCombs – Vishay Transducers

BOD 2005 Final Report
Appendix C3 – Verified Conformity Assessment Program

Introduction

- NTEP requires that certified devices must meet appropriate influence factors as identified in NIST Handbook 44
- Since device conformity, to these requirements, cannot be tested during initial verification, manufacturers must have a VCAP program in place to ensure that metrological devices and/or components are produced at a level consistent with that of the device and/or component submitted for NTEP evaluation

Working Group Responsibilities

- The responsibility of the VCAP Group is focused on the requirements and guidelines to support the program
- The intention is to establish a "level playing field" among manufacturers of metrological devices and/or components affected by these influence factors
- Certificate Holders must show evidence of conformance to influence factor testing capabilities

General

- The goal is to concentrate more on actual testing and test data than internal procedures
- This program will be site specific and will focus on the site that controls the "testing" of the device.
- Internal procedural audits are required

General

- ISO certification is a benefit but not a requirement
- Recommend yearly audit first three years, then merit would allow three year cycle thereafter (Change to policy, section c)

Registrar Responsibilities

- Registrar responsible to audit certificate holders site responsible for the testing of the device
- RAB or equivalent (FM, UL, etc.)
- International Representatives
- Certificate Holder able to choose Registrar according to above requirements

Certificate Holders Responsibilities

- Schedule stand alone audit, not part of ISO, FM, UL etc.
- Audit to be scheduled during an influence factor test so auditor can witness test, data recording, actions taken, etc.
- New Certificate Holder must have process capability audit prior to receiving certificate from NTEP

Certificate Holders Responsibilities

- A certificate Holder may appeal non-conformance items during the conformity assessment audit
- Manufacturer may appeal to NTEP Director prior to pulling a certificate if non-conformance warrants that action
- Time Frame to fix non-conformance issues is 90 days after audit is complete

NCWM Responsibilities

- Create Database to track audit dates, certification etc.
- Require VCAP Audit Report to be provided during annual maintenance
- List of default registrar for those not ISO
- VCAP certification required within a one year cycle of maintenance fee (example if VCAP approved in July, certification required by November of following year) This is to kickoff the audit cycle.

Sampling/Testing

- Sample plan to be in compliance with established sampling plans (refer to SMA plan as reference or MIL standard 105E)
- Model/family selection is in compliance with NTEP evaluation guidelines as established in appropriate sections of Publication 14 (Devices to be submitted for evaluation)

Sampling/Testing

- Objective evidence of testing when substitution of MSC's
- An engineering change system to control engineering/design changes affecting any MSC's including appropriate testing and methods to ensure changes are released to production

Open Issues

- The Policy is complete
- Checklist for Auditor to audit by
- Define Process Capability and Objective Evidence (test results)
- Definition of minor / major non-conformances

THIS PAGE LEFT INTENTIONALLY BLANK.

L&R Committee 2005 Final Report

Report of the Laws and Regulations Committee

Joe Gomez, Chairman
New Mexico Weights and Measures

Reference
Key Number

200 INTRODUCTION

This is the report of the Committee on Laws and Regulations (hereinafter referred to as "Committee") for the 90th Annual Meeting of the National Conference on Weights and Measures (NCWM). It is based on the Interim Report offered in the NCWM Publication 16, "Committee Reports," testimony at public hearings, comments received from the regional weights and measures associations and other parties, the addendum sheets issued at the Annual Meeting, and actions taken by the membership at the voting session of the Annual Meeting. The informational items presented below were adopted as presented when this report was approved.

Table A identifies the agenda items in the Report by Reference Key Number, title, and page number. The first three digits of the Reference Key Numbers of the items are assigned from the subject series listed below. Voting items are indicated with a "**V**" after the item number. Items marked with an "**I**" after the item number are informational. Items marked with a "**D**" after the key numbers are developing issues. The developing designation indicates an item has merit; however, the item is returned to the submitter for further development before any action is taken at the national level. Items marked "**W**" have been withdrawn from consideration. Table B lists the appendices to the report, and Table C provides a summary of the results of the voting on the Committee's items and the report in entirety.

This report contains recommendations to amend National Institute of Standards and Technology (NIST) Handbook 130, 2002 Edition, "Uniform Laws and Regulations," or NIST Handbook 133, "Checking the Net Contents of Packaged Goods," Fourth Edition. Proposed revisions to the handbook(s) are shown in **bold face print** by ~~striking out~~ information to be deleted and **underlining** information to be added. New items proposed for the handbooks are designated as such and shown in **bold face print**. Text presented for information only is shown in *italic* print. When used in this report, the term "weight" means "mass."

Subject Series

Introduction	200 Series
NIST Handbook 130 - General	210 Series
Uniform Laws	220 Series
Weights and Measures Law (WML)	221 Series
Weighmaster Law (WL)	222 Series
Engine Fuels, Petroleum Products, and Automotive Lubricants Inspection Law (EFL)	223 Series
Uniform Regulations	230 Series
Packaging and Labeling Regulation (PLR)	231 Series
Method of Sale Regulation (MSR)	232 Series
Unit Pricing Regulation (UPR)	233 Series
Voluntary Registration Regulation (VRR)	234 Series
Open Dating Regulation (ODR)	235 Series
Uniform National Type Evaluation Regulation (UNTER)	236 Series
Engine Fuels, Petroleum Products, and Automotive Lubricants Regulation (EFR)	237 Series
Examination Procedure for Price Verification	240 Series
Interpretations and Guidelines	250 Series
NIST Handbook 133	260 Series
Other Items	270 Series

L&R Committee 2005 Final Report

Table A
Index to Reference Key Items

Ref. Key No.	Title of Item	Page
200	INTRODUCTION	1
221	UNIFORM WEIGHTS AND MEASURES LAW	3
221-1 V Update	Terminology	3
232	METHOD OF SALE REGULATION	6
232-1 D Temperature	Compensation for Petroleum Products	6
234	UNIFORM REGULATION FOR THE VOLUNTARY REGISTRATION OF SERVICEPERSONS AND SERVICE AGENCIES	7
234-1 V Update	Terminology	7
237	ENGINE FUELS, PETROLEUM PRODUCTS, AND AUTOMOTIVE LUBRICANTS REGULATION	10
237-1 V	Biodiesel Fuel Identification and Labeling	10
237-2 I	Premium Diesel Lubricity	12
260	NIST HANDBOOK 133, CHECKING THE NET CONTENTs OF PACKAGED GOODS	13
260-1 W	Amend § 2.3 Basic Test Procedure, and Table 2-5	13
260-2 W	Amend § 3.11 and MAV Table 2-10	14
260-3 W	Make MAV Tables More Uniform	15
270	OTHER ITEMS	15
270-1 W	Tare on Case-Ready Packages of Meat	15

Table B
Appendices

Appendix	Title	Page
A	Sample List of Documentary Standards for Item 221-1	A1

Table C
Voting Results

Reference Key Number	House of State Representatives		House of Delegates		Results
	Yeas	Nays	Yeas	Nays	
221-1	33	5	23	7	Item Passed
234-1	36	1	33	0	Item Passed
237-1	37	0	38	0	Item Passed
200 - Entire Committee Report	37	0	38	0	Report Accepted

Details of all Items
(In order by Reference Key Number)

221 UNIFORM WEIGHTS AND MEASURES LAW

221-1 V Update   **Terminology**

(This item was adopted)

Source: Southern Weights and Measures Association (SWMA)

Recommendation: Amend the UWML as described below:

Amend the Table of Contents as shown:

Table of Contents

Section	Page
1. Definitions	21
~~1.4. Primary Standards~~	~~21~~
~~1.5. Secondary Standards~~	~~21~~
1.12. Standard, Field	23
1.13. Accreditation	23
1.14. Calibration	23
1.15. Traceability	23
1.16. Uncertainty	23
1.17. Verification	23
1.18. Recognition	23
1.19. Standard, Reference	23
1.20. Standard, Working	23

Delete Sections 1.4. and 1.5. as follows and renumber the remaining definitions in sequence:

~~1.4. Primary Standards. -- The term "primary standards" means the physical standards of the State that serve as the legal reference from which all other standards for weights and measures are derived.~~

1.5. Secondary Standards, Secondary. -- The term "secondary standards" means the physical standards that are traceable to the primary standards through comparisons, using acceptable laboratory procedures, and used in the enforcement of weights and measures laws and regulations.

Add these definitions:

1.12. Standard, Field. - A physical standard that meets specifications and tolerances in NIST 105-series standards (or other suitable and designated standards) and is traceable to the reference or working standards through comparisons, using acceptable laboratory procedures, and used in conjunction with commercial weighing and measuring equipment (1.13).
(Added 2005)

1.13. Accreditation. - A formal recognition by a recognized Accreditation Body that a laboratory is competent to carry out specific tests or calibrations or types of tests or calibrations. NOTE: Accreditation does not ensure compliance of standards to appropriate specifications.
(Added 2005)

1.14. Calibration. - A set of operations which establishes, under specified conditions, the relationship between values indicated by a measuring instrument or measuring system, or values represented by a material measure, and the corresponding known values of a measurand.

Also: Comparison of a measurement standard or instrument with another standard or instrument to detect, correlate, report, or eliminate by adjustment any inaccuracy of the compared.
(Added 2005)

1.15. Traceability. - The property of the result of a measurement or the value of a standard whereby it can be related to stated references, usually national or international standards, through an unbroken chain of comparisons all having stated uncertainties.
(Added 2005)

1.16. Uncertainty. - A parameter associated with the result of a measurement that characterizes the dispersion of the values that could reasonably be attributed to the measurand.
(Added 2005)

1.17. Verification. - The formal evaluation of a standard or device against the specifications and tolerances for determining conformance.
(Added 2005)

1.18. Recognition. - A formal recognition by NIST Weights and Measures Division that a laboratory has demonstrated the ability to provide traceable measurement results and is competent to carry out specific tests or calibrations or types of tests or calibrations.
(Added 2005)

1.19. Standard, Reference. - A standard, generally of the highest metrological quality available at a given location, from which measurements made at that location are derived. The term "reference standards" means the physical standards of the State that serve as the legal reference from which all other standards for weights and measures within that State are derived.
(Added 2005)

1.20. Standard, Working. - A standard that is usually calibrated against a reference standard, and is used routinely to calibrate or check material measures, measuring instruments, or reference materials. The term "working standards" means the physical standards that are traceable to the reference standards through comparisons, using acceptable laboratory procedures, and used in the enforcement of weights and measures laws and regulations.
(Added 2005)

L&R Committee 2005 Final Report

Amend Section 3 as shown:

Section 3. Physical Standards

Weights and measures that are traceable to the U.S. prototype standards supplied by the Federal Government, or approved as being satisfactory by the National Institute of Standards and Technology, shall be the State ~~primary~~ **reference and working** standards of weights and measures, and shall be maintained in such calibration as prescribed by the National Institute of Standards and Technology **as demonstrated through laboratory accreditation or recognition**. All ~~secondary~~ **field** standards may be prescribed by the director and shall be verified upon their initial receipt, and as often thereafter as deemed necessary by the director. **(Amended 2005)**

Amend Sections 12a, 12h, and 12p as follows:

Section 12. Powers and Duties of the Director

The Director shall:

a. maintain traceability of the State standards ~~to the national standards in the possession of the National Institute of Standards and Technology as~~ **demonstrated through laboratory accreditation or recognition;**
(Amended 2005)

h. ~~test annually the~~ **verify the field** standards for weights and measures used by any **city or county jurisdiction** within the State, **before being put into service, tested annually or as often thereafter as deemed necessary by the director based on statistically evaluated data,** and approve the same when found to be correct;
(Amended 2005)

p. provide for the training of weights and measures personnel, and may establish minimum training and performance requirements which shall then be met by all weights and measures personnel, whether county, municipal, or State. The director may adopt the training standards of the National Conference on Weights and Measures' National Training Program **and the laboratory metrology standards specified by the NIST accreditation and/or recognition requirements**; and
(Added 1991; Amended 2005)

Discussion: This item came to the Southern Weights and Measures Association from the NIST Handbook Update Work Group in conjunction with Item 234-1 and Specifications and Tolerances (S&T) Committee Item 360-2. It is the intent of the work group that these three items be considered together.

One of the reasons for these proposals is to update the terminology used in Handbooks 130 and 44 to conform to international definitions. The terms "primary standard" and "secondary standard" have been eliminated to avoid confusion with the international usage of these terms. Terms like "reference standard," "field standard," "traceability," and "uncertainty" have been added to reflect their use within these documents. The proposed changes also allow state directors to exercise more discretion when evaluating calibration intervals, referencing documentary standards, and accepting calibration reports.

This particular proposal allows state directors to change the calibration interval for field standards (which are now required to be calibrated annually). This proposal permits a jurisdiction to collect historical calibration data, including "as-found" measurements, to evaluate whether or not an annual calibration interval is appropriate for a particular type of standard. Based on a statistical analysis of its historical data, a lab may find that its stainless steel field weights only need to be calibrated once every 5 years, while their cast iron weights need to be calibrated every 6 months. The intent is to save jurisdictions time and money by setting calibration intervals at suitable frequencies rather than at arbitrary fixed intervals. This should also lead to improved inspection accuracy by ensuring field standards are within tolerance during the entire calibration interval. Laboratory metrologists should be familiar with adjusting calibration intervals for laboratory standards and may be a useful resource for both providing data and doing the statistical analysis. Jurisdictions that need more information or assistance with statistical approaches to changing calibration intervals may consult the National Conference of Standards Laboratories International (NCSLI) Recommended Practice (RP) #1, "Establishment & Adjustment of Calibration Intervals."

These proposed changes would have relatively little effect on state and local weights and measures programs. There is no mandate for a jurisdiction to change the way it currently operates. The proposed changes would serve only to increase control and flexibility when evaluating field standard calibration intervals, the acceptance of accredited private lab calibration reports, and other similar topics. Much of what is being proposed reflects practices already occurring in jurisdictions across the country. The Committee discussed this item in a joint session with the Specifications and Tolerances Committee and met with both NIST and several metrologists to resolve questions related to the meaning of the definitions.

The Committee received a comment expressing reservations about the appropriateness of all the new definitions proposed but concluded the new definitions were appropriate and submitted the item for adoption.

232 METHOD OF SALE REGULATION

232-1   D   Temperature Compensation for Petroleum Products

Source: Southern Weights and Measures Association (SWMA). (See Item 232-4 in the Report of the 89th NCWM Annual Meeting in 2004.)

Recommendation: Amend the Method of Sale Regulation in Handbook 130 as shown below:

> 2.XX. Temperature Correction for Petroleum Products Other Than LPG. - All petroleum products other than LPG shall be sold by liquid volume.
>
> > 2.XX.1. Petroleum products sold in volumes greater than 18,927 liters (5,000 U.S. gallons) may be corrected to the volume at 15 °C (60 °F), provided:
> >
> > > 2.XX.1.1. The correction is made through automatic means; and
> > >
> > > 2.XX.1.2. The measuring device and all associated documents clearly indicate the volume has been corrected for temperature.
> >
> > 2.XX.2. Petroleum products sold in volumes less than or equal to 18,927 liters (5,000 U.S. gallons) through (list specific device(s)) may be corrected to the volume at 15 °C (60 °F), provided:
> >
> > > 2.XX.2.1. The correction is made through automatic means;
> > >
> > > 2.XX.2.2. The measuring device and all associated documents clearly indicate the volume has been corrected for temperature; and
> > >
> > > 2.XX.2.3. All sales by the same vendor within a state are corrected over at least a 12-month period.
> >
> > 2.XX.3. The volume of petroleum products sold through retail motor-fuel devices and in all transactions not covered in 2.XX.2. or 2.XX.3. shall be the volume at the conditions at the time of sale. Products shall not be artificially heated prior to sale.

Discussion: Selling fuel adjusted to the volume at 15 °C (60 °F) throughout the distribution system is the most equitable way fuel can be sold without the buyer or seller gaining a competitive advantage. Allowing a distributor to buy product at wholesale by gross volume and sell it at retail by net volume is not equitable. A single method of sale should be required so a prospective customer can make a value comparison. There is no practical way customers can make value comparisons when some locations sell product temperature compensated and other locations sell the same product without temperature compensation.

This item is considered in conjunction with a temperature compensation item that is before the Specifications and Tolerances (S&T) Committee, Item 331-1, although that item is limited to vehicle-tank meters. The Committee believes this is an important issue that should be given careful consideration and that it must be discussed with parties that may be affected by its adoption. The Committee has requested authorization and funding from the Board of Directors to establish a work group to bring together interested parties and build a consensus on the best way to resolve this issue.

A similar proposal was made by NEWMA in 2000 that mirrored a temperature compensation item before the S&T Committee at the time. In 2000 NEWMA noted that Pennsylvania, New Hampshire, Maine, and Canada permit temperature compensation in sales of products like home heating fuel and retail gasoline. In 2001 the Committee withdrew that item after several jurisdictions opposed its adoption.

At the 2005 Interim Meeting the Committee heard several comments opposing the original language of this item and received an alternate recommendation from NEWMA. The Committee agreed to accept and circulate the NEWMA language for comments.

Regarding the NEWMA language, the Committee heard a comment that the 5,000-gallon threshold proposed in section 2.XX.2. is too large because, although the capacity of a tanker truck is more than 5,000 gallons, many trucks are compartmentalized. The compartmentalization of the trucks results in the delivery of a single product (e.g., grade of fuel) that is significantly less than 5,000 gallons. 1,500 gallons was proposed as an appropriate alternative. The Committee also received a comment that language would need to be inserted into section 2.XX.3. to recognize the need to heat certain viscous products, like Heating Oil #4 and Heating Oil #6, in order to allow them to flow properly.

The Committee also received comments opposing the permissive nature of the NEWMA language while others supported the voluntary nature of the requirement. One concern is that permitting temperature compensation without mandating it will encourage some companies to compensate while others will not. How is a consumer to make an informed purchasing decision when faced with choosing between competitors who are selling the same product using different methods of sale? Related to this, the Committee heard an alternate proposal to go back to the original language but mandate temperature compensation for those devices capable of pumping at a rate in excess of 20 gallons per minute, and prohibit temperature compensation for everything else. This would effectively require temperature compensation for all vehicle-tank meters, wholesale and terminal meters, and large volume diesel dispensers while prohibiting it for standard retail motor-fuel devices. Some comments expressed concern about the burden of educating consumers about what temperature compensation is and how it will affect their evaluation of options when making purchasing decisions.

The Committee will retain this item as a developing item until a consensus can be reached on the language to be proposed and will send the item back to all of the regional associations for further consideration.

234 UNIFORM REGULATION FOR THE VOLUNTARY REGISTRATION OF SERVICEPERSONS AND SERVICE AGENCIES

234-1 V Update   Terminology
                                        (This item was adopted)

Source: Southern Weights and Measures Association

Recommendation: Amend Sections 1 (Policy), 5 (Minimum Equipment), 8 (Placed in Service Report), and 9 (Examination of Calibration or Certification of Standards and Testing Equipment) in Handbook 130 as follows:

Section 1. Policy

For the benefit of the users, manufacturers, and distributors of commercial weighing and measuring devices, it shall be the policy of the Director of Weights and Measures, hereinafter referred to as "Director," to accept registration of (a) an individual and (b) an agency providing acceptable evidence that he, she, or it is fully qualified by training or experience to install, service, repair, or recondition a commercial weighing or measuring device; has a thorough working knowledge of all appropriate weights and measures laws, orders, rules, and regulations; and has possession of, or has available for use, and will use **suitable and** calibrated weights and measures **field** standards and testing equipment appropriate in design and adequate in amount. (An employee of the government shall not be eligible for registration.)

The Director will check the qualifications of each applicant. It will be necessary for an applicant to have available sufficient **field** standards and equipment (see § 5).

It shall also be the policy of the Department to issue to qualified applicants, whose applications for registration are approved, a "Certificate of Registration." This gives authority to remove rejection seals and tags placed on Commercial and Law-Enforcement Weighing and Measuring Devices by authorized weights and measures officials, to place in service repaired devices that were rejected, or to place in service devices that have been newly installed.

The Director is NOT guaranteeing the work or fair dealing of a Registered Serviceperson or Service Agency. He will, however, remove from the registration list any Registered Serviceperson or Service Agency that performs unsatisfactory work or takes unfair advantage of a device owner.

Registration with the Director shall be on a voluntary basis. The Director shall reserve the right to limit or reject the application of any Serviceperson or Service Agency and to revoke his, her, or its permit to remove rejection seals or tags for good cause.

This policy shall in no way preclude or limit the right and privilege of any individual or agency not registered with the Director to install, service, repair, or recondition a commercial weighing or measuring device (see § 7).

(Added 1966; Amended 1984**, and 2005**)

Section 5. Minimum Equipment

Applicants must have available sufficient standards and equipment to adequately test devices as set forth in the Notes section of each applicable code in NIST Handbook 44, "Specifications, Tolerances, and Other Technical Requirements for Weighing and Measuring Devices." ~~When applicable, t~~**T**his equipment will meet the specifications of National Institute of Standards and Technology Handbook 105- ~~1, "Specifications and Tolerances for Reference Standards and Field Standard Weights and Measures, Specifications and Tolerances for Field Standard Weights (NIST Class F)," National Institute of Standards and Technology Handbook 105-2, "Specifications and Tolerances for Reference Standards and Field Standard Weights and Measures, Specifications and Tolerances for Field Standard Measuring Flasks," or National Institute of Standards and Technology Handbook 105-3, "Specifications and Tolerances for Reference Standards and Field Standard Weights and Measures, Specifications and Tolerances for Graduated Neck Type Volumetric Field Standards."~~ **series standards (or other suitable and designated standards). This section shall not preclude the use of additional field standards and/or equipment, as approved by the Director, for uniform evaluation of device performance.** See also § 9.

(Added 1984**; Amended 2005**)

Section 8. Placed in Service Report

The Director shall furnish each Registered Serviceperson and Registered Service Agency with a supply of report forms to be known as "Placed in Service Reports." Such a form shall be executed in triplicate, shall include the assigned registration number, and shall be signed by a Registered Serviceperson or by a serviceperson representing a Registered Agency for each rejected device restored to service and for each newly installed device placed in service. Within 24 hours after a device is restored to service or placed in service, the original of the properly executed Placed in Service Report, together with any official rejection tag removed from the device, shall be ~~mailed~~ **forwarded** to the Director at ~~(address)~~. The duplicate copy of the report shall be handed to the owner or operator of the device, and the triplicate copy of the report shall be retained by the Registered Serviceperson or Registered Service Agency.

(Added 1966~~;~~ **Amended 2005**)

Section 9. Examination and Calibration or Certification of Standards and Testing Equipment

All **field** standards that are used for servicing and testing weights and measures devices for which competence is registered shall be submitted to the Director for ~~initial and subsequent examination and certification~~ **verification and calibration** at intervals determined by the director. A Registered Serviceperson or Registered Service Agency shall not use in servicing commercial weighing or measuring devices any **field** standards or testing equipment that have not been ~~certified~~ **calibrated or verified** by the Director. ~~Equipment calibrated by another State weights and measures laboratory that can show evidence of measurement traceability to the National Institute of Standards and Technology will also be recognized as equipment that is suitable for use by Registered Servicepersons or Registered Service Agencies in this State.~~ **In lieu of submission of physical standards the Director may accept calibration and/or verification reports from any laboratory that is formally accredited or recognized. The Director shall maintain a list of organizations from which the State will accept calibration reports. The State shall retain the right to periodically monitor calibration results and/or to verify field standard compliance to specifications and tolerances when field standards are initially placed into service or at any intermediate point between calibrations.**

(Added 1966; Amended 1984~~, and~~ 1999 **and 2005**)

Discussion: This item came to the Southern Weights and Measures Association from the NIST Handbook Update Work Group in conjunction with Item 221-1 and Specifications and Tolerances (S&T) Committee Item 360-2. It is the intent of the work group that these three items be considered together.

One of the reasons for these proposals is to update the terminology used in Handbooks 130 and 44 to conform to international definitions. The terms "primary standard" and "secondary standard" have been eliminated to avoid confusion with the international usage of these terms. Terms like "reference standard," "field standard," "traceability," and "uncertainty" have been added to reflect their use within these documents. The proposed changes allow state directors to exercise additional discretion when evaluating calibration intervals, referencing documentary standards, and accepting calibration reports.

This particular proposal grants state directors the freedom to reference ASTM, OIML, or other suitable documentary standards, in addition to NIST documents, when defining specifications for field standards. Currently, some standards being used in the field have no corresponding NIST document defining their specifications. Allowing ASTM, OIML, or other suitable documentary standards to be referenced would fill this void. State directors must be able to evaluate the impact of a field standard that deviates from documentary standards and assess how it might affect measurement results, functionality, efficiency, and safety. State directors would have the authority and flexibility to accept and designate field standards and to grandfather or otherwise allow deviations from standard specifications. State directors may choose to require unique calibration intervals for these deviant field standards, or they may reject and/or confiscate the deviant standard based on evaluation results. For further guidance on documentary standards that may be used as specifications and tolerances for field standards, please see Appendix A.

In addition, this proposal would allow state directors to accept calibration reports from accredited industry laboratories in addition to NIST WMD-recognized state laboratories. If a private laboratory is accredited by a National Cooperation for Laboratory Accreditation (NACLA)-approved accreditation body, or recognized by NIST WMD as capable of providing traceable measurement results, a state director may decide whether or not s/he wants to accept the calibration reports of the lab after evaluating the scope of accreditation and assessing the lab's measurement uncertainty. Initial verification of field standards may still be required, however, since a calibration report provides no guarantee the equipment meets specifications. Accreditation is not conformity assessment and should not be used for that purpose. State metrologists and technical experts at NIST may be able to assist in evaluating the acceptability of outside calibration reports.

These proposed changes would have relatively little effect on state and local weights and measures programs. There is no mandate for a jurisdiction to change the way that it currently operates. The proposed changes would serve only to increase local control and flexibility when evaluating things like field standard calibration intervals and the acceptance of accredited private lab calibration reports. Much of what is being proposed reflects practices already occurring in jurisdictions across the country. The Committee discussed this item in a joint session with the Specifications and Tolerances Committee and met with both NIST and several metrologists to resolve questions related to the meaning of the definitions.

The Committee did not receive any comments opposing this item.

237 ENGINE FUELS, PETROLEUM PRODUCTS, AND AUTOMOTIVE LUBRICANTS REGULATION

237-1   V   Biodiesel Fuel Identification and Labeling
(This item was adopted)

Source: Central Weights and Measures Association (CWMA). (See item 237-3B in the Report of the 89th NCWM Annual Meeting in 2004.)

Recommendation: Amend Handbook 130 Engine Fuels, Petroleum Products, and Automotive Lubricants Regulation by adding the following.

3.15 Biodiesel.

   3.15.1 Identification of Product. - Biodiesel and biodiesel blends shall be identified by the capital letter B followed by the numerical value representing the volume percentage of biodiesel fuel. (Examples: B10; B20; B100)

   3.15.2 Labeling of Retail Dispensers Containing Between 5 % and 20 % Biodiesel. - Each retail dispenser of biodiesel blend containing more than 5 % and up to and including 20 % biodiesel shall be labeled with either:

      3.15.2.1 The capital letter B followed by the numerical value representing the volume percentage of biodiesel fuel and ending with 'biodiesel blend.' (Examples: B10 biodiesel blend; B20 biodiesel blend), or;

      3.15.2.2 The phrase "biodiesel blend between 5 % and 20 %" or similar words.

   3.15.3 Labeling of Retail Dispensers Containing More Than 20 % Biodiesel. - Each retail dispenser of biodiesel or biodiesel blend containing more than 20 % biodiesel shall be labeled with the capital letter B followed by the numerical value representing the volume percentage of biodiesel fuel and ending with either 'biodiesel' or 'biodiesel blend.' (Examples: B100 biodiesel; B60 biodiesel blend).

   3.15.4 Documentation for Dispenser Labeling Purposes. - The retailer shall be provided, at the time of delivery of the fuel, with a declaration of the volume percent biodiesel on an invoice, bill of lading, shipping paper, or other document. This documentation is for dispenser labeling purposes only; it is the responsibility of any potential blender to determine the amount of biodiesel in the diesel fuel prior to blending.

   3.15.5 Exemption. - Biodiesel blends containing 5 % or less biodiesel by volume are exempted from the requirements of Section 3.15.

Discussion: The Committee has been working on this item since 2002 and has been monitoring the activities of the American Society for Testing and Materials (ASTM) with regard to biodiesel fuels. The Committee has decided to move forward with identification and labeling requirements for biodiesel blends containing more than 5 % biodiesel by volume. The Committee agrees it is important for consumers to be properly informed about what is being offered for sale so they can make informed purchases. The Committee has been informed that ASTM is considering changing the "Fill and Go" specifications in D 975 to include biodiesel blends of 5 % or less. Existing laws and regulations require accurate and adequate information to be placed on commodities to allow consumers to make price and quantity comparisons. Consumers must also be able to rely on manufacturers' product "claims" and products must conform to specifications.

When the first biodiesel specification was introduced at ASTM in 1993, it proposed a specification for biodiesel used as a pure fuel, called B100. However, several engine manufacturers had reservations about B100 biodiesel because they had no experience using blends over 20 % (B20). Engine manufacturers recommend that users consult with their engine manufacturer before using biodiesel blends above 5 % (B5) as concerns related to costs, rubber and gasket compatibility, and cold flow properties exist with these blends. While experience over the last 10 years and 40 million on-road miles has shown that biodiesel blends up to 20 % (B20) do not require modifications to the fuel systems of conventional diesel engines, the manufacturers of these engines still promote caution when using biodiesel blends over 5 % (B5). In 2002 ASTM adopted ASTM D 6751, Standard Specification for Biodiesel Fuel (B100) Blend Stock for Distillate Fuels. This specification is for use as a blend component with diesel fuel oils defined in Specification D 975.

ASTM is considering classifying biodiesel blends up to B5 as "Fill and Go" since generally they do not require changes to the engine or fuel system. ASTM is also considering adding a separate specification for B20 blends. Biodiesel levels higher than B20 may need to have different gaskets and hoses. While blends of biodiesel over 20 % are not readily available in today's marketplace, they may be in the not-too-distant future. Therefore, the biodiesel industry supports accurate labeling for all fuel dispensers and encourages the NCWM to adopt these recommendations.

An issue that remains, however, is the opportunity for fraud that may occur if inaccurate percentages of biodiesel are claimed. Biodiesel blends cost significantly more than conventional diesel fuels. As such, there is a possibility that an unscrupulous fuel distributor might unfairly profit from claiming a higher concentration of biodiesel than they actually deliver. If a distributor claims that they are selling B20 and they are putting in only 1 %, then the distributor is misrepresenting the product. The biodiesel industry claims this is not a pump labeling issue but an enforcement issue.

Part of the problem with a strict percentage labeling requirement is that as biodiesel blends become more "mainstream" the percentage of biodiesel added may vary from day to day depending on the needs of the distributor. Currently this practice is discouraged by the relatively high cost of biodiesel. However, as the price of biodiesel moves closer to the price of diesel fuel, it becomes just one of the myriad of compounds which could make up conventional diesel fuel. Refiners could blend in biodiesel to reduce the sulfur content or aromatic content of the finished blend. They could use it to replace their existing lubricity additives. If the price of biodiesel was more equal to diesel, then they may add 1 % today, 5 % the next day, and 20 % the following day. Theoretically, as long as the finished blend meets the ASTM D 975 "Fill and Go" specification, the level of biodiesel could range as high as 5 % without consequence. Labeling requirements that are too restrictive would eliminate the flexibility of the "Fill and Go" concept and could significantly reduce the amount of biodiesel that is eventually used.

ASTM is currently developing a Biodiesel "Fill and Go" specification for D 975 that is not based on the parent fuels, but on the finished fuel and what is satisfactory for operation in a diesel engine. This may also mean changes to D 6751, which is a stand-alone specification. The current thinking is that the upper biodiesel concentration limit for the D 975 "Fill and Go" specification will be 5 % although it is possible that it could ultimately be higher or lower. Whatever the concentration of biodiesel, if the finished blend meets the D 975 "Fill and Go" specification, the fuel is D 975-grade diesel fuel and would have to be labeled as such. Some industry members believe that existing labeling requirements in Handbook 130 are sufficient to address this situation.

The National Biodiesel Board supports this proposal. The Committee did not receive any comments opposing this item.

237-2 I Premium   Diesel Lubricity

Source: Southern Weights and Measures Association (SWMA)

Recommendation: Forward the following proposal to the Petroleum Subcommittee to review and consider.

Amend § 2.2.1. in Handbook 130 as follows:

2.2.1. Premium Diesel Fuel - All diesel fuels identified on retail dispensers, bills of lading, invoices, shipping papers, or other documentation with terms such a premium, super, supreme, plus, or premier must conform to the following requirements:

(a) Cetane Number - A minimum cetane number of 47.0 as determined by ASTM Standard Test Method D 613.

(b) Low Temperature Operability - A cold flow performance measurement which meets the ASTM D 975 tenth percentile minimum ambient air temperature charts and maps by either ASTM Standard Test Method D 2500 (Cloud Point) or ASTM Standard Test Method D 4539 (Low Temperature Flow Test, LTFT). Low temperature operability is only applicable October 1 - March 31 of each year.

(c) Thermal Stability - A minimum reflectance measurement of 80 % as determined by ASTM Standard Test Method D 6468 (180 min, 150 °C).

(d) Lubricity - A maximum wear scar diameter of 520 μm as determined by ASTM D 6079. ~~If an enforcement jurisdiction's singe test of more than 560 μm is determined, a second test shall be conducted. If the average of the two tests is more than 560 μm, the sample does not conform to the requirements of this part.~~

Discussion: A member of the petroleum industry believes that the test and associated tolerances for lubricity on premium diesel specified in 2.2.1.(d) are inconsistent with that for regular diesel. Effective January 1, 2005, the test tolerance for regular diesel lubricity will be the ASTM D 6079 reproducibility of 136 μm (see ASTM D 975-04b). The NCWM has chosen to accept the ASTM reproducibility limits for all diesel (D 975) and gasoline (D 4814) properties (see § 7.2.2., Reproducibility), but has chosen a different reproducibility limit for premium diesel lubricity without providing any explanation as to why the ASTM reproducibility limit is insufficient. If the NCWM intends to impose a stricter lubricity requirement for premium diesel, it should designate a tighter specification for this property instead of a different test tolerance (e.g., for regular and premium gasoline, premium has a different octane specification than regular but the test tolerance is the same). ASTM reproducibility limits are, by definition, based on establishing a 95 % probability that product that should pass, will pass. Applying an average test as specified in 2.2.1.(d) reduces this probability to only 80 %.

The Committee received comments from several members of the Premium Diesel Work Group (Work Group) who do not support the item as presented by the petroleum industry member. The Work Group members felt that the process that led to the current definition was very thorough and complete, and that the premium diesel lubricity requirements were established with a full understanding of their implications. The work group members felt that very knowledgeable individuals provided input to the process, which lead to the consensus position contained in the current regulation. The work being done by the work group was reported at meetings of ASTM Subcommittee E-2 every six months. The current regulation has been endorsed by the American Petroleum Institute, the Engine Manufacturer's Association, and the NCWM.

Prior to this requirement being adopted, the ASTM Lubricity Task Force conducted a great deal of research on this topic. Based on their research, the ASTM Lubricity Task Force concluded that a limit of 520 microns would meet the requirements of equipment in the field. Since the passage of this model regulation, ASTM included a lubricity requirement for No. 1 and No. 2 diesel fuel effective January 1, 2005. The ASTM requirement is also 520 microns.

The work group members reported that when this regulation was being written fuels with adequate lubricity provided a functional benefit to the end user. The work group agreed with the ASTM Lubricity Task Force that

520 microns was the correct limit to set for premium diesel. However, the work group's review process also indicated increased pump wear for fuels with High-Frequency Reciprocating Rig (HFRR) values greater than 560 microns. The current reproducibility value of the HFRR test method would have placed enforcement well beyond the 560 micron level, essentially allowing fuels with little lubricity protection to be sold as Premium. The work group felt it could not recommend a premium fuel standard that would permit excessive pump wear. Using the statistical tools provided in ASTM D 3244, the work group evaluated an enforcement limit of 560 microns. The statistical tools indicated that a single laboratory reporting the assigned test value would have an enforcement limit of approximately 80 % probability of acceptance, while the average of two separate laboratories reporting the assigned test value would have an enforcement limit of approximately 90 % probability of acceptance. It was agreed that for a premium fuel the average of two test results was the best approach given the current test methods and precision available. Therefore, if a test exceeds 560 microns, then a second test must be run. The average of the two tests must exceed 560 microns before a violation would occur. At this time, the work group members believe this remains the best approach.

The Committee believes that it lacks the expertise necessary to adequately evaluate this proposal. The Committee voted to forward this proposal to the Petroleum Subcommittee for its review and consideration, and requests that the Subcommittee provide the Committee with a recommendation and justifications for its adoption.

260 NIST HANDBOOK 133, CHECKING THE NET CONTENTS OF PACKAGED GOODS

260-1 W Amend § 2.3 Basic Test Procedure, and Table 2-5

Source: Central Weights and Measures Association (CWMA). (See Item 260-4 in the Report of the 89th NCWM Annual Meeting in 2004.)

Recommendation: Amend Handbook 133 § 2.3 as follows:

Where are Maximum Allowable Variations found?

Find the MAV values for packages labeled by weight, volume, count, and measure in the tables listed below in Appendix A.

- Packages labeled by weight — **See Table 2-5**
- Packages labeled by volume liquid or dry — **See Table 2-6**
- Packages labeled by count — **See Table 2-7**
- Packages labeled by length (width), or area — **See Table 2-8**
- Packages ~~labeled with~~ **bearing a** USDA seal of inspection - Meat and Poultry **when labeled weight is provided by the USDA-inspected facility** — **See Table 2-9**
- Textiles, polyethylene sheeting and film, mulch and soil labeled by volume, packaged firewood, and packages labeled by count with less than 50 items — **See Table 2-10**

Amend the Header of Table 2-5 in Handbook 133 as follows:

Table 2-5. Maximum Allowable Variations (MAVs) for Packages Labeled by Weight
~~Do Not Use This Table f~~**E**or Meat and Poultry Products ~~subject to USDA Regulations~~ **when Labeled Weight is Provided by USDA-Inspected Facility** – Use Table 2-9
For Polyethylene Sheeting and Film, see Table 2-10. Exceptions to the MAVs.

Discussion: This proposal was originally intended to more clearly define when the USDA lower limits should apply (Table 2-9) and when MAVs should apply (Table 2-5) to packages of meat and poultry. This item was informational on the Committee's agenda in 2004 and NIST was granted editorial privileges to amend

Handbook 133 to include this proposal. However, after researching the issue NIST believes this proposal is in conflict with language adopted by the USDA. The USDA requires that Table 2-9 lower limits be applied to any "meat and poultry product subject to USDA requirements." The language adopted by the USDA does not distinguish between packages packed and weighed at a USDA plant and packages packed at a USDA plant but weighed elsewhere; it simply requires that any package subject to USDA jurisdiction be tested with the USDA lower limits. NIST cannot include language in Handbook 133 that is in conflict with federal regulations.

NIST contacted the USDA about this item and was advised that USDA does not support the changes recommended in this proposal. Subsequently, all of the regional associations have withdrawn their support for this proposal and the Committee voted to withdraw this item.

260-2 W Amend § 3.11 and MAV Table 2-10

Source: Western Weights and Measures Association (WWMA). (See Item 260-6 in the Report of the 89th NCWM Annual Meeting in 2004.)

Recommendation: Amend the application and header of Handbook 133 Table 2-10 as follows to allow the MAVs that apply to Mulch and Soil to also apply to similar products, such as Wood Shavings and Animal Bedding:

Table 2-10. Exceptions to the Maximum Allowable Variations for
Textiles, Polyethylene Sheeting and Film, Mulch ~~and~~, Soil**, and Other Similar Products** Labeled by Volume,
Packaged Firewood, and
Packages Labeled by Count with Less than 50 Items

Amend Handbook 133 § 3.11 to read:

3.11. Mulch ~~and~~, Soil**, and Other Similar Products** Labeled by Volume

Discussion: A manufacturer of wood fiber products believes wood shavings, labeled by volume, should receive the same MAV exceptions as mulch, soils or peat moss. The wood fiber products in question could conceivably be used as animal bedding, insulation, mulch (a horticultural above-ground dressing), etc. Item 250-10, which was adopted at the 83rd National Conference on Weights and Measures in 1998 and was entitled "Bark Mulch and Other Organic Products - Maximum Allowable Variations," discussed the reasoning and the necessity for expanded MAVs in certain circumstances, and some of this rationale may apply to other wood fiber products.

The Committee believes that the manufacturer seeking this additional allowance has not provided sufficient data to support its position. There is an established procedure for evaluating MAVs and the manufacturer has not followed it. The Committee feels this item needs to be further developed by the manufacturer in conjunction with a regulatory agency to provide reliable data upon which to base any decision.

In addition, concerns have been raised about the expansion of the mulch, soil, and peat moss sections to "Other Similar Products." What are "Other Similar Products?" Are they products that are used in similar applications? If so, and if "Other Similar Products" is intended to extend to pet beddings made of wood shavings, should it also be extended to pet beddings made of paper (also a wood product)? What about pet beddings made from other substances (clay, straw, etc.)? It is believed that the language proposed is overly broad and needs to be better defined to capture the product under consideration without including products that do not require the larger MAV.

The Committee has received several comments opposing this item. The Committee has no received additional information from the original proponent of this item to justify its adoption and voted to withdraw this item.

260-3 W Make MAV Tables More Uniform

Source: Northeast Weights and Measures Association (NEWMA)

Recommendation: To evaluate whether or not the MAV tables in Handbook 133 should be revised to be more uniform with other national and global standards.

Discussion: The Committee heard from several manufacturers and packers that meeting the different MAVs in the global marketplace is not generally a problem for them. While most of the comments heard did not directly oppose this item, the overall sentiment was that this was not a high priority issue for manufacturers and packers. The Committee voted not to pursue the establishment of new MAVs through the collection of data. However, the Committee believed there may be merit in seeking to make Handbook 133 MAVs more uniform with other MAVs in the global marketplace. Subsequently, all of the regional associations have withdrawn their support for this item. The Committee voted to withdraw this item.

270 OTHER ITEMS

270-1 W Tare on Case-Ready Packages of Meat

Source: Central Weights and Measures Association (CWMA)

Recommendation: The NCWM should petition the USDA to request a rule change that would require packers of case-ready consumer-sized packages of beef and pork to print the individual consumer package tare weights on the outside of the shipping case.

Discussion: For several years the USDA has required packers of case-ready poultry to print the individual consumer package tare weights on the outside of the shipping case. This proposal would extend this requirement to packers of case-ready meat (beef and pork) products.

As retail stores reduce or eliminate on-site meat cutting and processing, weights and measures officials are seeing more packages of meat that are shipped case-ready (i.e., the meat is already portioned into individual packages, wrapped, and labeled with all required information except weight). Retailers are required to label these packages with the correct weight before making them available for sale. However, retailers don't know what tare deduction to take and are reluctant to open a reasonable sample of packages to determine an average tare weight. This has led to inaccurate tares being used with these products.

NIST believes that the current requirement for poultry has taught us that placing tare weights on shipping cases is an imperfect system. Inspections have shown that tare weights printed on poultry shipping cases are often inaccurate—packers use unused dry tare for this determination and don't always include the weight of all the tare materials. Retailers often rely on these tares to their detriment. Jurisdictions may have difficulty determining from whom to seek compliance—the retailer (for selling a short-weight product) or the packer (for declaring an inaccurate tare). The fact that the packer falls under USDA jurisdiction may also cause additional hurdles. In addition, NIST is also concerned that inspectors may mistakenly rely on the accuracy of these tares when performing inspections. If the tares are inaccurate but inspectors rely on them to perform audit tests, will the inaccuracy ever be discovered? Inspectors must remain vigilant about checking the actual tare of these packages and not rely on the packer for this information. Enforcement action must only be taken on packages where the average used or unused dry tare has been determined.

The Committee received comments opposing this item. Several manufacturers and packers stated that tare materials and weights change on a regular basis and would be difficult to pre-stamp on cases. In addition, packers stated that tare weight information is already provided to the retailers and recommended that retailers who are not receiving this information should contact the packer. A national retailer stated that they receive updated tare information from their packers in an electronic format on a regular basis, and that putting tare information on the shipping case would provide little benefit to them. The Committee voted to withdraw this item at its 2005 Interim Meeting.

Joe Gomez, New Mexico, Chairman
Joe Benavides, Texas
James Cassidy, Cambridge, Massachusetts
Vicky Dempsey, Montgomery County, Ohio
Dennis Johannes, California

Vince Orr, ConAgra Foods, Associate Member Representative
Brian Lemon, Canada, Technical Advisor
Doug Hutchinson, Canada, Technical Advisor
Tom Coleman, NIST, Technical Advisor
Kathryn Dresser, NIST, Technical Advisor

Laws and Regulation Committee

Appendix A

Sample List of Documentary Standards for Item #221-1

Physical Standard	Documentary Standard	Device Calibration	Interval	Notes
Cast Iron Weights	Handbook 105-1	Class III, III L, IV scales	6 months to 1 year	
Stainless Steel Weights	Handbook 105-1	Class III, III L, IV scales	5 years	
Class F1 Weights Class 2 Weights	OIML R111 ASTM E 617-97	Class II scales	1 year	
Glassware Handbook	105-2	Package testing	10 years	
Test Measures (hand-held and 5-gallon truck or trailer mounted)	Handbook 105-3	Gas pumps	1 year	
Large Provers	Handbook 105-3	Meters	1 year	
LPG Provers	Handbook 105-4	LPG meters	1 year	
Stopwatches Handbook	105-5	Taxi meters, timing devices, parking meters, Laundromats	1 year	
Thermometers Handbook	105-6	Temperature corrections, refrigeration specifications, package checking	5 years	Annual inspection required
Small Volume Provers	Handbook 105-7	Meters	6 months to 1 year	Need EPO for field testing
Master Meters	API document in development	Master meters for petroleum		
Proving Rings and Load Cells	ASTM E 74	Wheel load weighers, weight carts, large mass standards	Rings: 5 years Cells: 6 months if used for wheel load weighers; evaluate with use for substitution weighing	Depends on use
Weight Carts	Handbook 105-8	Vehicle scales	6 months to 1 year	Needs to be recalibrated with any repair. Need EPO for field use
Hydrometers ASTM	E 100	Petroleum products; bulk oil meters	1 year	
Length Standards, Tapes	GGG-standard	Taxi meters, fabric scale decks, firewood, lobster gauges	5 years	Inspect before use
Containers Handbook	133	Bulk mulch		
Berry Baskets	Handbook 44	Berry quantity		

THIS PAGE LEFT INTENTIONALLY BLANK.

S&T Committee 2005 Final Report

Report of the
Committee on Specifications and Tolerances

Jack Kane, Chairman
Bureau of Weights and Measures
Department of Labor and Industry
Montana

300 INTRODUCTION

This is the final report of the Committee on Specifications and Tolerances (S&T) (Committee) for the 90th Annual Meeting of the National Conference on Weights and Measures (NCWM). The report is based on the 90th Interim Report offered in NCWM Publication 16, "Committee Reports," the Addendum Sheets issued at the Annual Meeting, and actions taken by the membership at the Voting Session of the Annual Meeting.

Table A identifies the agenda items in the report by Reference Key Number, Item Title, and Page Number. The item numbers are those assigned in the Interim Meeting Agenda. Voting items are indicated with a "**V**," or if the item was part of the consent calendar by the suffix "**VC**" after the item number. Items marked with an "**I**" after the reference key numbers are information items. Items marked with a "**D**" after the key numbers are developing issues. The developing designation indicates an item that while it has merit, it may not be adequately developed for action at the national level. Developing items inform parties about issues that are developing in different localities or in the regional associations. A developing item is returned to the submitter to develop further before any action is taken at the national level. The Committee withdrew items marked with a "**W**." Items marked with a "**W**" generally will be referred to the regional weights and measures associations because they either need additional development, analysis, and input, or did not have sufficient Committee support to bring them before the NCWM. Table B lists the Appendices to the report, and Table C provides a summary of the results of the voting on the Committee's items and the report in entirety.

This Report contains many recommendations to revise or amend National Institute of Standards and Technology (NIST) Handbook 44 (HB-44), 2005 Edition, "Specifications, Tolerances, and Other Technical Requirements for Weighing and Measuring Devices." Proposed revisions to the handbook(s) are shown in **bold face print** by striking out information to be deleted and underlining information to be added. Proposed nonretroactive requirements are printed in **bold-faced italics.**

Note: The policy of NIST is to use metric units of measurement in all of its publications; however, recommendations received by the NCWM technical committees have been printed in this publication as they were submitted and may, therefore, contain references to inch-pound units.

Table A
Index to Reference Key Items

Reference Key No.		Title of Item	Page
300		INTRODUCTION	1
310		GENERAL CODE	4
310-1	W	G-A.1. Commercial and Law Enforcement, G-S.1. Identification; Built-for-Purpose Software Based Devices, Table G-S.1. Identification, G-S.1.1. Location of Marking Information for Not Built-For-Purpose, Software-Based Devices, and Appendix D; Definition of Built-for-Purpose Device, Measuring Device (General), Measuring System (General), Electronic Devices, Not-Built-for-Purpose Device, Metrological Software Version (Revision), and Weighing Device (Instrument)	4
310-2	I	G-T.1. (e) Acceptance Tolerances	8

320 SCALES 9
    320-1   I   S.1.1. (c) Zero Indication; Requirements for Markings or Indications for Other than Digital
                       Zero Indications 9
    320-2   VC   S.1.8.4. Recorded Representations, Point-of-Sale Systems; Footnote 1 11
    320-3   I   UR.1.6. Computing Scale Interfaced to a Cash Register 12
    320-4   VC   S.2.1.3. Scales Equipped with an Automatic Zero-Setting Mechanism (Zero Tracking),
                       S.2.1.3.1. For Scales Manufactured Between January 1, 1981 and January 1, 2007; Maximum
                       Load Rezeroed, S.2.1.3.2. For Scales Manufactured On or After January 1, 2007; Maximum
                       Load Rezeroed, and S.2.1.3.3. Automatic Zero-Setting Mechanism (Zero Tracking) on Class
                       III L Devices 14
    320-5   VC   Table S.6.3.b. Notes For Table S.6.3.a. Note 3; Nominal Capacity and Value of the Scale
                       Division and Appendix D; Definition of Reading Face 16
    320-6   I   N.1.3.1. Bench or Counter Scales, N.1.3.8. All Other Scales Except Crane Scales, Hanging
                       Scales, Hopper Scales, Wheel–Load Weighers, and Portable Axle-Load Weighers, and
                       Appendix D; Definitions of Bench Scale and Counter Scale 19
    320-7   I Table   6 Tolerances 22
    320-8   V   T.N.4.5. Time Dependence, General, T.N.4.5.1. Time Dependence; Class II, III, and IIII Non-
                       automatic Weighing Instruments, T.N.4.5.2. Time Dependence; Class III L Non-automatic
                       Weighing Instruments, T.N.4.6. Time Dependence (Creep) for Load Cells During Type
                       Evaluation, T.N.4.6.1. Permissible Variations of Readings, T.N.4.6.2. Apportionment Factors,
                       and Definitions of D_{max}, E_{max}, and Non-automatic Weighing Instrument 23
    320-9   I   List of International Symbols Noted as Acceptable 27

321 BELT-CONVEYOR SCALE SYSTEMS 29
    321-1   VC   UR.3.4. Diversion or Loss of Measured Product 29

322 AUTOMATIC BULK WEIGHING SYSTEMS 30
    322-1   W Tolerances 30

330 LIQUID-MEASURING DEVICES 32
    330-1   V   S.1.6.1. Indication of Delivery; Electronic Devices 32
    330-2   VC   N.4.2.2. Retail Motor-Fuel Devices 33

331 VEHICLE-TANK METERS 35
    331-1   I Temperature   Compensation 35
    331-2   VC   S.1.4.1. Display of Unit Price 38
    331-3   VC   S.2.4. Zero Set-Back Interlock, Vehicle-Tank Meters, Electronic 39
    331-4   VC   N.4.2. Special Tests (Except Milk-Measuring Systems), N.4.5. Product Depletion Test, T.4.
                       Product Depletion Test, and Table T.4. Tolerances for Vehicle-Tank Meters n Product
                       Depletion Tests, Except Milk Meters 39

336 WATER METERS 41
    336-1   I   Table N.4.2. Flow Rate and Draft Size for Water Meters Special Tests 41

360 OTHER ITEMS 42
    360-1   V   Proposed Section 5.59. Electronic Livestock, Meat, and Poultry Evaluation Systems and/or
                       Devices -Tentative Code 42
    360-2   V   Appendix A Fundamental Considerations 3. Testing Apparatus; 3.1 Adequacy, 3.2 Tolerances
                       for Standards and Footnote 2, and 3.3 Accuracy of Standards 45
    360-3   I International   Organization of Legal Metrology (OIML) Report 47
    360-4   I   Add International Terms that are Synonymous to NIST Handbook 44 Terms in Appendix D;
                       Definitions 47
    360-5   D Developing   Issues 48

Table B
Appendices

Appendix	Title	Page
A	Item 360-1: Proposed Section 5.59 Electronic Livestock, Meat, and Poultry Evaluation Systems and/or Devices – Tentative Code	A1
B	Item 360-2: Appendix A Fundamental Considerations 3. Testing Apparatus; 3.1 Adequacy, 3.2 Tolerances for Standards and Footnote 2, and 3.3 Accuracy of Standards	B1
C	Item 360-5: Developing Issues	C1
	Part 1, Item 1 General Code: G-S.5.6.1. Recorded Representation of Metric Units on Equipment with Limited Character Sets	C1
	Part 2, Item 1 Scales: Table 4. Minimum Test Weights and Test Loads	C1

Table C
Voting Results

Reference Key Number	House of State Representatives		House of Delegates		Results
	Yeas	Nays	Yeas	Nays	
300 (Consent Calendar)	36	0	36	0	Passed
320-8 27		10	28	8	Passed
330-1 37		0	36	0	Passed
360-1 32		3	31	3	Passed
360-2 37		0	33	1	Passed
300 (Report in its Entirety Voice Vote)	All Yeas	No Nays	All Yeas	No Nays	Passed

Details of all Items
(In order by Reference Key Number)

310 GENERAL CODE

310-1 W   G-A.1. Commercial and Law Enforcement, G-S.1. Identification; Built-for-Purpose Software Based Devices, Table G-S.1. Identification, G-S.1.1. Location of Marking Information for Not Built-For-Purpose, Software-Based Devices, and Appendix D; Definition of Built-for-Purpose Device, Measuring Device (General), Measuring System (General), Electronic Devices, Not-Built-for-Purpose Device, Metrological Software Version (Revision), and Weighing Device (Instrument)

(This item was withdrawn.)

Source: Carryover Item 310-1. (This proposal first appeared on the Committee's 2003 agenda.)

Recommendation: Amend General Code paragraph G-A.1. Commercial and Law Enforcement Equipment as follows:

> **G-A.1. Commercial and Law Enforcement Equipment. -** These specifications, tolerances, and other technical requirements apply as follows:
>
> (a) To commercial ~~weighing and~~ measuring **devices or systems** ~~equipment~~; that is, to weights, and measures, and ~~weighing and~~ measuring devices **or systems** commercially used or employed in establishing the size, quantity, extent, area, or measurement of quantities, ~~things, produce, or articles~~ for distribution or consumption, purchased, offered, or submitted for sale, hire, or award, or in computing any basic charge or payment for services rendered on the basis of **quantity determination.** ~~weight or measure.~~
>
> (b) To any accessory attached to or used in connection with a commercial ~~weighing or~~ measuring device when such accessory is so designed that its operation affects the accuracy of the device.
>
> (c) To ~~weighing and~~ measuring **devices or systems** ~~equipment~~ in official use for the enforcement of law or for the collection of statistical information by government agencies.
>
> (These requirements should be used as a guide by the weights and measures official when, upon request, courtesy examinations of noncommercial equipment are made.)
> **(Amended 200X)**

Amend General Code paragraph G-S.1. Identification as follows:

> **G-S.1. Identification. -** All equipment, except weights and separate parts necessary to the measurement process but not having any metrological effect, shall be clearly and permanently marked **in accordance with Table G-S.1** for the purposes of identification with the following information:
>
> (a) the name, initials, or trademark of the manufacturer or distributor;
>
> (b) a model designation that positively identifies the pattern ~~, or~~ design, **or metrological version or revision** of the device ~~in accordance with Table G-S.1~~;
>
> > 1. The model designation shall be prefaced by the term "Model," "Type," or "Pattern." These terms may be followed by the term "Number" or an abbreviation of that word. The abbreviation for the word "Number" shall, as a minimum, begin with the letter "N" (e.g., No or No.). The abbreviation for the word "Model" shall be "Mod" or "Mod." Prefix lettering may be initial capitals, all capitals or all lower case.
> > [Nonretroactive as of January 1, 2003]
> > (Added 2000) (Amended 2001)
>
> **(Amended 200X)**

(c) a nonrepetitive serial number, except for equipment with no moving or electronic component parts and not built-for-purpose, ~~software-based~~ electronic devices;
[Nonretroactive as of January 1, 1968]
(Amended 2003 and 200X)

1. *The serial number shall be prefaced by words, and abbreviation, or a symbol, that clearly identifies the number as the required serial number.*
   [Nonretroactive as of January 1, 1986]

2. *Abbreviations for the word "Serial" shall, as a minimum, begin with the letter "S," and abbreviation*
   for the word "Number" shall, as a minimum, begin with the letter "N" (e.g., S/N, SN, Ser. No., and S. No.).
   [Nonretroactive as of January 1, 2001]

~~(d) the current software version designation for not built-for-purpose, software-based devices;~~
~~[Nonretroactive as of January 1, 2004]~~
~~(Added 2003)~~

(~~e~~d) **an NTEP Certificate of Conformance (CC) number or a corresponding CC Addendum Number for devices that have a CC. The CC Number or a corresponding CC Addendum Number shall be prefaced by the terms "NTEP CC," "CC," or "Approval." These terms may be followed by the term "Number" or an abbreviation of that word. The abbreviation for the word "Number" shall, as a minimum, begin with the letter "N" (e.g., No or No.)**
[Nonretroactive as of January 1, 2003]

The required information shall be so located that it is readily observable without the necessity of the disassembly of a part requiring the use of any means separate from the device.
(Amended 1985, 1991, 1999, 2000, 2001 and 2003)

Delete General Code paragraph G-S.1.1. Location of Marking Information for Not-Built-for-Purpose, Software-based Devices and renumber G-S.1.2. Remanufactured Devices and Remanufactured Main Elements as follows:

~~**G-S.1.1. Location of Marking Information for Not-Built-for-Purpose, Software-based Devices.** - For not-built-for-purpose, software-based devices, the following shall apply:~~

~~(a) the manufacturer or distributor and the model designation shall be continuously displayed or marked on the device (see note below), or~~

~~(b) the Certificate of Conformance (CC) Number shall be continuously displayed or marked on the device (see note below), or~~

~~(c) all required information in G-S.1. Identification. (a), (b), (c), and (e) shall be continuously displayed. Alternatively, a clearly identified "view only" System Identification, G-S.1. Identification, or Weights and Measures Identification shall be accessible through the "Help" menu. Required information includes that information necessary to identify that the software in the device is the same type that was evaluated.~~

~~Note: Clear instructions for accessing the remaining required G-S.1. information shall be listed on the CC. Required information includes that information necessary to identify that the software in the device is the same type that was evaluated.~~
~~[Nonretroactive as of January 1, 2004]~~
~~(Added 2003)~~

G-S.1.12. Remanufactured Devices and Remanufactured Main Elements. - *All remanufactured devices and remanufactured main elements shall be clearly and permanently marked for the purposes of identification with the following information:*

(a) The name, initials, or trademark of the last remanufacturer or distributor;

(b) The remanufacturer's or distributor's model designation if different than the original model designation.
[Nonretroactive as of January 1, 2002]
(Added 2001)

Note: Definitions for "manufactured device," "repaired device," and "repaired element" are also included (along with definitions for "remanufactured device" and "remanufactured element") in Appendix D, Definitions.

Add a new Table G-S.1. Identification as follows:

	Table G-S.1. Identification	
	Built-for-Purpose Instruments, Elements, or Systems	**Not-Built-for-Purpose Devices or Elements**
Name, initials, or trademark of the manufacturer or distributor	M	D[2]
Model designation	M[1]	D[2]
Specific model designation[3]	M[1] or D	
Serial number	M	Not required
Metrological version or revision designation[3]	N/A	D
Certificate of Conformance (CC) number	M or D	D[2]

M:	Physically and permanently marked
D:	Either: (1) displayed by accessing a clearly identified view only System Identification, G-S.1 Identification, or Weights and Measures Identification accessible through the "Help" menu. Required information includes that information necessary to identify the software in the device is the same type that was evaluated, or (2) continuously displayed. Note: For revision or software version number, clear instructions for accessing this information shall be listed on the CC in lieu of the "Help" menu. Required information includes that information necessary to identify the software in the device is the same or subsequent type that was evaluated. (Nonretroactive as of January 2004)
Note 1:	As a minimum, the model designation (positively identifying the pattern, design, type, series, generic or trademark designation) must be marked on the device. If the model designation changes with differing parameters such as size, features, options, intended application, not Handbook 44 compliant construction, etc., the specific model designation shall be physically marked or continuously displayed or be capable of being displayed. (Nonretroactive as of January 200X)
Note 2:	As a minimum, either the manufacturer or distributor and the model designation, or the CC Number shall be continuously displayed. Clear instructions for accessing the remaining required G-S.1. information shall be listed on the CC, which may be available as an unaltered copy of the CC or printed by the device or through another on-site device. (Nonretroactive as of January 200X)
Note 3:	Metrological version or revision designation for devices with downloadable or field programmable software.

(Table Added 200X)

Add new terms and definitions to Appendix d, Definitions, as follows:

~~measuring device (general) - A device (instrument) intended to be used to make measurements, alone or in conjunction with supplementary devices. (VIM)[1.10]~~

~~measuring system (general) - An instrument or group of instruments that serves to make measurements, alone or in conjunction with supplementary devices. (VIM)[1.10]~~

~~electronic devices - A device operating by the principles of electronics, which may consist of one or more subassemblies and performs a specific function(s). (ASTM)[1.10]~~

~~not-built-for-purpose device -- Any electronic peripheral or auxiliary device or element which was not originally manufactured with the intent that it be used as, or part of, a weighing or measuring device or system. [1.10]~~

~~metrological software version (revision) - A designation that specifically defines the metrological software version used in a measuring instrument, system, or peripheral/auxiliary device with field programmable or downloadable metrological software). [1.10]~~

~~weighing device (instrument) -- A measuring instrument that serves to determine the mass of a body by using the action of gravity on said body. The instrument may also be used to determine other quantities, magnitudes, parameters or characteristics related to the determined mass. According to its method of operation, a weighing instrument is classified as an automatic or non-automatic instrument. (OIML R76)[1.10]~~

Amend the definition for "built-for-purpose device" as follows:

built-for-purpose device - Any main ~~, peripheral, or auxiliary~~ device or element which was manufactured with the intent that it be used as, or part of, a ~~weighing or~~ measuring device or system.

Background/Discussion: In 2003, paragraph G-S.1.1. was added to allow manufacturers of "not-built-for-purpose" devices to "display" the markings required in paragraph G-S.1. as an alternative to physically marking the required information on the device. Manufacturers of "built-for-purpose" devices have requested that paragraph G-S.1. be amended to provide a similar option for the "display" of the paragraph G-S.1. required markings on "built-for-purpose" devices.

At the 2004 NCWM Annual Meeting, the Committee made this proposal an information item because of concerns stated by some manufacturers that "built-for-purpose" devices were being treated differently than "not-built-for-purpose" devices. In response to this concern, the Committee asked that the Weighing and Measuring Sectors develop language acceptable to both weighing and measuring device manufacturers.

At its Fall 2004 meeting, the Weighing Sector reviewed the information from the Committee, previous Sector recommendations, and information regarding international requirements. The Sector also reviewed an alternate recommendation from NIST Weights and Measures Division (WMD), which included changes to paragraph G-A.1. The most significant change to paragraph G-A.1. was the elimination of the term "weighing" and utilization of the more general term "measuring" for devices or systems that measure mass, length, or volume. The WMD alternate proposal included new and amended definitions and addressed concerns raised during the Committee's deliberations on this item. The WMD proposed definition for a "weighing device" describes it as a "measuring instrument" that serves to determine the mass of a body by using the action of gravity on said body. Although this change is a departure from conventional terminology for "scales," it is consistent with OIML recommendations and facilitates harmonization between Handbook 44 and international standards. WMD revised the definition for "not-built-for-purpose" devices to clarify that they are auxiliary or peripheral equipment devices and systems, but they are part of the weighing or measuring system process. Some of the private Sector members repeated their earlier comments that current technology permits the electronic display of required identification information and there is no technical justification for treating "built-for-purpose" devices differently than "not-built-for-purpose" devices. Additionally, WMD's proposed definitions would reclassify most measuring devices according to the physical property being measured. Since WMD's proposed definition for measuring devices applies to all types of devices, some concern was expressed that laws and regulations would need to be changed because many state statutes refer to both "weighing and measuring" devices. The Weighing Sector supported the WMD alternate proposal; however, the Sector changed the marking requirement for metrological version or revision designation in Table G-S.1. for "built-for-purpose" instruments, elements, or systems from WMD's proposed designation of "marked or displayed (M or D)" to "not applicable (NA)" and added a definition for "weighing device." The Weighing Sector agreed to send the WMD alternate proposal with these modifications to the NTETC Measuring Sector and regional associations for their review and comments.

At the October 2004 Northeastern Weights and Measures Association Meeting, several participants indicated that the requirements for "built-for-purpose" and "not-built-for-purpose" devices should be the same. An Associate member commented that manufacturers should be trusted to report metrological updates to software since requirements for reporting current software version numbers hampers innovations in software development.

At its October 2004 meeting, the Measuring Sector also reviewed the recommendation developed by WMD since that was the only alternate proposal ready for review. The members agreed that the majority of the changes proposed to include "built-for-purpose" devices are more applicable to weighing devices than they are to measuring devices. One member objected to the proposal to eliminate references in paragraph G-A.1. to the term "weighing" and the dual use of the term "measuring" to refer to all forms of measurement including weighing. The member stated that the proposal was in conflict with the historic use of the term "measurement" in the United States. The Sector agreed to forward a recommendation to the Committee that the proposal to include marking requirements for "built-for-purpose" devices in paragraph G-S.1. Identification be withdrawn from the S&T agenda.

At its October 2004 meeting, the Southern Weights and Measures Association (SWMA) S&T Committee did not include this or other items requiring further development on its agenda for a vote of the members; however, the SWMA did accept comments during the open hearings. The SWMA learned that the Scale Manufacturers Association (SMA) wanted the requirements in Table G-S.1. for "built-for purpose" instruments, elements, or systems to allow markings for name, model, and serial number to be either physically marked (M) or displayed (D) just like requirements in the table for specific model designation or CC. One manufacturer of retail motor-fuel dispensers supported the recommendation on the condition that the requirement for metrological revision designation for "built-for purpose" instruments, elements, or systems is changed from "M" or "D" to "N/A" as recommended by the Weighing Sector. The SWMA forwarded these comments to the Committee without taking a position on the proposal.

At the 2005 NCWM Interim Meeting, the SMA opposed this item because it did not treat "built-for-purpose" and "not-built-for-purpose" devices equally and recommended the NCWM form a Work Group to further develop the proposal. The Committee heard support for the alternate proposal as modified by the Weighing Sector. The Committee considered withdrawing this item due to a lack of support from the group of manufacturers that originally submitted the proposal. After some discussion the Committee agreed to retain the Weighing Sector's latest alternate language shown in the recommendation above as an information item and urged the NTETC Sectors and SMA to develop a proposal they all support prior to the 2006 Interim Meeting. If the NTETC Sectors and SMA do not provide an alternative proposal that resolves their concerns with the current proposal, the Committee may withdraw this item from its agenda.

At the 2005 NCWM Annual Meeting, the Committee concluded that there was no support for this proposal and decided to withdraw it. The regional associations, the NTETC Sectors, and associations of device manufacturers may develop and submit a new proposal if they are able to resolve the concerns discussed above.

For more background information, refer to the 2003 and 2004 S&T Final Reports.

310-2   I   G-T.1. (e) Acceptance Tolerances

Source: National Type Evaluation Technical Committee (NTETC) Measuring Sector:

Recommendation: Modify Section 1.10 Paragraph G-T.1. (e) Acceptance Tolerances as follows:

G-T.1. Acceptance Tolerances. - Acceptance tolerances shall apply to:

(a) equipment to be put into commercial use for the first time;

(b) equipment that has been placed in commercial service within the preceding 30 days and is being officially tested for the first time;

(c) equipment that has been returned to commercial service following official rejection for failure to conform to performance requirements and is being officially tested for the first time within 30 days after corrective service;

(d) equipment that is being officially tested for the first time within 30 days after major reconditioning or overhaul; and

(e) equipment undergoing type evaluation ~~(special test tolerances are not applicable)~~.
(Amended 1989 **and 2005**)

Discussion/Background: At its October 2004 Meeting, the NTETC Measuring Sector noted that the intent of paragraph G-T.1. (e) is to specify that acceptance tolerances apply to all equipment undergoing type evaluation; however, the language is not clear regarding what tolerance would apply during "special tests."

Special test tolerances recognize that a larger tolerance for test drafts conducted under certain conditions, such as at a slow flow rate, is appropriate for meters in normal service. Normal wear of the measuring elements frequently produces larger performance errors when testing at a slow flow rate, compared to testing at full flow rate. The Sector agreed that devices submitted for NTEP evaluation should be held to a higher standard than devices in normal service and special test tolerances should not be applicable during an NTEP evaluation. The Sector also agreed to forward the proposal to modify Handbook 44 paragraph G-T.1. (e) Acceptance Tolerances to the NCWM S&T Committee NCWM and Southern Weights and Measures Association for consideration.

At its October 2004 Meeting, the SWMA reviewed the recommendation and agreed to forward it to the Committee with the recommendation that it be a voting item on the 2005 NCWM S&T Agenda.

At the 2005 NCWM Interim Meeting, the Committee received no opposition to this item and, therefore, agreed to present it for a vote at the Annual Meeting.

At the 2005 NCWM Annual Meeting, members of the Meter Manufacturers Association (MMA) said that they had not understood that the proposal from the Measuring Sector would only apply to liquid measuring devices undergoing NTEP evaluation. They explained that without special test tolerances most meters, especially those installed in vehicle-mounted applications, would not meet tolerances for low flow tests during either field testing or NTEP evaluations. Based on this information the Committee agreed to make this an information item to allow the MMA and the Measuring Sector to further develop the proposal and submit it for reconsideration.

320 SCALES

320-1 I S.1.1. (c) Zero Indication; Requirements for Markings or Indications for Other than Digital Zero Indications

Source: Carryover Item 320-8. (This item originated from the Committee and first appeared on its 2004 agenda.)

Recommendation: Amend paragraph S.1.1. (c) as follows:

S.1.1. Zero Indication.

(a) On a scale equipped with indicating or recording elements, provision shall be made to either indicate or record a zero-balance condition.

(b) On an automatic-indicating scale or balance indicator, provision shall be made to indicate or record an out-of-balance condition on both sides of zero.

(c) A zero-balance condition may be indicated by other than a continuous digital zero indication, provided that an effective automatic means is provided to inhibit a weighing operation or to return to a continuous digital indication when the scale is in an out-of-balance condition **and is marked or includes supplemental indications or markings to indicate that the "other than digital zero indication" represents a no-load condition of the scale.**
Added 1987 (Amended 1993**, and 2005**)

**[Note: The markings or supplemental indications in S.1.1.(c) are not required if, prior to the start of a transaction: (1) operator intervention is required to verify the zero balance condition with a digital zero indication, or (2) the scale automatically represents the zero-balance condition with a digital zero indication.]
(Added 2005)**
(Amended 1987)

Background/Discussion: The Committee proposes to modify paragraph S.1.1.(c) to clarify the requirement's original intent for marking zero indications on scales and point-of-sale systems where a zero-balance condition is represented by other than a digital zero indication. The proposal is the Committee's response to the 2003 NTETC Weighing Sector's request for clarification on whether or not scales that use scrolling messages, dashes, etc., to indicate zero require additional markings or indications to: (1) inform customers that the scales are at a zero-balance condition and (2) properly identify the feature as specified in General Code paragraph G-S.6. Marking Operational Controls, Indications, and Features.

The proposal is consistent with other Handbook 44 code requirements adopted to ensure that customers have sufficient information to make an informed decision during a direct sale. These codes require marking and/or identification of values, graduations, units, and indications in the displayed and recorded transaction information. Handbook 44 includes requirements for clearly identifying operational controls and features used in weighing applications. Additionally, Handbook 44 requirements specify that the size, proximity, and position of that information shall be such that it is easily read and is appropriate for that application.

In 2003 the Weighing Sector reported there was ongoing disagreement among NIST Weights and Measures Division (WMD), the NTEP Participating Laboratories, and manufacturers regarding the interpretation of Handbook 44 General Code paragraph G-S.6. Marking Operational Controls, Indications, and Features; Scales Code paragraph S.1.1. Zero Indication; and related discussions in the 78th (1993) NCWM Specifications and Tolerances (S&T) Final Report Item 320-1 S.1.1. Zero Indication. These disagreements resulted in inconsistencies between type evaluations and field enforcement for scales and point-of-sale systems interfaced with scales that use methods such as screen savers, power savers, scrolling displays, and modes of operation other than a digital zero indication to indicate that a device is at a no-load condition. WMD and some representatives of several NTEP Participating Laboratories agreed that General Code paragraph G-S.6. requires weighing devices to be marked or provide an indication that states the zero-balance is represented by other than a digital zero indication. WMD and the representatives noted this interpretation was supported by the 1993 S&T Final Report, and NCWM Publication 14 clearly states such markings are required. Other Participating Laboratories and some manufacturers stated that the markings were not necessary because Handbook 44 paragraph S.1.1.(c) does not specifically state that the additional markings are required and the actions of the 78th NCWM to amend paragraph S.1.1.(c) provided sufficient customer protection for devices that use this feature.

Weights and measures officials indicated there may be "not-built-for-purpose" devices that do not comply with the proposed interpretation. These "not-built-for-purpose" devices are interfaced with approved devices; however, the system continues weighing when the scale is off zero. Consequently, officials questioned whether the proposed changes to paragraph S.1.1.(c) are intended to be nonretroactive requirements.

In July 2004 the Committee agreed that its proposal to modify paragraph S.1.1.(c) was consistent with the original intent of the requirement. After hearing comments about how some systems are designed to operate, the Committee decided that additional language was needed to clarify that no marking is required if operator intervention is necessary to verify a zero condition before the start of a transaction. In July 2004, the Committee made this an information item to provide sufficient time for input from the Weighing Sector (that did not have this proposal at its 2003 meeting) and to receive a proposal that addresses operator intervention.

The Committee believes the proposal provides a record of how to apply the requirement. The Committee agreed that the original intent of the requirement was that all primary indicators comply with paragraph S.1.1., therefore, the proposal should be a retroactive requirement.

At its August 2004 meeting the Weighing Sector agreed with the Committee's interpretation, but did not find it necessary to modify paragraph S.1.1.(c) because NCWM Publication 14 was expanded in 2003 to include in type evaluation checklist procedures criteria to verify that digital electronic scales equipped with other than a continuous digital zero-balance indication comply. Publication 14 test procedures specify methods for defining the zero indication when the zero condition of the scale is represented by other than a continuous digital zero indication. The Weighing Sector agreed the type evaluation aspects of this issue have been resolved.

The Northeastern Weights and Measures Association (NEWMA) indicated there is little support for this proposal. Many at NEWMA believe the NTEP laboratories already have the necessary information to properly perform evaluations.

The Central and Western Weights and Measures Associations recommended the proposal be withdrawn because appropriate protections and labeling criteria are applied during type evaluation.

The Scale Manufacturers Association agreed that the current type evaluation process based on paragraph S.1.1.(c) prevents facilitation of fraud.

During the 2005 NCWM Interim Meeting, the Committee agreed that past inconsistencies in the interpretation of paragraph S.1.1.(c) warrant clarifying the intent of the paragraph in Handbook 44. Even though the regional weights and measures associations recommended a different approach, their positions do not disagree with the technical content of the proposal. The Committee further modified paragraph S.1.1. to include a new note recommended by WMD to clarify that no markings are necessary when operator intervention is required to return the indication to a digital zero balance before conducting a transaction.

At the July 2005 NCWM Annual Meeting, the Committee changed the status of the item from "voting" to "information" to allow additional time to determine whether or not the markings could be displayed as part of the indication rather than being physically marked on the device. This will also allow additional time for the Committee to gather information on whether or not self-service systems provide information about the zero-balance condition of scales prior to each weighment.

320-2 VC S.1.8.4. **Recorded Representations, Point-of-Sale Systems; Footnote 1**
(This item was adopted.)

Source: National Type Evaluation Technical Committee (NTETC) Weighing Sector

Recommendation: Amend paragraph S.1.8.4. Recorded Representations, Point-of-Sale Systems; Footnote 1 as follows:

S.1.8.4. Recorded Representations, Point-of-Sale Systems. - The sales information recorded by cash registers when interfaced with a weighing element shall contain the following information for items weighed at the checkout stand:

(a) the net weight, [1]

(b) the unit price, [1]

(c) the total price, and

(d) the product class or, in a system equipped with price look-up capability, the product name or code number.

[1] ~~Weight values shall be identified by kilogram, kg, grams, g, ounces, oz, pound, lb, or the sign "#." For~~ devices interfaced with scales indicating in metric units, the unit price may be expressed in price per 100 grams. Weight values shall be identified by kilogram, kg, grams, g, ounces, oz, pound, or lb. The "#" symbol is not acceptable.
[Nonretroactive as of January 1, 2006]
(Amended 1995 and 2005)

Discussion/Background: In 1976, the Committee reviewed numerous examples of point-of-sale systems' transaction information and provided clarification on how that information should be formatted on recorded representations. At that time, the Committee indicated the "#" symbol was an acceptable representation for "pound" on point-of sale system's receipts. The Committee noted that the "#" symbol was acceptable because it was recognized in a widely used dictionary. In addition, printer technology at that time could better accommodate the "#" symbol since it required only one column, whereas the two characters in "lb" needed two columns.

Currently, NCWM Publication 14 "NTEP Technical Policy, Checklists and Test Procedures," Section 75, List of Acceptable Abbreviations/Symbols recognizes the "#" symbol as acceptable, but discourages using the "#" symbol for recorded representations for electronic cash registers (ECR) and point-of-sale (POS) systems. One manufacturer reasoned that if the symbol is suitable for recorded representations for ECRs, then there is no justification for prohibiting use of the "#" symbol for other recorded representations or markings. The manufacturer argued that the "#" symbol should be acceptable in all instances or not acceptable in any weighing applications, but was amenable to the Weighing Sector's proposal to remove the "#" symbol from Footnote 1.

The Committee considered several proposals to modify paragraph S.1.8.4. Footnote 1, including recommendations from the Western and Central Weights and Measures Associations outlined above and the Weighing Sector to remove reference to the "#" symbol as shown below:

[1] Weight values shall be identified by kilogram, kg, grams, g, ounces, oz, pound, or lb, or ~~the sign "#." For~~ devices interfaced with scales indicating in metric units, the unit price may be expressed in price per 100 grams.
(Amended 1995 and 200X)

The Weighing Sector proposed removing the "#" symbol from paragraph S.1.8.4. Footnote 1 because the symbol represented a multitude of terms used in many unrelated disciplines and because of advances in printer technology. The Western, Central, Northeastern, and Southern Weights and Measures Associations and Scale Manufacturers Association agreed the "#" symbol is no longer acceptable, but this should not be applied retroactively.

At the 2005 NCWM Annual Meeting the Committee heard unanimous support for removing reference to "#" from the list of acceptable symbols used to identify weight values. The Committee agreed to present the proposal as a voting item with an effective date of January 1, 2006. This prohibition on the use of the "#" will be nonretroactive.

320-3   I   UR.1.6. Computing Scale Interfaced to a Cash Register

Source: Southern Weights and Measures Association (SWMA)

Recommendation: Add a new paragraph UR.1.6. to the Scales Code as follows:

UR.1.6. Computing Scale Interfaced to a Cash Register. – A computing scale may interface with a cash register provided all displayed and recorded indications agree:

(a) the cash register only records (serves as printer) the information received from the scale,

~~(b) the computing scale has tare capability,~~

~~(c) the computing scale is not equipped with PLU capability,~~

~~(d) The electronic cash register does not have any input to the computing scale in the process of determining the total price of a weighed item.~~
~~(Added 200X)~~

Discussion: This proposal is intended to add new device-specific requirements to the Scales Code to address the interface of computing scales with electronic cash registers (ECR) and to clarify how each component must display transaction information. The requirements also prescribe how such devices must operate in taking tare and how Price-Look-Up (PLU) features must function. Currently, a General Code Specification (G-S.2.) specifying that weighing and measuring equipment and associated devices shall not facilitate fraud is not sufficient to clarify how a computing scale interfaced with an ECR must operate.

In Spring 2004, the NTEP Participating Laboratories learned that officials in one jurisdiction were finding computing scales interfaced with ECRs, where the ECR accepts weighing results from the computing scale and uses the ECR's price look-up (PLU) feature to retrieve tare and unit price information to calculate the total price. Officials reported that a different unit price, tare, and total price could be manually entered and displayed on the computing scale at the same time. In this instance, what the customer views on the computing scale as the net weight, unit price, and total price may not be what is actually used by the ECR to calculate the customer's charge. Additionally, the NTEP Certificate of Conformance (CC) for devices with such areas of noncompliance did not list the interface as an approved application.

The Participating Laboratories recognized that NCWM Publication 14 type evaluation criteria address how computing scales must interface with ECRs and decided to use that criteria to propose the following new specification for the Scales Code that would be used by field officials in their inspection and test of these systems:

~~S.1.8.5. Computing Scale Interfaced to a Cash Register. - A computing scale may interface with a cash register provided:~~

~~(a) the cash register only records (serves as printer) the information received from the scale,~~

~~(b) the computing scale has tare capability,~~

~~(c) the computing scale is not equipped with PLU capability, and~~

~~(d) the electronic cash register does not have any input to the computing scale in the process of determining the total price of a weighed item.~~

The proposal was distributed at the 2004 fall meetings of the NTETC Weighing Sector, Western Weights and Measures Associations (WWMA) and SWMA. The WWMA withdrew the item from its agenda because there was only minimal support for the proposal from the Weighing Sector. The Scale Manufacturers Association (SMA) opposed the proposed specification because SMA members believed it would, as worded, inadvertently impose design restrictions on devices. SMA recommended the following language as an alternative:

~~S.1.8.5. Computing Scale Interfaced to a Cash Register. - A computing scale may interface with a cash register provided all displayed and recorded indications agree.~~

The SWMA supported the original proposal because it provided clear guidance for officials and SWMA also believed it would be easier to enforce than G-S.2. Facilitation of Fraud. The SWMA agreed to forward the proposal to the NCWM S&T Committee for consideration as a voting item.

During the 2005 NCWM Interim Meeting, the Committee agreed that adding specific language to the Scales Code would make it easier for the field official to ensure that equipment is operating in an approved manner. The language clarifies that it is acceptable for the ECR and computing scale to communicate the total price, but not to the point where the input process involves the ECR calculating the total price. The Committee recommended that jurisdictions, if they have not already done so, establish specific examination procedures (e.g., enter a new price per pound at the ECR) so that officials verify that both the ECR and the computing scale interface are in compliance.

The Committee heard numerous comments opposing the proposed specification. Industry representatives said the proposal might limit future technology used to interface equipment and that it would be too restrictive when applied to a point-of-sale system that reads UPC codes and computes prices for frequent shopper discounted prices. The Committee was advised that, since type evaluation already verifies the requirements proposed in new paragraphs S.1.8.5.(a) through (d), that the Committee should consider an alternate proposal that only specifies "all indications must agree," similar to the language in the SMA proposal. The Committee also concluded that the term "input" should be expanded to more provide more detail to officials about how the interface must work and that a requirement was needed to ensure equipment in commercial use is interfaced as approved by NTEP and as intended by the manufacturer's design. Consequently, the Committee modified the proposal to make it a user requirement with the recommendation that it be adopted by the NCWM.

During the 2005 NCWM Annual Meeting, the Committee again heard that there are instances in which a computing scale may be interfaced with an ECR to create a point-of-sale system that is contrary to the device application covered on the device's Certificate of Conformance. Additionally, the Committee was told that neither of the proposals discussed above address computing scales with multiple sales accumulation capability. Several comments suggested that the current definition of point-of-sale system (POS) may also need modification to clarify the specific type of weighing element that is permitted as part of the POS assembly. Based on the comments it received the Committee believed that developing a new specification rather than a user requirement was the most appropriate way to address the problems that have been reported. Consequently, the Committee changed the item to "information" so that it can be further developed. The Committee recommends that the SWMA rework the proposal as a specification that (1) provides details to officials users about how cash registers must function, (2) provides guidance to assist device manufacturers who are considering design modifications to a computing scale or cash register, and (3) is not in conflict with requirements in related paragraphs such as S.1.8.4. Recorded Representations, Point-of-Sale Systems.

320-4 VC   **S.2.1.3. Scales Equipped with an Automatic Zero-Setting Mechanism (Zero Tracking), S.2.1.3.1. For Scales Manufactured Between January 1, 2007; Maximum Load Rezeroed, S.2.1.3.2. For Scales Manufactured On or After January 1, 2007; Maximum Load Rezeroed, and S.2.1.3.3. Automatic Zero-Setting Mechanism (Zero Tracking) on Class III L Devices**
(This item was adopted.)

Source: National Type Evaluation Technical Committee (NTETC) Weighing Sector

Recommendation: Modify paragraphs S.2.1.3. and S.2.1.3.1. and add new paragraphs S.2.1.3.2.and S.2.1.3.3.as follows:

    S.2.1.3. Scales Equipped with an Automatic Zero-Setting Mechanism **(Zero Tracking).** -Under normal operating conditions

       S.2.1.3.1 Zero-Tracking for Scales manufactured Between January 1, 1981 and January 1, 2007 .-T*the maximum load that can be "rezeroed," when either placed on or removed from the platform all at once* **under normal operating condition***s, shall be:*

          (a) for bench, counter, and livestock scales: 0.6 scale division;

          (b) for vehicle, axle-load, and railway track scales: 3.0 scale divisions; and

          (c) for all other scales: 1.0 scale division.
       (Amended 2005)

~~S.2.1.3.2. Zero-Tracking for Scales manufactured On or After January 1, 2007.~~ ~~The maximum load that can be "rezeroed," when either placed on or removed from the platform all at once under normal operating conditions, shall be:~~

~~(a) for vehicle, axle-load, and railway track scales: 3.0 scale divisions; and~~

~~(b) for all other scales: 0.5 scale division.~~
~~(Added 2005)~~

S.2.1.3.~~13~~. ~~Automatic Zero-Setting Mechanism~~ **Means to Disable Zero-Tracking on** Class III L **Devices** - *Class III L devices equipped with automatic zero setting mechanisms shall be designed with a sealable means to allow the automatic zero setting to be disabled during the inspection and test of the device.*
[Nonretroactive as of January 1, 2001]
(Added 1999) ~~(Amended 2005)~~

Discussion: This issue revisits the 2003 Weighing Sector's concerns about holding a device to different AZSM requirements based solely on whether or not it is located on a counter or floor. The confusion over how to apply AZSM requirements is compounded when a family of scales covered on an NTEP Certificate of Conformance includes both bench/counter scales and other platform-type scales. Currently, paragraph S.2.1.3. specifies a different maximum load that can be rezeroed under normal operating conditions for bench/counter scales (0.6 scale division) from that for all other scales (1.0 scale division).

The proposal is also intended to partially align the automatic zero tracking requirements in paragraph S.2.1.3. with those of Measurement Canada and OIML R76 "Non-automatic Weighing Instruments." AZSM requirements for Class III L vehicle, axle-load, and railway track scales will remain unchanged.

The Weighing Sector asked that the proposal be a developing item on the NCWM S&T Agenda while the regional weights and measures associations consider its effect on field evaluations. The Sector's public members questioned how field officials will determine the date of manufacture and whether training is needed. The Weighing Sector's industry members requested a delayed enforcement date to allow sufficient time for changes to be made to devices nearing the end of their production cycle.

The Western Weights and Measures Association (WWMA) believed there is sufficient time between September 2004 and July 2005 to gather data to determine if there will be enforcement issues. The WWMA agreed that while input from field officials is necessary the proposal should move forward as a voting item.

The Central Weights and Measures Association received no comments on the proposal and recommended it move forward as a voting item.

The Southern Weights and Measures Association agreed with the concern stated by public members of the Sector that it is difficult for field officials to determine when a device was manufactured and recommended the proposal be an information item.

NIST Weights and Measures Division (WMD) believes field officials will have no difficulty with enforcing the proposal based on the equipment manufacture date since officials already successfully establish that criteria when enforcing other nonretroactive requirements.

The Scale Manufacturers Association (SMA) believes the proposal has no technical merit and is only an attempt to harmonize United States and OIML requirements. SMA is concerned about the potential for unnecessarily increasing evaluation costs. However, the SMA supported this effort toward harmonization provided NTEP does not require reevaluation of devices already covered by NTEP Certificates of Conformance.

At the 2005 NCWM Interim Meeting, the Committee agreed that the proposal is a good move in the direction of harmonization of standards and should not lose momentum. The Committee concluded that sufficient data could be easily gathered by July 2005 on new production lots of existing products to demonstrate if a January 1, 2006, effective date was appropriate. The Committee encouraged manufacturers, officials, and Participating NTEP Laboratories to gather data since it is easy for each group to verify if bench, counter, livestock scales, and scales classified as other types can meet the proposed ASZM requirement during their regular duties. The Committee indicated it is willing to modify the date to January 1, 2007, if any group submitted data at the July 2005 NCWM Annual Meeting to support extending the period in which manufacturers have to comply. The Committee agreed with WMD's assessment that jurisdictions continually prove their ability to determine manufacture dates when devices are subject to nonretroactive requirements. The Committee indicated its full support of an NTEP policy that does not require additional evaluation for existing equipment since the proposal appears to have little effect on most bench or counter scales. Consequently, the Committee agreed the proposal was ready for a vote at the 2005 NCWM Annual Meeting.

During the July 2005 NCWM Annual Meeting, the Committee acknowledged that officials may experience delays during inspections if they have to verify the date that a device was manufactured. However, it believes these delays are manageable and are no different than those experienced when verifying compliance with other nonretroactive requirements. Typically, date of manufacture information is readily available from the manufacturer. The Committee heard opposition to an alternate SMA proposal that based the enforcement date on the Certificate of Conformance (CC) issue date. A CC can be updated or revised for any number of reasons consequently there are variations in subsequent CC numbers and model features that would require even more investigative work by officials. The Committee did not support the alternate proposal since it would also set a precedent for enforcing Handbook 44 nonretroactive requirements based on the CC issue date rather than the manufacture date. The Committee also recognized that there may be some models nearing the end of their production life, where it may not be economically practicable to modify them to meet the proposed maximum 0.5 d load requirement. The Committee heard from industry that most equipment is already designed to operate to the proposed standard and that large numbers of devices are not built in advance; however, additional time is necessary for existing field devices to reach the end of their life cycle. Consequently, the Committee modified the proposal to extend the enforcement date to January 1, 2007.

320-5   VC   Table S.6.3.b. Notes For Table S.6.3.a. Note 3; Nominal Capacity and Value of the Scale Division and Appendix D; Definition of Reading Face
(This item was adopted.)

Source: National Type Evaluation Technical Committee (NTETC) Weighing Sector

Recommendation: Amend Table S.6.3.b. Notes For Table S.6.3.a. Note 3 and revise the definition for "reading face" to include a reference to Scales Code Section 2.20 as follows:

3. **The device shall be marked with the nominal capacity.** The nominal capacity *and shall be shown together* **with the** *value of the scale division (e.g.,* 50 000 x 5 kg, 100 000 x 10 lb, *15 x 0.005 kg , or* 30 x 0.01 lb, **or capacity = 15 kg, d = 0.005 kg,** adjacent to the weight display **in a clear and conspicuous manner and be readily apparent when viewing the reading face of the scale indicator unless when the nominal capacity and value of the scale division are not immediately already** *apparent* **by the design of the device**. *Each scale division value or weight unit shall be marked on multiple range or multi-interval scales.*
[Nonretroactive as of January 1, 1983]
(Amended 2005)

reading face. That portion of an automatic-indicating weighing or measuring device that gives a visible indication of the quantity weighed or measured. A reading face may include an indicator and a series of graduations or may present values digitally, and may also provide money-value indications. [1.10, **2.20**]
(Amended 2005)

Discussion: The proposed change is intended to eliminate any differences in the interpretation of where to place the required nominal capacity and scale division markings on equipment. Currently, Table S.6.3.b. Note 3 specifies that the nominal capacity and the scale division shall be shown together adjacent to the weight display. In 1990, the Committee was unable to arrive at definitive guidelines on what is meant by "adjacent" and left the interpretation to

NTEP Participating Laboratories. Any manufacturer's challenge to the laboratory's interpretation was to be heard by the NTEP Board of Governors (now the NCWM NTEP Committee).

NCWM Publication 14, "NTEP Technical Policy, Checklists, and Test Procedures" for Digital Electronic Scales Section 2.13. states:

> 2.13. The nominal capacity by minimum scale division shall be clearly and conspicuously marked adjacent to the weight display. (Acceptable location depends on conspicuousness).

Repeated attempts by the NTEP Laboratories and manufacturers to uniformly apply this marking requirement have resulted in conflicting interpretations. The NTEP Laboratories believe the criteria in paragraph 2.13. implies that "conspicuousness" should be the primary objective, rather than proximity of the information. However, the NTEP Laboratories agree that until the term "adjacent" is removed from Handbook 44 Table S.6.3.b. Note 3, the Laboratories are tied to requiring the nominal capacity and scale division values be marked adjacent to the weight display as shown below in Example 1.

The NTEP Laboratories maintain that the information must be marked next to the weight display on the face of a scale, as shown below in Example 1, but that they continue to receive devices with the required markings located elsewhere on the face of the scale such as shown below in Example 2.

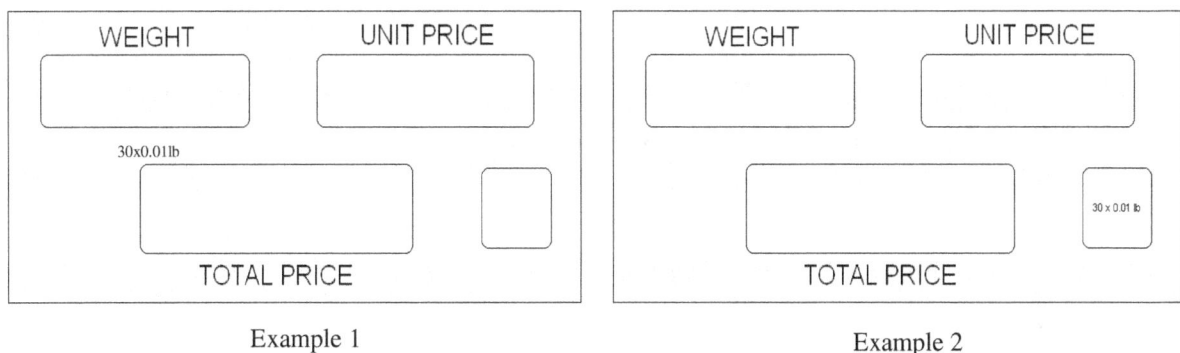

Example 1   Example 2

The NTEP Laboratories agreed that at this point in time Example 2 shown above is incorrect according to Handbook 44 because the markings do not appear adjacent to or as close as practical to the weight display as required in General Code paragraph G-S.5.2.4. Values. The NTEP Laboratories believe that the operator is already familiar with the device and the customer does not fully understand the significance of this information. The NTEP Laboratories also believe that the markings in the examples above are "conspicuous" enough for the inspector and service technician who rely most heavily on the information. However, Example 2 is only acceptable if Note 3 could be amended to allow for placing the markings conspicuously on the face of the indicating portion of the scale.

The Weighing Sector agreed with the Laboratories that both Example 1 and 2 represent the acceptable placement of markings since they are either adjacent to or conspicuous on the reading face of the weight display. The Weighing Sector also proposed to modify the existing definition of "reading face" to include a reference to Section 2.20. Scales Code since the term would also apply to scale indications.

The Central Weights and Measures Association and Scale Manufacturers Association (SMA) supported the Sector's proposal shown in the recommendation above. The Scale Manufacturers Association asked for further clarification on the meaning of the phrase "already apparent by the design."

The Western Weights and Measures Association (WWMA) discussed how paragraph G-S.5.2.4. requirements for values are not intended to apply to the nominal capacity statement and do little to help the customer determine the acceptability of a weight value. The WWMA agreed to the same wording shown in the Weighing Sector's proposal and recommended the proposal move forward as a voting item.

The Northeastern Weights and Measures Association concluded that this is an NTEP issue and "adjacent" is the correct terminology since it represents "abutting" or "next to."

The Southern Weights and Measures Association (SWMA) agreed with the Weighing Sector's proposal provided the unit of weight is identified in a manner that is consistent with requirements in paragraph G-S.5.2.4. Values for placing, as close as practicable, adequate and sufficient information to define graduations, indications, or recorded representations. The SWMA agreed that Example 2 is not correct; however, the placement of the nominal capacity and division marking would be correct if the unit of weight were properly marked adjacent to the weight display shown in Example 3.

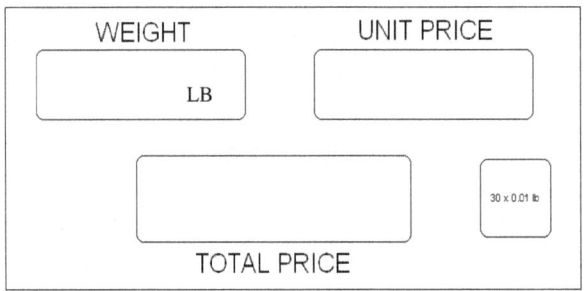

Example 3

The NIST Technical Advisor to the Weighing Sector requested that the Sector consider an alternate NIST Weights and Measures Division (WMD) proposal amending Note 3 in Table S.6.3.b. to require markings "near" the weight display that do not reference the reading face as follows:

3. *The nominal capacity and value of the scale division shall be shown together (e.g., ~~50 000 x 5 kg, 100 000 x 10 lb,~~ 15 x 0.005 kg , or 30 x 0.01 lb) near ~~adjacent to the~~ weight display when the nominal capacity and value of the scale division are not immediately apparent. Each scale division value or weight unit shall be marked on multiple range or multi-interval scales.*
[Nonretroactive as of January 1, 1983]
~~(Amended 200X)~~

The WMD proposal would also more closely align U.S. terminology with that used in OIML R76 "Non-automatic Weighing Instruments" paragraph 7.1.4 Presentation of descriptive markings, which specifies the descriptive markings shall be grouped together shall identify the Max, Min, e, and d, if "d" does not equal "e", and shall be shown near the display of the weight result if they are not already located there.

WMD was concerned that the Sector's proposal deviates from the intent of General Code paragraph G-S.5.2.4. Values, which specifies that values shall be adequately defined and placed as close as practicable to the corresponding indication. WMD noted the Sector's proposal allows information to be placed further away from the display and this becomes more difficult to locate as the font size of the lettering decreases. WMD disagreed with the premise that consumers do not value this information. WMD believes the information should be available to the customer as well as officials and service representatives. As currently written, Note 3 is not in conflict with the General Code paragraph G-S.5.2.4. Values. However, the proposal creates a conflict since it would permit markings that may not be placed as close as practical to the weight display.

The Committee agreed that the Sector's proposal shown above is acceptable and ready for a vote since it provides guidelines on the required information, yet allows some flexibility in the placement of that information. The Committee concurred with officials that the phrase "already apparent by the design" is a carryover from language developed to address mechanical beam and dial type scales, where the beam capacity and its "d" and the complete revolution of the dial and its "d" provided the nominal capacity and value of the scale division without the need for additional markings. The Committee concluded that Example 1 and Example 3 both comply with the proposal and show acceptable ways to mark the nominal capacity and value of the scale division (d) even though there is a difference in where the information is placed on the display. Example 2 is not encouraged since it is the conspicuous supplemental marking of "LB" on the weight display that makes all of the information crystal clear.

During the July 2005 NCWM Annual Meeting, the Committee modified the proposal to also recognize formats used in international markings to designate the capacity and d, such as "max = 15 kg, d = 0.005 kg, where text or abbreviations may identify the required capacity and division size information. Marking the capacity and division information in the alternate format also requires that the information is located near the weight display.

320-6   I   N.1.3.1. Bench or Counter Scales, N.1.3.8. All Other Scales Except Crane Scales, Hanging Scales, Hopper Scales, Wheel–Load Weighers, and Portable Axle-Load Weighers, and Appendix D; Definitions of Bench Scale and Counter Scale

Source: National Type Evaluation Technical Committee (NTETC) Weighing Sector

Recommendation: Delete paragraph N.1.3.1. and renumber subsequent paragraphs.

N.1.3. Shift Test.

> ~~N.1.3.1. Bench or Counter Scales. - A shift test shall be conducted with a half-capacity test load centered successively at four points equidistant between the center and the front, left, back, and right edges of the load-receiving element.~~

Renumber and amend paragraph N.1.3.8. All Other Scales Except Crane Scales, Hanging Scales, Hopper Scales, Wheel–Load Weighers, and Portable Axle-Load Weighers as follows:

N.1.3.~~8~~1. All Other Scales Except Crane Scales, Hanging Scales, Hopper Scales, Wheel-Load Weighers, and Portable Axle-Load Weighers. A shift test shall be conducted using the following prescribed test loads and test patterns.

> (**a**) For ~~livestock~~ scales ~~, the~~ with a nominal capacity greater than 150 kg (300 lb), a shift test load ~~shall not exceed one-half the rated section~~ may be conducted by either using one-third nominal capacity ~~or one-half the rated concentrated load~~ test load centered as nearly as possible at the center of each quadrant of the load-receiving element as shown in Figure 1 below, or by using one-quarter nominal capacity, ~~whichever is applicable. A shift test shall be conducted using either:~~ load centered as nearly as possible, successively over each corner of the load-receiving element as shown in Figure 2 below.

> (~~a~~**b**) ~~A one-quarter~~ For scales with a nominal capacity of 150 kg (300 lb) or less, a shift test load ~~shall be conducted using one-third nominal capacity test load. The~~ centered as nearly as possible, ~~successively over each main~~ load shall be applied centrally in the quadrant if a single weight is used, or applied uniformly over the quadrant, if several weights are used ~~support as shown in the diagram below; or~~

> (~~b~~**c**) ~~A one-half nominal capacity~~ For livestock scales, the shift test load ~~centered as nearly as possible, successively at the center of each quarter of the load-receiving element~~ shall not exceed one-half the rated section or concentrated load capacity using the prescribed test pattern as shown in ~~the diagram~~ Figure 1, or one quarter the section or concentrated load capacity as shown in Figure 2 below.
> (Added 2003)
> (Amended 1987, ~~and~~ 2003, and 200X)

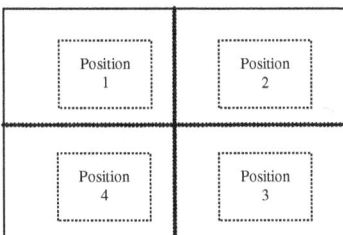

Figure 1   **Figure 2**

Delete Appendix D definitions for "bench scale" and "counter scale" as follows:

~~bench scale. See "counter scale." [2.20]~~

~~counter scale. One that, by reason of its size, arrangement of parts, and moderate nominal capacity, is adapted for use on a counter or bench. Sometimes called "bench scale." [2.20]~~

The Central Weights and Measures Association (CWMA) recommended an alternate proposal to modify paragraph N.1.3.8. as follows:

N.1.3.~~8~~7. **All Other Scales Except Crane Scales, Hanging Scales, Hopper Scales, Wheel-Load Weighers, and Portable Axle-Load Weighers.** A shift test shall be conducted using the following prescribed test loads and test patterns.

    (~~a~~) For ~~livestock~~ scales~~,~~ ~~the~~ **with a nominal capacity greater than 150 kg (300 lb) a** shift test ~~load shall not exceed one-half the rated section~~ **may be conducted by either using one-third nominal** capacity ~~or one-half the rated concentrated load~~ **test load centered as nearly as possible at the center of each quarter of the load-receiving element as shown in Figure 1 below, or by using one-quarter nominal** capacity~~, whichever is applicable. A shift test shall be conducted using either:~~ **load centered as nearly as possible, successively over each corner of the load-receiving element as shown in Figure 2 below.**

    (~~a~~**b**) ~~A one-quarter~~ **For scales with a** nominal capacity **of 150 kg (300 lb) or less, a shift** test ~~load shall be conducted using one-third nominal capacity test load. The~~ **centered as nearly as possible, successively over each main** load **shall be applied centrally in the segment if a single weight is used, or applied uniformly over the segment, if several small weights are used** support as shown ~~in the diagram~~ **Figure 1 below**~~, or~~**.**

    (~~b~~**c**) ~~A one-half nominal capacity~~ **For livestock scales the shift** test load ~~centered as nearly as possible, successively at the center of each quarter of the load-receiving element~~ **shall not exceed one-half the rated section or concentrated load capacity using the prescribed test pattern** as shown in ~~the diagram~~ **Figure 1, or one-quarter of the section or concentrated load capacity as shown in Figure 2** below.

(Added 2003)
(Amended 1987~~,~~ ~~and~~ 2003**, and 200X**)

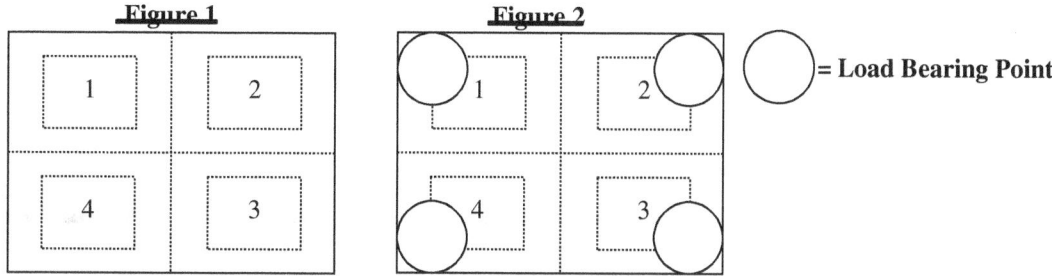

Discussion: The Committee was requested to reconsider a 2003 Weighing Sector proposal to clarify the appropriate shift test pattern and test loads for bench/counter scales and other platform-type scales. Currently, bench and counter scale shift tests are conducted with a one-half capacity test load centered successively at four points equidistant between the center and the front, left, back, right edges of the load-receiving element. Other platform scale shift tests are conducted with a one-half capacity test load centered, as nearly as possible, successively at the center of each quadrant. The proposal eliminates the bench and counter scale device types and prescribes the shift test load and test pattern based on either the scale's nominal capacity or because the scale is used to weigh livestock. It should be noted that the proposal does not permit corner testing for scales with a nominal capacity less than or equal to 150 kg. Corner testing is allowed within permissible load limits if the scale has four load supports for scales with a nominal capacity greater than 150 kg. Currently, Table 4 Minimum Test Weights requires that scales with a capacity of 150 kg or less have test weights up to 100 % of the scale capacity.

The Scale Manufacturers Association (SMA) supported the Sector's proposal, but pointed out that Figure 2 was inconsistent with the proposed requirement that describes the location of the test load. Consequently, the SMA recommended an alternate Figure 2, where the test loads were located on the outer corners of the platform. The SMA also noted other inconsistencies in the terminology in the proposal. Proposed paragraph N.1.3.7.(a) included the term "quarter," whereas proposed paragraph N.1.3.7.(b) specified the term "segment." The SMA recommended replacing both terms with the word "quadrant."

The SMA agreed that the Sector's proposal provided for a shift test that is independent of the device's design. The proposal is an improvement over the corresponding R76 requirement, which is design dependent. In keeping with the spirit of harmonization, the SMA recommended that NIST Weights and Measures Division (WMD) submit a similar proposal to OIML.

The Committee heard similar comments from all regional weights and measures associations indicating that additional study is needed before presenting the issue for a vote. The associations indicated that additional data should be collected on shift tests to verify that the proposed test loads and positions are equivalent to existing test loads. On a general note regarding harmonization with OIML, the Northeastern Weights and Measures Association believes there may be instances where OIML should harmonize with U.S. requirements. Participants at the regional meetings were advised that all shift test data comparing existing and proposed test loads and positions should be sent to Steve Cook, NIST Technical Advisor to the NTETC Weighing Sector, at steven.cook@nist.gov, by fax at 301-926-0647 or at NIST WMD, 100 Bureau Drive MS 2600, Gaithersburg, MD 20899-2600.

The Committee made the proposal an information item to allow sufficient time for comparison of data using existing and the proposed shift test procedures to ensure that devices passing current tests also meet the proposed requirements. The Committee acknowledged that the Weighing Sector proposal addressed the Committee's 2004 requests for a procedure where the official was not required to determine the scale's design in order to conduct a shift test. In the spring of 2005, the proposal was posted on the Weights and Measures List Server to generate further discussion and data. The Committee agreed that the corrections noted by SMA to the Figure 2 diagram and terminology were appropriate and, therefore, modified the proposals accordingly.

During the July 2005 NCWM Annual Meeting, the Committee further modified Figure 2 by showing the test loads as squares because circles are used in other sections of Handbook 44 to represent load bearing points. The Committee kept the proposal as an information item to enable officials and the NTEP Laboratories to continue forwarding data on the proposed and current shift tests to the NIST Technical Advisor for evaluation.

320-7 I   **Table 6 Tolerances**

Source: NIST Weights and Measures Division (WMD)

Recommendation: Amend Table 6 Maintenance Tolerances as follows:

Table 6. ~~Maintenance~~ Tolerances (All values in this table are in ~~verification~~ scale divisions ~~e~~)					
Tolerance in ~~verification~~ scale divisions ~~e~~					
1 2 3 5					
Class Test			Load		
I	0 - 50 000	50 001 - 200 000	200 001 +		
II	0 - 5 000	5 001 - 20 000	20 001 +		
III	0 - 500	501 - 2 000	2 001+ ~=~	~~1 000~~	~~1 001 +~~
IIII	0 - 50	51 - 200	201+ ~=~	~~100~~	~~101 +~~
III L	0 - 500	501 - 1 000	(Add 1 ~~d~~e for each additional 500 ~~d~~e or fraction thereof)		

~~(Amended 200X)~~

Discussion: During an August 2003 meeting, the U.S. National Work Group (USNWG) for R76 "Non-automatic Weighing Instruments" discussed the differences in the tolerances for Class III and IIII weighing instruments. The USNWG reconfirmed that the original intent of the step tolerances was to provide a relationship between scale accuracy and scale resolution. The USNWG agreed that NIST Handbook 44 Class III and Class IIII tolerances should be aligned with OIML R76. The manufacturers present reported that they build identically performing instruments and load cells for both U.S. and international markets.

In September 2004 Hobart Corporation provided "production data" comparing different Class III tolerances. Hobart's data demonstrated that their production scales would comply with Handbook 44 Table 6 tolerances up to 10 000 e and OIML R76 tolerances up to approximately 7000 e. Hobart also reported that many scales and load cells with an n_{max} greater than 5000 e would have difficulty in complying with the temperature effect on zero in both Handbook 44 and OIML R76 standards. Currently, a scale's performance takes advantage of the extra step in Handbook 44, and that is contrary to the intended relationship of scale resolution to accuracy.

The NIST technical advisor to the Weighing Sector requested that it discuss whether or not there is any need to retain the Handbook 44 Accuracy Class III L tolerance or for proposing this tolerance be incorporated into OIML R76. The Class III L tolerance structure in Handbook 44 deviates from the intent of step tolerances since there is little relation of the value of the scale division (i.e., e = 20 lb resolution) to the accuracy required (i.e., ± 8 e at 80 000 lb maintenance tolerance). It should be noted that the tolerance values, zero-tracking limit, and motion detection requirements in Handbook 44 are roughly equivalent to an R76 instrument when e = 50 lb.

The NTETC Weighing Sector withdrew this proposal from its agenda since it was not developed in response to problems encountered with Publication 14 test procedures and, hence, not under its purview. The Sector recommended the WMD and USNWG proposal become either an information item or developing item that is reviewed by the regional weights and measures associations as well as the NCWM S&T Committee. Several regional associations recommended that more data is needed before the proposal can move to a vote.

Additional test data is needed to determine the effect of the proposed tolerances on Class III and IIII scales and on the apportionment of errors for single and multiple load cell applications. It is also recommended that consideration be given to the international recommendations for the apportionment of error and that further analysis be made on the proposal's possible impact on load cells, separable weighing elements, and existing scales. One regional association noted that the Class III L scale tolerances for test loads greater than the proposed 1000 verification scale divisions (e) are based on a test load value measured in scale divisions (d) rather than the proposed "e." That association questioned whether these tolerances should be in "e;" however, it recognized that further modification may only add to the confusion.

During the 2005 NCWM Interim Meeting, the Committee agreed that the proposal has merit. However, it made the proposal an information item in response to requests for more time to examine data from test results using the proposed tolerances and to determine if there are devices that cannot comply, unless they are granted the 5 d tolerance being eliminated from Table 6. The Committee also modified the Class III L tolerance structure for test loads greater than 1000 e to include units of "e" rather than "d" since it is appropriate to have like units in Table 6.

During the 2005 NCWM Annual Meeting, the Scale Manufacturers Association (SMA) reiterated its opposition to the proposal because it believes a change of this magnitude is premature and should not take precedence over other harmonization issues.

320-8 V T.N.4.5. Time Dependence, General, T.N.4.5.1. Time Dependence; Class II, III, and IIII Non-automatic Weighing Instruments, T.N.4.5.2. Time Dependence; Class III L Non-automatic Weighing Instruments, T.N.4.6. Time Dependence (Creep) for Load Cells During Type Evaluation, T.N.4.6.1. Permissible Variations of Readings, T.N.4.6.2. Apportionment Factors, and Definitions of D_{max}, E_{max}, and Non-automatic Weighing Instrument
(This item was adopted.)

Source: Western Weights and Measures Association (WWMA)

Recommendation: Amend paragraph T.N.4.5. as follows:

T.N.4.5. Time Dependence. ~~General~~ - ~~At constant test conditions, the indication 20 seconds after the application of a load and the indication after 1 hour shall not differ by more than:~~ A time dependence test shall be conducted during type evaluation and may be conducted during field verification provided test conditions remain constant.

~~(a) one-half of the absolute value of the applicable tolerance for the applied load for class III L devices; and~~

~~(b) the absolute value of the applicable tolerance for the applied load for all other devices.~~
(Amended 1989 and 2005)

Add new paragraphs T.N.4.5.1. and T.N.4.5.2. as follows:

T.N.4.5.1. Time Dependence; Class II, III, and IIII Non-automatic Weighing Instruments. - A non-automatic weighing instrument of class II, III, and IIII shall meet the following requirements at constant test conditions:

(a) When any load is kept on an instrument, the difference between the indication obtained immediately after placing a load and the indication observed during the following 30 minutes shall not exceed 0.5 e.

(b) However, the difference between the indication obtained at 15 minutes and that at 30 minutes shall not exceed 0.2 e. If these conditions are not met, the difference between the indication obtained immediately after placing a load on the instrument and the indication observed during the following four hours shall not exceed the absolute value of the maximum permissible error at the load applied.

(c) The deviation on returning to zero as soon as the indication has stabilized, after the removal of any load which has remained on the instrument for 30 minutes, shall not exceed 0.5 e.

For a multi-interval instrument, the deviation shall not exceed 0.5 e_1 (first weighing segment)

On a multiple range instrument, the deviation on returning to zero from Max_____ (load in the applicable weighing range) shall not exceed 0.5 e_____ (interval of the weighing segment). Furthermore, after returning to zero from any load greater than Max_____ (capacity of the first weighing range) and immediately after switching to the lowest weighing range, the indication near zero shall not vary by more than e_____ (interval of the first weighing range) during the following 5 minutes.
(Added 2005)

T.N.4.5.2. **Time Dependence; Class III L Non-automatic Weighing Instruments.** - A non-automatic weighing instrument of class III L shall meet the following requirements:

(a) When any load is kept on an instrument, the difference between the indication obtained immediately after placing a load and the indication observed during the following 30 minutes shall not exceed 1.5 e.

(b) However, the difference between the indication obtained at 15 minutes and that at 30 minutes shall not exceed 0.6 e. If these conditions are not met, the difference between the indication obtained immediately after placing a load on the instrument and the indication observed during the following 4 hours shall not exceed the absolute value of the maximum permissible error at the load applied.

(c) The deviation on returning to zero as soon as the indication has stabilized, after the removal of any
load which has remained on the instrument for 30 minutes, shall not exceed one-half of the absolute value of the applicable tolerance for the applied load for class III L devices.
(Added 2005)

Add new paragraphs T.N.4.6., T.N.4.6.1., T.N.4.6.2., T.N.4.6.3 and Table T.N.4.6.2 to include tolerances for load performance and zero repeatability that are aligned with OIML R 60.

T.N.4.6. **Time Dependence (Creep) for Load Cells During Type Evaluation.** - A load cell (force transducer) marked with an accuracy Class shall meet the following requirements at constant test conditions:

(a) **Permissible Variations of Readings.** - With a constant maximum load for the measuring range (D_{max}) between 90 % and 100 % of maximum capacity (E_{max}) applied to the load cell, the difference between the initial reading and any reading obtained during the next 30 minutes shall not exceed the absolute value of the maximum permissible error (mpe) for the applied load (see Table T.N.4.6). The difference between the reading obtained at 20 minutes and the reading obtained at 30 minutes shall not exceed 0.15 times the absolute value of the mpe (see Table T.N.4.6).

(b) **Apportionment Factors.** - The mpe for creep shall be determined from Table T.N.4.6. Maximum Permissible Error (mpe)* for Load Cells using the following apportionment factors (p_{LC}):

p_{LC} = 0.7 for load cells marked with S (single load cell applications), and
p_{LC} = 1.0 for load cells marked with M (multiple load cell applications).
(Added 2005)

	Table T.N.4.6. Maximum Permissible Error (mpe)* for Load Cells During Type Evaluation			
	mpe in Load Cell Verifications Divisions (v) = p_{LC} x Basic Tolerance in v			
Class	p_{LC} x 0.5 v	p_{LC} x 1.0 v		p_{LC} x 1.5 v
I	0 - 50 000 v	50 001 v -	200 000 v	200 001 v +
II	0 - 5 000 v	5 001 v -	20 000 v	20 001 v +
III	0 - 500 v	501 v -	2 000 v	2 001 v +
IIII	0 - 50 v	51 v -	200 v	201 v +
III L	0 - 500 v	501 v -	1 000 v	(Add 0.5 v to the basic tolerance for each additional 500 v or fraction thereof up to a maximum load of 10 000 v)

v represents the load cell verification interval
p_{LC} represents the apportionment factors applied to the basic tolerance
p_{LC} = 0.7 for load cells marked with S (single load cell applications)
p_{LC} = 1.0 for load cells marked with M (multiple load cell applications)
* mpe = p_{LC} x Basic Tolerance in load cell verifications divisions (v)

(Table Added 2005)

Add new definitions of D_{max}, E_{max}, and amend the current definition of non-automatic weighing systems as follows:

D_{max} (maximum load of the measuring range). Largest value of a quantity (mass) which is applied to a load cell during test or use. This value shall not be greater than E_{max}. [2.20]

E_{max} (maximum capacity). Largest value of a quantity (mass) which may be applied to a load cell without exceeding the mpe [2.20]

non-automatic weighing ~~system~~ **instrument.** A weighing instrument or system that requires the intervention of an operator during the weighing process to determine the weighing result or to decide that it is acceptable. [**2.20**, 2.24]

Notes: Determining the weighing result includes any intelligent action of the operator that affects the result, such as deciding and taking an action when an indication is stable or adjusting the weight of the weighed load.

Deciding that the weighing result is acceptable means making a decision regarding the acceptance of each weighing result on observing the indication or releasing a print out. The weighing process allows the operator to take an action which influences the weighing result in the case where the weighing result is not acceptable. (Added 2004) **(Amended 2005)**

Background/Discussion: The NIST Weights and Measures Division believes that this recommendation is a small step in the work to align U.S. and international requirements. Another possible alternative for aligning Handbook 44 and Publication 14 with OIML R60 "Load Cells" is to consider incorporating OIML R60 chapters 1 through 7 by reference into Handbook 44 and OIML R60 Annexes A through E into Publication 14. Handbook 44 and Publication 14 could further include paragraphs that state which requirements are not adopted, are different than, or are in addition to OIML R60.

The following background information on the development of Handbook 44 Scales Code paragraph T.N.4.5. Time Dependence is provided by Mr. John Elengo (NIST Consultant), who prepared the comparison of Handbook 44, OIML R76 "Non-automatic Weighing Instruments," and OIML R60.

Prior to the adoption of Handbook 44 paragraph T.N.4.5., the United States had not established any requirements for "creep." At that time, the OIML requirement for a creep test was based on a 4-hour period, which was considered excessive since the error is primarily contributed by the load cells used in a scale. Generally, the greatest amount of load cell creep occurs during a short period (minutes) immediately following the application of the load on the scale. After that point, the output becomes increasingly constant. Hence, the United States adopted a requirement that specifies a 1-hour period rather than a 4-hour period. Years later, during the revision of OIML R60, it became evident that most international evaluation laboratories were not conducting the 4-hour test but a shorter one, and the creep proved to stabilize sufficiently during this shorter test. The assumption was made that a device passing the shorter test would meet the 4-hour requirement. This assumption was verified by sample tests. Based on this experience and that gained in the international comparison of load cell evaluations, the OIML International Work Group for R60 concluded that a 30-minute test is sufficient provided that, in addition to measuring the difference over a 30-minute period, the difference occurring in the last 10 minutes of this period is also measured. A more restrictive allowance than the total allowance for the 30-minute period is applied to the 10-minute period difference in order to assure that the creep is becoming increasingly constant and not increasing. The R60 30-minute requirement has been incorporated into OIML R76. Thus, the requirement now applies not only to the load cell, but also to the instrument as a whole. If main components other than the load cell are a source of creep, they can be accounted for using the principle of apportionment of errors (including the assignment of fractions "p_i" to those various separate main components of an instrument that can be evaluated separately). [Refer to R76-1 Section 3 Metrological Requirements paragraph 3.5.4. Apportioning of Errors.]

The NTEP Laboratories discussed this at the 2004 NTEP Participating Laboratories meeting and agreed to forward a proposal to align Handbook 44 with R76 and R60 to the Committee.

The National Type Evaluation Technical Committee (NTETC) Weighing Sector withdrew this proposal from its agenda since it was not developed in response to problems with Publication 14 test procedures (and, hence, not under its purview) and due to time constraints. A member of the Weighing Sector also noted that the proposal does not recognize tolerances for Class I scales.

The Western Weights and Measures Association recommended this item move forward as a voting item, but did not indicate its rationale for taking this position.

The Central Weights and Measures Association (CWMA) agreed the proposal was an issue for the Weighing Sector requiring further development. Consequently, CWMA recommended the proposal move forward as an information item.

The Northeastern Weights and Measures Association (NEWMA) recommended that for consistency the U.S. terms should be followed by the OIML equivalent terminology in parentheses. NEWMA also found that this is an example of the need for revising Handbook 44 into separate sections for field verification and type evaluation test procedures.

The Southern Weights and Measures Association recommended that the proposal become a developing item on the NCWM S&T Agenda.

The Scale Manufacturers Association (SMA) recommended only the proposed modification to current Scales Code paragraph T.N.4.5. as follows:

> T.N.4.5. Time Dependence, General. - ~~At constant test conditions, the indication 20 seconds after the application of a load and the indication after 1 hour shall not differ by more than:~~ A <u>time dependence test shall be conducted during type evaluation.</u>
>
> ~~(a) one-half of the absolute value of the applicable tolerance for the applied load for class III L devices; and~~
>
> ~~(b) the absolute value of the applicable tolerance for the applied load for all other devices.~~
> (Amended 1989 <u>and 2005</u>)

The SMA agreed with the proposed tolerances and recommended that the remaining proposed subparagraphs be added to NCWM Publication 14 through the Weighing Sector. The SMA agreed that Publication 14 requirements should be traceable to NIST Handbook 44; however, there is no need to add additional text to Handbook 44 to provide traceability. The SMA agreed that its alternate proposal provides the necessary traceability.

The SMA believes this is a harmonization issue. The SMA supports harmonization of U.S. and international requirements, but is concerned about the potential for unnecessarily increasing evaluation costs. However, the SMA does support this effort toward harmonization provided NTEP waives the resulting additional evaluation of existing devices.

The Committee noted that the proposed tolerances are absent from Handbook 44 and that tolerances usually appear in Handbook 44 rather than Publication 14. One added benefit to adopting the proposed creep test tolerances is that it harmonizes U.S. and international requirements. The Committee agreed with SMA's recommendation that time dependence test be performed as a type evaluation test and modified the proposal accordingly. Class I scales were intentionally omitted from the proposal because of the device's sensitivity to even minimal changes in environmental factors. The Committee supports the NTEP policy that existing devices will not be required to be reevaluated since most devices are expected to already comply with the proposal. To clarify all terminology in the proposed requirements that is not already defined in Handbook 44, the Committee made editorial changes to several terms; added two new definitions (D_{max} and E_{max}); amended the term "non-automatic weighing system" to read "non-automatic weighing instrument;" and included a reference to Section 2.20.

During the 2005 NCWM Annual Meeting, the Committee heard that there are jurisdictions that wish to continue to cite paragraph T.N.4.5. when a field inspection reveals an abnormal performance in a device's indications. In some cases, those devices are out of compliance with General Code paragraph G-UR.4.2. Abnormal Performance. The Committee acknowledged there may be other instances where it is appropriate to perform a time dependence test in the field under controlled conditions, based on a specific Scales Code requirement. Consequently, the Committee agreed to move forward with the entire proposal with modifications only to paragraph T.N.4.5. in the proposal to include provisions for conducting a time dependence test in the field when there are constant test conditions. The Committee notes that it may be necessary to exercise the load-receiving element prior to performing the time dependence test.

320-9 I List of International Symbols Noted as Acceptable

Source: Southern Weights and Measures Association (SWMA)

Recommendation: Add a new Appendix E as follows:

Appendix E

List of Acceptable Abbreviations/Symbols

Device Application	Term	Acceptable	Not Acceptable
The following symbols are intended for operator controls, indications, and features. When they are also intended for the customer (including customer-operated devices) they cannot be used without additional descriptions, directions, or marks displayed or marked on the device.			
	zero key or center of zero indicator	→0←	"z" alone is not acceptable unless term is defined on device
	Off (Power)	○	
	On (Power)	│	
	On/Off (Power)	⏻	

Device Application	Term	Acceptable	Not Acceptable
The following symbols are intended for operator controls, indications, and features. When they are also intended for the customer (including customer-operated devices) they cannot be used without additional descriptions, directions, or marks displayed or marked on the device.			
Operational Controls, Indications, Features:	Print	⊙	
	Weighing	⚖	
	Scale n (n = 1, 2, ...)	⚖n	
	Range n (n = 1, 2, ...)	→|n|←	
	High resolution	/HR/	
	enter key	↵	
	tare enter key	→⟨T⟩	
Operational Controls, Indications, Features:	tare clear key	T⟨⇐⟩	
	tare enter/tare clear	⟨↔T⟩	⟨↔ T⟩
	verify tare	⟨⇐T⟩	
	Not for direct sales to the public	👥⌀	
	Combined zero/tare – See S.2.1.6 for additional information	→0/T←	
	Taring	→|←	
	Mass/Weight	🏋	
	Money	◯◯◯	
	Price Per weight unit	◯/🏋	
	Piece count	⁘	
	Counter	|1|2|3|	
	Read Counter	↑ |1|2|3|	
	Print certificate	📄	
	Information	ℹ	

Discussion: The proposed list of symbols introduces officials to a set of international symbols for use in marking operator controls, indications, and device features. Recognition and use of these symbols is consistent with efforts to harmonize U.S. and international device requirements.

Currently, the list of symbols is part of NCWM Publication 14 "Technical Policy, Checklists, and Test Procedures" for Weighing Devices. NTEP uses international symbols whenever possible. Style differences such as variations in the shape of arrows are acceptable.

The Southern Weights and Measures Association (SWMA) heard several concerns about the initial use of international symbols. Most weights and measures officials do not have access to Publication 14 or other international documents. Consequently, it was suggested that NCWM and NIST Weights and Measures Division post the list on their websites and incorporate the symbols into bulletins, examination procedure outlines, and inspector training modules. The increased number of customer-operated devices would require additional markings or descriptions to describe the less familiar symbols. This is especially true for symbols that represent "Not for Direct Sales," "Total Money," and "Price per Unit Weight," which are not in widespread use in the United States. Once customers become familiar with the symbols, descriptions would no longer be necessary and the list of symbols would not be necessary in Handbook 44 or other documents.

The SWMA agreed that the proposed list of symbols would best serve field officials if placed in NIST Handbook 44 as an appendix.

The Committee agreed with SWMA on the need to familiarize officials with international symbols and recommended the proposed list of acceptable new symbols become a new Appendix E in Handbook 44. The Committee made several editorial changes to the table and agreed the proposal should be a voting item at the 2005 NCWM Annual Meeting.

During the 2005 NCWM Annual Meeting, the Committee agreed that unless the table references a specific code, then the table applies to all types of devices. The Committee believes that if the table is to be used as an enforcement tool, then only symbols in the proposed list would be considered acceptable. The Committee preferred an all-inclusive list of acceptable symbols over a WMD alternate proposal to develop a list of acceptable symbols that includes a statement indicating other symbols may be used without prior approval. SMA suggested an alternate proposal to designate the table as a list of commonly used international symbols. However, the Committee believes the intended scope of the list is much broader. If the table is intended to be all-inclusive, the other acceptable symbols currently in use for all device types, such as the dollar sign ($) on retail motor-fuel dispensers and taximeters must be added to the list. The Committee considered SMA's suggestion to eliminate the list of not acceptable symbols and retitle the columns to clarify that the symbols represents terms as well as functions. The Committee changed the status of the item from voting to an information item, to allow time to develop language that will link the table to specific codes and to assess whether or not the table should be all-inclusive.

321 BELT-CONVEYOR SCALE SYSTEMS

321-1 VC UR.3.4. Diversion or Loss of Measured Product
(This item was adopted.)

Source: Western Weights and Measures Association (WWMA)

Recommendation: Add new paragraph UR.3.4. as follows:

UR.3.4. Diversion or Loss of Measured Product. - There shall be no operation(s) or condition(s) of use that result in loss or diversion that adversely affects the quantity of measured product. (Added 2005)

Discussion: This proposal is intended to ensure that all product measured on the scale is delivered to the customer. There are several circumstances where the final amount of a commodity weighed on the system's scale can be affected by operator practices. For instance, taking commodity samples or movement of commodities on belt conveyors over long distances where product slippage from the belt can result in product loss before the customer has custody of the commodity. Without records, any major spillage results in an inaccurate payment for delivered product. The chain of custody of weighed material between the scale and the end point of a conveyor system should be maintained at all times. The diversion of a measured commodity by as much as 0.1 % becomes significant over a period of time and can affect royalty payments and taxes and can even have an environmental impact for some commodities.

Originally, the Western Weights and Measures Association (WWMA) and Central Weights and Measures Association (CWMA) considered an industry proposal to amend existing paragraphs UR.3.2. Maintenance and UR.3.3. Retention of Maintenance, Test, and Analog or Digital Recorder Information to address diversion of commodities by requiring this material be measured and recorded.

The WWMA heard comments from a manufacturer that supported the concept, but found the "measurable diversion of weighed material" somewhat ambiguous. The WWMA believed the intent of the proposal could be better stated and simplified. Consequently, the WWMA developed an alternate proposal similar in wording to the recommendation above adding a new paragraph UR.3.4. titled Diversion of Measured Product rather than suggest changes to existing paragraphs UR.3.2. and UR.3.3.

The CWMA withdrew the issue from its agenda because no data was provided to demonstrate there is an issue with diverted product.

At the 2005 NCWM Interim Meeting, the Committee further modified the language proposed by WWMA to clarify the requirement was intended to apply under conditions where weighed product is "loss" because it slips off the belt or is sampled and not returned to the end customer. The Committee agreed to present the item for a vote at the 2005 NCWM Annual Meeting.

322 AUTOMATIC BULK WEIGHING SYSTEMS

322-1 W Tolerances

(This item was withdrawn.)

Source: Carryover Item 322-1. (This item originated from the Northeastern Weights and Measures Association (NEWMA) and first appeared on the Committee's 2002 agenda.)

Recommendation: Delete paragraphs T.1.4., T.2., T.2.1, T.3.2. and T.3.3.:

~~T.1.4. To Tests Involving Digital Indications or Representations. - To the tolerances that would otherwise be applied, there shall be added an amount equal to one-half the value of the scale division. This does not apply to digital indications or recorded representations that have been corrected for rounding using error weights.~~

~~T.2. Minimum Tolerance Values. - The minimum tolerance value shall not be less than half the value of the scale division.~~

~~T.2.1. For Systems used to Weigh Construction Materials. - The minimum maintenance and acceptance tolerance shall be 0.1 % of the weighing capacity of the system, or the value of the scale division, whichever is less.~~

~~T.3.2. For Systems used to Weigh Grain. - The basic maintenance tolerance shall be 0.1 % of test load.~~

~~T.3.3. For all Other Systems. - The basic maintenance tolerance shall be 0.2 % of test load.~~

Renumber paragraph T.3. and renumber and modify T.3.1. as follows:

T.3.2. Basic Tolerance Values.

T.3.2.1. Acceptance Tolerance. -The basic acceptance tolerance shall be one-half the basic maintenance tolerance, but never less than 1 division.
(Amended 200X)

Add new paragraphs T.2.2., T.2.3., and T.2.3.1. and Table 1. and Table 2. as follows:

T.2.2. General - The tolerance applicable to devices not marked with an accuracy class shall have the tolerances applied as specified in Table 1 below.

Table 1. Tolerance for Unmarked Scales			
Type of Device	Tolerance	Decreasing Load Multiplier	Other applicable Requirements
Grain Hoppers	Class III, T.2.3 (table 2)	1.0	T.2.1, T.2.3.1
Other Systems	Class III L, T.2.3 (table 2)	1.0	T.2.1, T.2.3.1

(Added 200X)

T.2.3. Tolerances Applicable to Devices Marked III or III L.

T.2.3.1. Maintenance Tolerance Values - The maintenance tolerance values are specified in Table 2 below.

Table 2. Maintenance Tolerance for Marked Scales (All values in this table are in scale divisions)				
Tolerance in scale divisions				
	1	2	3	5
Class	Test Load			
III	0 - 500	501 - 2000	2001 - 4000	4001 +
III L	0 - 500	501 - 1000	(Add 1d for each additional 500 d or fraction thereof)	

(Added 200X)

Add a new footnote to Section 2.20 Scales Code Table 1.1.1. Tolerances for Unmarked Scales as follows:

ˣAutomatic bulk weighing systems see Section 2.22 for specifications and tolerances.
(Added 200X)

Discussion: Since 2002, the Committee has considered a proposal to change the automatic bulk weighing systems tolerances from a percentage basis to division values, which are based on the device's accuracy class. The proposal was intended to align tolerances in the Automatic Bulk Weighing Systems (ABWS) Code and the Scales Code.

The Committee has kept the proposal as an information item to allow interested parties sufficient time to work through issues surrounding the permissible system errors and other concerns. The U.S. Grain Inspection, Packers and Stockyard Administration (GIPSA) opposed the proposed tolerances because of concerns about the allowable cumulative error in a system's performance. GIPSA also cited its 17-year history of successful implementation of current ABWS code requirements.

The Western Weights and Measures Association heard no comments on the proposal, but remains concerned about the potential cumulative effect of allowable errors that are the result of the proposed step tolerances.

The Northeastern Weights and Measures Association (NEWMA) continues to welcome the opportunity for more discussion with the S&T Committee and GIPSA. NEWMA believes the minor differences in tolerance applications on a few borderline cases do not justify having a unique code for a device that is identical in design and performance to devices evaluated under the Scales Code. NEWMA provided two contacts if anyone wanted to discuss the proposal; Bill Wilson (Clinton County, New York) at 518-565-4681, by fax at 518-565-4694, or at wilsonperu@aol.com or contact Ross Andersen (New York) at 518-457-3146, by fax at 518-457-5693, or at ross.andersen@agmkt.state.ny.us.

The Central Weights and Measures Association (CWMA) expressed concern that the proposal might not have technical merit and was developed as the result of each regulatory agency's preference for a particular code format. The CWMA was also concerned that adopting the proposal would effect step tolerances to the point that older devices with an n_{max} greater than 4000 would not comply.

During the 2005 NCWM Interim Meeting, the Committee heard that NEWMA was continuing work on a survey to determine how officials apply the ABWS Code tolerances. The Committee decided at that time to keep the proposal an information item to allow GIPSA, NEWMA, the grain industry, and all other parties affected by the proposed changes to the ABWS tolerances additional time to compare data and agree on an appropriate set of tolerances for systems that fall under the ABWS Code. GIPSA did not comment at the meeting but it had reiterated its earlier opposition to the proposal to WMD in advance of the meeting. In anticipation that NEWMA would have the results of its survey at the July 2005 NCWM Annual Meeting the Committee kept this issue an information item, but planned to move the proposal to a developing item if no survey data was available in July 2005.

At the July 2005 NCWM Annual Meeting, there were no new developments and NEWMA and GIPSA, still held differing positions on the proposal. The results from the survey distributed by NEWMA in July 2005 were not available. The Committee decided to withdraw this item because, after 3 years of deliberations, no consensus could be reached by the parties affected by the proposal.

For more background information, refer to the 2002, 2003, and 2004 S&T Final Reports.

330 LIQUID-MEASURING DEVICES

330-1 V S.1.6.1. Indication of Delivery; Electronic Devices

(This item was adopted.)

Source: National Type Evaluation Technical Committee (NTETC) Measuring Sector

Recommendation: Modify Section 3.30. paragraph S.1.6.1. Indication of Delivery as follows:

S.1.6.1. Indication of Delivery. – The device shall automatically show on its face the initial zero condition and the quantity delivered (up to the nominal capacity).

(a) However, For electronic devices manufactured prior to January 1, 2006, the first 0.03 L (or 0.009 gal) of a delivery and its associated total sales price need not be indicated.

(b) For electronic devices manufactured on or after January 1, 2006, the measurement, indication of delivered quantity, and the indication of total sales price shall be inhibited until the fueling position reaches conditions necessary to ensure that the delivery starts at zero.
[Nonretroactive as of January 1, 2006]
(Added 2005)
(Amended 1982 and 2005)

Discussion/Background: At the 2004 NTETC Measuring Sector meeting, Maryland Weights and Measures stated that as the price for motor fuel nears or exceeds $2 per gallon, the number of complaints it receives regarding computer jump has increased. NIST Weights and Measures Division (WMD) has received numerous calls from jurisdictions related to this problem. It appears that the actual amount of jump or meter creep occurring because of internal pressure changes related to changes in temperature has not increased. However, at the higher unit prices this relatively small meter creep results in an indication of several cents. Concern was expressed that there was no guidance in Handbook 44 regarding criteria or tolerances for "computer jump." Prior to 1987 Handbook 44 had a test note (paragraph N.4.3.) and tolerance (paragraph T.2.4.) in the Liquid-Measuring Devices Code for conducting an elapsed time test. At the 1986 NCWM Annual Meeting the NCWM voted to delete those paragraphs. The discussion of that item indicates that a suggestion was received that all references to an elapsed time test should be removed because: (1) none are being conducted, and (2) the conditions that caused their inclusion in Handbook 44 have for the most part been eliminated. In 1986, if a consumer experienced a computer jump that resulted in an indication of money value prior to opening the nozzle, the consumer normally could return the dispenser to the off position and start the delivery from "zero." Currently, if a customer is making a fuel purchase using a credit or debit card at the pump, any indication of delivery is automatically charged to the customer's account; therefore, returning the dispenser to the "off" position and re-starting the delivery from "zero" does not resolve the problem and the consumer is charged for undelivered product. Maryland and WMD provided a proposal to eliminate the indication of computer jump for the Sector to consider. The Sector agreed with the proposal in principle, but recommended some changes to the language (including the use of the term "fueling position") as indicated in the recommendation and agreed to forward it to the NCWM and the Southern Weights and Measures Association (SWMA) S&T Committees for consideration. A manufacturer of retail motor-fuel dispensers stated that "fueling position" is a recognized industry term that is preferable in this case to the term "dispenser." Dispensers typically have hoses on two sides. The term "fueling position" is applicable to only one side at a time.

At its October 2004 meeting, the SWMA heard no opposition to the Measuring Sector proposal. The SWMA agreed to forward the proposal to the Committee with the recommendation that it be a voting item on the 2005 NCWM S&T Agenda. The SWMA also recommended that the Committee consider adding similar requirements to Handbook 44 Section 3.32. as appropriate.

At the 2005 Interim Meeting, several dispenser manufacturers expressed concern with the use of the term "normal delivery pressure," in the original proposal, since the pressure within a system can vary during normal use. The Committee met with three dispenser manufacturers to develop new nonretroactive language in which the word "pressure" is changed to "condition" as indicated in the Recommendation. The new requirement does not allow the measurement of product until the fueling position reaches normal delivery condition (packed hose) up to the nozzle. If the system meets the new requirement, the dispenser will indicate zero until the nozzle is opened and product begins to flow. The Committee agreed that making the requirement nonretroactive was appropriate to provide manufacturers time to develop a mechanism for eliminating computer jump on new devices. For devices already in the field, officials can use paragraph UR.3.1. Return of Indicating and Recording Elements to Zero and General Code paragraph G-S.2. Facilitation of Fraud to require that the primary indicating element be returned to zero prior to the start of each delivery. The Committee agreed this item should be presented for a vote at the 2005 NCWM Annual Meeting.

At the 2005 NCWM Annual Meeting, the Committee agreed that paragraph S.1.6.1. should be modified as shown in the recommendation above to clarify when the suppresion (masking) of indications is permitted and when the inhibition (prevention) of measurement and indication is required. The Committee further amended the proposal to clarify what is meant by "normal delivery conditions." The Committee believes the proposal would eliminate "computer jump" on new devices installed in the field and over time will eliminate the problem on most retail motor fuel dispensers, similar to the near elimination of scales being found "off zero" after the automatic zero-setting mechanism requirement was added to the Scales Code. During the voting session, an official requested that additional language be added to the discussion to clarify how a dispenser would operate if this item were adopted. The Committee agreed to add the following language to the discussion: "To comply with the new requirement, a dispenser shall operate as follows. Begin with the valve in the nozzle "closed" and activate the dispenser. After initialization (i.e., first indication of zero) of the dispenser is complete, the display of volume and total price shall indicate "zero" and shall increment only in coincidence with product flow after the valve in the nozzle is opened."

330-2   VC   N.4.2.2. Retail Motor-Fuel Devices
(This item was adopted.)

Source: National Type Evaluation Technical Committee (NTETC) Measuring Sector

Recommendation: Modify Section 3.30. paragraph N.4.2.2. Retail Motor-Fuel Devices as follows:

N.4.2.2. Retail Motor-Fuel Devices.

(a) Devices with **out** a **marked minimum** flow-rate ~~capacity less than 100 L (25 gal) per minute sh~~all have a "special" test performed at the slower of the following rates:

   (1) 19 L (5 gal) per minute, or

   (2) ~~the minimum discharge rate marked on the device, or~~

   ~~(3)~~ the minimum discharge rate at which the device will deliver when equipped with an automatic discharge nozzle set at its slowest setting.

(b) Devices **marked** with a **marked minimum** flow-rate ~~capacity 100 L (25 gal) or more per minute~~ shall have a "special" test performed at **or near** the **marked minimum flow rate**. ~~slowest of the following rates:~~

   ~~(1) the minimum discharge rate marked on the device, or~~

   ~~(2) the minimum discharge rate at which the device will deliver when equipped with an automatic discharge nozzle set at its slowest setting.~~

(Added 1984) **(Amended 2005)**

Discussion/Background: At its October 2004 meeting, the NTETC Measuring Sector discussed a test scenario in which a retail motor-fuel device (RMFD) was marked with flow rates of 60 gpm maximum and 12 gpm minimum, where the actual flow rate on the lowest setting of the automatic nozzle was 6 gpm. The laboratory posed the following questions regarding this situation:

Paragraph S.4.4.1. Discharge Rates, requires that RMFDs with a designed maximum flow rate of 30 gpm or greater be marked with a minimum and maximum flow rate. RMFDs with a designed maximum flow rate of less than 30 gpm are not required to have a maximum and minimum flow rate marking, but such a marking is not prohibited. Paragraph N.4.2.2. (b) in the LMD Code states that "Devices marked with a flow-rate capacity of 100 L (25 gal) or more per minute shall have a "special" test performed at the slowest of the following rates: (1) the minimum discharge rate marked on the device, or (2) the minimum discharge rate at which the device will deliver when equipped with an automatic discharge nozzle set at its slowest setting." The question is if a RMFD is marked with a minimum flow rate, is it appropriate to operate the device below the marked minimum flow rate?

There appears to be a conflict between the test notes and the user requirements for RFMDs that are marked with a maximum and minimum flow rate. General Code paragraph G-UR.3.1. Method of Operation states that a device is to be used in the manner that is indicated by instructions on the equipment. Paragraphs N.4.2.2. (a) and (b) both contain testing procedures that instruct a weights and measures official to conduct a test of a dispenser at a flow rate that is less than the minimum flow rate that may be marked on the device. The manufacturers of RMFDs present at the 2004 Measuring Sector meeting stated that it is not appropriate to require accuracy for a device when it is operated below the marked minimum flow rate.

The Sector agreed that officials should not test below the minimum flow rate marked on the device because the device is not designed to operate accurately at lesser flow rates. The Sector also agreed to propose changing the flow rate of 25 gpm in paragraph N.4.2.2. to 30 gpm to agree with the marking requirements in paragraph S.4.4.1. The Sector agreed to forward a proposal that both issues to the NCWM and Southern Weights and Measures Association (SWMA) for consideration.

At its October 2004 meeting, the SWMA heard concerns with the proposed changes to paragraph N.4.2.2. Retail Motor-Fuel Devices. The SWMA recommended that officials not test at a flow rate less than the minimum flow rate marked on a device. However, the Sector's proposal as worded creates conflicts with other requirements in paragraph N.4.2.2. Consequently, the SWMA agreed that the proposal should not be forwarded to the Committee.

Following the SWMA meeting, NIST Weights and Measures Division (WMD) developed the alternative shown above to address the concerns of the SWMA with the original Measuring Sector proposal.

When first adopted, paragraph N.4.2.2. contained only two test criteria which stipulated that the slow flow test be made at the slower of 19 L (5 gal) per minute or the minimum flow rate marked on the device. In 1971, the Committee received several communications that RMFDs equipped with an automatic nozzle were often operated at a discharge rate established by the automatic nozzle when set at its slowest setting. Paragraph N.4.2.2. was modified to include the provision for testing with an automatic nozzle set on the lowest notch, if the flow rate at that setting was less than 19 L (5 gal) per minute, or the minimum flow rate marked on the device. In 1971 few, if any, RMFDs were marked with a minimum flow rate and the information provided by the manufacturer (and sometimes marked on the device) typically stated that the device was accurate at any flow rate.

In 1984, when "high gallonage" dispensers gained popularity in the marketplace, paragraph S.4.4. Marking Requirements/For Retail Devices Only, (now paragraph S.4.4.1. Discharge Rates), was added to require dispensers with a maximum flow rate of 25 gpm or greater to be marked with maximum and minimum flow rates. At that time paragraph N.4.2.3., which later became the present paragraph N.4.2.2. (b), was added to the Handbook. It was the view of the Committee that the minimum flow rate for these dispensers would be greater than 5 gallons per minute so that specific flow rate was not included in the test criteria of new paragraph N.4.2.2.

General Code paragraph G-UR.2.3. Installation, states "that equipment shall be operated only in the manner that is indicated by instructions on the equipment (minimum flow rate)." Some dispensers are equipped with a latch on the nozzle lever which, when set at its lowest setting, may cause the dispenser to operate below the marked minimum flow rate. WMD noted that the Committee may want to consider a user requirement in the LMD Code that does not allow a latch on the nozzle to create this situation since such a component would facilitate inappropriate and inaccurate use of the device.

At the 2005 Interim and Annual Meeting, the Committee received no comments on this item. The Committee agreed that the alternate proposal prepared by WMD resolved the issue of what flow rates are appropriate when conducting a field examination of a RMFD and agreed to present the item for a vote.

331 VEHICLE-TANK METERS

331-1 I   Temperature Compensation

Source: Carryover Item 331-1 (This item originated from the Western Weights and Measures Association (WWMA) and first appeared on the Committee's 2000 agenda.)

Recommendation: Modify Section 3.31. Vehicle-Tank Meters (VTM) Code by adding the following new paragraphs to recognize temperature compensation as follows:

S.2.4. Automatic Temperature Compensation for Refined Petroleum Products.

S.2.4.1. Automatic Temperature Compensation for Refined Petroleum Products. - A device may be equipped with an automatic means for adjusting the indication and registration of the measured volume of product to the volume at 15 °C (60 °F), where not prohibited by State Law.

S.2.4.2. Provision for Deactivating. - On a device equipped with an automatic temperature-compensating mechanism that will indicate or record only in terms of liters (gallons) compensated to 15 °C (60 °F), provision shall be made for deactivating the automatic temperature-compensating mechanism so that the meter can indicate and record, if it is equipped to record, in terms of the uncompensated volume.

S.2.4.3. Gross and Net Indications - A device equipped with automatic temperature compensation shall indicate and record, if equipped to record, both the gross (uncompensated) and net (compensated) volume for testing purposes. If both values cannot be displayed or recorded for the same test draft, means shall be provided to select either the gross or net indication for each test draft.

S.2.4.4. Provision for Sealing Automatic Temperature-Compensating Systems. - Adequate provision shall be made for an approved means of security (e.g., data change audit trail) or physically applying security seals in such a manner that an automatic temperature-compensating system cannot be disconnected and that no adjustment may be made to the system.

S.2.4.5. Temperature Determination with Automatic Temperature Compensation. - For test purposes, means shall be provided (e.g., thermometer well) to determine the temperature of the liquid either:

    (a) In the liquid chamber of the meter, or

    (b) Immediately adjacent to the meter in the meter inlet or discharge line.
(Added 200X)

S.5.6. Temperature Compensation for Refined Petroleum Products. - If a device is equipped with an automatic temperature compensator, the primary indicating elements, recording elements, and recording representation shall be clearly and conspicuously marked to show that the volume delivered has been adjusted to the volume at 15 °C (60 °F).
(Added 200X)

    N.4.1.3. Automatic Temperature-Compensating Systems for Refined Petroleum Products. - On devices equipped with automatic temperature-compensating systems, normal tests shall be conducted:

        (a) by comparing the compensated volume indicated or recorded to the actual delivered volume corrected to 15 °C (60 °F); and

        (b) with the temperature-compensating system deactivated, comparing the uncompensated volume indicated or recorded to the actual delivered volume.

The first test shall be performed with the automatic temperature-compensating system operating in the "as found" condition. On devices that indicate or record both the compensated and uncompensated volume for each delivery, the tests in (a) and (b) may be performed as a single test.
(Added 200X)

N.5. Temperature Correction for Refined Petroleum Products. - Corrections shall be made for any changes in volume resulting from the differences in liquid temperatures between the time of passage through the meter and time of volumetric determination in the prover. When adjustments are necessary, appropriate petroleum measurement tables should be used.
(Added 200X)

    T.2.1. Automatic Temperature-Compensating Systems. - The difference between the meter error (expressed as a percentage) for results determined with and without the automatic temperature-compensating system activated shall not exceed:

        (a) 0.4 % for mechanical automatic temperature-compensating systems; and

        (b) 0.2 % for electronic automatic temperature-compensating systems.

The delivered quantities for each test shall be approximately the same size. The results of each test shall be within the applicable acceptance or maintenance tolerance.
(Added 200X)

UR.2.5. Temperature Compensation for Refined Petroleum Products.

UR.2.5.1. Automatic.

UR.2.5.1.1. When to be Used. - In a State that does not prohibit, by law or regulation, the sale of temperature-compensated product a device equipped with an operable automatic temperature compensator shall be connected, operable, and in use at all times. An electronic or mechanical automatic temperature-compensating system may not be removed, nor may a compensated device be replaced with an uncompensated device, without the written approval of the responsible weights and measures jurisdiction.

[Note: This requirement does not specify the method of sale for product measured through a meter.]

UR.2.5.1.2. Invoices. - An invoice based on a reading of a device that is equipped with an automatic temperature compensator shall show that the volume delivered has been adjusted to the volume at 15 °C (60 °F).
(Added 200X)

Discussion/Background: When this item was originally submitted, several officials reportedly were confused about the specific meter applications covered by an NTEP Certificate of Conformance for a meter that included the temperature-compensation feature. The Western Weights and Measures Association (WWMA) acknowledged some jurisdictions permit temperature-compensated deliveries in applications that are not addressed by NIST Handbook 44. Some states do not allow the use of automatic temperature compensation for the delivery of products using a VTM.

At the 2002 and 2003 NCWM Annual Meetings, this item did not achieve a majority vote to pass or fail and was, therefore, returned to the Committee for further consideration.

At the 2004 NCWM Annual Meeting, the Committee stated its position on Item 331-1 as follows:

The Committee believed that the Specifications, Test Notes, Tolerances, and User Requirements contained in the proposal are technically correct and provide both weights and measures officials and the NTEP laboratories with the proper criteria to use when evaluating a vehicle-tank meter (VTM) with temperature-compensation capability. The addition of this language to the VTM Code does not require, approve, nor solicit any jurisdiction to either prohibit or accept the use of temperature compensation in that jurisdiction. The Committee further stated that the adoption of a nationally accepted method of sale for temperature compensation by all jurisdictions will not be obtainable in the foreseeable future and encouraged each jurisdiction to adopt by either statute, rule, or regulation requirements that prohibit, permit, or require temperature compensation in their jurisdiction.

The Committee agreed there were a sufficient number of states that needed the new requirements as an inspection tool to warrant adding the proposal to NIST Handbook 44 at that time without waiting for method of sale requirements to be added to NIST Handbook 130.

At the 2004 NCWM Annual Meeting, this item did not achieve a majority vote to pass or fail and was, therefore, returned to the Committee for further consideration.

At its September 2004 Interim Meeting, the Central Weights and Measures Association (CWMA) agreed with the Committee that nothing in this proposal requires a jurisdiction to permit or prohibit the sale of petroleum products that have been temperature compensated. The CWMA recognized the technical merit of the proposal and felt that requirements are needed in Handbook 44; however, the CWMA further agreed that this is also a "method of sale" issue and that the proposal should be retained as an information item until an accompanying method of sale requirement is added to Handbook 130.

At its September 2004 meeting, the WWMA agreed with the Committee that nothing in this proposal requires a jurisdiction to permit or prohibit the sale of petroleum products that have been temperature compensated. The

WWMA continues its strong support of this proposal and recommends that this item go forward for adoption by the NCWM.

At its October 2004 meeting, the Northeastern Weights and Measures Association (NEWMA) members were informed that the L&R Committee requested that the Board of Directors fund a work group to determine if requirements for temperature compensation should be added to Handbook 130 and, if so, what wholesale and retail areas should be covered. Several participants believed a work group was unnecessary and that work groups should not be created just because a subject is controversial. These members felt there were other items where work groups could be better used. NEWMA also suggested removing the words "recognition of" from the title of Item 331-1.

At the 2005 NCWM Interim Meeting, the Committee participated in a combined open hearing with the L&R Committee for discussion of this item and L&R Item 232-1 Temperature Compensation for Petroleum Products. A special forum was also held on the first day of the Interim Meeting to discuss temperature compensation issues. At both the forum and open hearing, the Committee received little or no new information on this item and considered withdrawing it from its agenda. However, the Committee was informed that the L&R Committee kept its Item 232-1 as a developing issue. The L&R Committee considered modifying Item 232-1 to become two separate Items: 232-1A and 232-1B; Item 232-1A would address VTMs and Item 232-1B would address other meter types. However, the L&R Committee decided not to split the item. Instead, the L&R Committee modified Item 232-1 to allow temperature compensation for the sale of petroleum products other than LPG and products sold through retail motor-fuel devices and changed the status of the item to a "Developing" issue.

During the 2005 NCWM Annual Meeting S&T Committee's open hearing, a manufacturer stated that the number of requests from retailers for retail motor-fuel dispensers with temperature-compensation capability is increasing. The Committee agreed to keep the item on the agenda until the L&R Item 232-1 was further developed. (See L&R Item 232-1.)

For additional background on this item, see the NCWM 2000 through 2004 S&T Final Reports.

331-2   VC   S.1.4.1. Display of Unit Price

(This item was adopted.)

Source: National Type Evaluation Technical Committee (NTETC) Measuring Sector

Recommendation: Modify Section 3.31. paragraph S.1.4.1. Display of Unit Price as follows:

> **S.1.4.1. Display of Unit Price.** - In a device of the computing type, means shall be provided for displaying ~~on the outside of the device~~, in a manner clear to the operator and an observer, the unit price at which the device is set to compute. **The unit price is not required to be displayed continuously.**
> (Amended 1983 and **2005**)

Discussion/Background: At the 2004 Measuring Sector meeting, a manufacturer of vehicle-tank meters (VTM) asked the Sector to provide input on the intent of Handbook 44 Section 3.31. paragraph S.1.4.1. Display of Unit Price. The Sector was asked to determine whether or not the unit price must be displayed continuously. The manufacturer referred to the final report of the 1983 NCWM S&T Committee. In that report under S&T Item 304-2 the Committee stated its view that it is appropriate for a digital electronic indicating element associated with a VTM to utilize a shared display; that is, the same display area can be used to indicate the volume delivered, the unit price, and the total price. However, the information is not required to be displayed simultaneously. The Sector agreed the intent of the S&T Committee was clear and it decided to forward to the NCWM and the Southern Weights and Measures Association (SWMA) for consideration a recommendation to add text to clarify S.1.4.1.

At its October 2004 meeting, the SWMA agreed with the Measuring Sector's interpretation of the intent of S.1.4.1. and agreed to forward the recommendation shown above to the Committee as a voting item.

At the 2005 NCWM Interim and Annual Meetings, the Committee heard no opposition to this item and agreed to present it for a vote.

331-3   VC   S.2.4. Zero Set-Back Interlock, Vehicle-Tank Meters, Electronic
(This item was adopted.)

Source: Carryover Item 331-3. (This item originated from the Southern Weights and Measures Association (SWMA) and first appeared on the Committee's 2004 agenda.)

Recommendation: Add a new paragraph S.2.4. to Section 3.31. Vehicle-Tank Meters (VTM) as follows:

S.2.4. Zero-Set-Back Interlock, Vehicle-Tank Meters, Electronic. – Except for vehicle-mounted metering systems used solely for the delivery of aviation fuel, a device shall be so constructed that after an individual or multiple deliveries at one location have been completed, an automatic interlock system shall engage to prevent a subsequent delivery until the indicating and, if equipped, recording elements have been returned to their zero position. For individual deliveries, if there is no product flow for 3 minutes the transaction must be completed before additional product flow is allowed. The 3-minute timeout shall be a sealable feature on an indicator.
[Nonretroactive as of January 1, 2006]
(Added 2005)

Background/Discussion: The original SWMA proposal applied to both mechanical and electronic registers in VTM applications. The manufacturers of VTM registers agreed that it is not economically practical to modify existing mechanical registers to include a zero set-back interlock or to add that feature to new production of mechanical registers. At the October 2004 meeting of the Measuring Sector, the members developed an alternate recommendation to add a new paragraph S.2.4. to Handbook 44, Section 3.31. Vehicle-Tank Meters that applies only to electronic registers. The Sector agreed to forward the proposal to the NCWM S&T and the SWMA Committees for consideration.

At its October 2004 meeting, the SWMA reviewed the Measuring Sector's recommendation. The SWMA agreed with the proposal provided, that the 3-minute time-out feature be sealable and agreed that the word "may" be changed to "shall" in the last sentence. The SWMA agreed to forward its modified proposal to the S&T Committee with the recommendation that it be a voting item on the Committee's 2005 Agenda.

At the 2005 NCWM Interim Meeting, one official stated that mechanical registers should be included in the requirement for a zero-set-back interlock. The Committee believes it is not practical to modify the mechanical registers currently in use in vehicle-tank meter applications and that attempting to include them in this requirement would significantly delay adoption of any requirement for a zero-set-back interlock. The Committee also believes the number of new mechanical registers being installed is declining and will continue to do so. The Committee recognizes that, while it is more difficult to detect and take enforcement action, paragraph UR.2.3. Ticket in Printing Device, provides a mechanism for stopping the "riding of tickets" between deliveries. The Committee agreed with the SWMA recommendation to modify the Measuring Sector's proposal and to present the modified proposal in the recommendation above for a vote at the 2005 NCWM Annual Meeting.

For additional background on this item, see the NCWM 2004 S&T Final Report.

At the 2005 NCWM Annual Meeting, the Committee heard no opposition to this item.

331-4   VC   N.4.2. Special Tests (Except Milk-Measuring Systems), N.4.5. Product Depletion Test, T.4. Product Depletion Test, and Table T.4. tolerances for Vehicle-Tank Meters on Product Depletion Tests, Except Milk Meters
(This item was adopted.)

Source: Carryover Item 331-2. (This item originated from the Northeastern Weights and Measures Association (NEWMA) and first appeared on the Committee's 2003 agenda.)

Recommendation: Amend paragraph N.4.2. Special Tests (Except Milk-Measuring Systems) as follows:

N.4.2. Special Tests (Except Milk-Measuring Systems). - "Special" tests shall be made to develop the operating characteristics of a measuring system and any special elements and accessories attached to or associated with the device. Any test except as set forth in N.4.1. **and N.4.5** shall be considered a special test. Special tests of a measuring system shall be made ~~as follows:~~

~~(a)~~ at a minimum discharge rate of 20 % of the marked maximum discharge rate or at the minimum discharge rate marked on the device whichever is less~~;~~.
(Amended 2005)

~~(b) to develop operating characteristics of the measuring system during a split compartment delivery.~~

Add new paragraphs N.4.5. Product Depletion Test and T.4. Product Depletion Test and Table T.4. Tolerances as follows:

N.4.5. Product Depletion Test. - Except for vehicle-mounted metering systems used solely for the delivery of aviation fuel, the effectiveness of the vapor eliminator or vapor elimination means shall be tested by dispensing product at the normal flow rate until the product supply is depleted and continuing until the lack of fluid causes the meter indication to stop completely for at least 10 seconds. If the meter indication fails to stop completely for at least 10 seconds, continue to operate the system for 3 minutes. Finish the test by switching to another compartment with sufficient product to complete the test on a multi-compartment vehicle or by adding sufficient product to complete the test to a single compartment vehicle. When adding product to a single compartment vehicle, allow appropriate time for any entrapped vapor to disperse before continuing the test. Test drafts shall be of the same size and run at approximately the same flow rate.
(Added 2005)

T.4. Product Depletion Test. - The range of the test results for the normal test and the product depletion test shall not exceed the tolerance shown in Table T.4. Test drafts shall be of the same size and run at approximately the same flow rate.

[Note: The result of the product depletion test may fall outside of the applicable test tolerance as specified in Table T.2.]
(Added 2005)

Table T.4. Tolerances for Vehicle-Tank Meters on Product Depletion Tests, Except Milk Meters	
Meter Size	**Maintenance and Acceptance Tolerances**
Up to but not including 50 mm (2 in)	1.70 L (104 in^3)[1]
From 50 mm (2 in) up to but not including 75 mm (3 in)	2.25 L (137 in^3)[1]
75 mm (3 in) or larger	3.75 L (229 in^3)[1]
[1] Based on a test volume of at least 1 minute flow in accordance with N.3.	

(Table Added 2005)

Discussion: The measurement of vapor when product is depleted during the vehicle-tank meter (VTM) "split compartment" test (product depletion test) is a system problem and the amount of vapor measured is not related to the size of the test draft. The proposal requires a product depletion test for single compartment vehicles to verify the performance of the air elimination mechanism. Currently paragraph N.4.2.(b) refers only to a "split-compartment" delivery, implying that the test should only be conducted on multi-compartment vehicles. The proposal recommends modifying the tolerances so that the applicable tolerance is based on the meter's flow rate and remains constant regardless of the size of the test draft and modifies the language to clarify that the product depletion test is to be conducted on both single- and multi-compartment vehicles.

At its October 2004 meeting, the NTETC Measuring Sector reviewed an alternate proposal for a new Table T.4. developed by Maryland Weights and Measures and NIST WMD based on the Measurement Canada tolerance structure that categorizes meters by size (pipe diameter) for product depletion tests. The VTM manufacturers present at the meeting verified that there is a definite correlation between the meter size and the achievable maximum flow rate. The Sector agreed with the alternate proposal and provided an example of how the product depletion test would be applied and a note stating that the results of the product depletion test could fall outside of the applicable tolerance if the meter being tested were included in Table T.4. as shown in the recommendation above. The Sector agreed to forward the alternate proposal to the Southern Weights and Measures Association (SWMA) and the Committee for consideration.

At the October 2004 NEWMA meeting, New York proposed that an NCWM work group be formed to research this item and supplied a discussion paper in support of the proposal. NEWMA agreed to forward its recommendation for a work group and the paper to the Committee for consideration.

At its October 2004 Meeting, the SWMA heard no opposition to the Measuring Sector's proposal. One official asked if a similar requirement should be added to the Section 3.30. Liquid-Measuring Devices for wholesale meters and to Section 3.32. LPG and Anhydrous Ammonia Liquid-Measuring Devices. The SWMA agreed to forward the proposal to the NCWM S&T Committee with the recommendation that it be a voting item on the Committee's 2005 Agenda. The SWMA also recommended that the Committee consider adding similar appropriate requirements to Sections 3.30. and 3.32. for testing the effectiveness of vapor elimination means.

Following the 2004 fall meetings of NEWMA, SWMA, and the NTETC Measuring Sector, New York Weights and Measures worked with WMD to add another category of meter sizes to the proposed Table T.4. from the NTETC Measuring Sector as shown in the recommendation above. This change was based on New York's concern that a large number of vehicle-tank meters less than 2.0 inches are still in use in that state. The tolerance for meters smaller than 2.0 inches was developed based on the current tolerance for a draft of at least 1 minute's flow for a typical meter of that size. However, the tolerance is not directly related to draft size and remains unchanged even if the draft size is increased.

At the 2005 NCWM Interim Meeting, the Committee heard support for the proposal with the changes recommended by New York and WMD and agreed to present the modified proposal for a vote at the 2005 Annual Meeting.

During the open hearing at the 2005 NCWM Annual Meeting, a manufacturer of vehicle-tank meters informed the Committee of safety concerns with conducting a product depletion test on an aircraft refueling system. The creation of vapor within the system during the conduct of a product depletion test can cause an explosion hazard. The technical advisor to the Committee from Measurement Canada concurred with this comment and advised that Measurement Canada no longer conducts such tests on meters used for aircraft refueling. The Committee agreed that, because there is a safety concern and that many aircraft refueling systems use effective means other than a "vapor eliminator" to prevent the passage of vapor or air though the meter, aircraft refueling systems should be exempt from the product depletion tests and proposed modifying paragraph N.4.5. Product Depletion Test, as shown in the recommendation above.

For additional background on this item, see the NCWM 2003 and 2004 S&T Committee Final Reports.

336   WATER METERS

336-1   I   Table N.4.2. Flow Rate and Draft Size for Water Meters Special Tests

Source: Northeastern Weights and Measures Association (NEWMA)

Recommendation: Amend Table N.4.2. as follows:

Table N.4.2. Flow Rate and Draft Size for Water Meters Special Tests						
Meter size (inches)	Intermediate Rate			Minimum Rate		
	Rate of flow (gal/min)	Meter indication/Test Draft		Rate of flow (gal/min)	Meter indication/Test Draft	
		gal	ft^3		gal	ft^3
Less than or equal to 5/8	2	10	1	1/4	~~5~~10	1
3/4	3	10	1	1/2	~~5~~10	1
1	4	10	1	3/4	~~5~~10	1
1 1/2	8	50	5	1 1/2	10	1
2	15	50	5	2	10	1
3	20	50	5	4	10	1
4	40	100		10	7	~~50~~100	5
6	60	100		10	12	~~50~~100	5

(Table Added 2003) **(Amended 200X)**

Discussion/Background: At the fall 2004 NEWMA meeting, a manufacturer submitted the proposal revisions to Table N.4.2. shown above. The manufacturer explained that a test draft of 5 gallons is not large enough to provide repeatability for dial indicating water meters sized 1 inch and smaller. The dial indicator for these devices has 100 graduations of 1/10 gallon, which means one complete revolution equals 10 gallons. The effect of parallax on the reading and gear backlash both contribute to the lack of repeatability of indications when using a 5-gallon test draft. The manufacturer recommended that any test of the device include, at a minimum, at least one complete revolution of the dial indicator. None of the jurisdictions represented at the NEWMA meeting routinely test water meters; therefore, they could not provide any input on the technical merits of the proposal. However, NEWMA agreed to forward the proposal to the Committee for consideration.

At the 2005 NCWM Interim Meeting, the only concern the Committee heard was that the time required for some tests would increase significantly. The submitter of the proposal did not attend the Interim Meeting. The Committee agreed to make the proposal an information item to provide an opportunity for review and comment from the regional associations, especially jurisdictions routinely conducting water meter tests. If additional support and comments are not received by the 2006 NCWM Interim Meeting, the Committee may withdraw this item.

At the 2005 NCWM Annual Meeting, there was no discussion on this item.

360 OTHER ITEMS

360-1 V Proposed Section 5.59. Electronic Livestock, Meat, and Poultry Evaluation Systems and/or Devices -Tentative Code

(This item was adopted.)

Source: Southern Weights and Measures Association (SWMA)

Recommendation: Add a Tentative Code Section 5.59. Livestock, Meat, and Poultry Evaluation Systems and/or Devices as follows:

Sec. 5.59. Electronic Livestock, Meat, and Poultry Evaluation Systems and/or Devices - Tentative Code. - This tentative code has only a trial or experimental status and is not intended to be enforced. The requirements are designed for study prior to the development and adoption of a final Code for Livestock, Meat, and Poultry Evaluation Systems and/or Devices. Officials wanting to conduct an official

examination of a device or system are advised to see paragraph G.A.3. Special and Unclassified Equipment.
(Tentative Code Added 2005)

A. Application

A.1. This code applies to electronic devices or systems for measuring the composition or quality constituents of live animals, livestock and poultry carcasses, and individual cuts of meat or a combination thereof for the purpose of determining value.

A.2. See also Sec. 1.10; General Code requirements.

A.3. This code does not apply to scales used to weigh live animals, livestock and poultry carcasses, and individual cuts of meat unless the scales are part of an integrated system designed to measure composition or quality constituents. Scales used in integrated systems must also meet NIST Handbook 44 Section 2.20. requirements.

S. Specifications

S.1. Design and Manufacture. - All design and manufacturing specifications shall comply with ASTM Standard F 2342 Standard Specification for Design and Construction of Composition or Quality Constituent Measuring Devices or Systems.

N. Notes

N.1. Method of Test. - Performance tests shall be conducted in accordance with ASTM Standard F 2343 Test Method for Livestock, Meat, and Poultry Evaluation Devices.

N.2. Testing Standards. - ASTM Standard F 2343 requires device or system users to maintain accurate reference standards that meet the tolerance expressed in NIST Handbook 44 Fundamental Considerations, paragraph 3.2. (i.e., one third of the smallest tolerance applied.)

N.3. Verification. - Device or system users are required to verify and document the accuracy of a device or system on each production day as specified by ASTM Standard F 2341 Standard Practice of User Requirements for Livestock, Meat, and Poultry Evaluation Devices or Systems.

N.3.1. Official Tests. - Officials are encouraged to periodically witness the required "in house" verification of accuracy. Officials may also conduct official tests using the on-site testing standards or other appropriate standards belonging to the jurisdiction with statutory authority over the device or system.

T. Tolerances

T.1. Tolerances on Individual Measurements. - Maintenance and acceptance tolerances on an individual measurement shall be as shown in Table T.1.

Table T.1. Tolerances	
Individual linear measurement of a single constituent	$\forall$ 1 mm (0.039 in)
Measurement of area	$\forall$ 1.6 cm^2 (0.25 in^2)
For measurements of other constituents	As specified in ASTM Standard F 2343

UR User Requirements

UR.1. Installation Requirements.

UR.1.1. Installation. - All devices and systems shall be installed in accordance with manufacturer's instructions.

UR.2. Maintenance of Equipment.

UR.2.1. Maintenance. - All devices and systems shall be continually maintained in an accurate condition and in accordance with the manufacturer's instructions and ASTM Standard F 2341.

UR.3. Use requirements.

UR.3.1. Limitation of Use. - All devices and systems shall be used to make measurements in a manner specified by the manufacturer.

UR.4. Testing Standards. - The user of a commercial device shall make available to the official with statutory authority over the device testing standards that meet the tolerance expressed in Fundamental Considerations, paragraph 3.2. (i.e., one third of the smallest tolerance applied). The accuracy of the testing standards shall be verified annually or on a frequency as required by the official with statutory authority and shall be traceable to a national standard.

Discussion: In 2000 the Grain Inspection, Packers, and Stockyards Administration (GIPSA) branch of the United States Department of Agriculture (USDA) approached NIST Weights and Measures Division (WMD) and the NCWM to discuss the development of standards for devices used to measure fat content in animal carcasses. Because neither the NCWM nor NIST had the resources needed to develop such a standard, the American Society for Testing and Materials (ASTM) was asked to facilitate development of a standard. The ASTM agreed to develop standards, (now known as ASTM Standard F10) for Livestock, Meat, and Poultry Evaluation Systems for the measurement of fat and other quality constituents in animal carcasses. Some of these devices or systems will measure only a single constituent, which will be used to determine the value of the carcasses or primal cuts. Other systems may integrate the measurement of several constituents such as fat, lean, marbling, pH, and color, to determine carcass value.

The NCWM agreed that if USDA was able to develop standards for these devices outside of the NCWM, the NCWM would consider adopting these standards as a tentative code in NIST Handbook 44. The code in Handbook 44 is needed to provide an enforcement tool for USDA and other jurisdictions wanting to have a mechanism for conducting inspections of these devices and approving or rejecting them according to the results of the inspection. The ASTM Standards are voluntary standards that only have the effect of law when they are adopted into regulation by a jurisdiction with statutory authority over these devices. Including or referencing such standards in Handbook 44 provides a method for that adoption.

At its October 2004 meeting, the SWMA reviewed a draft tentative code for livestock, meat, and poultry evaluation systems and devices prepared by WMD. The SWMA agreed to forward the proposal to the Committee for addition to Handbook 44 as a tentative code with the recommendation that it be a voting item on the 2005 NCWM S&T Agenda.

At the 2005 NCWM Interim Meeting, the Committee heard no opposition to this proposal and agreed to present it for a vote at the 2005 NCWM Annual Meeting.

At the 2005 NCWM Annual Meeting, one official stated that the proposal was not ready for adoption and would not be used by weights and measures officials. Another official stated that Handbook 44 should not apply to devices used for grading purposes. Several individuals stated that the purpose of a tentative code is to provide a trial period and to facilitate necessary changes prior to making a code "permanent." Attendees at the 2005 NCWM Annual Meeting and at the Spring 2005 Central and Northeastern Weights and Measures Associations Annual Meetings were provided with a list of "frequently asked questions and answers" relating to Electronic Livestock, Meat, and

Poultry Evaluation Systems and/or Devices; these FAQs are included in Appendix B. The FAQs were also posted on the Weights and Measures Directors' list server in June 2005. After consideration of the comments it received the Committee decided to recommend the item for adoption by the NCWM.

360-2 V Appendix A Fundamental Considerations 3. Testing Apparatus; 3.1 Adequacy, 3.2 Tolerances for Standards and Footnote 2, and 3.3 Accuracy of Standards
(This item was adopted.)

Source: Western Weights and Measures Association (WWMA)

Recommendation: Amend Appendix A Fundamental Considerations 3.Testing Apparatus as follows:

Add amended Footnote 2 to paragraph 3.1 Adequacy as follows:

3. Testing Apparatus

3.1. Adequacy. ^{2} - Tests can be made properly only if, among other things, adequate testing apparatus is available. Testing apparatus may be considered adequate only when it is properly designed for its intended use, when it is so constructed that it will retain its characteristics for a reasonable period under conditions of normal use, when it is available in denominations appropriate for a proper determination of the value or performance of the commercial equipment under test, and when it is accurately calibrated.

> ^{2} ~~Recommendations regarding the specifications and tolerances for suitable field standards may be obtained from the Weights and Measures Division of The~~ numerical values of the tolerances ~~recommended by~~ the National Institute of Standards and Technology,. ~~for the s~~Standards will meet the specifications of **length, mass, and capacity used by weights and measures officials, may be obtained upon request from the** ~~Weights and Measures Division of the~~ National Institute of Standards and Technology **Handbook 105-Series standards (or other suitable and designated standards). This section shall not preclude the use of additional field standards and/or equipment, as approved by the Director, for uniform evaluation of device performance.**

Amend paragraphs 3.2 Tolerances for Standards and 3.3 Accuracy of Standards as follows:

3.2. Tolerances for Standards. ^{2} - ~~The error in a standard used by a weights and measures official should be known and corrected for when the standard is used; or if the standard is to be used without correction, its error should be not greater than one-third of the smallest tolerance to be applied when the standard is used. The reason for this is to keep at a minimum the proportion of the tolerance on the item tested that will be used up by the error of the standard. Expressed differently,~~ **Except** ~~for work of relatively high precision, it is recommended that the accuracy of standards used in testing commercial weighing and measuring equipment be established and maintained so that the use of corrections is not necessary.~~ **When the standard is used without correction, its combined error and uncertainty must be less than one-third of the applicable device tolerance.**

Device testing is complicated to some degree when corrections to standards are applied. When using the correction of the standard, the uncertainty associated with the corrected value must be less than one-third of the applicable device tolerance. t~~T~~he reason **for this requirement** is to give the **item** ~~device~~ being tested as nearly as practicable the full benefit of its own tolerance.

~~Field testing operations are complicated to some degree when corrections to standards are applied. Except for work of relatively high precision, it is recommended that the accuracy of standards used in testing commercial weighing and measuring equipment be so established and maintained that the use of corrections is not necessary. Also, whenever it can readily be done, it will be desirable to reduce the error on a standard below the one-third point previously mentioned.~~

3.3. Accuracy of Standards. - Prior to the official use of testing apparatus, its accuracy should invariably be verified. **Field S**~~s~~tandards should be **re-verified** ~~calibrated~~ as often as circumstances require. By their nature, metal volumetric **field** standards are more susceptible to damage in handling than are standards of some other types. A **field** standard should be re-calibrated whenever damage is known or suspected to have occurred or significant repairs have been made. In addition, **field** standards, particularly volumetric standards, should be re-calibrated with sufficient frequency to affirm their continued accuracy, so that the official may always be in an unassailable position with respect to the accuracy of his testing apparatus. Secondary **field** standards, such as special fabric testing tapes, should be verified much more frequently than such basic standards as steel tapes or volumetric provers to demonstrate their constancy of value or performance.

Accurate and dependable results cannot be obtained with faulty or inadequate **field** standards. If either the service person or official is poorly equipped, their results cannot be expected to check consistently. Disagreements can be avoided and the servicing of commercial equipment can be expedited and improved if service persons and officials give equal attention to the adequacy and maintenance of their testing apparatus.

Discussion: In July 2000, the Metrology Subcommittee began formal discussions on inconsistencies in laboratory calibration practices for ensuring the traceability of field standards. A NIST work group further developed the Subcommittee's recommendations into proposals to modify NIST Handbook 44 as shown in the recommendation above. It also submitted proposals for changes to the requirements in NIST Handbook 130 "Uniform Laws and Regulations" to include guidelines for suitable reference standards, test procedures, and practices for determining whether or not to allow the use of field standards as test apparatus.

Both Handbooks required updating for consistency and to recognize current accepted accreditation and recognition practices for field standards, where applicable. The Handbooks should be modified to align international and national metrological terminology and to adequately define and clarify terms already in use that relate to field standard verification such as: accreditation, calibration, recognition, standards (field, primary, reference, secondary, and working), traceability, uncertainty, and verification. The proposal added the term "field" to distinguish the type of physical standard in use for testing of devices. The proposal also specifies the appropriate documentary standards and specifies that the field standard's combined error and uncertainty must be less than one-third of the applicable device tolerance.

The Subcommittee recommended corresponding modifications to Handbook 130 (see L&R Agenda Item 221-1 and Item 234-1). Metrological terminology would be updated and, where permitted, calibration interval adjustments based on statistical data would be allowed to improve the accuracy of field standards in use and provide more cost-effective use of resources. The Subcommittee further recommended that Handbook 130 reference the entire NIST Handbook 105 Series as well as other suitable designated standards. To expedite matters and recognize the latest technology, proposed amendments would permit "Placed in Service Reports" for registered service agencies to be forwarded electronically to the State Director rather than mailed. Finally, to ensure measurements are allowable, organizations issuing calibration reports must be recognized by NIST or approved by an accreditation body.

The WWMA recommended the proposal as a voting item.

The Central Weights and Measures Association (CWMA) believes that device tolerances already allow for uncertainties, which field officials find difficult to determine. The CWMA also believes that use of the term "calibrated" changes the intent of paragraph 3.3. Consequently, the CWMA withdrew the proposal from its Interim Agenda.

The Northeastern Weights and Measures Association recommended the proposal become a developing item, but did not provide a rationale for taking that position.

During the 2005 NCWM Interim Meeting, the Committee met jointly with the L&R Committee to discuss and to take testimony on this proposal. The Committee heard only a request that the terms "initial verification" and "subsequent verification" be identified in the corresponding L&R proposal. Both Committees agreed that the proposal will eliminate inconsistencies and provide for recognition of current metrological practices. Consequently, the Committee agreed that the issues should move forward for a vote in July 2005. Modifications were planned for L&R Item 221-1 to include adding new definitions of "initial verification" and "subsequent verification" since both terms are referenced in the proposed guidelines for examination and calibration or certification of standards and testing equipment.

A list of frequently asked questions (FAQs) was distributed at the July 2005 NCWM Annual Meeting and distributed on the Weights and Measures Directors list server in June 2005 to provide additional background information on the changes proposed to NIST Handbooks 130 and 44; these FAQs are included in Appendix C. One point not specified in the FAQs or proposal is the expanded uncertainty to an approximate 95 % confidence level. The three interrelated items passed with several modifications to L&R items that addressed the definitions of primary and secondary standards and the examination and certification of test standards. For more details on this item, see the 2005 L&R Final Report.

360-3   I   International Organization of Legal Metrology (OIML) Report

Many issues before the OIML, the Asian-Pacific Legal Metrology Forum (APLMF), and other international groups are within the purview of the S&T Committee. Additional information on OIML activities is available in Appendix A of the 2005 Board of Directors Final Report and on the OIML website at http://www.oiml.org. NIST Weights and Measures Division (WMD) provided updates on OIML activities during the open hearing session on Monday, July 18, 2005. For more information on specific OIML device activities contact the WMD staff listed in the table below:

| NIST Weights and Measures Division Contact List ||||
Staff	Telephone	Email Device	Type	Postal Mail or Fax
Steven Cook (LMD)	301-975-4003	steven.cook@nist.gov	Automatic Weighing Systems Weighing Devices	NIST WMD 100 Bureau Dr MS 2600 Gaithersburg, MD 20899-2600 Fax: 301-926-0647
Richard Harshman (LMD)	301-975-8107	richard.harshman@nist.gov	R134 "Weighing Road Vehicles In-Motion" R60 "Load Cells"	
Diane Lee McGowan (LMD)	301-975-4405	diane.lee@nist.gov	R51 Grain Moisture Meters Near Infrared Grain Analyzers	
Ralph Richter (ILM)	301-975-4025	ralph.richter@nist.gov	R117 "Measuring Systems for Liquids Other Than Water" R105 "Direct Mass Flow Measuring Systems for Quantities of Liquids" and Gas Meters	
Wayne Stiefel (ILM)	301-975-4011	s.stiefel@nist.gov	Measuring Devices	
Dr. Ambler Thompson (ILM)	301-975-2333	ambler@nist.gov	Electronic Measuring Devices	
Juana Williams (LMD)	301-975-3989	juana.williams@nist.gov	R21 Taximeters	
LMD - Legal Metrology Devices Group ILM - International Legal Metrology Group			

360-4   I   Add International Terms that are Synonymous to NIST Handbook 44 Terms in Appendix D; Definitions

Source: Carryover Item 360-4. (This item originated from the Northeastern Weights and Measures Association (NEWMA) and first appeared on the Committee's 2002 agenda.)

Discussion: Many Handbook 44 and OIML technical concepts and procedures are in harmony, yet there are significant differences in the terminology used. The harmonization of language is not necessary to harmonize requirements, provided a state of equivalence exists; however, improvements should be promoted where the language is confusing or has the potential for misinterpretation. Currently, the U.S. National Work Group (USNWG) on R76 "Non-automatic Weighing Instruments" is working on a proposal to amend NIST Handbook 44 Appendix D, Definitions to include international terminology that is synonymous with Handbook 44 definitions. This item is intended to familiarize the public and private sectors with the proposed approach to modify Appendix D. The USNWG will identify Handbook 44 terms or definitions that are equivalent to international vocabulary by placing the corresponding OIML term in parentheses adjacent to the Handbook term.

The development of this proposal will also clarify terminology for international participants in the proposed Mutual Acceptance Arrangement (MAA) (see the 2005 Board of Directors Final Report, Appendix A for more information), where it is imperative that all parties are aware of and understand each other's requirements. Similar terms can have a different meaning in Handbook 44 than they do in R76. Handbook 44 is also inconsistent in the use of many terms such as "division," "increment," and "interval." One additional goal is to eliminate any confusion about other frequently used terms such as "device," "element," "mechanism," "scale," "weigher," and "balance."

NEWMA supports this item and views it as a first step toward familiarizing officials and other users of the Handbook with new terminology and believes that future efforts should include work to place terms in Handbook 44 with the goal of having one mutually acceptable set of terminology.

At its 2004 meeting, the Western Weights and Measures Association requested that the USNWG continue to develop the terms and asked that the proposal remain an information item.

The Central Weights and Measures Association (CWMA) believes international terms serve no purpose for the field official. The CWMA believes this is an issue for NCWM Publication 14, "NTEP Technical Policy, Checklists, and Test Procedures;" therefore, the proposal should be withdrawn from the S&T Agenda.

The Scale Manufacturers Association supports the efforts of the USNWG and looks forward to reviewing the final proposal as an information item.

The Committee concurred with NEWMA's assessment that the proposal is a necessary step for harmonizing U.S. and international terminology and later standards. The Committee heard support from industry for the proposal. Industry requested an opportunity to review the final product. The Committee decided to keep this proposal as an information item on its agenda to update the weights and measures community on this important work in the harmonization of standards and to allow the work group sufficient time to complete its comparison of Handbook 44 General Code and Scales Code terms with equivalent international terminology.

360-5   D   Developing Issues

The NCWM established a mechanism to disseminate information about emerging issues that have merit and are of national interest. Developing issues have either not received sufficient review by parties affected by the proposal or may be insufficiently developed to warrant action by the Committee. These issues are currently under review by at least one regional association or technical committee. The developing issues are listed in Appendix A according to the specific NIST Handbook 44 Code Section under which they fall.

The S&T Committee encourages interested parties to examine the proposals included in Appendix A and send their comments to the contact listed in each item. The Committee also asks that the regional weights and measures associations and National Type Evaluation Technical Committee Sectors continue their work to fully develop each proposal. Should an association or Sector decide to discontinue work on a developmental item, the Committee asks that it be notified.

Jack Kane, Montana, Chairman
Clark Cooney, Oregon
Carol P. Fulmer, South Carolina
Todd R. Lucas, Ohio
Michael J. Sikula, New York

Ted Kingsbury, Canada, Technical Advisor
Richard Suiter, NIST, Technical Advisor
Juana Williams, NIST, Technical Advisor

Committee on Specifications and Tolerances

S&T Committee 2005 Final Report
Appendix A - Item 360-1: Proposed Section 5.59

Appendix A

Item 360-1: Proposed Section 5.59. Electronic Livestock, Meat, and Poultry Evaluation Systems and/or Devices -Tentative Code

Electronic Meat Evaluation Systems Frequently Asked Questions	
1. Why did ASTM develop these standards?	In 2000, U.S. Department of Agriculture Grain Inspection and Packers and Stockyard Administration (GIPSA) approached NIST & NCWM to request the development of a standard for carcass evaluation devices. When it was determined that neither the NCWM nor NIST had the resources needed to develop such a standard, ASTM was asked to guide the task. After an initial meeting with representatives from GIPSA, NCWM, and NIST, ASTM agreed to form the Committee F10 to develop standards for devices and systems for the measurement of fat and other quality constituents in Livestock, Meat, and Poultry.
2. What standards did ASTM develop?	The ASTM Committee F10 developed four separate standards to address design, use, testing, and predictive accuracy for these devices and systems. They are designated as: F2340 – 04 "Standard Specification for Developing and Validating Prediction Equation(s) or Model(s) Used in Connection with Livestock, Meat, and Poultry Evaluation Devices(s) or System(s) to Determine Value" F2341 – 03 "Standard Practice for User Requirements for Livestock, Meat, and Poultry Evaluation Devices or Systems" F2342 – 03 "Design and Construction of Composition or Quality Constituent Measuring Devices or Systems" F 2343 – 04 "Standard Test Method for Livestock, Meat, and Poultry Evaluation Devices"
3. What does the term "Predictive Accuracy" mean?	The original title for the draft standard developed by ASTM Subcommittee F10 – 40 was "Predictive Accuracy." The title of the final document F2340 – 04 was changed to "Standard Specification for Developing and Validating Predication Equation(s) or Model(s)." The new title better describes statistical procedures and the scientific approach that system/device manufacturers must follow to establish equations, algorithms, etc., that predict fat content for an entire carcass. Manufacturers may use sampling methods, limited measurements, and formula similar to those used to determine quality constituents such as moisture, starch, or oil content, in grain.
4. Were all interested parties involved in the standards development process?	The F10 Committee and Subcommittees included representatives from device manufacturers, meat packers, livestock producer associations, GIPSA, USDA Agriculture Marketing Service (AMS), NIST, NCWM, and University Meat Science Programs.
5. Do the ASTM standards follow the same format as NIST Handbook 44?	Three of the Standards are each similar in format to the Specifications (F2342 – 03), Test Notes and Tolerances (F 2343 – 04), and User Requirements (F2341 – 03), sections of a Handbook 44 code. The Standard for Prediction of Value (F 2340 - 04) is not; however, this is not a weights and measures issue.
6. Why should a tentative code for these devices be added to Handbook 44?	The devices and systems covered by these standards are commercial devices that have impacted over 80 % of the sale and harvesting of over 100 million hogs and over 35 million cattle with a value of billions of dollars (the latest estimate [2005] is $38.8 billion). ASTM standards are voluntary standards and are only "legal requirements" when they are cited in a law or regulation. Having a code in Handbook 44 will provide States who wish to include these devices in their registration and inspection programs with the legal authority to do so through the adoption of Handbook 44.

S&T Committee 2005 Final Report
Appendix A - Item 360-1: Proposed Section 5.59

7. Will W&M jurisdictions have to purchase the ASTM standards?	States may want to have one reference set of some or all four of the standards in their main office. W&M Regional training funds left over at the end of the year could also be used to purchase copies of the standards. The cost is currently $28 each.
8. Why shouldn't the NCWM/NIST just develop a new code for Handbook 44?	Resources are still not available to conduct what would now be a duplication of effort.
9. What is "in it" for weights and measures?	Similar to regulation of other commercial devices, programs will be able to verify the accuracy of the devices and systems that measure the constituents used to determine the value of livestock, meat, and poultry being produced and sold within their jurisdiction.
10. Won't weights and measures officials require training to be able to test these devices? Who will provide the necessary training?	Yes – GIPSA and NIST plan to discuss the development of a training program for these devices. The scope of the training will be developed in these discussions.
11. What types of certified standards are necessary to verify device accuracy?	The manufacturers of various devices can supply calibration standards with the devices at time of installation. The users of the devices are required to have the standards verified annually, to an appropriate tolerance (#1/3 of device tolerance), at an appropriate laboratory.
12. What additional equipment must be purchased in order to test these devices?	The users of the devices are required to have appropriate certified standards on site for testing the devices. Weights and measures jurisdictions may want to, but will not be forced to, have their own standards in order to conduct inspections
13. If devices use different technologies to make similar measurements will the end result be the same?	The standards were written to be applicable regardless of the type of measurement technology utilized. If two different technologies are used to make the same type of measurement (either within the same facility or at two different facilities) and the same formula is used to determine value, the end result should be the same.
14. Why doesn't USDA GIPSA just test these devices themselves?	Similar to livestock scales and in-motion monorail scales GIPSA will have requirements for accuracy verification of these devices. GIPSA will test these devices during investigations; however, GIPSA does not have the manpower to handle the routine inspections.
15. Why isn't there a standard formula for calculating the price adjustments made based on measurements from these devices?	At present, different packing companies have different criteria for what they consider to be their preferred characteristics for the animals they purchase. In the future competition may drive "standard formula" to be adopted across the industry.
16. If the formula can vary from packer to packer what is the value of testing the measurement devices?	Equity in the transactions begins with, and can only be assured with, accurate devices. From that point, the livestock producer can determine which packing company provides the best pricing structure for the particular characteristics of the animals he or she offers for sale.
17. Will the USDA GIPSA require these devices to be tested?	Yes, GIPSA is drafting regulations similar to those that require livestock scales and monorail scales to be tested for accuracy on a regular basis. These regulations will reference NIST Handbook 44 requirements.

Appendix B

Item 360-2: Appendix A Fundamental Considerations
3. Testing Apparatus; 3.1 Adequacy, 3.2 Tolerances for Standards and Footnote 2, and 3.3 Accuracy of Standards

Frequently Asked Questions (FAQs)
Proposed NIST Handbook (HB) 44 Changes for Test Standards

A work group was formed to review and modify the original proposed technical updates to NIST Handbooks 130 and 44. This group carefully reviewed each change, modified wording to assure clarity and brevity, and evaluated the effect of each change on individual weights and measures programs. Changes are proposed for NIST Handbook 130 "Uniform Laws and Regulations" Weights and Measures Law and Voluntary Registration Regulation, and NIST Handbook 44 "Specifications, Tolerances, and Other Technical Requirements for Weighing and Measuring Devices, Appendix A Fundamental Considerations.

What are the key points of the changes?

Specifically, one change would update terminology in both handbooks. Updates were planned for terms such as "primary" and "secondary" standard to reflect the international usage of each term. Additional terms and their definitions would be added, such as "reference standard," "field standard," "traceability," and "uncertainty." Terms would be added only if they are used elsewhere in the document.

Some of the proposed changes would allow State directors more discretion when evaluating calibration intervals, referencing documentary standards, and accepting calibration reports. Handbook 130 currently states that field standards must be calibrated annually. The proposed language would allow adjustment of field standard calibration intervals based on historical calibration data. Intervals could be increased for standards such as stainless steel weights or decreased for standards such as weight carts or cast iron weights. State directors would also be able to reference documentary standards other than in NIST documents when defining specifications for field standards. Currently, there are some standards used in the field with no corresponding NIST document defining their specifications. Allowing American Society for Testing and Materials (ASTM), International Organization of Legal Metrology (OIML) or other documentary standards to be referenced would fill this void. Finally, State directors would be able to accept calibration reports from both State laboratories and accredited industry laboratories recognized by NIST Weights and Measures Division (WMD). Some states are already accepting accredited calibrations from private industry. The new language would provide guidance for making the decision about which labs are acceptable and what additional information is necessary before accepting their calibration reports.

Another change clarifies the uncertainty to tolerance ratios required when selecting field standards. The tolerance ratio is currently described as a "3 to 1" ratio, with no additional explanation. The new language clearly defines what this means and will help State directors and weights and measures officials select appropriate equipment when conducting field tests.

Why are these changes being proposed?

Changes are being proposed to these sections of Handbook 130 and Handbook 44 for several reasons. First, there is a need to update terminology in both handbooks in order to conform to international definitions. Second, many states have changed calibration intervals on field standards. Allowing for adjustment of calibration intervals based on statistical data is in alignment with reality, and is sound rationale for varying from annual intervals. Third, expanding acceptable references to a generic list of documentary standards allows jurisdictions to adopt industry or international standards, in addition to the standards developed by NIST. Fourth, allowing states to determine which calibration reports are acceptable for calibration of field equipment gives more options to each jurisdiction. It is especially important to understand that the concept of traceability is evaluated by formal accreditation and recognition methods. Self-declaration and the use of NIST test numbers are no longer considered acceptable indications of traceability. Finally, the tolerance ratios described in Handbook 130 need additional explanation and clarification.

S&T Committee 2005 Final Report
Appendix B - Item 360-2: Fundamental Considerations

What does this mean to our State program?

These proposed changes would have a relatively small effect on state and local weights and measures programs. There is no mandate for a jurisdiction to change the way it currently operates; however, the changes would allow local control and flexibility with respect to field standards and their calibration intervals. Additionally, the new language documents what is already being done in practice in many states. It promotes international uniformity and would allow the use of industry and international documentary standards in addition to NIST Handbooks.

How do I set appropriate calibration intervals?

When setting initial calibration intervals, it is recommended that a jurisdiction set a base interval of one year. For additional information on setting initial intervals for a variety of field standards, see the list of recommendations at the end of this document. In order to adjust or change a calibration interval, it is necessary to have sufficient historical calibration data, which includes "as-found" measurement data. In addition to data, it is also necessary to have a statistically valid approach for modifying the intervals. The laboratory metrologist should be familiar with adjusting calibration intervals for laboratory standards, and may be a useful resource for both providing data and statistical analysis. For more information on statistical approaches to changing calibration intervals, consult National Conference of Standards Laboratories International (NCSLI) RP #1 on Setting and Adjusting Calibration Intervals. It is important to remember that suitable care and handling is essential when using field standards. Jurisdictions may require verification and oversight of field standards even if not providing a full calibration.

Why should we allow adjustment of calibration intervals?

One of the reasons for allowing the adjustment of calibration intervals is to save money and time by having calibrations done at suitable frequencies rather than at arbitrary fixed intervals. It will also lead to improved accuracy, by ensuring that field standards are within tolerance during the entire calibration interval. The goal is to "calibrate the day before an item goes out of tolerance," but the reality is simply cost-effective risk management. Accurate analysis of calibration intervals can provide evidence needed to defend the tolerance of field standards, but this requires calibration data, analysis, and accompanying documentation of the program.

How do I know which documentary standards to reference?

When referencing documentary standards, refer to the sample list provided with this document and consult your laboratory metrologist for input. For unique equipment, it may be necessary to consult the manufacturer. NIST, OIML, and ASTM provide many field standard specifications. Determine if suitable industry or international standards are available. If no documentary standard exists for a field standard, it may be necessary to write one. To do this, the specifications, tolerances, and requirements must be identified and documented. It may be useful to consult the manufacturer when writing the specifications. The State director must also assess uncertainties for the field standard and its measurement impact, and evaluate their laboratory's ability to calibrate or obtain a calibration for the field standard.

What do we do with field standards that don't meet the specifications? What about measurement areas where we don't have documentary standards?

When a field standard does not meet specifications outlined in an accepted documentary standard, a State director must evaluate the impact of the deviation on the measurement results, as well as the functionality, efficiency, and safety of the device. State directors have local authority and flexibility to accept and designate field standards and to allow grandfathering and deviations from standard specifications. They may require unique calibration intervals for these field standards or they may reject and/or confiscate the standard based on evaluation results.

How do I know if a laboratory's calibration reports are acceptable? How do we create the "accepted list?"

In order to determine which calibration reports are acceptable, several criteria must be evaluated. First, determine if the laboratory providing the calibration report is accredited by a National Cooperation for Laboratory Accreditation (NACLA) approved accreditation body or recognized by WMD as capable of providing traceable measurement results. If the lab passes this first step, evaluate the scope of accreditation or recognition and assess the laboratory's best measurement uncertainty to make sure that they can provide the services needed. Be sure that the calibration report provided contains values and associated uncertainties. State metrologists or technical experts at NIST may be able to assist in evaluating the acceptability of outside calibration reports.

Why do we need to have initial verification of field standards?

Even when a laboratory provides an accredited calibration report meeting the uncertainty to tolerance requirements specified, there is no guarantee that the field equipment meets specifications. It may be necessary for field standards to have an initial evaluation by a weights and measures jurisdiction before being put into service. It is the responsibility of a weights and measures agency to ensure that suitable field standards are used for official inspections. Accreditation is not conformity assessment and should not be used for that purpose. New field standards must be evaluated for compliance with specifications and for impact on measurement results.

How do we evaluate the uncertainties versus the tolerance requirements in the Fundamental Considerations? Where can I get more information?

In determining the suitability of a field standard, it is necessary to evaluate the uncertainty to tolerance ratio. In order to do this, both the uncertainty of the field standard and the tolerance of the device to be tested must be known. Additionally, it is important to know whether or not the field standard has been adjusted to its nominal value. If an adjustment has been made, a comparison between the uncertainty and tolerance is all that is necessary. Here, the uncertainty should be no more than one-third of the tolerance. The calibration report for the field standard should contain the uncertainty of the measurement. If the field standard has been left with an associated correction, the correction and the uncertainty must be combined before making the comparison with the tolerance. Both the correction and the uncertainty should be listed on the calibration report. When added together, their sum should be no more than one-third of the tolerance of the device under test. State metrologists should be able to provide additional information regarding evaluating uncertainties of field standards.

Sample list of documentary standards that can be used as specifications and tolerances for "field standards."

Sample List of Documentary Standards and Calibration Intervals			
Standards Device		**Calibration Interval**	**Comments**
HB 105-1, Cast iron	Class III, IIII, IV scales	6 month to 1 year	
HB 105-1, Stainless steel	Class III, IIII, IV scales	5 year	
OIML R111, Class F1 ASTM E 617-97, Class 2	Class II scales	1 year	
HB 105-2, glassware	Package testing	10 year	
HB 105-3, test measures (hand-held and 5 gal truck/trailer mounted)	Gas pumps	1 year	
HB 105-3, large provers	Meters	1 year	
HB 105-4, LPG provers	LPG meters	1 year	
HB 105-5, stopwatches	Taxi meters, timing devices, parking meters, Laundromats	1 year	
HB 105-6, thermometers ASTM E1	Temperature corrections, refrigeration specs, package checking	5 year	Inspection required annually
HB 105-7, small volume provers	Meters	6 months, extendable to 1 year	Need EPO for field testing.
API document in development	Master Meters for petroleum		

| Sample List of Documentary Standards and Calibration Intervals ||||
Standards	Device	Calibration Interval	Comments
ASTM E 74, proving rings and load cells	Wheel load weighers, weight carts, large mass standards	Rings: 5 years Cells: 6 months if used for wheel load weighers; evaluate with use for substitution weighing	Depends on use.
HB 105-8, weight carts	Vehicle scales	6 months to 1 year; recalibration for any repair	Need EPO for field use.
ASTM E 100, hydrometers	Petroleum products; bulk oil meters	1 year	
Federal Specification GGG – standard; Length standards, tapes	Taxi meters, fabric, scale decks, firewood, lobster gauges	5 years; inspection before use	
Containers (HB 133)	Bulk mulch		
HB 44, Berry Baskets	Berry quantity		
API - American Petroleum Institute HB 105 Series - A series of NIST technical documents that include "Specifications and Tolerances for Reference Standards and Field Standard Weights and Measures" HB 133 - A NIST technical document that includes specifications and other requirements for "Checking the Net Contents of Packaged Goods"			

S&T Committee 2005 Final Report
Appendix C - Item 360-5: Developing Issues

Appendix C

Item 360-5: Developing Issues

Part 1, Item 1 General Code: G-S.5.6.1. Recorded Representation of Metric Units on Equipment with Limited Character Sets

Source: Western Weights and Measures Association (WWMA)

Recommendation: Modify paragraph G-S.5.6.1. as follows:

G-S.5.6.1. ~~Recorded Representation of Metric Units on Equipment with Limited Character Sets~~ <u>Acceptable Abbreviations for Recorded and Indicated Representation of Units on Equipment</u>. - The appropriate defining symbols are shown in Table 1.

Add the following new abbreviations to Table 1 Representation of Units to the General Code:

Name of Unit	Common Use Symbol	Representation			Name of Unit	Common Use Symbol	Representation		
		Form I (double case)	Form II (single lower case)	Form II (single case upper)			Form I (double case)	Form II (single lower case)	Form II (single case upper)
Inches in	In	in	IN	deciliter	dL	dL			
Foot ft	ft	ft	FT	Kiloliter	kL	kL			
Yard yd	yd	yd	YD	cubic meter	M^3	m^3	m^3	M^3	
milligram mg	mg	mg	cubic inches in	in^3	in^3	in^3	IN^3		
megagram Mg	Mg	cubic foot ft	ft^3	ft^3	ft^3	FT^3			
Grain gr	gr	gr	cubic yard yd	yd^3	yd^3	yd^3	YD^3		
Dram dr	dr	dr	Gills gi	gi	Gi	GI			
Ounce oz	oz	oz	OZ	Pint pt	pt	pt	PT		
Pound lb	lb	lb	LB	Quart qt	qt	qt	QT		
hundredweight	cwt	cwt	CWT	Gallon gal	gal	gal	GAL		
pennyweight dwt	dwt	dwt	DWT	Ampere A		A	A	I	
ounce troy oz	t oz	t oz	t OZ	resistance ohms	ohms	ohms	OHMS		
milliliters mL	mL								
centiliter cL	cL								

Discussion: The WWMA notes that the current General Code Table 1 Representation of Units does not include many units that are in common use today.

At its 2004 meeting, the WWMA indicated that unless it receives a report on the development of the table, the proposal will be withdrawn from its September 2005 agenda.

To provide input on this proposal, contact Gary Castro, California Division of Measurement Standards, by at (916) 229-3018, by fax at (916) 229-3015, or at gcastro@cdfa.ca.gov.

Part 2, Item 1 Scales: Table 4. Minimum Test Weights and Test Loads

Source: Northeastern Weights and Measures Association (NEWMA)

Recommendation: Modify Table 4. Minimum Test Weights and Test Loads as follows:

S&T Committee 2005 Final Report
Appendix C - Item 360-5: Developing Issues

Table 4. Minimum Test Weights and Test Loads[1]			
Device capacity	**Minimums (in terms of device capacity)**		**(where practicable)**
	Test weights (greater of)	**Test loads[2]**	
0 to 150 kg (0 to 300 lb)	100 %		Test weights to dial face capacity, 1 000 d, or test load to used capacity, if greater than minimums specified
151 to 1 500 kg (301 to 3 000 lb)	25 % or 150 kg (300 lb)	75 %	
1 501 to 20 000 kg (3 001 to 40 000 lb)	12.5 % or 500 kg (1 000 lb)	50 %	
20 001 kg to 250 000 kg (40 001 lb to 500 000 lb)	12.5 % or 5 000 kg (10 000 lb)	25 %[3]	During initial verification, a scale should be tested to capacity.

[1] If the amount of test weight in Table 4 combined with the load on the scale would result in an unsafe condition, then the appropriate load will be determined by the official with statutory authority.

[2] The term "test load" means the sum of the combination of field standard test weights and any other applied load used in the conduct of a test using substitution test methods. Not more than three substitutions shall be used during substitution testing, after which the tolerances for strain load tests shall be applied to each set of test loads.

[3] The scale shall be tested from zero to at least 12.5 % of scale capacity using known test weights, and then to at least 25 % of scale capacity using either a substitution or strain load test that utilizes known test weights of at least 12.5 % of scale capacity. Whenever practical, a strain load test should be conducted to the used capacity of the scale. When a strain load test is conducted, the tolerances apply only to the test weights or substitution test loads. (Amended 1988, 1989, 1994, and 2003 and 200X)

Discussion: Jurisdictions encounter scales with 1 000 000 lb nominal capacity and must determine the minimum test load. NEWMA finds that NIST Handbook 44 is flexible, but does not provide any definitive guidelines on test loads for large-capacity scales. NEWMA modified its original proposal by reducing the scale maximum capacity from 1 000 000 lb to 500 000 lb and removing a proposed new footnote that permitted officials to establish the minimum test load. Industry and other regional associations have developed alternate proposals to address their concerns that the proposal does not address the minimum test load and test weights requirements for a scale with a nominal capacity greater than 500 000 lb.

The Committee agreed that Table 4 is the appropriate place in Handbook 44 to provide guidance on the appropriate minimum test load for tests on scales that exceed capacities of 400 000 lb. The Committee believes this issue is a high priority but requires further review and input from both the public and private sectors.

To provide input on this proposal contact Michael Sikula, New York Bureau of Weights and Measures at (518) 457-3452, by fax at (518) 457-2552 or at mike.sikula@agmkt.state.ny.us.

PDC 2005 Final Report

Report of the Professional Development Committee

Kenneth Deitzler, Chairman
Pennsylvania Department of Agriculture Bureau of Ride and Measurement Standards
Harrisburg, Pennsylvania

Reference
Key Number

400 INTRODUCTION

This is the report of the Professional Development Committee (hereinafter referred to as "Committee" or PDC) for the 90th Annual Meeting of the National Conference on Weights and Measures (NCWM). It is based on the Interim Report offered in NCWM Publication 16, testimony heard at public hearings, comments received from the Regional Weights and Measures Associations and other parties, the Addendum Sheets issued at the Annual Meeting, and actions taken by the membership at the Voting Session of the Annual Meeting. The informational items presented below were adopted as presented when the Committee's report was approved.

Table A identifies the agenda items in the Report by Reference Key Number, Item Title, and Page Number. The item numbers are those assigned in the Interim Meeting Agenda. A voting item is indicated with a "V" after the item number. An item marked with an "I" after the reference key number is an information item. An item marked with a "D" after the reference key number is a developing issue. The developing designation indicates an item has merit; however, the item was returned to the submitter for further development before any action can be taken at the national level. An item marked with a "W" was withdrawn by the Committee and generally will be referred to the regional weights and measures associations because it either needs additional development, analysis, and input or does not have sufficient Committee support to bring it before the NCWM.

Note: The policy of NIST is to use metric units of measurement in all of its publications; however, recommendations received by the NCWM technical committees have been printed in this publication as they were submitted and may, therefore, contain references to inch-pound units.

Table A
Index to Reference Key Items

Reference Key Number		Title of Item	Page
400		**INTRODUCTION**	1
401 EDUCATION			2
401-1	I	National Training Program (NTP)	2
401-2	W	Professional Development	3
401-3	W	Identify Partners	3
401-4	I	Create a Curriculum Plan	3
401-5	W	Curriculum Coordination	4
401-6	W	Training Innovations	5
401-7	D	Instructor Improvement	5
401-8	D	Certification	5
401-9	W	NCWM Training	7
401-10	D	Recommended Topics for Conference Training	8
402		**PROGRAM MANAGEMENT**	8
402-1	W	Voluntary Quality Assurance Assessment	8
402-2	W	NCWM Associate Membership Scholarships	9
402-3	I	Safety Awareness	9
402-4	I	Standard Categories of Weighing and Measuring Devices	9

PDC 2005 Final Report

Table B
Appendix

Appendix Title Page

A   Strategic Direction for the Professional Development Committee..A1

Details of All Items
(In Order by Reference Key Number)

401 EDUCATION

401-1   I   National Training Program (NTP)

Source: The Committee

The Board of Directors established the Committee at the 2003 NCWM Annual Meeting in Sparks, Nevada. The first critical charge given to the Committee was to develop a national weights and measures professional development program in cooperation with its partners including:

- State and local weights and measures departments;
- Private industry at all levels; and
- Technical advisors from NIST Weights and Measures Division and Measurement Canada

The NTP will address the following tasks in order of priority:

1. The education and professional development of weights and measures officials and the promotion of uniformity and consistency in the application of weights and measures laws and regulations;
2. The education of industry personnel with regard to weights and measures laws and regulations, including all areas from device manufacturer to service technician;
3. Quality standards for weights and measures activities and programs;
4. Safety awareness for weights and measures-related activities; and
5. Development of a firm partnership with the state and local weights and measures departments, private industry at all levels, and the NCWM. It is critical that NIST Weights and Measures Division (NIST WMD) partner with the Committee and, where appropriate, provide technical advice. Measurement Canada is also encouraged to participate in Committee activities.

Discussion: The Committee began developing the concept of a National Certification Program for weights and measures officials during the 2004 NCWM Annual Meeting (see developmental Item 401-8 below). In December 2004 several Committee members met in Harrisburg, Pennsylvania, to further develop the Committee's overall strategic direction of a National Certification Program. The participants agreed that the NTP should take the following directions:

- The training responsibility should fall directly on state and local jurisdictions.
- Administrator training must be added to the curriculum.
- The Committee should consider looking outside the NCWM for training and structure.
- The Central Weights and Measures Association (CWMA) will assist the Committee in determining what knowledge and prerequisites are required for three tiers of the NTP: beginning, intermediate, and advanced.
- The Western Weights and Measures Association (WWMA) recommended the Committee establish identifiable course outlines that would result in shorter training courses.

The strategic direction is summarized in Appendix A.

At the Annual Meeting comments from the floor indicated support for the Committee's direction on the item. Other comments indicated that the Committee should not lose sight of training of supervisors, managers, and service personnel. A recommendation was made to set parameters and benchmarks and let the states do the work in training the inspectors.

401-2 W Professional Development

Source: The Committee

Discussion: The Committee withdrew this item because the scope and content of this item is inherent in the tasks outlined in the information items on the agenda.

The Committee created and distributed an informational survey during the 2004 Annual Meeting to identify the needs of jurisdictions and to create a consensus position in the development of the National Training Program. The Committee reported the results of the survey at the 2005 Interim Meeting. The data showed that a Handbook 44 course was a top priority followed by a course on small scales. The state of California offered its support and the training material used in that state. The CWMA agreed that Committee's efforts to establish a training and certification program should be the first step of providing professional development for all NCWM stakeholders.

401-3 W Identify Partners

Source: The Committee

Identify appropriate roles in implementing an educational process for each of the partners (e.g., NCWM, state and local weights and measures jurisdictions, private industry at all levels, NIST Weights and Measures Division, and Measurement Canada).

Discussion: The development of a training program should follow the steps listed below:

1. Study training programs of outside agencies, as well as those of state and local jurisdictions.
2. Establish knowledge goals for weights and measures officials and administrators.
3. Develop curriculum based upon the findings and results of the steps 1 and 2.
4. Develop exams or tests.

The Committee moved "the development of training program steps" to Item 401-4 and withdrew this item.

401-4 I Create a Curriculum Plan

Source: The Committee

The Committee agreed the following steps must be addressed for the NTP to be viable:

(a) Develop and maintain a curriculum plan in cooperation with our partners that establishes uniform and consistent training objectives for weights and measures professionals in all fields and at all levels.

(b) Develop objectives of the curriculum plan representative of a consensus of our partners and organize those objectives by scope, sequence, and level of complexity to assist those developing the curriculum materials.

The development of a training program should follow the steps below:

1. Study training programs of outside agencies, as well as those of state and local jurisdictions.

2. Establish knowledge goals for weights and measures officials and administrators.

3. Develop curriculum based upon the findings and results of the steps 1 - 2 above.

   (a) Coordinate the development of curriculum materials to be used in the delivery of training (i.e., lesson plans, digital presentations, slide shows, testing guides, etc.) using a variety of formats (e.g., self-study, traditional instruction).

   (b) Consider creating a network of interested parties to establish priorities, share training resources, foster cooperation to reduce redundancy, and promote uniformity and consistency.

4. Develop examinations, quizzes or tests based on the content of the materials developed under Item 3.

5. Gather and share information from trainers on highly effective techniques, visual aids and other materials that have been used to facilitate learning. Use as many of these resources as available.

The Committee reviewed the notes from the NIST-sponsored administrators' workshops held in Denver, Colorado, and Baltimore, Maryland, and plans to explore many of these ideas.

Discussion: During the 2004 Annual Meeting, the Committee discussed the idea of using work groups to develop courses that could be used for self-study or for traditional classroom settings. The Committee agreed that the initial priority should be high profile devices (e.g., motor-fuel dispensers and retail computing scales). The Committee will study the survey results to determine the membership's needs and desires.

There were several recommendations submitted by the regional associations. The CWMA commented that the Committee should draw upon other sources, both external and internal, for establishment of curricula. The WWMA recommended the Committee review current training courses on the NIST website at http://www.nist.gov/owm to establish and identify various levels of training. They also suggested the Committee review and update all existing NIST training courses and post them on the NIST website. The Northeast Weights and Measures Association (NEWMA) recommended the Committee set standards for education that include provisions for field tests.

During the 2005 Interim Meeting the Committee received recommendations to develop course curriculum with specific learning objectives and develop tests to determine mastery of the learning objectives. The responsibility for providing training to meet the objectives would rest with the jurisdictions. It was also recommended the Committee develop tests to be administered at the end of each course. Upon successful completion of the tests, individuals would be issued certificates. Schemes for controlling the tests and preserving the integrity of the system would need to be developed.

At the 2005 Annual Meeting the State of New York indicated that it will provide the Committee with information on this subject.

401-5   W   Curriculum Coordination

Source: The Committee

In order to achieve the goal of curriculum development, the Committee discussed the following:

(a) Coordination of the development of curriculum materials to be used in the delivery of training (i.e., testing guides, digital presentations, slide shows, lesson plans, etc.) using a variety of formats (e.g., self-study, traditional instruction).

(b) Creation of a network of interested parties to establish priorities, share training resources, foster cooperation to reduce redundancy, and promote uniformity and consistency.

The Committee should consider curricula from other sources to develop a National Training Program. The CWMA agreed that the Committee should draw upon several sources, both external and internal, for the establishment of curricula.

Discussion: Since this item had substantial overlap with the preceding item, the Committee withdrew it and placed portions of it in Item 401-4.

401-6   W   Training Innovations

Source: The Committee

To achieve the objective of developing creative training innovations, the Committee agreed to gather and share information from trainers on highly effective techniques, visual aids, etc., that have been used to facilitate learning and to use as many resources as available. The Committee reviewed the notes from the NIST-sponsored administrators' workshops held in Denver and Baltimore and plans to explore many of these ideas.

The CWMA Professional Development Committee recommends focus groups be used to identify training innovations and that each group be assigned at least one person with teaching or training background to ensure different learning styles are recognized and utilized in developing the final product.

Discussion: The Committee incorporated some information from Item 401-6 into Item 401-4 and withdrew this item.

401-7   D   Instructor Improvement

Source: The Committee

One goal of the Committee is to coordinate with all interested parties activities to improve the competence of instructors and the uniformity of delivery of the curriculum.

Discussion: The Committee concluded there are two parts of an instructor—improvement strategy. The first part is educating trainers in effective methods of instruction. A variety of courses and training methods are available from state, federal, and private sources to develop instructional skills and techniques. Jurisdictions are encouraged to seek out and send selected staff to this type of training.

The second area of instructor improvement is to provide trainers with the knowledge of the technical aspects of all types of devices. The Committee will look to NIST WMD for leadership and participation as a valuable asset in this aspect of training and recommends that WMD assume the task of providing the technical training of instructors. The Committee will look to WMD as a resource to consult with trainers and to work with the Committee on keeping the curricula current as changes to the Handbooks occur, new technologies are deployed, and emerging issues develop. The Committee invites discussion from WMD on this topic. The Committee decided this is currently a low priority for 2005. However, the item will be retained as a developing item.

At the Annual Meeting industry representatives offered continued support on training for the new weighing and measuring device technology. WMD indicated that they would continue to provide technical training for the trainers.

401-8 D Certification

Source: The Committee

The Committee believes that an NCWM certification program should be developed based on the curriculum plan with measurable levels of competency.

Discussion: The Committee agrees that weights and measures officials must pass written examinations to receive certification. Certificates could be presented at the Annual Meeting to administrators and weights and measures officials who complete training classes and pass the course examination. In 2004 Chairman Dennis Ehrhart expressed his support for certification and indicated the Board of Directors would consider requests to fund training. The Committee is exploring certification of weights and measures officials as a means to demonstrate competency.

PDC 2005 Final Report

The WWMA and CWMA submitted extensive comments and recommendations regarding this item prior to the 2004 NCWM Annual Meeting. The Committee has designated this item as developmental.

At the Annual Meeting the Committee considered and agreed to include the following proposal on state-issued certification.

State-Issued NCWM Certification Proposal

Background

The PDC strategic direction has established a plan for a certification program for individuals and programs. The Professional Development Committee has been charged with developing an NCWM certification program based on the curriculum plan with measurable levels of competency.

A full certification proposal was developed and submitted for consideration at the NCWM 2005 Interim Meeting. Questions were raised over the availability of NCWM resources needed to maintain a full NCWM certification program. Feedback from the membership in attendance showed there was interest in development of the state-issued certificate of competency since the states already have responsibility for maintaining training records and are ultimately responsible for the competency of inspectors in their jurisdictions. This proposal is for a state-issued certificate based upon a National certification testing program.

During the open discussion some members indicated they would prefer NCWM issue the certificates and the states be responsible for the training.

Implementation

Step One: Each State Director will identify a State Certification Coordinator (SCC) for its state to work with the PDC and NCWM. The SCC would be the main state contact and collection point for materials and information related to certification. The SCC would be responsible for:

1. Assisting the PDC in developing:
    a. Test questions (or recommending work group members who could)
    b. Test protocol
    c. Certification criteria
    d. Certification templates
2. Implementing certification testing in their state.
3. Maintaining confidentiality of testing and test materials
4. Scoring certification tests
5. Issuing state certificates
6. Reviewing their state's submitted questions annually for adherence to the handbook changes
7. Maintaining state certification files

Step Two: The PDC will establish work groups to identify core competencies and knowledge requirements for basic (beginning) and advanced (journey level) inspectors for a general W&M inspector, for specific devices and W&M disciplines as identified in the training outline already developed by the PDC. The PDC and SCC can work together to assist in establishing work groups for specialty areas to ensure the correct level of expertise.

Step Three: The work groups will develop certification tests and field competency verification methods to test the core competencies and knowledge requirements as established in step two. Allow members of the work groups to utilize a secure area of the NCWM website to conduct their work without having costly meetings or conference calls. Each work group would submit questions to be used in the development of the test that would demonstrate the core competencies and knowledge requirements. This will establish a pool of potential questions for the PDC and SCC to use in development of certification tests. Use the ISWM 900-Question model and others for "developing," "recycling" and "updating" test questions as needed. SCCs should review the questions they developed annually and update if necessary. This will ensure that as handbook requirements change all questions will remain current and in agreement with the conference documents. Reviewing only a few questions should not be overly burdensome on any one jurisdiction or organization. Development of the tests must also include the testing minimums for certification of every test for each device and discipline for certification (i.e., must pass 75 % of the questions to be certified).

PDC would maintain a master list of questions for each test to be given, who submitted each question, when it was last reviewed and then generate the test questions using a random selection method. The test would be changed annually. Once a test has been developed, the PDC would submit the test questions (along with the answers) to the SCC for their use in certification.

Step Four: The PDC will establish confidentiality, testing and field verification protocol for the tests to ensure the integrity of the test and testing validity are maintained. This is crucial given the wide scope of testing and the need to offer testing in every state. This ISWM testing protocol and other successful testing procedures should be studied to build on current successes. PDC or BOD determines what, if any, involvement the NCWM will have in the actual printing and issuance of Certificates and what recognition, if any, the NCWM will give to certificate holders. The SCC in each state will be responsible for printing all testing materials and instructions, giving the tests, and grading the tests, the SCC must monitor to see that testing protocol is followed.

Certification program expected outcome: consistency of enforcement, uniformity, respect, integrity, and acceptance of end product. Inspectors will be able to compete in marketplace for fair wages and be recognized as professionals in their field.

Other things to consider:

1. Each state must also ensure field competency along with certification.
2. Should certificates be required to be renewed?
3. Should there be a fee associated with certification as a revenue source or to cover the basic cost of administering the test?
4. Should study guides or workshops be developed as a revenue source for the NCWM or as increased value to NCWM membership and attendance at meetings?

401-9 W NCWM   Training

Source: Western Weights and Measures Association (WWMA)

Recommendation: The WWMA recommended that the NCWM establish and maintain a database of classroom training programs completed by individual weights and measures officials where the training uses NCWM courses (or equivalent) and certified trainers. The NCWM should also issue certificates to individual weights and measures officials for course completion.

Background: The WWMA recognized the value of formal training for inspection staff and the credibility these programs provide. Some jurisdictions have formal licensing programs for weights and measures staff and rely on informal programs. The WWMA recognized that the NCWM is a logical entity to provide standardized training and accreditation programs.

Discussion: The Committee acknowledges the comments from WWMA. Such comments will be taken under advisement during the formulation of any training effort. The Committee would like to know if NIST will participate in the NCWM training and certification program and would like to see a NIST liaison added to the Committee. The Committee would like to maintain NIST involvement with the National Training Program. NIST reported they have and will continue to develop training materials that will be made available for use in a wide variety of training classes. The standards used to inspect devices are technical; therefore, the training and development of these standards require a wide variety of technical expertise. NEWMA stated technical and administrative support for the Committee should come from NIST. The Committee will solicit partnerships with other interested parties.

During the 2005 Interim Meeting, it appeared there was a consensus among the membership that this should be a responsibility of the states. Based on that consensus, the Committee withdrew this item.

401-10 D   Recommended Topics for Conference Training

At the 2005 Interim Meeting, the Committee recommended a number of topics for possible training seminars, round tables or symposia that would be suitable for presentation at the 2006 National Conference.

They are:

- Risk-based inspections,
- Marketplace surveys,
- Auditing the performance of field staff,
- Device inspections using a sampling model, and
- Emerging issues.

Will Wotthlie, MD, volunteered to lead a session on auditing field staff.

Robert Williams, TN, volunteered to present their state's RMFD testing program.

Jerry Buendel, WA, volunteered to lead a session on marketplace surveys.

All members are encouraged to submit their ideas for topics to the Committee members and to volunteer to lead, present or moderate a topic.

402 PROGRAM   MANAGEMENT

402-1 W   Voluntary Quality Assurance Assessment

Source: The Committee

The Committee will continue to promote the development of quality programs through the Voluntary Quality Assurance Assessments (VQAA). The Committee would like to see more participation in the VQAA. The Committee discussed the use of the ISO/IEC/EN 17025 *"General Requirements for the Competence of Calibration and Testing Laboratories"* for state and local field enforcement programs but concluded that the ISO 17025 standard does not apply to state and local field enforcement programs. The Committee recommends that the NCWM develop its own certification standards for state and local field enforcement programs. The Committee encourages all member states to utilize the VQAA and provide information to the Committee. The assessments can be a valuable tool in determining training needs. The Committee noted that in 2003 several certificates were presented at the Annual Meeting, but no requests for review were received in 2004. The Committee would like to remind the membership that the VQAA forms and other information are available on the NCWM website and the results are confidential. The CWMA believes jurisdictions interested in having the assessments made have already done so and reported that there is no interest among its membership in developing additional VQAAs checklists.

Discussion: The Committee has withdrawn this item because of inactivity or lack of interest for the past three years. The forms can still be obtained on the NCWM website or by contacting one of the Committee members.

PDC 2005 Final Report

402-2 W NCWM Associate Membership Scholarships

Source: The Committee

In past years when funding was available from the Associate Membership Committee (AMC), the Committee oversaw a system to evaluate applications and award scholarships. The Committee then provided a report on the scholarships awarded each year. No funds were made available for scholarships for the calendar year 2004. Guidelines for the Associate Membership Committee scholarships can be found in NIST Special Publication 992, Report of the 87th NCWM (2003). Continued interest in scholarships has been expressed by several state and local jurisdictions. The WWMA expressed appreciation to the AMC for its continued support of various NCWM needs and encourages the associate membership to fund training scholarships in the future if possible.

Discussion: The Committee withdrew this item. The Associate Membership Committee will decide how its money is to be used and define the criteria for applying for the funds and the NCWM's management company will provide administrative support.

402-3 I Safety Awareness

Source: The Committee

In the past the Committee's responsibility extended to the identification of safety issues in the weights and measures field and included efforts to increase safety awareness.

Recommendation: This is an area where activities should be increased to promote safety awareness.

Discussion: Past-Chairman Dennis Ehrhart explained that the Voluntary Quality Assurance Assessment program, the NCWM Associate Membership Scholarships, and Safety Awareness efforts were carryover items from the Committee on Administration and Public Affairs and recommended that the Committee make training its highest priority.

The Committee encourages jurisdictions to send the safety reports and issues to their regional safety liaison, who in turn forwards them to Charles Gardner, the NCWM Safety Coordinator, who recommends the reports or summaries of the reports be published in the NCWM newsletter. At the 2005 Interim Meeting a CD-ROM on safety produced for the U.S. Environmental Protection Agency was made available for review. The Committee agreed to ensure that safety awareness is a part of every aspect of training for NCWM stakeholders.

402-4 I Standard Categories of Weighing and Measuring Devices

Source: Western Weights and Measures Association

Discussion: The Western Weights and Measures Association (WWMA) Administration and Public Affairs (A&P) Committee recommended that standard categories of weighing and measuring devices be adopted to facilitate development of technical standards, inspector training, data collection, and program management.

Background: The final report of the *Survey of Inspection Statistics Collected by State Weights and Measures Programs [2002]*, conducted during mid-2003, observed the absence of standard categories for weighing and measuring devices was a serious obstacle to data collection. For example, the way weights and measures programs categorize scales by type, use, or capacity and capacity ranges often vary considerably. Retail motor-fuel dispensers are currently being counted either by dispenser, grade, or number of hoses or meters. The need for reliable weights and measures statistics is summarized in the final report conclusion as follows:

> Accurate statistics would be helpful in many ways at both the state and national level. For instance, it is difficult to develop performance measures without statistics. Also, work plans require accurate and detailed statistics. In addition, budget, staffing, and other elements of each state program demand statistics on inspection workloads. Finally, neither individual states nor the NCWM will be able to estimate and advertise the value of the nation's weights and measures programs unless reliable statistics are available.

To correct this problem, the WWMA has developed *Standard Categories for Weighing and Measuring Devices* and recommends that standard categories for weighing and measuring devices be adopted to facilitate the development of technical standards, inspector training, inspection data collection, and weights and measures program management.

At the 2005 Interim Meeting the Committee agreed this item should remain informational at this time because standardized categories of weighing and measuring devices have merit and should be considered in the future.

At the Annual Meeting NEWMA recommended use of the categories from Handbook 44 instead of recreating new ones. The WWMA Administrative and Public Affairs Committee drafted the following recommendation for consideration by the Committee. The standard categories of weighing and measuring devices are based on capacity ranges rather than type or use. It is assumed that the inspection test procedures for scales and meters within these capacity ranges are generally similar. Weights and measures programs can adopt the recommended standard categories without changing the manner in which they presently keep records of device inspections by simply adding an extra data field.

NCWM DEVICE CATEGORY CODES

DEVICE CODE	CATEGORY	CAPACITY	EXAMPLES
SP	Scale, Precision	< 5 g scale division	jewelry, prescription scales
SS	Scale, Small	< 100 lbs.	retail computing scales
SM	Scale, Medium	100 – 5000 lb	dormant, platform scales
SL	Scale, Large	> 5000 lb	livestock, recycler scales
SV	Scale, Vehicle	>40 000 lb	vehicle, railway track scales
MS	Meter, Small <30	gpm[1]	retail motor fuel dispensers
MM	Meter, Medium	30-100 gpm	loading rack, vehicle-tank meters
ML	Meter, Large >100	gpm	agri-chemical meters
MF	Meter, Mass Flow	All	heated tanks of corn syrup (soft drinks)
MW	Meter, Water	All	water sub-meters for mobile homes & apartments
MG	Meter, LPG	All propane	sales
MT	Meter, Taxi All Taximeters		
DT	Device, Timing	All	clocks in parking garages
DL	Device, Length Measuring	All	cordage meters

Two-letter device category codes could be employed to categorize devices in weights and measures jurisdictions for reporting to the NCWM during annual surveys. Otherwise, the data collection procedures already in place would be unaffected. It would be helpful also to add the two-letter device category code to inspection reports.

Other measuring devices (e.g., MFM, LPG, LMD, etc.) may not require capacity-based categories like scales or liquid measuring devices.

This briefing paper was provided by the WWMA to serve as a basis for further discussion and development of this item.

---

[1] Retail motor-fuel dispenser counts should be based on meters except that mid-grades should be added for blenders.

Additional Considerations:

The Committee recognized that many aspects of their work would need to be documented and presented. The Committee and Board should consider the publication of a handbook or similar document.

Kenneth Deitzler, Pennsylvania, Chairman
Celeste Bennett, Michigan
Jerry Buendel, Washington
Agatha Shields, Franklin County, Ohio
Stuart Strnad, Texas
Richard W. Wotthlie, Maryland
C. Gardner, Suffolk County, New York, Safety Liaison
NCWM Executive Staff: Beverly I. Levy, CAE

Professional Development Committee

THIS PAGE LEFT INTENTIONALLY BLANK.

Appendix A

Strategic Direction for the Professional Development Committee

The Committee developed their strategic direction to define its roles and responsibilities to the NCWM and the weights and measures community. The Committee members wrote principles to guide them in their deliberations and defined four main areas to focus their efforts. The Committee recognizes that its direction and responsibilities may be changed by the Board of Directors.

The guiding principles of the group were:

- Keep things simple,
- Develop programs that are realistic and achievable,
- Minimize redundancy and administrative tasks,
- Recognize that no one size fits all, and
- Meet the needs of W&M officials, service companies, industry and manufacturers.

The four main areas for focusing their efforts were:

National Training Program – the focus of the national training program would be to increase technical knowledge, strengthen credibility and improve the professionalism of the individual weights and measures official. A strong national training program will work to promote uniformity across the nation.

National Certification System – a national certification system would be developed to recognize or accredit weights and measures programs as competent or capable. The program would include requirements around individual training, proper test standards, use of national handbooks and a data gathering system.

Conference Training Topics – the Committee would be the focal point for gathering and recommending workshops or symposia on leadership, management and emerging issues to be presented during the annual conference. These topics would provide a forum for the exchange of ideas and discussion of changes in the marketplace.

Uniformity of Data – the Committee would work to develop standard categories for devices and inspection areas so that such things as the number of devices, compliance rates, frequency of inspection and other areas could be compiled and compared at the national level. These statistics could be used to benchmark organizations and to communicate the value of weights and measures to the public and to decision makers (see Item 402-4).

THIS PAGE LEFT INTENTIONALLY BLANK.

Report of the
National Type Evaluation Program (NTEP) Committee

Jim Truex
Chief
Ohio Department of Agriculture, Weights and Measures

Reference
Key Number

500 INTRODUCTION

The National Type Evaluation Program (NTEP) Committee ("Committee") submits its Report for consideration by the 90th National Conference on Weights and Measures (NCWM). This consists of the Interim Report presented in NCWM Publication 16 as amended in the Addendum Sheets issued during the Annual Meeting that was held July 10-14, 2005, in Orlando, Florida. The Committee considered communications received prior to and during the 90th Annual Meeting that are noted in this report

Table A identifies the agenda items in the Report by Reference Key Number, Item Title, and Page Number. The item numbers are those assigned in the Committee's Interim Meeting Agenda. A voting item is indicated with a **"V"** after the item number or, if the item was part of the consent calendar, by the suffix **"VC"**. An item marked with an **"I"** after the reference key number is an information item. An item marked with a **"W"** was withdrawn by the Committee and generally will be referred to the regional weights and measures associations because it either needs additional development, analysis, and input or does not have sufficient Committee support to bring it before the NCWM. Table B lists the appendices to the report, and Table C provides a summary of the results of the voting on the Committee's items and the report in entirety.

This Report contains many recommendations to revise or amend National Conference on Weights and Measures (NCWM) Publication 14, Administrative Procedures, Technical Policy, Checklists, and Test Procedures or other documents. Proposed revisions to the publication(s) are shown in **bold face print** by ~~striking out~~ information to be deleted, and **underlining** information to be added. Requirements that are proposed to be nonretroactive are printed in *italics*.

Note: The policy of NIST is to use metric units of measurement in all of its publications; however, recommendations received by the NCWM technical committees have been printed in this publication as they were submitted and may, therefore, contain references to inch-pound units.

Table A
Index to Reference Key Items

Reference Key Number	Title of Item	Page
	Introduction	1
1.	Test Data Exchange Agreements	2
2.	Adoption of Uniform Regulation for National Type Evaluation by States	3
3.	NTEP Participating Laboratories and Evaluations Reports	3
4.	NTETC Sector Reports	3
5.	NTEP Participation in U.S. National Work Group on Harmonization of NIST Handbook 44, NCWM Publication 14 and OIML R 76 and R 60	5
6.	Mix and Match Elements	5
7.	Software Evaluations	6

Table B
Appendices

Appendix Title Page

A NTEP Participating Laboratories and Evaluations Report..A1
B NTETC - GMM and NIR Sector Annual Meetings, Summary of Decisions..B1
C NTETC - Measuring Sector Annual Meeting, Summary of Decisions..C1
D NTETC - Weighing Sector Annual Meeting, Summary of Decisions...D1
E Provisional Committee on Participation Review (CPR) Meeting Summary..E1

Table C
Voting Results

Reference Key Number	House of Representatives		House of Delegates		Results
	Yeas	Nays	Yeas	Nays	
500 (Report in Its Entirety) Voice Vote	All Yeas	No Nays	All Yeas	No Nays	Passed

Details of All Items
(In Order by Reference Key Number)

1. Test Data Exchange Agreements

Background/Discussion: This item was included on the Committee's agenda in 1998 to provide an update on NTEP's work to establish bilateral and multilateral agreements. Under such agreements and arrangements, manufacturers would be able to submit their equipment to any of the participating countries for testing to OIML-recommended requirements. The resulting test data would be accepted by other participants as a basis for issuing each country's own type approval certificate. Following is a report on the three types of test data exchange agreements:

Mutual Acceptance Arrangement (MAA):
Stephen Patoray reported on the first meeting of the MAA Committee on Participation Review (CPR) during June 15 - 16, 2005, in Lyon, France. A copy of the report is contained in Appendix E General Summary of the June 2005 Provisional CPR Meeting in Lyon, France.

The NCWM will notify the BIML of any decision made by the NCWM regarding becoming a "Utilizing Participant" or "Issuing Participant" for R76, "Non-automatic Weighing Instruments" and R60, "Metrological Regulation for Load Cells."

See related BOD Agenda Item 10 for additional information on the MAA.

Bilateral Agreements: No additional discussions have been held on this topic. Additional discussions may be held pending the outcome of the MAA discussions.

NTEP-Canada Mutual Recognition Program (MRA): No additional discussions or meetings have been held on this subject. Future discussions may include extending the MRA to include Multiple Dimension Measuring Devices.

2. Adoption of Uniform Regulation for National Type Evaluation by States

Background/Discussion: The Scale Manufacturers Association (SMA) hosted NTEP adoption and implementation meetings for state directors at each regional weights and measures association conference. These meetings enable jurisdictions to share information about adopting and implementing NTEP in their respective jurisdictions, encourage non-NTEP jurisdictions to adopt the regulation, and allow current NTEP jurisdictions to share ideas on how to make enforcement more effective and uniform among the States. The meetings also provide NTEP management with information related to areas in which the operation and implementation of the program can be improved. Several questions have been posed at these meetings regarding issues associated with NTEP interpretation or practice. Comments from 1997 to 2004 have been summarized, without attribution, and are available for review and download on the SMA website at http://www.scalemanufacturers.org.

SMA representative, Darrell Flocken, updated the NTEP Committee on the status of SMA's drive to assist States to adopt the Uniform Regulation for National Type Evaluation (URNTE) and the Uniform Regulation for the Voluntary Registration of Servicepersons and Service Agencies (VRSA). Mr. Flocken indicated the SMA decided it would be more useful to show which States require NTEP Certificates before allowing weighing and measuring devices to be certified as legal for trade regardless of their adoption of the NIST/NTEP URNTE. SMA developed a new map that shows that status. The SMA, deciding that it would be more useful to show which States require Registration of Service Agencies and Service Personnel regardless of their adoption of VRSA, developed separate maps that show that status. Such maps are available for review and download on the SMA website at http://www.scalemanufacturers.org.

At the request of the SMA, the NTEP Committee is considering discontinuing this item from the Agenda.

3. NTEP Participating Laboratories and Evaluations Reports

NTEP Director, Steve Patoray provided the Committee with a report of the NTEP Laboratory and administrative activities since the October 1, 2002, to June 2005. Additionally, he provided the NCWM an update on the status on the update of NCWM Publication 14 checklists for Automatic Weighing Systems (AWS) and Multiple Dimension Measuring Devices (MDMD) as a result of the change in the status of the AWS and MDMD codes from provisional to full code status in NIST Handbook 44. In addition, several MDMD devices are currently undergoing NTEP evaluation.

A report of the activities was distributed to the NTEP Committee at the 2004 NCWM Annual Meeting and is included in the Final Report of the NTEP Committee as Appendix A.

The laboratory meeting was held April 3 through 6, 2005, in Columbus, OH.

4. NTETC Sector Reports

The Committee received an update on the activities of the National Type Evaluation Technical Committee (NTETC) Sectors at the 2005 NCWM Interim Meeting. Outlined below is a brief summary of Sector activities since the 2004 NCWM Annual Meeting.

The NTEP Committee accepted recommendations from the Weighing Sector, the Measuring Sector, and the Grain Analyzer Sector.

There was additional discussion on editorial updates to the Taximeter section of NCWM Publication 14. These updates were reviewed and accepted by the NTEP Committee.

There was also discussion on the accepted section of NCWM Publication 14 Checklist for Cash Acceptors for weighing devices. After the sector recommended cash acceptor checklist language, a device incorporating cash acceptors was submitted for evaluation. During the evaluation, it became evident to the NTEP laboratory evaluator that some items in the recommended checklist were either vague or missing from the proposed Publication 14 language. The items identified by the laboratory were:

(1) insufficient paper to print a receipt and complete a transaction, and
(2) insufficient funds to return the correct change or return the correct amount inserted into the machine should a transaction be canceled.

The NIST technical advisor, Steve Cook, proposed some additional language. This language attempts to ensure that in case of an error the customer would receive information regarding the error in a printed receipt or be informed that they need to contact an attendant or store manager. The NTEP Committee agreed to add the additional language as "ad hoc" language in the 2005 update of NCWM Publication 14. The Committee discussed several additional "cash acceptor" issues that may require clarification or additional checklist requirements. An agenda item will be presented during the 2005 meeting of the Weighing Sector to address these issues. These items may also need to be addressed in other sections of NCWM Publication 14.

The NTEP Committee discussed an additional issue brought forward by a manufacturer regarding the title of Section 8.2 of NCWM Publication 14 Digital Electronic Scales, Additional criteria for vehicle scales, railway track scales, combination vehicle/railway track scales, and other platform scales greater than 200 000 lb. Information from the 1998 and 2000 Sector meetings was reviewed. The NTEP Committee instructed the NTEP director to correct the Publication 14 language to reflect previous decisions of the sectors, identify the changes clearly in the Publication 14, and place this item on the agenda for the 2005 meeting of the Weighing Sector for additional comments and recommendations.

The NTEP Committee reviewed a request from the Grain Moisture Meter and Near-Infrared Protein Analyzer Sectors to combine the two sectors and change the name to "Grain Analyzer Sector." The Committee accepted these recommendations.

Grain Analyzer Sector: The NTETC Grain Moisture Meter and NIR Protein Analyzer Sectors held a joint meeting in Kansas City, MO, on August 26 - 27, 2004.

The next meeting of the Grain Analyzer Sector is scheduled for August 24 - 25, 2005, in Kansas City, MO. For questions on the current status of Sector work or to propose items for a future meeting, please contact the Sector technical advisors:

Diane Lee	Jack Barber
NIST WMD	J.B. Associates
100 Bureau Drive – Stop 2600	10349 Old Indian Trail
Gaithersburg, MD 20899-2600	Glenarm, IL 62536
Phone: 301-975-4405	Phone: 217-483-4232
Fax: 301-926-0647	e-mail: jbarber@motion.net
e-mail: diane.lee@nist.gov	

Measuring Sector: The NTETC Measuring Sector met October 21 - 22, 2004, in Gulfport, MS.

The next meeting of the Measuring Sector is scheduled for October 21 - 22, 2005, in Nashville, TN, conjunction with the Southern Weights and Measures Association's Annual Meeting. For questions on the current status of Sector work or to propose items for a future meeting, please contact the Sector technical advisor:

Richard Suiter
NIST WMD
100 Bureau Drive – Stop 2600
Gaithersburg, MD 20899-2600
Phone: 301-975-4406
Fax: 301-926-0647
e-mail: rsuiter@nist.gov

Weighing Sector: The NTETC Weighing Sector met August 29 - 31, 2004, in Ottawa, Canada.

The next Weighing Sector meeting is scheduled for September 25 - 27, 2005, in Columbus, OH. For questions on the current status of Sector work or to propose items for a future meeting, please contact the Sector technical advisor:

> Steven Cook
> NIST WMD
> 100 Bureau Drive – Stop 2600
> Gaithersburg, MD 20899-2600
> Phone: 301-975-4003
> Fax: 301-926-0647
> e-mail: stevenc@nist.gov

NTETC Sector Summaries: Past NTETC Sector summaries are available upon request from NCWM and the NIST Sector technical advisors:

> NCWM Inc. or
> Phone: 240-632-9454
> email: ncwm@mgmtsol.com
>
> NIST WMD Technical Advisor, Steve Cook
> (See contact information above)

5. NTEP Participation in U.S. National Work Group on Harmonization of NIST Handbook 44, NCWM Publication 14 and OIML R 76 and R 60

Steve Cook, NIST Weights and Measures Division (WMD), reported during the BOD meeting that NIST WMD, with input from the U.S. National Work Group (USNWG), submitted several comments on the 1st Committee Draft (1st CD) of OIML R76-1 "Non-automatic Weighing Instruments" and that WMD voted against advancing the CD to a Draft Recommendation Status. The Secretariat for OIML TC9/SC1 recently submitted the result of the vote and a list of comments received from the participating members of the subcommittee. The result of the vote was 20 Participating (P) members voted YES, four P members voted NO, and one P member abstained. Although there was a two-thirds majority in favor, the Secretariat decided to develop a 2nd CD due to the number of comments. The Secretariat anticipates completion of the 2nd CD by the end of October 2005. Steve Cook further reported that meeting of the USNWG was held on Sunday, July 10, 2005, during the Annual Meeting of the NCWM. The purpose of the meeting was to review comments that may result in amendments to the 1st CD that may prevent the United States from supporting the 2nd CD. The attendees included three manufacturers, two regulators, Measurement Canada, and NIST WMD.

6. Mix and Match Elements

In 2004 Ross Andersen provided the Committee with an update on this item. He indicated that some U.S. manufacturers had questioned him about the possibility of using the OIML system of apportionment of errors in the evaluation of separate main elements (OIML calls them modules). The U.S. system applies a 0.7 fraction of the tolerance to any weighing/measuring or indicating element. In contrast, the OIML system recognizes that there may be more than two elements in the system that contribute error. The OIML allows the manufacturer to apply different fractions of error to each element (module), from 0.3 to 0.8, provided the sum of the squares is less than or equal to 1 for the combined system. OIML also has specific criteria for evaluating compatibility of elements. At present NTEP Certificates specify that the separate main elements must be interfaced with compatible equipment but provide no guidance on how to evaluate compatibility. It appears that this issue will become more important over time. Mr. Andersen advised that the United States should be looking closely at the issues involved and the changes that might be required in NIST Handbook 44 to allow the OIML system to be used here.

There have been no additional comments or alternate proposals since the 2004 Annual Meeting. This item needs to be submitted as a specific agenda item to a regional Specifications and Tolerances Committee or to the NTETC Weighing Sector for additional action if there is continued interest.

7. Software Evaluations

The NTEP Committee discussed the pros and cons of software evaluation. General concerns relate to difficulties identifying software and determining traceability to an NTEP Certificate of Conformance during field verification and providing NTEP laboratories with a meaningful and functional checklist for evaluating software security and functions.

NCWM staff gathered the costs involved with forming a Sector and the costs to conduct a Sector meeting. This information, along with a detailed action plan for the development of the sector charges, were presented and reviewed by the NCWM Board of Directors at its meeting in March 2005.

At the 2004 NCWM Annual Meeting, the NTEP committee heard various comments from the floor both supporting and questioning the merits of forming an NTEP technical committee, sector or subcommittee. Also, there were comments regarding the importance of this project and if it should have a higher or lower priority than other current projects being considered by the BOD.

Based on the comments from the floor, Chairman Jim Truex reported that the NTEP Committee has three possible alternatives:

1. Leave the Status Quo
2. Create an NTETC Software Sector
3. Create an S&T Subcommittee

The NTEP Committee discussed this item after the open hearing discussions. The Committee unanimously supports the formation of a NTETC Software Sector. The Committee believes that the Conference Chair, the NTEP Chair and the NTEP Director will provide the Sector with initial guidance and direction on scope and purpose of their charge.

Jim Truex, OH, NTEP Committee Chair
Wes Diggs, VA
Don Onwiler, NB
Charles Carroll, MA
Stephen Pahl, TX

NTEP Technical Advisor, S. Patoray, NTEP Director
NTEP Technical Advisor, S. Cook, NIST WMD

National Type Evaluation Program Committee
THIS PAGE LEFT INTENTIONALLY BLANK.

Appendix A

NTEP Participating Laboratories and Evaluations Report

NTEP Application Statistics			
	2003 - 2004 10/1/03 - 6/13//04	**2004 - 2005 10/1/04 - 6/13/05**	**Grand Total 10/1/00 - 6/13/05**
Applications Processed (Reactivations)	(1) 188	(2) 198	(44) 1232
Applications Completed	140	53	865
New Certificates Issued	165	131	1073
Certificates Distributed to State Directors	228	134	1055
Certificates Posted to Web Site	219	134	3592
Active NTEP Certificates			1532
	Average	**Median**	
Time for NCWM to Assign an Evaluation	10 days	8 days	
Time for NCWM to Review a Draft Certificate	8 days	6 days	
Time For Complete Evaluation	166 days	112 days	

THIS PAGE LEFT INTENTIONALLY BLANK.

Appendix B

National Type Evaluation Technical Committee (NTETC)
Grain Moisture Meter (GMM) and NIR Sector Annual Meetings

August 26-27, 2004 - Kansas City, Missouri
Summary of Decisions

Agenda Items

1. Report on GIPSA/NIST Interagency Agreement Renewal...1
2. Report on OCP (Phase II) Testing..2
3. Publication 14 – GMM Tolerances for Calibration Performance..2
4. Proposed Change to Publication 14 – Test Weight per Bushel Range for Test Weight Accuracy, Precision and Reproducibility Tests...6
5. Proposed Change to Publication 14 – Repeatability Tolerances for Test Weight..................9
6. Handbook 44, § 5.56(a) Paragraph S.2.6. Determination of Quantity and Temperature....10
7. Report on OIML IR 59 "Moisture Meters for Cereal Grains and Oilseeds".........................11
8. Report on NTEP Type Evaluations..12
9. Should the Grain Moisture Meter Sector and the NIR Grain Analyzer Sectors Merge?......13
10. Report on the 2004 NCWM Annual Meeting...13
11. Multiple Application Certificates...14
12. Time and Place for Next Meeting..15

Appendix A – NTETC Grain Moisture Meter Sector
Recommendations for Amendments to Publication 14..16

Note: Because of common interest, agenda items 8 through 12, above, were considered in a joint session of the NIR Grain Analyzer and the Grain Moisture Meter Sectors.

Details of All Items
(In Order by Reference Key Number)

---

1. Report on GIPSA/NIST Interagency Agreement Renewal

Background: The current five-year Interagency Agreement between GIPSA and NIST that provides funding for the Grain Moisture Meter On-going Calibration Program (OCP) expires at the end of the Federal Government's Fiscal Year (FY) 2004 (September 30, 2004). Under the terms of the present agreement NIST and GIPSA each contribute one-third the cost of the program subject to an annual maximum of $18,000 each. The balance of costs is borne by manufacturers and depends on the number of meter models in the NTEP "pool" according to a fee schedule. The fee schedule has remained fixed since October 1, 1999. NIST and GIPSA have reviewed costs associated with the program and a revised fee schedule has been proposed. At the Sector's 2003 meeting Dr. Richard Pierce, GIPSA, briefed the Sector on the proposed fee schedule, a draft of which is shown below. Implementation of the proposed fee schedule, which would become effective at the start of FY 2005 (October 1, 2004), is subject to approval by both agencies. Dr. Pierce reported that the fee schedule in the proposed agreement has been the subject of serious discussion at GIPSA. GIPSA has had to increase its hourly fees for services by 50 % to 100 % over the rates used when the proposed fee schedule was calculated. However, at the time of the Sector meeting, it appeared likely that GIPSA would agree to absorb the added costs at least for the coming year. Costs will be reviewed at the end of each year and manufacturers are likely to see a fee increase in subsequent years even if the number of meters remained constant. A copy of the proposed agreement has been forwarded for signing, but as of September 11, 2004, no signatures were in place.

NTEP Committee 2005 Interim Report
Appendix B – NTETC - GMM and NIR Sectors

Proposed NTEP On-Going Calibration Program Fee Schedule For Fiscal Year 2005 to 2009							
(1) Total Meters (including official meter)	(2) Meters in NTEP Pool	(3) Cost per NTEP Pool Meter	(4) Total Program Cost	Funding Contribution from Participants			(8) Cost per Meter Type
				(5) NIST	(6) GIPSA	(7) Manufacturers (total funding from mfg's)	
2	1	19,875	19,875	6,625	6,625	6,625	3,315
3	2	19,875	39,750	13,250	13,250	13,250	4,415
4	3	19,875	59,625	19,875	19,875	19,875	4,970
5	4	19,875	79,500	26,500	26,500	26,500	5,300
6	5	19,875	99,375	26,500	26,500	46,375	7,730
7	6	19,875	119,250	26,500	26,500	66,250	9,465
8	7	19,875	139,125	26,500	26,500	86,125	10,765
9	8	19,875	159,000	26,500	26,500	106,000	11,775

2. Report on OCP (Phase II) Testing

Phase II On-going Calibration Program (OCP) data for the 2003 crop year was in manufacturers' hands by February 1, 2004. Cathy Brenner of the Grain Inspection, Processors and Stockyards Administration (GIPSA, formerly FGIS), the NTEP Participating Laboratory for Grain Moisture Meters, reported that billing for the 2004 cycle was sent out in June 2004 based on the Interagency Agreement currently in place. Five models will be enrolled in Phase II for the 2004 harvest.

DICKEY-john		GAC2100
	Foss	Infratec 1229, Infratec 1241
Seedburo		1200A
Steinlite		SL95

3. Publication 14 – GMM Tolerances for Calibration Performance

Background: To address concerns that different meter types were not as closely aligned with the air oven as they could be, the Sector, at their August 2003 meeting, recommended a change to Publication 14 that would require a calibration to meet Phase I tolerances (without the application of a confidence interval) for each 2 % interval of the basic 6 % moisture range in order for that calibration to remain on the Certificate of Conformance.

During the discussion on this issue, Dr. Charles Hurburgh, Jr., Iowa State University, pointed out that if there is a statistically significant bias between two meters and both meet "Approved" tolerances, then the tolerance is too broad. It was suggested that statistics are needed to show that meters as a cluster are aligned with each other in addition to aligning with the air oven. A subcommittee was formed to look at approval tolerances and uniformity among meters. When the subcommittee met, it became clear that a major obstacle to further study this matter by the committee would be greatly hindered by the fact that manufacturers consider On-going Calibration Program (OCP) data proprietary, and the NTEP Laboratory is not free to release this data. Dr. Richard Pierce, GIPSA (the NTEP Laboratory), offered to look further into the matter and have GIPSA's statistician prepare a report.

Discussion: Dr. Pierce presented data showing the performance of NTEP meters compared to the air oven. These data were based on the last three crop years (2001 - 2003) using calibrations updated for use during the 2004 harvest season. Dr. Pierce reported that the data for the most recent three-year period is similar to data presented to the Sector five years ago. Addressing the results for corn, Dr. Pierce conceded that alignment (between meters) could be improved. With the exception of one model, agreement between meters was good over the basic 6 % moisture range. Dr. Hurburgh pointed out that each point on the graphs represents an average of a significant number of samples; thus, there is an implied "error bar" for each point. As a result, on individual samples there could be a wide dispersion in measurements between two different meter models. The results for corn, soybeans, and hard red winter wheat are shown graphically below.

NTEP Committee 2005 Annual Report
Appendix B – NTETC - GMM and NIR Sectors

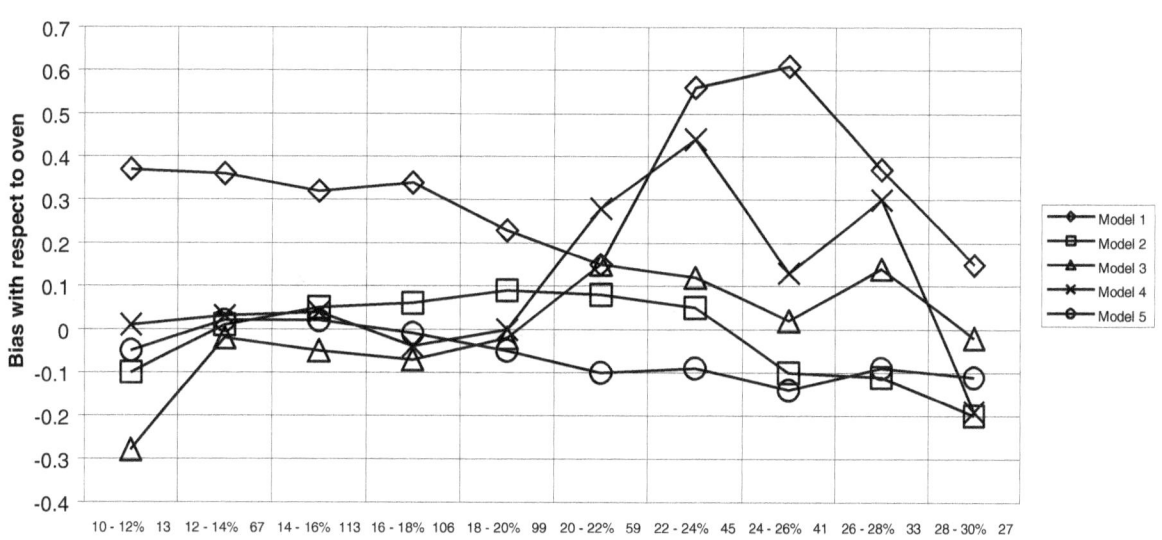

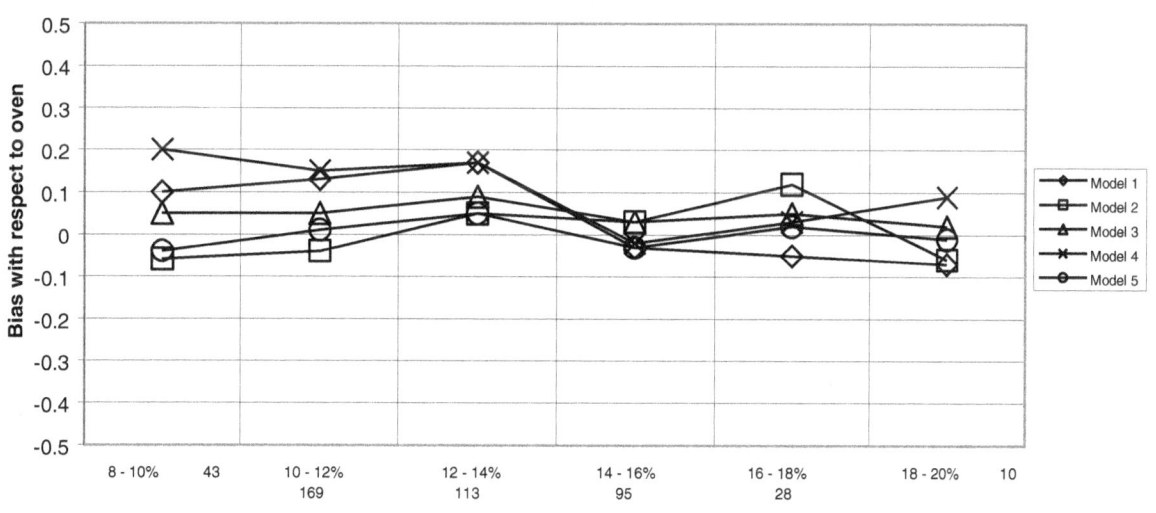

NTEP - B3

NTEP Committee 2005 Interim Report
Appendix B – NTETC - GMM and NIR Sectors

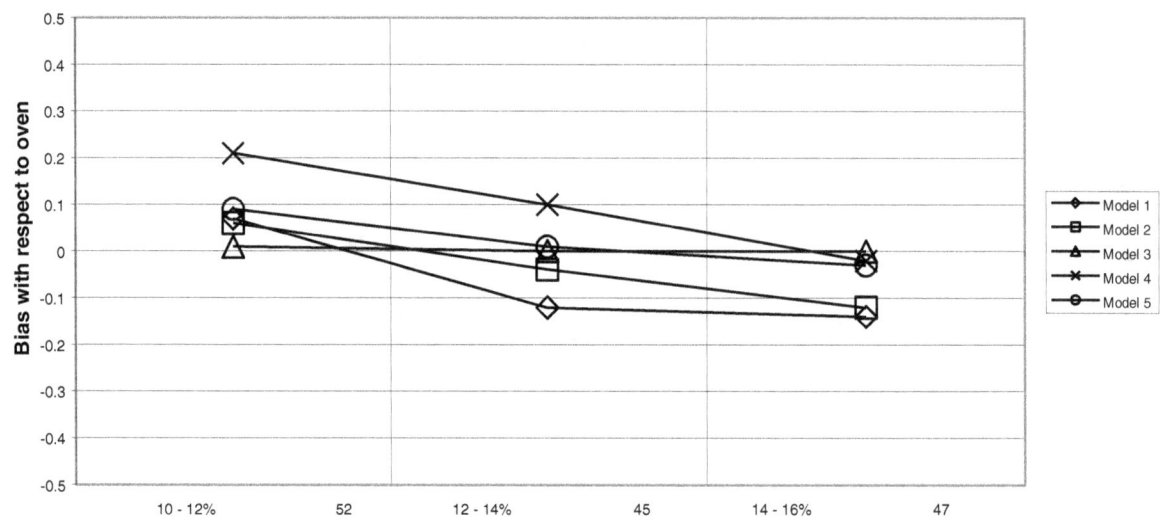

Dr. Pierce explained that wet corn is a problem. Above 20 % moisture, the number of available samples drops significantly with each 2 % interval of increasing moisture. In addition, year-to-year variability can be significant. In response to a suggestion that a tighter tolerance be applied to a three-year rolling average of the bias for each 2 % interval above 20 % moisture, Dr. Pierce replied that the problem lies in the imperfect sample set for moistures above 20 % moisture where meters show the most year-to-year variability. There are a limited number of samples, and the samples are not fully representative of the population. As a result, even three-year rolling averages may vary from year to year for each 2 % interval above 20 % moisture. This is the reason that Publication 14 applies confidence intervals to the tolerances for each 2 % interval above the basic 6 % moisture range.

Calling attention to the substantial difference between Models 1 and 5 on corn, Rich Flaugh, GSF, Inc., urged the Sector to work harder on this issue, noting that GSF had performed studies showing that the discrepancies above 20 % moisture (on corn) have been present for a number of years. He also pointed out that 2 to 4 million bushels of corn run through one meter (with a + 0.6 % bias) could cost producers $250,000 in excess shrink and drying charges.

It was suggested that the alignment problem could be solved if comparative data identifying each model by manufacturer were to be published. (Such data is presently considered proprietary according to the terms of the interagency agreement.) An informal poll of manufacturers indicated they were generally opposed to publishing this data or including a chart or graph of biases for their individual meters on the Certificate of Conformance. There was concern that this data might be misinterpreted and might lead to unnecessary calibration changes. Dr. Pierce cautioned that tolerances should not be so tight as to require calibration changes every year. Calibration changes to the official meter are upsetting to the grain trade as they can have a substantial effect on the value of grain inventories.

As presently written, there is nothing in the Grain Moisture Meter chapter of Publication 14 to force a calibration change for a meter exhibiting bias characteristics similar to those shown for meter Model 1 on corn moisture. Dr. Pierce suggested the Sector might want to consider an "overall bias" requirement similar to GIPSA's "Rule for sustained biases" cited below, but with a 0.20 limit on overall bias:

A calibration is considered for bias correction when all of the following conditions are met:

(1) The three-year average calibration bias (the three-year average bias over the entire range) exceeds 0.15 % moisture,
(2) The most recent three-year average calibration bias exceeds twice the standard deviation of past three-year average calibration biases.

One Sector member originally opposed an "overall bias" rule, believing this would not improve performance of meters in the field. This opposition was withdrawn when it was explained that: 1) moisture meter calibrations are always based on historical data; 2) although based on raw data collected over a three-year period, a calibration having a smaller bias with respect to air oven on that data has a greater probability of exhibiting a smaller bias on next year's crop; and 3) assuming that meters of like type in the field are aligned with the NTEP laboratory meter, the bias of meters in the field will also be reduced. Another member originally opposed an "overall bias" rule on the grounds that it was trying to hit a moving target. This objection was also withdrawn after considering that any proposed rule would incorporate a bias tolerance wider than the 0.15 % moisture used by GIPSA. The Sector then agreed to consider a written proposal to add an "overall bias" rule to Publication 14.

During discussion of proposed wording, questions were raised about handling new meters where less than three years of data were available. It was recognized that calibrations for a new meter might have to change each year until enough data could be accumulated. One Sector member recalled that this, in fact, did happen for some meters in the first few years of the OCP. The Sector agreed that an "overall bias" rule should apply to all available OCP data for the most recent three-year period. If only one year of data is available, the rule will apply to that year's data. The requirement that the most recent three-year average calibration bias exceed twice the standard deviation of past three-year average calibration biases was dropped for two reasons: 1) at least four years of data are required before this requirement can be evaluated, and 2) an overall average calibration bias limit of 0.20 would catch the worst offenders and would not cause unnecessary calibration changes.

Conclusion and Recommendation: The Sector agreed to recommend the addition of an overall calibration bias requirement based on up to three years of available Ongoing Calibration Program data collected by the NTEP Laboratory to § **IV. Tolerances for Calibration Performance** of the Grain Moisture Meter Chapter of the 2004 edition of Publication 14 as shown below:

IV. Tolerances for Calibration Performance

Calibration performance must be tested against established criteria at the following stages of the type evaluation process:

1. Evaluation of the calibration data supplied by the manufacturer with the application for type evaluation.

2. Evaluating instrument and calibration performance over the 6 % moisture range for corn, HRW wheat and soybeans (accuracy test discussed earlier).

3. Initial calibration approval for grains other than corn, HRW wheat, and soybeans.

4. Review of ongoing calibration data collected as part of the national calibration program.
   •
   •
   •

New calibrations will be approved based upon the re-predicted moisture values. Approval tolerances will be one-half of the Handbook 44 acceptance tolerance and will be applied in 2 % intervals over the range of available data. Additionally, for up to three years of available data:

NTEP Committee 2005 Interim Report
Appendix B – NTETC - GMM and NIR Sectors

a. The difference between the average bias to air oven for all samples in a given year and the average bias to air oven for any other year shall not exceed: 0.90 for corn; 0.80 for rice, oats, sunflowers and sorghum; and 0.70 for wheat, soybeans, and barley.

b. The range of year-to-year differences in bias to air oven shall not exceed the Handbook 44 tolerances for three or more consecutive 2 % moisture intervals. Only moisture intervals consisting of five or more samples per year will be considered for this comparison.

c. The average calibration bias with respect to air oven shall not exceed 0.20 % moisture, calculated using the most recent calibration and all available raw data collected within the last 3 years for the entire moisture range.

Failure to meet the requirements in either item a, b, or c above will cause a "No Longer Approved for Use" status to be assigned to the affected grain type(s) on the NTEP Certificate of Conformance (CC) for that instrument. Calibration coefficients will not be listed for any calibration failing these requirements.

.
.
.

4. Proposed Change to Publication 14 – Test Weight per Bushel Range for Test Weight Accuracy, Precision and Reproducibility Tests

Background/Discussion: Publication 14 stipulates that samples used for Test Weight per Bushel (TW) type approval tests for accuracy, precision, and reproducibility are to be selected to meet the following conditions:

a) A total of 12 samples are required per grain type;
b) Samples should be selected from the same 6 % moisture range used for GMM Phase I tests;
c) No less than 8 samples should come from the lowest two-thirds of the 6 % moisture range;
d) No less than 2 samples should come from the highest one-third of the 6 % moisture range;
e) The range of sample TWs should be no less than the range that is grade determining; and
f) Samples should represent a distribution of Test Weights per Bushel (TW) that minimizes the correlation between TW and moisture.

The specific requirements for the test samples are spelled out for each grain type in a table in § VII. B. of the 2004 Edition of the Grain Moisture Meters chapter of Publication 14.

In an attempt to assemble a set of test samples, the NTEP Laboratory screened a group of samples from the 1998 – 2003 Phase II moisture survey supplemented by additional samples collected from GIPSA field offices to eliminate those not within the specified 6 % moisture range. From the remaining samples, attempts were made to meet the distribution requirements by first selecting those with TWs close to the low end of the specified TW range in each 2 % moisture interval. There were problems locating samples of sufficient volume (the quart kettle reference method for TW requires "enough grain to overflow the kettle) within the specified moisture range, test weight range, and correlation requirements. The following table shows the current Publication 14 TW ranges, the percentage of Phase II samples in those ranges, and the actual TW range of the sets the Lab was able to use for evaluation purposes.

Type of Grain	Moisture Range	Publication 14 Min Test Weight per Bushel Range	% Useable Within Current TW Range	Range used for Sets
Corn	12 - 18 %	52 - 56	8	52.6 - 57.3
Soybeans	10 - 16 %	52 - 56	11	51.5 - 56.9
Hard Red Winter Wheat	10 - 16 %	56 - 60	17	57.2 - 61.4
Durum Wheat	10 - 16 %	56 - 60	21	57.3 - 61.9
Soft White Wheat	10 - 16 %	56 - 60	22	57.1 - 62.1
Hard Red Spring Wheat	10 - 16 %	55 - 58	6	55.2 - 59.5
Soft Red Winter Wheat	10 - 16 %	56 - 60	37	55.6 - 60.1
Hard White Wheat	8 - 14 %	56 - 60	4	56.6 - 63.6
Two-Row Barley	10 - 16 %	43 - 47	4	45.8 - 52.6
Six-Row Barley	10 - 16 %	43 - 47	31	43.5 - 48.6
Oats	10 - 16 %	30 - 36	31	31.4 - 38.2
Sunflower Seed	6 - 12 %	24 - 27	3	26.5 - 31.3
Long Grain Rough Rice	10 - 16 %	42 - 46	50	42.0 - 46.7
Medium Grain Rough Rice	10 - 16 %	44 - 48	56	44.2 - 48.6
Grain Sorghum	10 - 16 %	53 - 57	4	56.0 - 60.9

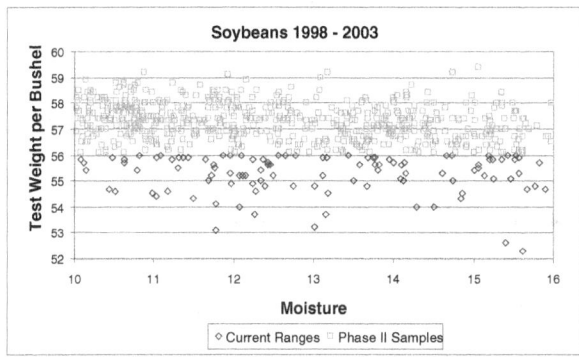

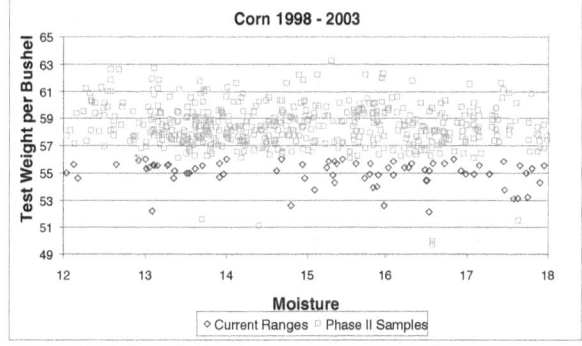

The difficulty in locating samples of sufficient size for the quart kettle reference test weight measurement within the moisture range, test weight range, and correlation requirement can be seen by examining graphs of TW vs. moisture for Phase II samples from the six most recent crop years (1998 – 2003) for corn, soybeans, and hard red winter wheat. It is even more difficult to locate qualified samples for some of the less widely traded grains. Samples represented by diamonds on the graphs are samples that meet the current selection criteria.

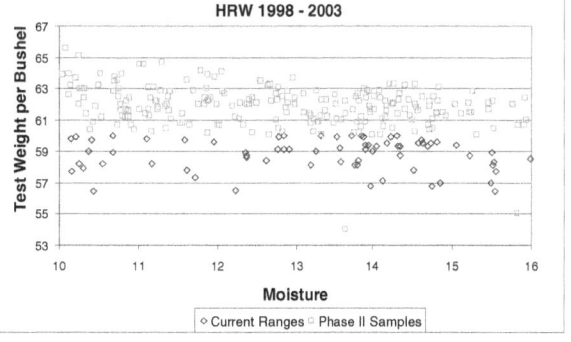

By changing the TW Range required for the test sample sets, many more samples could be made available for selection. The following chart shows the grade-determining minimum TWs for grades 1, 2, and 3 (or in parenthesis the current Publication 14 range if different); the proposed TW range (which in most cases includes the minimum TWs for grades 1 and 2); and the percentage of 1998 – 2003 Phase II samples that would be available for selection with the proposed TW range compared to the percentage available with the current range.

NTEP Committee 2005 Interim Report
Appendix B – NTETC - GMM and NIR Sectors

Grain Type	Minimum TW for Grade (pounds/bushel)			Proposed Range	Percent Available with Proposed Range	Percent Available with Current Range
	Grade 3	Grade 2	Grade 1	--- --- --		
Corn	52	54	56	54 - 58	26	8
Soybeans	52	54	56	55 - 59	73	11
Hard Red Winter Wheat	56	58	60	59 - 63	54	17
Durum Wheat	56	58	60	59 - 63	50	21
Soft White Wheat	56	58	60	58 - 62	50	22
Hard Red Spring Wheat	55	57	58	58 - 61	37	6
Soft Red Winter Wheat	56	58	60	56 - 60	37	37
Hard White Wheat	56	58	60	60 - 64	28	4
Two-Row Malting Barley (43-47)	48	48	50	47 - 51	32	4
Six-Row Barley	43	45	47	43 - 47	31	31
Oats	30	33	36	33 - 39	47	31
Sunflower Seed (24-27)		25	25	28 - 31	32	3
Long Grain Rough Rice	(42-46)	43 - 47	60	50		
Medium Grain Rough Rice	(44-48)	44 - 48	56	56		
Grain Sorghum	53	55	57	58 - 62	56	54

One Sector member expressed concern that meters won't be evaluated in the range where (for corn) discounts are most likely to be applied. The user presumes that the meter has been evaluated over the entire operating range, when, in fact, it will have been evaluated only at the upper range of operation. Dr. Hurburgh, explained that the main use of test weight (for corn) is in certifying warehouse volume. TW is not widely discounted for corn. Low TW for corn is a rare occurrence, which is why low TW corn samples are difficult to obtain. Furthermore, in contrast to moisture, the measurement of TW is inherently linear. There is not a problem extrapolating to lower TWs.

The Sector agreed to the following recommendation.

Recommendation: Change the Minimum Test Weight per Bushel Range in the Table in § VII.B. of the 2004 Edition of the Grain Moisture Meters chapter of Publication 14 on the following page:

Type of Grain	Moisture Range	Minimum Test Weight per Bushel Range	Criteria for Sample Selection
Corn	12 - 18 %	54 - 58	a). No less than 8 samples should come from the lowest two-thirds of the 6 % moisture range. b). No less than 2 samples should come from the highest one-third of the 6 % moisture range. c). Samples should represent a distribution of Test Weights per Bushel (TW) that minimizes the correlation between TW and moisture.
Soybeans	10 - 16 %	55 - 59	
Hard Red Winter Wheat	10 - 16 %	59 - 63	
Durum Wheat	10 - 16 %	59 - 63	
Soft White Wheat (except White Club)	10 - 16 %	58 - 62	
Hard Red Spring Wheat (and White Club)	10 - 16 %	58 - 61	
Soft Red Winter Wheat	10 - 16 %	56 - 60	
Hard White Wheat	8 - 14 %	60 - 64	
Two-Row Barley	10 - 16 %	47 - 51	
Six-Row Barley	10 - 16 %	43 - 47	
Oats	10 - 16 %	33 - 39	
Sunflower Seed (Oil Type)	6 - 12 %	28 - 31	
Long Grain Rough Rice	10 - 16 %	43 - 47	
Medium Grain Rough Rice	10 - 16 %	44 - 48	
Grain Sorghum or Milo	10 - 16 %	58 - 62	

5. Proposed Change to Publication 14 – Repeatability Tolerances for Test Weight

Discussion: The tolerance for the Test Weight per Bushel repeatability test of Publication 14 is marginally too tight for corn and for oats. The present limit is 0.4 times the absolute value of the Handbook 44 acceptance tolerance of 0.8 pounds per bushel for corn and oats. At the time the Sector recommended a multiplier of 0.4 for repeatability, which translates to a tolerance of 0.32 pounds per bushel, it was a "best estimate" value with little data available to show if this limit would be marginal with the sample test set specified in Publication 14. Subsequent testing indicates that 0.40 pounds per bushel is a more realistic repeatability tolerance for corn and oats.

Certificates of Conformance have been issued for the 2004 crop year. One device met the present repeatability tolerance for corn (admittedly by a very small margin). No devices have met the present repeatability tolerance for oats.

The Sector agreed by consensus to recommend the following change in repeatability tolerances for Test Weight in Publication 14.

Recommendation: Change tolerances for repeatability for corn and oats in § VII. B. of the Grain Moisture Meter chapter of the 2004 edition of Publication 14 as follows:

Tolerances for repeatability for all grain types except corn and oats are 0.4 times the absolute value of the Handbook 44 acceptance tolerance. The tolerance for repeatability for corn and oats is 0.5 times the absolute value of the Handbook 44 acceptance tolerance. Specific tolerances are:

NTEP Committee 2005 Interim Report
Appendix B – NTETC - GMM and NIR Sectors

Grain Type	Tolerance
Corn, oats	0.40 pounds per bushel
All wheat classes	0.20 pounds per bushel
Soybeans, barley, rice, sunflower, sorghum	0.28 pounds per bushel

6. Handbook 44, § 5.56(a) Paragraph S.2.6. Determination of Quantity and Temperature

Background: In August 2002 the Sector considered whether their recommended changes to NIST Handbook 44, § 5.56(a), paragraph S.2.6., relating to a means of sensing adequate sample volume, should be retroactive or nonretroactive. Discussion centered on the requirement that meters measuring TW must provide some means to ensure that measurements of TW are not allowed to be displayed or printed when insufficient sample volume has been supplied. (Although the code does not specify how this is to be accomplished, it is generally assumed that the means will include a sensor of some sort installed in either the sample hopper or the test cell.)

Those favoring making the proposed code retroactive reminded the Sector that although moisture measurements are not significantly affected when samples are not of sufficient size to completely fill the measuring cell of a GMM, the TW measurement is greatly affected when the cell is not filled. Measurement of TW requires determination of two parameters: volume and mass. The vast majority of GMM's with TW capability presently in the field do not have means to assure that the measuring cell is completely full. If the cell is not filled completely, TW indications will be lower than they should be to the disadvantage of the producer selling grain. Some sector members favoring making the code nonretroactive felt that GMM's with a window, through which the test cell could be seen, provided adequate means to verify that the cell had been filled. A grain industry member expressed the belief that compared to how test weight measurements are being made now, the worry about a sensor was trivial. As long as the GMM could produce an accurate TW measurement when properly used, whether or not the hopper had a sensor, was not important. Some thought this was a facilitation of fraud issue and favored making the sensor requirement retroactive. Others thought that making the code retroactive would unfairly penalize users of existing NTEP meters with TW capability. By a vote of 9 to 4, the Sector agreed that the addition to paragraph S.2.6. relating to a means of sensing adequate sample volume should be nonretroactive. As adopted by the Conference, this paragraph currently reads:

> **S.2.6. Determination of Quantity and Temperature. -** The moisture meter system shall not require the operator to judge the precise volume or weight and temperature needed to make an accurate moisture determination. External grinding, weighing, and temperature measurement operations are not permitted. In addition, if the meter is capable of measuring test weight per bushel, determination of sample volume and weight for this measurement shall be fully automatic *and means shall be provided to ensure that measurements of test weight per bushel are not allowed to be displayed or printed when an insufficient sample volume is available to provide an accurate measurement.*
> (Added 1994)(Amended 1995 and 2003)
> *[Nonretroactive as of January 1, 2004]*

Discussion: Handbook 44, § 1.10. General Code, Paragraph G-A.6. states:

Nonretroactive Requirements. "Nonretroactive" requirements are enforceable after the effective date for:

(a) devices manufactured within a State after the effective date;
(b) both new and used devices brought into a State after the effective date; and
(c) devices used in noncommercial applications which are placed into commercial use after the effective date.

Nonretroactive requirements are not enforceable with respect to devices that are in commercial service in the State as of the effective date or to new equipment in the stock of a manufacturer or a dealer in the State as of the effective date.
(Nonretroactive requirements are printed in italic type)]
(Amended 1989)

Thus, as Handbook 44 is currently written, a State can test the TW feature of any GMM placed into commercial service in that State prior to January 1, 2004, and approve or reject it, whether or not the device has the means to ensure that sufficient volume is available for an accurate test. However, some States have indicated they will not allow the use of a TW feature unless an active Certificate of Conformance (CC) covers the TW feature of the device. NCWM, Inc., is accepting applications for NTEP testing for TW capability for only those GMMs incorporating a volume sensor.

During development of the Handbook 44 Code relating to TW, several Sector members made a strong case for requiring that GMMs with TW capability be able to prevent a TW indication and printout if insufficient volume of grain is present for an accurate reading.

The Sector considered the following questions:

- How are states enforcing this requirement?
- Are meters without a volume sensor being tested for TW?
- If a volume sensor is important for accurate TW measurement, should this requirement be retroactive (perhaps with a future effective date) or should it remain nonretroactive?

Diane Lee, NIST WMD, reported that based on the calls she had received from State W&M personnel, the states were not enforcing this portion of the code uniformly. One State W&M representative reported that to date they have not been approving meters for TW if they did not have volume sensors. For survey purposes, they had tested a group of meters not having volume sensors. A large portion of that group did not pass the tests for TW. It was suggested that these failures were most likely due to poor maintenance rather than inadequate volume of sample. Although a W&M representative was not present from Illinois, it was reported that Illinois was conducting TW tests on all meters in place before January 1, 2004, whether or not they had volume sensors. Illinois was reportedly testing only with wheat. There was concern that testing with a single grain might not be adequate indication the device would perform accurately on other grains as some devices are adjusted to grain type. This "adjustment to type" frequently takes the form of grain-specific TW calibration constants (slope or bias terms) that compensate for differences in packing density between the GMM test cell and the standard TW quart cup for each grain. This concern is most serious with devices that haven't received NTEP approval for TW. Devices that have been NTEP approved for TW will be using TW calibrations that have been evaluated for each grain type, so testing with a single grain at least verifies the weighing mechanism is functioning properly.

Conclusion: The Sector agreed that its earlier decision to make the requirement for a volume sensor nonretroactive was correct, and it will stand.

7. Report on OIML IR59 "Moisture Meters for Cereal Grains and Oilseeds"

Background: At an OIML TC17/SC1 meeting in Berlin on June 22, 2001, the U.S. delegation put forth a series of proposals to revise OIML IR59 "Moisture Meters for Cereal Grains and Oilseeds." These proposals were well received, and it was requested that the U.S. prepare a draft based on the U.S. NTEP program. A rough draft of this document was reviewed at the August 2002 GMM Sector meeting. A working draft, incorporating changes suggested by the Sector, was submitted to U.S. and International Work Groups in February 2003 for comment. NIST Weights and Measures Division (WMD), now responsible for U.S. participation and representation in the technical activities of the OIML, compiled comments to the working draft for review by representatives of the U.S. National Work Group (USNWG). The working draft was modified to address comments where it was judged appropriate. The modified working draft and a table of responses to the comments received to the working draft were distributed to USNWG members May 28, 2003. Subsequently, the Secretariat (the Peoples Republic of China) distributed the revised working draft as the "First Committee Draft" (1 st CD) to OIML TC17/SC1 for review and comment by the member states of the subcommittee. Comments to the 1 st CD were addressed by OIML TC17/SC1 at a meeting held in Beijing October 15 – 16, 2003. A revised 1 st CD, dated April 2004 incorporating changes agreed to at the Beijing meeting has been distributed to member countries. USNWG members were asked to return their comments on the latest draft to Diane Lee, NIST WMD, no later than July 30, 2004.

NTEP Committee 2005 Interim Report
Appendix B – NTETC - GMM and NIR Sectors

A meeting of TC17/SC1 was held September 20 - 21, 2004, in Paris to discuss the latest draft of R59.

Discussion: Diane Lee reported that Japan had objected to the required minimum sample size of 100 g or 400 kernels or seeds, which ever is smaller, for dielectric meters (and 20 g for near-infrared meters), because it ruled out meters based on the electrical resistivity of grain. These meters are used mainly for small grains, but at least one type can also measure moisture in soybeans. About 70 % of the grain moisture meters in Asia are of this type. During the Sector's discussion of this issue, it was reported that the sample size for these meters, on small grains, was 0.5 g. Some members questioned this size, wondering if a larger sample might be ground up and mixed before 0.5 g was extracted and placed between electrodes for measurement. Subsequent to the meeting, at least two models of resistive meters were found to utilize only 18 – 22 kernels when measuring short grain brown or white rice, which approximates 0.4 g.. The April 2004 draft had included the following note to address Japan's concerns about sample size:

> (Note: if another meter technology is used which requires a smaller sample size than noted above, additional testing is required to ensure that proper sampling techniques can be applied to the measurement to ensure that the measurement is representative of the grain sample.)

It was suggested that a class of "small sample size" instruments might be needed to address Japan's concerns with that class being excluded from use in the U.S. Steve Patoray, NTEP Director, pointed out that should the U.S. enter into a grain moisture meter mutual recognition agreement with OIML, the U.S. would have to have sound technical basis for excluding this class from U.S. use.

Subsequent to the Sector meeting, comments on the April 2004 draft of R59 were received from other OIML member countries. Comments were for the most part positive. The most serious objections were from Japan. They included:

1) In clause 6.1.5 the meaning of "representative size grain sample" is not clear because the statistical population is not defined in this draft. Meters could not be designed to measure the moisture content of representative size of grain samples because representativeness does not depend on the size of sample but on preparation such as mixing sample and on way of measurement. Therefore this clause should be deleted, or we should just note that the sample should be homogeneous.

2) The present draft seems to require all types of grain moisture meters to measure the temperature of a loaded sample. As we pointed out at the meeting in Beijing, it is almost impossible for resistance type moisture meters to comply with the requirement due to geometrical and mechanical restriction. Therefore the present descriptions concerning temperature measurement of the sample, if they are not changed, would lead to exclude the resistance type moisture meters, whose market share is about 70 % in Asian countries.

Japan proposed removing all requirements regarding inhibiting display of moisture value when certain grain or instrument temperature limits had been exceeded.

Diane Lee has compiled the comments received from other OIML member countries and circulated a comment form to the U.S. work group soliciting comments in hopes of receiving feedback on the comments prior to the next meeting of OIML TC17/SC1 scheduled for September 20 – 21, 2004, in Paris, France.

8. Report on NTEP Type Evaluations

Cathy Brenner of the Grain Inspection, Processors and Stockyards Administration (GIPSA, formerly FGIS), the NTEP Participating Laboratory for Grain Analyzers (Grain Moisture Meters and Near-Infrared Grain Analyzers) reported on Type Evaluation activity. In addition to regular grain moisture meter calibration updates, two certificates were updated to add new features following successful evaluations:

1. CC 01-063A4 – Foss Infratec 1241
    a) added protein and oil for corn and soybeans
    b) added protein for the following wheats: Durum, HRS, HRW, Hard White, SRW, Soft White; and for both 6-row and 2-row Barley

2. CC 97-073A7 – Steinlite SL95 (only units with funnel sensor are approved for TW)
   a) added test weight per bushel for all grains except Oats

Evaluations are currently underway for two additional devices: one for test weight per bushel and one for protein and oil combined.

9. Should the Grain Moisture Meter Sector and the NIR Grain Analyzer Sectors Merge?

Discussion: The Grain Moisture Meter Sector and the Near-Infrared Grain Analyzer Sector (originally the Near-Infrared Protein Analyzer) first met in Kansas City in December 1991. Since their beginning, the two Sectors have met separately on successive days, often meeting jointly for part of that time to consider items of common interest. The advent of CCs listing multiple applications evaluated under either or both the Grain Moisture Meter Code and the Near-Infrared Analyzer Code has increased the number of issues common to both groups. Furthermore, the Sector chair, the technical advisors, and the vast majority of Sector members are common to both Sectors. These facts suggest that it would be more efficient for the two Sectors to merge into a single new Sector called the "Grain Analyzer Sector." In the past, when items required in-depth consideration of technical matters or development of detailed procedures, *ad hoc* subcommittees or work groups were formed to develop background information and to suggest action for consideration by the Sectors. It is envisioned that such sub-committees or work groups can be of equal or greater importance to a merged Sector dealing with more mature issues.

Following are few of the benefits of merging into a single sector:

- One meeting agenda instead of two;
- One meeting summary instead of two;
- More flexibility in dealing with items of common interest;
- Consistency between GMM and NIR Code and Checklists.

Recommendation: By consensus the Sector agreed to recommend that the NCWM Board of Directors merge the Grain Moisture Meter Sector and the Near-Infrared Grain Analyzer Sector into a new Sector to be called the Grain Analyzer Sector.

10. Report on the 2004 NCWM Annual Meeting

Background/Discussion: The 89th Annual Meeting of the National Conference on Weights and Measures (NCWM) was held July 11 - 15, 2004, in Pittsburgh, Pennsylvania.

No Grain Moisture Meter (GMM) or Near-Infrared (NIR) Grain Analyzer items appeared in the Specifications and Tolerances (S&T) Committee Interim Report for consideration by the NCWM at the 2004 Annual Meeting.

The National Type Evaluation Program (NTEP) Committee Interim Report contained an item relating to NTEP's work to establish bilateral and multilateral test data exchange agreements. Under such agreements and arrangements, manufacturers would be able to submit their equipment to any of the participating countries for testing to OIML-recommended requirements. The resulting test data would be accepted by other participants, as a basis for issuing each country's own type approval certificate. One such agreement or arrangement is the Mutual Acceptance Arrangement (MAA) on OIML Type Evaluations recently adopted by the International Committee on Legal Metrology (CIML) at their November 2003 meeting. For additional background refer to *Committee Reports for the 89th Annual Meeting,* NCWM Publication 16.

By way of background, Steve Patoray, NTEP Director, explained that the U.S. and Canada have a bilateral MAA covering weighing devices. Under this MAA, a U.S. NTEP test report on a weighing device can be sent to Canada where a Canadian Certificate of Approval will be issued without further testing (and vice versa). A bilateral MAA agreement covering retail motor-fuel dispensers has been signed recently between the U.S. and Canada, but to date no dispensers have been evaluated under this MAA.

NTEP Committee 2005 Interim Report
Appendix B – NTETC - GMM and NIR Sectors

Mr. Patoray also reported that progress was being made to establish an OIML MAA program. An additional International Bureau of Legal Metrology (BIML) staff member will be hired by January 1, 2005, to undertake the new tasks resulting from the implementation of the MAA. Initially this MAA will cover R76 (non-automatic weighing devices) and R60 (load cells). A four-year time plan has been set for implementation. This will be a multilateral agreement with many countries signing a declaration of mutual confidence. Much work has yet to be done to harmonize NTEP requirements with the OIML recommendations for these devices. A major issue in establishing MAAs is confidence in the data. Testing laboratories will be assessed either by accreditation or peer assessment using criteria that comply with ISO/IEC 17025.

With OIML International recommendations still in the draft stage for GMMs and NIR analyzers, it will be some time before MAAs are in place for these devices. This is, however, an issue that the Sector members may want to watch closely to see how MAAs might impact future type evaluation testing and certification of GMMs and NIR Grain Analyzers.

11. Multiple Application Certificates

Background: During the 2003 NCWM Interim Meeting in Jacksonville, Florida, the NTEP Committee reviewed the Sector's recommendation to issue a single Certificate of Conformance to devices evaluated using two inter-related codes. Since that time there has been the possibility of dual certification for moisture plus protein and oil, and now test weight per bushel. The first dual certificates became effective July 1, 2004, (97-073A7 and 01-063A4). The two areas of change are in the "For:" box on page 1 and on the last page with the calibration information.

In the "For:" box, the certificates now identify the device as a Grain Analyzer instead of a Grain Moisture Meter or Near-Infrared Grain Analyzer. The device type is then followed by the Application(s) that the device is approved for, in alphabetical order (Moisture, Oil, Protein, Starch, Test Weight). This information matches the current NTEP Certificate of Conformance searchable database.

The page for the calibration information also lists the applications in alphabetical order. For example, if a meter were approved for moisture, oil, protein, and test weight per bushel for corn, the calibration listing for corn would be listed as:

Corn
    Designation: CORN
    Moisture: ABC123
    Moisture Range - Approved: 10 % to 30 %
    Moisture Range - Pending: 8 % to 40 %
    Oil: BCD234
    Protein: CDE345
    Native Moisture Basis: 0 %
    Test Weight per Bushel: Approved

Discussion: The Sectors reviewed the new dual certificates. The Sector agreed that the revised certificates generally looked good and commended Cathy Brenner for a job well done. The following suggestions were made to clarify some of the information on the Calibration page:

a. Separate the moisture calibration information from the information on calibrations for other constituents (Protein, Oil, Starch), perhaps using a dotted line.
b. Make it clear that the Approved and Pending moisture ranges apply only to moisture measurements. An approved moisture range of 8 % to 40 % does NOT mean that accurate Protein measurements can be made on samples having 40 % moisture.
c. Make it clear that the Intercept (Bias) note "Varies by instrument" applies only to calibrations for constituents other than moisture (e.g., Protein, Oil, Starch). It does NOT apply to the Moisture calibration. If a moisture bias term is used, it MUST be part of the grain moisture calibration and be the same for all instruments of like type. [Ref., Handbook 44, § 5.56(a), Paragraph S.2.4.3.].

In a related matter, it was pointed out that the revised application form for NTEP testing is unclear. Steve Patoray, NTEP Director, suggested that information could be added to the "Evaluation Description" section to indicate which parts of the form must be completed when a box was checked for the type of evaluation being requested.

Questions were also raised about fees involved in Phase I evaluations and Phase II (Ongoing Calibration Program). These fees (for NCWM members) and their frequency are summarized in the table below:

			NTEP Laboratory fees	Frequency
Phase I NTEP Evaluation	Non-refundable application fee $800	Certificate processing fee $150	At NTEP Lab hourly rates based on actual hours. ($10,000 -$25,000 and up depending on tests involved.)	Once per type/pattern.
Maintenance fee	$350			Annually
Phase II Ongoing Calibration Program. (applicable to grain moisture meters only)		Certificate processing fee $150	Per Interagency Agreement. Depends on total number of meter types in the OCP	Annually

12. Time and Place for Next Meeting

The next meeting is tentatively planned for the week of August 22, 2005, in the Kansas City, MO, area. Meetings will be held in one of the meeting rooms at the National Weather Service Training Center if available. The meeting room will be reserved for Wednesday, August 24 and Thursday, August 25. Sector members are asked to hold both these days open pending determination of exact meeting times and meeting duration. Final meeting details will be announced by late April 2005.

If you would like to submit an agenda item for the 2005 meeting, please contact Steve Patoray, NTEP technical director, at spatoray@mgmtsol.com, G. Diane Lee, NIST technical advisor, at diane.lee@nist.gov, or Jack Barber, technical advisor, at jbarber@motion.net by April 1, 2005.

Appendix A – NTETC Grain Moisture Meter Sector Recommendations for Amendments to Publication 14

\multicolumn{4}{c}{**Grain Moisture Meters** Recommended Amendments and Changes to the 2004 Edition of Publication 14}
Section Number	**Amendment/Change**	**Page**	**Source**
Section IV. Tolerances for Calibration Performance	Add item c. to establish an overall calibration bias requirement based on up to three years of available data. Change wording in paragraph preceding item a. and in paragraph following item c. to reflect addition of item c.	GMM-5 through GMM-6	08/04 GMM Sector Item 3
Section VII.B. Accuracy, Precision, and Reproducibility	Change the Minimum Test Weight per Bushel Ranges in the Table in § VII.B. to facilitate selection of test-set samples.	GMM-11	08/04 GMM Sector Item 4
Section VII.B. Accuracy, Precision, and Reproducibility	Change tolerances for repeatability (precision) for Corn and Oats to more realistic value.	GMM-13	08/04 GMM Sector Item 5

NTEP Committee 2005 Annual Report
Appendix B – NTETC - GMM and NIR Sectors

National Type Evaluation Technical Committee (NTETC)
Near-Infrared (NIR) Grain Analyzer Sector Annual Meeting

August 26 - 27, 2004 - Kansas City, Missouri
Draft Summary of Decisions

Agenda Items

1. Report on NTEP Type Evaluations...17
2. Should the Grain Moisture Meter Sector and the NIR Grain Analyzer Sectors Merge?.........................17
3. Report on the 2004 NCWM Annual Meeting..18
4. Multiple Application Certificates...18
5. Time and Place for Next Meeting..20
6. Report on OIML TC17/SC8 IR for Protein Measuring Instruments for Cereal Grain...........................20

Note: Because of common interest, items 1 through 5, above, were considered in a joint session of the NIR Grain Analyzer and the Grain Moisture Meter Sectors

Details of All Items
(In Order by Reference Key Number)

1. Report on NTEP Type Evaluations

Cathy Brenner of the Grain Inspection, Processors and Stockyards Administration (GIPSA, formerly FGIS), the NTEP Participating Laboratory for Grain Analyzers (Grain Moisture Meters and Near-Infrared Grain Analyzers) reported on Type Evaluation activity. In addition to regular grain moisture meter calibration updates, two certificates were updated to add new features following successful evaluations:

1) CC 01-063A4 – Foss Infratec 1241
   a) added protein and oil for Corn and Soybeans
   b) added protein for the following wheats: Durum, HRS, HRW, Hard White, SRW, Soft White; and for both 6-row and 2-row Barley

2) CC 97-073A7 – Steinlite SL95 (only units with funnel sensor are approved for TW)
   a) added test weight per bushel for all grains except Oats

Evaluations are currently underway for two additional devices: one for test weight per bushel and one for protein and oil combined.

2. Should the Grain Moisture Meter Sector and the NIR Grain Analyzer Sectors Merge?

Discussion: The Grain Moisture Meter Sector and the Near-Infrared Grain Analyzer Sector (originally the Near-Infrared Protein Analyzer) first met in Kansas City in December 1991. Since their beginning, the two Sectors have met separately on successive days, often meeting jointly for part of that time to consider items of common interest. The advent of CCs listing multiple applications evaluated under either or both the Grain Moisture Meter Code and the Near-Infrared Analyzer Code has increased the number of issues common to both groups. Furthermore, the Sector chair, the technical advisors, and the vast majority of Sector members are common to both Sectors. These facts suggest that it would be more efficient for the two Sectors to merge into a single new Sector called the "Grain Analyzer Sector." In the past, when items required in-depth consideration of technical matters or development of detailed procedures, *ad hoc* subcommittees or work groups were formed to develop background information and to suggest action for consideration by the Sectors. It is envisioned that such sub-committees or work groups can be of equal or greater importance to a merged Sector dealing with more mature issues.

NTEP Committee 2005 Interim Report
Appendix B – NTETC - GMM and NIR Sectors

A few of the benefits of merging into a single sector:

- One meeting agenda instead of two;
- One meeting summary instead of two;
- More flexibility in dealing with items of common interest;
- Consistency between GMM and NIR Code and Checklists.

Recommendation: By consensus the Sector agreed to recommend that the NCWM Board of Directors merge the Grain Moisture Meter Sector and the Near Infrared Grain Analyzer Sector into a new Sector to be called the Grain Analyzer Sector.

3. Report on the 2004 NCWM Annual Meeting

Background/Discussion: The 89th Annual Meeting of the National Conference on Weights and Measures (NCWM) was held July 11 - 15, 2004, in Pittsburgh, Pennsylvania.

No Grain Moisture Meter (GMM) or Near Infrared (NIR) Grain Analyzer items appeared in the Specifications and Tolerances (S&T) Committee Interim Report for consideration by the NCWM at the 2004 Annual Meeting.

The National Type Evaluation Program (NTEP) Committee Interim Report contained an item relating to NTEP's work to establish bilateral and multilateral test data exchange agreements. Under such agreements and arrangements, manufacturers would be able to submit their equipment to any of the participating countries for testing to OIML recommended requirements. The resulting test data would be accepted by other participants, as a basis for issuing each country's own type approval certificate. One such agreement or arrangement is the Mutual Acceptance Arrangement (MAA) on OIML Type Evaluations recently adopted by the International Committee on Legal Metrology (CIML) at their November 2003 meeting. For additional background refer to *Committee Reports for the 89th Annual Meeting,* NCWM Publication 16.

By way of background, Steve Patoray, NTEP Director, explained that the U.S. and Canada have a bilateral MAA covering weighing devices. Under this MAA, a U.S. NTEP test report on a weighing device can be sent to Canada where a Canadian Certificate of Approval will be issued without further testing (and vice versa). A bilateral MAA agreement covering retail motor-fuel dispensers has been signed recently between the U.S. and Canada, but to date no dispensers have been evaluated under this MAA.

Steve also reported that progress was being made to establish an OIML MAA program. An additional International Bureau of Legal Metrology (BIML) staff member will be hired by January 1, 2005, undertake the new tasks resulting from the implementation of the MAA. Initially this MAA will cover R76 (Non-automatic weighing devices) and R60 (Load Cells). A four-year time plan has been set for implementation. This will be a multilateral agreement with many countries signing a declaration of mutual confidence. Much work has yet to be done to harmonize NTEP requirements with the OIML recommendations for these devices. A major issue in establishing MAAs is confidence in the data. Testing laboratories will be assessed either by accreditation or peer assessment using criteria that comply with ISO/IEC 17025.

With OIML International recommendations still in the draft stage for GMMs and NIR analyzers, it will be some time before MAAs are in place for these devices. This is, however, an issue that the Sector members may want to watch closely to see how MAAs might impact future type evaluation testing and certification of GMMs and NIR Grain Analyzers.

4. Multiple Application Certificates

Background: During the 2003 NCWM Interim Meeting in Jacksonville, Florida, the NTEP Committee reviewed the Sectors' recommendation to issue a single Certificate of Conformance to devices evaluated using two inter-related codes. Since that time there has been the possibility of dual certification for moisture plus protein and oil, and now test weight per bushel. The first dual certificates became effective July 1, 2004 (97-073A7 and 01-063A4). The two areas of change are in the "For:" box on page 1 and on the last page with the calibration information.

In the "For:" box, the certificates now identify the device as a Grain Analyzer instead of a Grain Moisture Meter or Near Infrared Grain Analyzer. The device type is then followed by the Application(s) that the device is approved for, in alphabetical order (Moisture, Oil, Protein, Starch, Test Weight). This information matches the current NTEP Certificate of Conformance searchable database.

The page for the calibration information also lists the applications in alphabetical order. For example, if a meter were approved for moisture, oil, protein, and test weight per bushel for corn, the calibration listing for corn would be listed as:

> **Corn**
> Designation: CORN
> Moisture: ABC123
> Moisture Range - Approved: 10 % to 30 %
> Moisture Range - Pending: 8 % to 40 %
> Oil: BCD234
> Protein: CDE345
> Native Moisture Basis: 0 %
> Test Weight per Bushel: Approved

Discussion: The Sectors reviewed the new dual certificates. The Sector agreed that the revised certificates generally looked good and commended Cathy Brenner for a job well done. The following suggestions were made to clarify some of the information on the Calibration page:

a. Separate the moisture calibration information from the information on calibrations for other constituents (Protein, Oil, Starch), perhaps using a dotted line.
b. Make it clear that the Approved and Pending moisture ranges apply only to moisture measurements. An approved moisture range of 8 % to 40 % does NOT mean that accurate Protein measurements can be made on samples having 40 % moisture.
c. Make it clear that the Intercept (Bias) note "Varies by instrument" applies only to calibrations for constituents other than moisture (e.g., Protein, Oil, Starch). It does NOT apply to the Moisture calibration. If a moisture bias term is used, it MUST be part of the grain moisture calibration and be the same for all instruments of like type. [Ref., Handbook 44, § 5.56(a), Paragraph S.2.4.3.].

In a related matter, it was pointed out that the revised application form for NTEP testing is unclear. Steve Patoray, NTEP Director, suggested that information could be added to the "Evaluation Description" section to indicate which parts of the form must be completed when a box was checked for the type of evaluation being requested.

Questions were also raised about fees involved in Phase I evaluations and Phase II (Ongoing Calibration Program). These fees (for NCWM members) and their frequency are summarized in the table below:

			NTEP Laboratory fees	Frequency
Phase I NTEP Evaluation	Non-refundable application fee $800	Certificate processing fee $150	At NTEP Lab hourly rates based on actual hours. ($10,000 -$25,000 and up depending on tests involved.)	Once per type/pattern.
Maintenance fee	$350			Annually
Phase II Ongoing Calibration Program. (applicable to grain moisture meters only)		Certificate processing fee $150	Per Interagency Agreement. Depends on total number of meter types in the OCP	Annually

NTEP Committee 2005 Interim Report
Appendix B – NTETC - GMM and NIR Sectors

5. Time and Place for Next Meeting

The next meeting is tentatively planned for the week of August 22, 2005, in the Kansas City, MO, area. Meetings will be held in one of the meeting rooms at the National Weather Service Training Center if available. The meeting room will be reserved for Wednesday, August 24 and Thursday, August 25. Sector members are asked to hold both these days open pending determination of exact meeting times and meeting duration. Final meeting details will be announced by late-April 2005.

If you would like to submit an agenda item for the 2005 meeting, please contact Steve Patoray, NTEP technical director, at spatoray@mgmtsol.com, G. Diane Lee, NIST technical advisor, at diane.lee@nist.gov, or Jack Barber, technical advisor, at jbarber@motion.net by April 1, 2005.

6. Report on OIML TC17/SC8 IR for Protein Measuring Instruments for Cereal Grain

Background:

OIML TC17/SC8, charged with developing an International Recommendation (IR) for Protein Measuring Instruments for Cereal Grain, held its first meeting May 31 and June 1, 2004, in Sydney, Australia. Representatives from Australia, Japan, New Zealand, and the United States attended the meeting. Australia, as the secretariat of the subcommittee, developed an outline of the Recommendation on Protein Measuring Instruments for Cereal Grain (March 2004) that was circulated to participating nations (Australia, Brazil, Canada, Czech Republic, Germany, Japan, Poland, Republic of Korea, Russia and the United States) for comments. In the U.S. the document was circulated to the U.S. National Work Group (USNWG) for comments. The comments received from the U.S. and Germany were discussed at the TC17/SC8 meeting in Australia. The comments for the most part were accepted. Additionally, TC17/SC8 agreed to the following changes:

   a. The scope will be expanded to include wheat, barley, corn, soybeans and rice

   b. Maximum permissible errors (MPE) and Moisture Basis: Publication 14 will be used to establish the maximum permissible errors for wheat, barley, corn and soybeans. China will provide information for tolerances on rice. Moisture basis will be determined by the national measurement authority.

   c. The section for sampling will be updated to address the U.S. comments.

   d. The technology for protein measurements will not be specific.

   e. The standard will incorporate appropriate sections of OIML D9

   f. The instrument monitoring process will be left up to the national measurement authority.

   g. The document will be updated so that the April 2004 Final Draft of the **International vocabulary of basic and general terms in metrology** (VIM) definitions are included.

   h. The reference method will be determined by the national measurement authority.

   i. The Recommendation on protein measuring instruments will be drafted as close as possible with the latest draft of OIML R59.

   j. The document will include susceptibility to dust.

   k. Decision to test non-indirect measuring devices will be at the discretion of the national measurement authority.

Discussion: A revised draft incorporating the changes agreed upon at the Sydney meeting was distributed with the Agenda for the Sector's August 2004 meeting. Australia, the Secretariat of TC17/SC8, used portions of the NIR

Grain Analyzer Chapter of Publication 14 in this draft outline recommendation. As of the Sector meeting, Diane Lee, NIST WMD reported that comments had been received only from Randy Burns, Arkansas Bureau of Standards. Randy's comments were mostly editorial in nature. Dr. Charles Hurburgh, Iowa State University, mentioned that **NIR 2005,** the 12th International Conference on Near Infrared Spectroscopy, would be held April 10 - 15, 2005, in Auckland, New Zealand. He suggested that this would be an ideal time for TC17/SC8 to meet because all the recognized names in the field of Near Infrared Spectroscopy would be present. Dr. Hurburgh offered the following comments on the latest draft:

- There should be explicit mathematical descriptions in addition to statements for many terms.
- The MEPS in the table of tolerances are extremely tight for the United States where there is not variety release control and therefore much more variation in germplasm.
- There are many places where the basis of determination (i.e., the number of samples used) is not stated. The background statistics are always based on some number of observations.
- The draft defines a networked instrument as one that is linked, either electronically or manually under a quality system, to a certified measuring instrument and/or a whole grain certified reference material and/or the reference method of Annex A so that its performance may be monitored on a daily basis or according to a schedule set by the quality system administrator. I don't think the United States is ready to accept that a company with a certified quality management system is metrologically the same as if the instruments are actually electronically linked. This would be a huge policy change/modification for the UnitedSstates. I think it is the way to move, but not sure we are ready yet.
- The draft also states that networked instruments subject to a quality control system may be adjusted within the range of MPES to improve the accuracy of the instrument. This would not be consistent with U.S. metrological practice.
- The draft does not cover the case where calibrations have been derived on a moisture basis equal to Mref.
- Only one unit is required for type evaluation. One unit is not sufficient to verify that production meets type, nor does it allow testing for calibration transfer methods.

Dr. Hurburgh will be sending a complete write-up of his comments with detailed comments/suggestions to Diane Lee.

Because several of the members of TC17/SC8 are also members of TC17/SC1 (OIML R59 Moisture Meters For Cereal Grain and Oilseeds), which met in Paris in September 20 - 21, 2004, it had been proposed that the next meeting of TC17/SC8 to discuss the latest draft of the "Outline of a Recommendation on Protein Measuring Instruments for Cereal Grain" be held in Paris the day following the TC17/SC1 meeting. The TC17/SC8 meeting was not held following the TC17/SC1 meeting.

NTEP Committee 2005 Interim Report
Appendix B – NTETC - GMM and NIR Sectors

2004 GMM/NIR Sector Meeting Attendees
Kansas City, MO - August 26 & 27

John W. Barber
J B Associates
10349 Old Indian Trail
Glenarm, IL 62536
(217)483-4232, FAX:
Email: jbarber@motion.net

Cathleen Brenner
USDA GIPSA FGIS
10383 North Ambassador Drive
Kansas City, MO 64153-1394
(816)891-0486, FAX: (816)891-8070
Email: Cathleen.A.Brenner@usda.gov

Victor Gates
Shore Sales Company
1112 Enterprise Drive
Rantoul, IL 61866
(217)892-2544, FAX: (217)892-4281
Email: vgates_shore@msn.com

Andrew Gell
Foss North America
11 Edvac Drive, Unit 10
Brampton, Ontario L6S 5W5
CANADA
(905)793-6440, FAX: (905)793-6719
Email: agell@fossnorthamerica.com

Charles R. Hurburgh, Jr.
Iowa State University
1541 Food Science
Ames, IA 50011-1061
(515)294-8629, FAX: (515)294-6383
Email: tatry@iastate.edu

John Kennedy
Perten Instruments
6444 South 6th Street Road
Springfield, IL 62707
(217)585-9440, FAX: (217)585-9441
Email: jkennedy@perten.com

David James Krejci
Grain Elevator & Processing Society
301 Fourth Avenue S PO Box 15026
Minneapolis, MN 55415-0026
(612)339-4625, FAX: (612)339-4644
Email: david@geaps.com

G. Diane Lee
NIST
Building 820, 100 Bureau Drive MS 2600
Gaithersburg, MD 20899-2600
(301)975-4405, FAX: (301)926-0647
Email: diane.lee@nist.gov

Stephen Patoray
National Conf. on Weights & Measures
1239 Carolina Drive
Tryon, NC 28782
(828)859-6178, FAX: (828)859-6180
Email: spatoray@mgmtsol.com

Richard Pierce
USDA GIPSA Tech Services Division
Inspection Systems Engineering Branch
10383 North Ambassador Drive
Kansas City, MO 64153-1394
(816)891-0430, FAX: (816)891-8070
Email: Richard.O.Pierce@usda.gov

Cassie Eigenmann Pierson
DICKEY-john Corporation 5200
Dickey-john Road Auburn, IL 62615
(217)438-2294, FAX: (217)438-2635
Email: ceigenmann@dickey-john.com

James Rampton
USDA GIPSA FCIS
10383 N. Ambassador Drive
Kansas City, MO 64153-1394
(816)891-0450, FAX: (816)891-8070
Email: James.H.Rampton@usda.gov

Thomas E. Runyon
Seedburo Equipment Co
1022 W Jackson Blvd
Chicago, IL 60607-2990
(312)738-3700, FAX: (312)738-3544
Email: trunyon@seedburo.com

Bob Sadler
Dickey-john Corporation
5200 Dickey-john Road
Auburn, IL 62615
(217)438-2615, FAX: (217)438-6012
Email: bsadler@dickey-john.com

Cheryl A. Tew
North Carolina Department of Agriculture
Consumer Services Bldg.
1001 Mail Service Center
Raleigh, NC 27699-1050
(919)733-4411, FAX: 919-733-8804
Email: cheryl.tew@ncmail.net

NTEP Committee 2005 Interim Report
Appendix C – NTETC - Measuring Sector

Appendix C

National Type Evaluation Technical Committee
Measuring Sector Annual Meeting

October 21 - 22, 2004, Gulfport, Mississippi
Summary of Decisions

National Type Evaluation Technical Committee..1
1. Recommendations to Update to NCWM Publication 14 to Reflect Changes to NIST Handbook 44............1
Carry-over Items:...3
2. On-Screen Display of G.S.1. Requirements for Software-Based Built-for-Purpose Devices..........................3
3. Testing Required for an Electronic Indicator with a CC Interfaced with a Measuring Element with a CC Not Previously Evaluated Together..7
4. Tolerance for Product Depletion Test..9
5. Product Family Tables for MAG Meters...11
6. Acceptable Symbols or Wording to Identify Unit Price, Total Price, and Quantity on a Retail Motor-Fuel Dispenser..12
New Items:..12
7. Section E Meter Sizes to be Included on a Certificate of Conformance...12
8. Products to be covered on a Certificate of Conformance for a Meter Tested with Gasoline and/or Diesel Fuel...13
9. NTEP Tolerances for Meters with Different Flow Rates when Using Different Size Provers...................15
10. Testing Required to Upgrade a RMFD from Audit Trail Category 2 to Category 3..................................17
11. Specific Gravity Range to be Covered on a Certificate of Conformance Based on Products Tested........20
12. Computer Jump on RMFD...20
13. Section D Product Family for Mass Flow Meters – Specific Gravity Range 0.1 Above and 0.1 Below Products Tested...21
14. Section D Product Family for Mass Flow Meters – Multi-product Applications......................................22
15. Next Meeting..24
Additional Items..24
16. ECRs Approved for Dispensers from Multiple Manufacturers...24
17. Zero Set-back Interlocks on Vehicle-tank Meters...24
18. Wireless Communication Systems...25
19. Display of Unit Price on Vehicle-Tank Meters...25
20. Evaluations Using Simulated Input Devices...25
21. Modifications to Pre-NTEP Certificates:..26

Details of All Items
(In Order by Reference Key Number)

1. Recommendations to Update to NCWM Publication 14 to Reflect Changes to NIST Handbook 44

Source: NIST/WMD

Background: The 89th National Conference on Weights and Measures (NCWM) adopted the following items that will be reflected in the 2005 Edition of NIST Handbook 44 and NCWM Publication 14. These items are part of the agenda to inform the Measuring Sector of the NCWM actions and recommend changes to NCWM Publication 14.

Recommendation: The Sector will review and, if acceptable, recommend to the NTEP Committee adoption of the following changes to Publication 14 based on changes to NIST Handbook 44:

A. S.2.2.1. Multiple Measuring Devices with a Single Provision for Sealing

Background: During its 2004 Annual Meeting, the NCWM agreed to add a new paragraph to NIST Handbook 44, Section 3.30. Liquid-Measuring Devices S.2.2.1. Multiple Measuring Elements with a Single Provision for Sealing as follows:

> S.2.2.1. Multiple Measuring Elements with a Single Provision for Sealing. - A change to the adjustment of any measuring element shall be individually identified.
> [Nonretroactive as of January 1, 2005]
>
> Note: Examples of acceptable identification of a change to the adjustment of a measuring element include but are not limited to:
>
> (a) a broken, missing, or replaced physical seal on an individual measuring element,
> (b) a change in a calibration factor for each measuring element,
> (c) display of the date of or the number of days since the last calibration event for each measuring element or,
> (d) a counter indicating the number of calibration events per measuring element.

Recommendation: Add a new Code Reference S.2.2.1. to Section 9, of the Liquid-Measuring Devices Checklist and Test Procedures of NCWM Pulication 14, Measuring Devices, 2004 edition as follows:

Code Reference: S.2.2.1. Multiple Measuring Devices with a Single Provision for Sealing

> 9.6 S.2.2.1. Multiple Measuring Elements with a Single Provision for Sealing. - A change to the adjustment of any measuring element shall be individually identified.
>
> Note: Examples of acceptable identification of a change to the adjustment of a measuring element include but are not limited to:
>
> (a) a broken, missing, or replaced physical seal on an individual measuring element,
> (b) a change in a calibration factor for each measuring element,
> (c) display of the date of or the number of days since the last calibration event for each measuring element or,
> (d) a counter indicating the number of calibration events per measuring element.

Renumber succeeding Section 9 paragraphs accordingly.

B. S.4.4.2. Location of Marking Information

Background: During its 2004 Annual Meeting, the NCWM agreed to amend Handbook 44 Section 3.30. Liquid-Measuring Devices paragraph S.4.4.2. Location of Marking Information as follows:

> **S.4.4.2. Location of Marking Information; Retail Motor-Fuel Dispensers.** - *The required marking information in the General Code, Paragraph G-S.1. shall appear as follows:*
>
> (a) ~~Placement of this information shall not be on a portion of the device that can be readily removed or interchanged without the use of a tool separate from the device.~~ shall be within 24 to 60 inches from the base of the dispenser;
>
> (b) ~~The information shall appear 24 to 60 inches from the base of the dispenser when placed on the outside of the device.~~

may be internal and/or external provided the information is permanent and easily read;

(c) ~~When placed behind an access door or panel the information shall appear 24 inches to 60 inches from the base of the dispenser in a readily legible position. The use of a dispenser key shall not be considered a tool separate from the device.~~ shall be on a portion of the device that cannot be readily removed or interchanged (i.e., not on a service access panel).

~~Note: the use of a dispenser key or tool to access internal marking information is permitted.~~

[Nonretroactive as of January 1, 2003]
(Added 2002) (Amended 2004)

Recommendation: Modify Section 11, paragraph 11.3. of the Liquid-Measuring Devices Checklist and Test Procedures of NCWM Pulication 14, Measuring Devices, 2004 edition as follows:

Code Reference: S.4.4.2. Location of Marking Information

11.3. The required marking information in the General Code, paragraph G-S.1. shall be located as follows:

(a) ~~Placement of this information shall not be on a portion of the device that can readily removed or interchanged without the use of a tool separate from the device.~~ shall be within 24 to 60 inches from the base of the dispenser;

(b) ~~When placed on the outside to the device the information shall appear 24 to 60 inches from the base of the dispenser.~~ may be internal and/or external provided the information is permanent and easily read;

(c) ~~When placed behind an access door or panel the information shall appear 24 inches to 60 inches from the base of the dispenser in a readily legible position. The use of a dispenser key shall not be considered a tool separate from the device.~~ shall be on a portion of the device that cannot be readily removed or interchanged (i.e., not on a service access panel).

Note: the use of a dispenser key or tool to access internal marking information is permitted.

Decision: The Sector reviewed, accepted, and recommends the NTEP Committee adopt the proposed changes to NCWM Publication 14.

Carry-over Items:

2. On-Screen Display of G.S.1. Requirements for Software-Based Built-for-Purpose Devices

Source: Returned from NCWM S&T Committee

Background: At its 2003 Annual Meeting, the NCWM adopted a proposal that provides alternate methods, other than physical marking, for meeting some of the requirements of Handbook 44 G-S.1. for "not-built-for-purpose" devices. At that meeting the NCWM S&T Committee also reviewed an SMA proposal that provided similar alternate marking methods for "built-for-purpose" devices. The S&T Committee concluded that the proposal for "built-for-purpose" devices required further review and development by the NTETC Technical Sectors and the regional weights and measures associations.

Prior to the October 2003 NTETC Measuring Sector Meeting, the WMD NTETC technical advisors developed an alternate proposal to modify G.S.1. and add a Table G.S.1. that provided alternate methods other than physical markings for meeting some of the requirements of G-S.1. for both "not-built-for-purpose" and "built-for-purpose" devices.

At its 2003 meeting, the Measuring Sector agreed with the WMD proposal in principle, but recommended some small changes to simplify the table. The Sector agreed to forward the modified proposal for G-S.1. in tabular format to the NCWM S&T Committee for consideration.

At the 2004 NCWM Annual Meeting during the open hearing, the SMA stated that S&T Item 310-1, the proposal to modify G-S.1., should not go forward for a vote because a ballot of the Weighing Sector on the proposal failed to provide clear support for the item. A manufacturer stated that the term "microprocessor" is not appropriate because their devices contain numerous microprocessors. Another manufacturer stated that the requirement for marking the current software version number would place an unrealistic burden on their company. The Committee agreed that sufficient opposition and questions were raised during the open hearing to demonstrate the item is not sufficiently developed to be a voting item at that meeting. The Committee agreed to make Item 310-1 an information item to be returned to the Weighing and Measuring Sectors for further development.

Recommendation: G-S.1. Identification. - WMD has revised language in the 2004 S&T Agenda Item 310-1. Additions and changes to the proposal to the 2004 S&T Agenda Item 310-1 are highlighted in gray text.

Add new General Code Terms and Definitions as follows:

> **measuring device (general)** – a device (instrument) intended to be used to make measurements, alone or in conjunction with supplementary devices. (VIM)
>
> **measuring system (general)** - an instrument or group of instruments that serve to make measurements, alone or in conjunction with supplementary devices. (VIM)
>
> **electronic devices** – a device operating by the principles of electronics, which may consist of one or more subassemblies and perform a specific function(s). (ASTM)
> or
> **electronic measuring device** – a measuring instrument intended to measure a quantity using electronic means and/or equipped with electronic devices. (D11)
>
> **not-built-for-purpose device.** Any electronic peripheral or auxiliary device or element which was not originally manufactured with the intent that it be used as, or part of, a weighing or measuring device or system.
>
> **metrological revision** – a revision to a measuring instrument, device, or system that affects its metrological integrity (e.g., physical modifications or modifications to embedded, programmable, or downloadable software).

Amend the definition of built-for-purpose device as follows:

> **built-for-purpose device** – any main, ~~peripheral, or auxiliary~~ device or element which was manufactured with the intent that it be used as, or part of, a ~~weighing or~~ measuring device or system.

Amend General Code paragraph G-A.1. Commercial and Law Enforcement Equipment as follows:

> **G-A.1. Commercial and Law Enforcement Equipment.** - These specifications, tolerances, and other technical requirements apply as follows:
>
> > (a) To commercial ~~weighing and measuring devices or systems~~ equipment, that is, to weights and measures ~~weighing~~ and measuring devices ~~or systems~~ commercially used or employed in establishing the ~~size,~~ quantity, ~~extent, area, or~~ measurement of quantities, things, ~~produce, or articles for~~ distribution or consumption, purchased, offered, or submitted for sale, hire, or award, or in computing any basic charge or payment for services rendered on the basis of quantity determination weight or measure.

(b) To any accessory attached to or used in connection with a commercial weighing or measuring device when such accessory is so designed that its operation affects the accuracy of the device.

(c) To weighing and measuring devices or systems equipment in official use for the enforcement of law or for the collection of statistical information by government agencies.

(These requirements should be used as a guide by the weights and measures official when, upon request, courtesy examinations of noncommercial equipment are made.)

Amend General Code paragraph G-S.1. Identification as follows:

G-S.1. Identification. - All equipment, except weights and separate parts necessary to the measurement process, but not having any metrological effect, shall be clearly marked **in accordance with Table G-S.1**, for the purposes of identification, with the following information:

(a) the name, initials, or trademark of the manufacturer or distributor;

(b) a model designation that positively identifies the pattern, or design, or metrological revision of the device;

(c) the model designation shall be prefaced by the term "Model," "Type," or "Pattern." These terms may be followed by the term "Number" or an abbreviation of that word. The abbreviation for the word "Number" shall, as a minimum, begin with the letter "N" (e.g., No or No.). The abbreviation for the word "Model" shall be "Mod" or "Mod."
[Nonretroactive January 1, 2003]
(Added 2000) (Amended 2001)

[Note: Prefix lettering may be initial capitals, all capitals or all lower case.]

(d) except for equipment with no moving or electronic component parts and not-built-for-purpose, software-based electronic devices, a nonrepetitive serial number;
[Nonretroactive as of January 1, 1968]

(e) for not-built-for-purpose, software-microprocessor-based devices the current software version designation or revision number;
(Added 2003)

(ef) the serial number shall be prefaced by words, an abbreviation, or a symbol, that clearly identifies the number as the required serial number; and
[Nonretroactive as of January 1, 1986]

(fg) the serial number shall be prefaced by the words "Serial Number" or an abbreviation of that term. Abbreviations for the word "Serial" shall, as a minimum, begin with the letter "S," and abbreviations for the word "Number" shall, as a minimum, begin with the letter "N" (e.g., S/N, SN, Ser. No, and S No.).
[Nonretroactive as of January 1, 2001]

(gh) for devices that have an NTEP Certificate of Conformance (CC), the CC Number or a corresponding CC addendum number prefaced by the terms "NTEP CC," "CC," or "Approval." These terms may be followed by the term "Number" or an abbreviation of that word. The abbreviation for the word "Number" shall, as a minimum, begin with the letter "N" (e.g., No or No.).
[Nonretroactive as of January 1, 2003]

The required information shall be so located that it is readily observable without the necessity of the disassembly of a part requiring the use of any means separate from the device.
(Amended 1985, 1991, 1999, 2000, 2001 and 2003)

Delete General Code paragraph G-S.1.1. Location of Marking Information for Not-Built-for-Purpose, Software-Based Devices and renumber G-S.1.2. Remanufactured Devices and Remanufactured Main Elements as follows:

G-S.1.1. Location of Marking Information for Not-Built-for-Purpose, Software-Based Devices. - For not-built-for-purpose, software-based devices, the following shall apply:

~~(a) the manufacturer or distributor and the model designation shall be continuously displayed or marked on the device (see note below); or~~

~~(b) the Certificate of Conformance (CC) Number shall be continuously displayed or marked on the device (see note below); or~~

~~(c) all required information in G-S.1. Identification. (a), (b), (c), (e), and (h) shall be continuously displayed. Alternatively, a clearly identified "view only" System Identification, G-S.1. Identification, or Weights and Measures Identification shall be accessible through the "Help" menu. Required information includes that information necessary to identify that the software in the device is the same type that was evaluated.~~

~~Note: Clear instructions for accessing the remaining required G-S.1. information shall be listed on the CC. Required information includes that information necessary to identify that the software in the device is the same type that was evaluated.~~
~~[Nonretroactive as of January 1, 2004]~~
~~(Added 2003)~~

G-S.1.1~~2~~. Remanufactured Devices and Remanufactured Main Elements. - *All remanufactured devices and remanufactured main elements shall be clearly and permanently marked for the purposes of identification with the following information:*

(a) the name, initials, or trademark of the last remanufacturer or distributor;

(b) the remanufacturer's or distributor's model designation if different than the original model designation.
[Nonretroactive as of January 1, 2002]
(Added 2001)

Note: Definitions for "manufactured device," "repaired device," and "repaired element" are also included (along with definitions for "remanufactured device" and "remanufactured element") in Appendix D, Definitions.

Add new Table G-S.1. Identification as follows:

	Table G-S.1. Identification	
	Built-for-Purpose Instruments, Elements, or Systems	Not-Built-for-Purpose Devices or Elements
Name, initials, or trademark of the manufacturer or distributor	~~M~~ D	$-^2$
Model designation ~~M~~	$-^1$	D^2
Specific model designation	M^1 or D	
Serial number ~~M~~	—	Not required
Metrological revision designation^3	~~M or D~~ D	—
Certificate of Conformance (CC) number	~~M or D~~ D	$-^2$

Table G.S.1 Identification		
	Built-for-Purpose Instruments, Elements, or Systems	Not-Built-for-Purpose Devices or Elements
M:	Physically and permanently marked	
D:	Either: (1) displayed by accessing a clearly identified "view only" System Identification, G.S.1 Identification, or Weights and MeasuresIdentification accessible through the "Help" menu. Required information includes that information necessary to identify that the software in the device is the same type that was evaluated, or (2) continuously displayed. Note: For revision or software version number, clear instructions for accessing this information shall be listed on the CC in lieu of the "Help" menu. Required information includes that information necessary to identify that the software in the device is the same or subsequent type that was evaluated. (Nonretroactive as of January 2004)	
Note 1:	As a minimum, the model designation (positively identifying the pattern, design, type, series, generic, or trademark designation) must be marked on the device. If the model designation changes with differing parameters such as size, features, options, intended application, not Handbook 44 compliant, construction, etc., the specific model designation shall be physically marked or continuously displayed or be capable of being displayed. (Nonretroactive as of January 200X)	
Note 2:	As a minimum, either the manufacturer or distributor and the model designation, or the CC Number shall be continuously displayed. Clear instructions for accessing the remaining required G.S.1 information shall be listed on the CC, which may be available as an unaltered copy of the CC printed by the device or through another on-site device. (Nonretroactive as of January 200X)	
Note 3:	Metrological revision designation may include hardware or software revision (version).	

Decision: The Sector discussed the amended WMD proposal and the recommendations of the 2004 Weighing Sector and agreed to forward a recommendation the NCWM S&T Committee that Item 310-1 be withdrawn from the 2005 S&T Agenda.

3. Testing Required for an Electronic Indicator with a CC Interfaced with a Measuring Element with a CC Not Previously Evaluated Together

Source: Returned from NCWM S&T Committee

Background: Prior to the October 2003 Measuring Sector Meeting, a work group submitted a proposal to add a new paragraph N.X. to Handbook 44 Sections 3.30., 3.31., 3.32., and 3.37. and an alternate proposal to add a new Section T. to Publication 14, for consideration. The work group proposed a new section 44 to be added to the Liquid-Measuring Devices Checklist and Test Procedures of Publication 14, 2003 Edition.

At its 2003 meeting, the Measuring Sector agreed to forward the following Proposal 1 for addition to Publication 14 to the NCWM NTEP Committee for consideration, and the following Proposal 2 to the NCWM S&T Committee for consideration. The Sector strongly believed that, for the benefit of weights and measures officials, the proposed test notes for determining the compatibility of the various components of a weighing of measuring system need to be added to the General Code Section of Handbook 44.

Proposal 1. Add a new section "T" to Publication 14 to guide NTEP Inspectors as to when additional testing is necessary to determine compatibility between components as follows:

Testing Required to Interface Components with Individual CC's that were Not Previously Tested Together.

Additional testing by an NTEP Participating Laboratory is not required if an electronic indicator is interfaced to a measuring element provided all of the following are true:

a) the communication means for the input to the electronic indicator (pulse, frequency, serial, etc.) has been previously tested with a measuring element listed on a CC;
b) the communication means for the output of the measuring element (pulse, frequency, serial, etc.) has been previously tested with an electronic indicator listed on a CC;
c) the communication means to be used for the electronic indicator input is the same as the communication means to be used for the measuring element output (pulse-pulse, frequency-frequency, serial-serial, etc.) and both devices are being used within the current parameters listed on their respective CCs;
d) the devices are communicating with each other and the system in which they are installed can be accurately calibrated; and
e) if required, Handbook 44 compliant tickets can be printed.

Note: NTEP may require initial or complete evaluation of new technologies or applications.

Add additional checklist section 44 (Page LMD XX) to Publication 14 as follows:

44. Additional Checklist and Test Procedures for Interfacing Components

When examining the interface between electronic indicator and a measuring element, the following must be considered:

44.1	Does the electronic indicator have a CC?	Yes ☐ No	☐
44.2	Is the electronic indicator being used within the application limits of the CC?	Yes ☐ No	☐
44.3	Does the measuring element have a CC?	Yes ☐ No	☐
44.4	Is the measuring element being used within the application limits of the CC?	Yes ☐ No	☐
44.5	Can the system in which both devices are installed be accurately calibrated?	Yes ☐ No	☐
44.6	Can a ticket (if required) be properly printed?	Yes ☐ No	☐
44.7	Are interfaces, other than mechanical or pulse interfaces (e.g., 4-20 mA or frequency interfaces), being used as defined by the appropriate CC?	Yes ☐ No	☐

Proposal 2. Add a new paragraph G-N.3. Compatibility of Indicators and Weighing or Measuring Elements to Handbook 44 to clarify what requirements must be met to interface an indicating element and a weighing or measuring element when each element has its own CC listing compatible communication specifications, but such elements have not been previously evaluated together on a single NTEP CC.

G-N.3. Compatibility of Indicators and Weighing or Measuring Elements. – To be considered compatible, the following conditions shall be met:

(a) the communication means used for the input to the electronic indicator (analog, digital, pulse, frequency, serial, etc.) has been previously evaluated with a weighing or measuring element;

(b) the communication means used for the output of the weighing or measuring element (analog, digital, pulse, frequency, serial, etc.) has been previously evaluated with an electronic indicator;

(c) the communication means used for the electronic indicator input is the same as the communication means used for the weighing and measuring element output (analog-analog, digital-digital, pulse-pulse, frequency-frequency, serial-serial, etc.);

(d) **the elements are communicating with each other and the device or system into which they are installed can be accurately calibrated; and**

(e) **if required, Handbook 44 compliant tickets can be printed.**

At the 2004 NCWM Interim Meeting, the NTEP Committee approved the addition of the information contained in Proposal 1 above to the 2004 Edition of Publication 14. The S&T Committee heard several comments indicating that the proposal to add a new paragraph G-N.3. Compatibility of Indicators and Weighing or Measuring Elements to Handbook 44 is not sufficiently developed to move forward. One manufacturer stated that his company manufactures measuring and indicating elements or components that can be interfaced to provide a complete measuring system. He believes this item needs to be in Handbook 44 for the use of the field official and that the proposal as written provides at least some guidance on compatibility of components. The Committee agreed that the item is not sufficiently developed to move forward. The Committee decided to withdraw the proposal from the S&T Committee agenda until it is further developed and resubmitted by the NTETC Weighing and Measuring Sectors.

Recommendation: The Sector needs to determine if it wants to continue to develop language to be added to Handbook 44 or if the information added to Publication 14 is sufficient to address the original concerns of manufacturers regarding when additional testing is necessary to determine compatibility between components.

Decision: The members generally agreed that the language added to Publication 14 last year was sufficient to address the original concerns of manufacturers regarding when additional testing is necessary to determine compatibility between components. The Sector did not propose any new language for Handbook 44 be submitted to the NCWM S&T Committee for consideration. The Sector agreed that the item should be dropped from the Measuring Sector's Agenda.

4. Tolerance for Product Depletion Test

Source/Background: At its October 2003 meeting, the Sector agreed to forward the following proposal to the NCWM S&T Committee for consideration.

N.4.2. Special Tests (Except Milk-Measuring Systems), N.4.5. Product Depletion Test, and T.5. Product Depletion Test

N.4.2. Special Tests (Except Milk-Measuring Systems). - "Special" tests shall be made to develop the operating characteristics of a measuring system and any special elements and accessories attached to or associated with the device. Any test except as set forth in N.4.4.1. or N.4.5. shall be considered a special test. Special tests of a measuring system shall be made ~~as follows:~~

~~(a)~~ ~~A~~at a minimum discharge rate of 20 % of the marked maximum discharge rate or at the minimum discharge rate marked on the device, whichever is less.

~~(b) To develop operating characteristics of the measuring system during a split compartment delivery.~~

N.4.5. Product Depletion Test. - The effectiveness of the vapor eliminator shall be tested by depleting the product supply and continuing until the lack of fluid causes the meter indication to stop completely for at least 10 seconds. If the meter indication fails to stop completely for at least 10 seconds, continue to operate the system for 3 minutes. The test shall be completed by switching to another compartment with sufficient product on a multi-compartment vehicle, or by adding sufficient product to a single-compartment vehicle. When adding product to a single-compartment vehicle, allow appropriate time for any entrapped vapor to disperse before continuing the test.
(Added 200X)

~~T.5. Product Depletion Test. - The difference in the delivered volumes for the normal test and the product depletion test shall not exceed the tolerance shown in Table T.5, and all test results shall be within applicable tolerances.~~

~~Table T.5. Tolerances For Vehicle Tank Meters On Product Depletion Tests, Except Milk Meters~~

~~Manufacturer's rated capacity (Maximum gpm)~~	~~Maintenance and acceptance tolerances~~
~~Up to 125 125~~	~~in³~~
~~126 to 250 200~~	~~in³~~
~~251 to 500 300~~	~~in³~~
~~501 to 750 400~~	~~in³~~
~~Over 751 600~~	~~in³~~

At the 2004 NCWM Interim Meeting, the Meter Manufacturers Association (MMA) voiced support for the intent of the alternative proposal submitted by the NTETC Measuring Sector provided T.4. is modified by removing the words "and all test results shall be within applicable tolerances." A Maryland Weights and Measures official noted that the proposal if modified as the MMA recommends provides a substantial change in tolerance; however, Maryland is in favor of the concept because the tolerance for a given meter is not linked to the size of the prover used for testing. A New York official stated that a product depletion test should be viewed as the test of a "disturbance," similar to a test for radio frequency interference (RFI) on a scale. New York preferred a tolerance expressed as a flat percentage and suggested a tolerance of 0.5 % of the meter's marked maximum flow rate over the step tolerances in the proposed Table T.5. A representative from Measurement Canada indicated there is an opportunity for the United States and Canada to harmonize the requirement for a product depletion test. Canada is currently using a tolerance of 0.25 % of the meter's marked maximum flow rate applied to the product depletion test results; however, Measurement Canada is still conducting a study to determine if the 0.25 % tolerance is appropriate. The Committee agreed that Item 331-2 should remain an information item and be returned to the NTETC Measuring Sector for review and further development at its fall 2004 meeting.

Recommendation: Will Wothlie (Maryland NTEP Laboratory) and Dick Suiter (NIST) have developed a new proposal for consideration by the Sector. The amended proposal will harmonize Handbook 44 tolerances for product depletion tests with the Measurement Canada tolerances. The Sector was asked to review the following proposal and if the members agreed forward it to the NCWM S&T Committee for consideration.

   N.4.2. Special Tests (Except Milk-Measuring Systems). - "Special" tests shall be made to develop the operating characteristics of a measuring system and any special elements and accessories attached to or associated with the device. Any test except as set forth in N4.4.1. or **N.4.5.** shall be considered a special test. Special tests of a measuring system shall be made as follows:

   ~~(a)~~ ~~A~~at a minimum discharge rate of 20 % of the marked maximum discharge rate or at the minimum discharge rate marked on the device whichever is less;

   ~~(b) To develop operating characteristics of the measuring system during a split compartment delivery.~~

N.4.5. Product Depletion Test. - The effectiveness of the vapor eliminator shall be tested by depleting the product supply and continuing until the lack of fluid causes the meter indication to stop completely for at least 10 seconds. If the meter indication fails to stop completely for at least 10 seconds, continue to operate the system for 3 minutes. The test shall be completed by switching to another compartment with sufficient product on a multi-compartment vehicle, or by adding sufficient product to a single compartment vehicle. When adding product to a single compartment vehicle, allow appropriate time for any entrapped vapor to disperse before continuing the test.
   (Added 200X)

   T.5. Product Depletion Test. - The difference in the delivered volumes for the normal test and the product depletion test shall not exceed the tolerance shown in Table T.5.

Table T.5. Tolerances For Vehicle Tank Meters On Product Depletion Tests, Except Milk Meters	
Meter size	Maintenance and acceptance tolerances
Up to but not including 75 mm (3.0 inches)	2.25 liters (137 in^3)[1]
75 mm (3.0 inches) or larger	3.75 liters (229 in^3)[2]
[1] Based on a test volume of approximately 900 liters (238 gal)	
[2] Based on a test volume of approximately 1500 liters (396 gal)	

Example: "+ 25 cu in" error normal test, + or – 137 cu in, for product depletion total error; + 162 cu in or – 112 cu in.
Note: The result of the product depletion test may fall outside of the applicable test tolerance.

Decision: The Sector agreed to forward the proposal to the NCWM and Southern Weights and Measures Association S&T Committees for consideration, with the addition of an example and a note stating that the result of the product depletion test may fall outside of applicable tolerance as shown above.

5. Product Family Tables for MAG Meters

Source: Liquid Controls LLC

Background/ Discussion: At the 2002 Sector Meeting, a working group was formed to address the issue of product family criteria. The Sector will consider the recommendations of the work group.

Prior to the 2003 Sector Meeting the technical advisor was informed that this work group was not ready to present a recommendation; however, the work group requested that the item remain on the agenda for further development.

At the 2003 Sector Meeting, the Sector agreed that an expanded work group should be formed to develop family product tables for Mag Meters, Ultrasonic Meters, and Turbine Meters for consideration by the Sector at its next meeting. The members of the new work group are: Charlene Numrych (Liquid Controls), Chair; Richard Miller (FMC); Joe Buxton (Daniel Measurement & Control); and Randy Byrtus (Measurement Canada). Charlene volunteered to contact other manufacturers to invite them to participate in the work group.

The work group formed at the 2003 Sector Meeting identified four turbine meter manufacturers that could provide data on a variety of products measured using this type of meter. Only one mag meter manufacturer of three manufacturers identified has a certificate for products other than milk. No information has been gathered regarding manufacturers of ultrasonic meters. The work group does not have a proposal to present at this time, but plans to continue its work. A new Chair is needed for the work group because Charlene Numrych (Liquid Controls) is no longer available to perform that function.

Decision: The Sector agreed that a work group to develop a family products table limited to only turbine meters should be formed. The members of the new work group are: Joe Buxton (Daniel Measurement & Control), Chair; Ray Kalivoda (FMC); Joseph Beyer (Liquid Controls); Gary Castro (California NTEP); and Christian Lachance (Measurement Canada).

The Sector also agreed to form a separate work group to develop a family products table for mag meters. The members of the Mag Meter work group are: Joseph Beyer (Liquid Controls), Chair; Wade Matar (Invensys/Foxboro); Christian Lachance (Measurement Canada); and Michael Keilty (Endress+Hauser).

6. Acceptable Symbols or Wording to Identify Unit Price, Total Price, and Quantity on a Retail Motor-Fuel Dispenser

Source: Maryland NTEP Laboratory

Background: At the June 2002 NTEP Laboratory Meeting, one of the participating laboratories requested guidance on acceptable symbols or wording to identify the unit price, total sale, and quantity delivered on a retail motor-fuel dispenser. The laboratories recommended the question be added to the 2002 Measuring Sector Agenda.

At the 2002 Sector Meeting, a work group was formed to address this issue. The Sector will consider the recommendations of that work group.

No input has been received from the work group assigned to develop this issue following the 2002 Sector Meeting. If the Sector agrees, this item will be dropped from the agenda until a proposal is submitted for consideration.

Decision: The Sector agreed the work group should be disbanded and the NTEP Laboratories should develop a list of acceptable symbols at the next laboratory meeting. The Sector will review and consider the list of symbols at its 2005 meeting.

New Items:

7. Section E Meter Sizes to be Included on a Certificate of Conformance

Source: NTEP Director and NIST/WMD

Background: Section E states that "based upon the test of a meter (or meters) of only one size, meters one size larger and one size smaller than the meter that is tested and meeting the following criteria may be covered by the Certificate." In several cases Certificates of Conformance have been issued for a family of meter sizes where one meter size larger and/or one meter size smaller has been included above and/or below the largest and smallest meters that were actually tested. In some cases a manufacturer has asked to add an additional meter size to an existing CC where the "one size smaller or larger" has already been included and an additional larger or smaller meter, not on the existing CC, was submitted for evaluation.

Recommendation: The Sector is asked to determine if the current practice of adding additional sizes is acceptable and if Section E should be amended to provide criteria for adding additional sizes to a family of meter sizes based on meters tested.

Decision: The Sector agreed to forward the following amended Section E to the NTEP Committee for consideration.

    E. **Meter Sizes to be Included on a Certificate of Conformance**

~~To cover a family of meters on a Certificate of Conformance, if there are more than three meter sizes in a family, the largest and smallest meters in the family shall be submitted for evaluation. It is suggested that these meters represent the meter with the lowest minimum rated flow and the meter with the highest rated flow rate. Depending upon the range between the largest and smallest meters, additional meters may be required to be submitted for testing.~~

Based upon the test of a meter (or meters) ~~of only one size~~, meters ~~one size~~ larger and ~~one size~~ smaller than the meter(s) ~~that is~~ tested and meeting the following criteria may be covered by the Certificate:

1. meter sizes with rated maximum flow rates of 50 % to 200 % of the rated maximum flow rate of the meter tested; and

2. meter sizes with rated minimum flow rates of 50 % to 200 % of the rated minimum flow rate of the meter tested.

The maximum flow rate achieved in an installation is considered to be 80 % of the maximum flow rate to be listed on the Certificate of Conformance.

8. Products to be covered on a Certificate of Conformance for a Meter Tested with Gasoline and/or Diesel Fuel

Source: NTEP Laboratories

Background: Several Certificates of Conformance have been issued with a statement in the application section that states that the Retail Motor-fuel Device (RFMD) is approved for dispensing all motor fuels based on the testing of gasoline and diesel fuel. In many cases the RMFDs have been used for dispensing blends of gasoline and oxygenates such as ethanol, methanol, or MTBE with no problems. More recently RMFDs have been used for blends of petroleum diesel fuel and vegetable oil referred to as Biodiesel. The product family tables in Publication 14 have family categories and subgroups for refined petroleum products, vegetable oils, and for alcohols; however, there is no family or subgroup for blended products. Most gasoline ethanol blends (gasohol) are a blend of approximately 90 % gasoline and 10 % ethanol. For methanol blends and MTBE the percentage of oxygenate is typically less than 5 %. Biodiesel is typically a blend of up to 20 % vegetable-based oil with petroleum-based diesel fuel. However, there are alcohol/gasoline blends available where the ratio is reversed, such as E85 and M85 which are comprised of 85 % alcohol and 15 % gasoline. The question from the laboratories is "at what point is a Certificate no longer applicable to a blended product?"

The Sector was asked to provide guidelines on testing required for adding products, such as alcohol blends up to 10 % or Biodiesel blends up to 20 % to an existing certificate for a meter tested with gasoline and/or diesel fuel. Additional subgroups for the product family tables may be required to provide guidance as to when devices must be reevaluated to include the higher ratios of blended alcohols or vegetable oils.

Decision: The Sector agreed to forward the following amended product family tables for positive displacement meters in NCWM Publication 14 to the NTEP Committee for consideration.

C. Product Families for Positive Displacement Meters

Product Family	Product Subgroup	Typical Products[1]	Viscosity (Centipoise)	Specific Gravity[2]	% Abrasive Solids
Fuel Lubricant, Oil Products and Edible Oil Products	Refined Products	Diesel Fuel, Distillate[3], Gasoline[3,4], Fuel Oil, Kerosene, Light Oil, Spindle Oil, Lubricating Oils, SAE Grades, Bunker Oil, 6 Oil, Crude Oil, Asphalt, Vegetable Oil, etc.	0.3 to 2500	0.68 to 1.1	None
	Aviation Fuels	AVgas, Jet A, Jet A-1, Jet B, JP4, JP5, JP7, JP8, etc.	0.4 to 3.6	0.68 to 0.85	None
	Vegetable Oils	Cooking Oils, Sunflower Oil, Soy Oil, Peanut Oil, Olive Oil, etc.	20 to 300	0.8 to 1.0	None
Solvents	Solvents General	Acetates, Acetone, Esters, Ethylacetate, Hexane, MEK, Naphtha, Toluene, Xylene, etc.	0.3 to 7	0.6 to 1.6	None
	Solvents Chlorinated	Carbon Tetra-Chloride, Methylene-Chloride, Perchloro-Ethylene, Trichloro-Ethylene, etc.	0.3 to 7	0.6 to 1.6	None

Product Family	Product Subgroup	Typical Products[1]	Viscosity (Centipoise)	Specific Gravity[2]	% Abrasive Solids
Alcohol & Glycols	Alcohols, Glycols, & Water Mixes Thereof	Ethanol, Methanol, Butanol, Isopropyl, Isobutyl, Ethylene glycol, Propylene glycol, etc.	0.3 to 7	0.6 to 1.6	None
Liquefied Compressed Gases	Fuels and Refrigerants	LPG, Propane, Butane, Ethane, Freon 11, Freon 12, Freon 22, etc.	0.1 to 0.5	0.3 to 0.65	None
	NH_3	Anhydrous Ammonia	0.1	0.56 to 0.68	None
Water	Water	Tap Water, Deionized, Demineralized, Potable	1.0	1.0	None
Agricultural Liquids	Clear Liquid				
	Fertilizers	Nitrogen Solution; 28 %, 30 % or 32 %; 20 % Aqua-Ammonia; Urea; Ammonia Nitrate; N-P-K solutions; 10-34-0; 4-10-10; 9-18-9; etc.	10 to 400	1.0 to 1.45	None
	Crop Chemicals	Herbicides: Round-up, Touchdown, Banvel, Treflan, Paraquat, Prowl, etc	4 to 400	0.7 to 1.2	None
		Fungicides, Insecticides, Adjuvants, Fumigants	0.7 to 100	0.7 to 1.2	None
	Flowables	Dual, Bicep, Marksman, Broadstrike, Doubleplay, Topnotch, Gaurdsman, Harness, etc.	20 to 900	1 to 1.2	Nil to 3 %
	Crop Chemicals	Fungicides			
		Micronutrients			
	Suspensions				
	Fertilizers	3-10-30; 4-4-27, etc.	20 to 900	1.0 to 1.6	Nil to 4 %
	Liquid Feeds	Liquid Molasses; Molasses plus Phos Acid and/or Urea; etc.	10 to 50 000	1.2 to 1.5	Nil to 4 %
Chemicals	Chemicals	Sulfuric Acid, Hydrochloric Acid, Phosphoric Acid, etc	1.0 to 296	1.1 to 1.85	None

[1] NOTE: The Typical Products listed in this table are not limiting or all-inclusive; there may be other products and product trade names, which fall into a product family and product subgroup.

[2] The specific gravity of a liquid is the ratio of its density to that of water at standard conditions, usually 4 °C (or 20 °C) and 1 atm. The density of water at standard conditions is approximately 1000 kg/m^3 (or 998 kg/m^3)

[3] Diesel fuel blends (biodiesel) with up to 20 % vegetable or animal fat/oil.
[4] Gasoline includes oxygenated fuel blends with up to 15 % oxygenate.
Source for some of the viscosity value information is in the Industry Canada - Measurement Canada "Liquid Products Group, Bulletin V-16-E (rev. 1), August 3, 1999."

9. NTEP Tolerances for Meters with Different Flow Rates when Using Different Size Provers

Source: Maryland NTEP Laboratory

Background: During a recent evaluation of a high gallonage RMFD with marked flow rates of 60 gpm maximum and 12 gpm minimum, the Maryland NTEP laboratory found that the actual flow rate on the lowest setting of the automatic nozzle was 6 gpm. Several questions need to be addressed regarding this situation.

LMD Code paragraph N.4.2.2 (b) states "Devices marked with a flow-rate capacity of 100 L (25 gal) or more per minute, shall have a "special" test performed at the slowest of the following rates: (1) the minimum discharge rate marked on the device, or (2) the minimum discharge rate at which the device will deliver when equipped with an automatic discharge nozzle set at its slowest setting." Is it appropriate to operate the device below the marked minimum flow rate?

If a 10-gallon test measure is used, what is the appropriate tolerance applicable? LMD Code paragraph Table T.2. stipulates that the special test tolerance is 0.5 % or 11.55 cubic inches on a 10-gallon test draft; however, there is a footnote that states that the applicable acceptance tolerance when using a 10-gallon test draft is 5.5 cubic inches. Which tolerance should be applied during an NTEP evaluation? If a prover with a capacity greater than 10 gallons is used, does it provide a tolerance advantage over tests conducted with a 10-gal test measure?

General Code paragraph G-T.1. (e) states that acceptance tolerances apply to all equipment undergoing type evaluation. Does that mean that special test tolerances are not applicable during NTEP testing?

Recommendation: The Sector needs to determine what tolerances are appropriate for NTEP evaluations. The Sector may also want to recommend changes to Handbook 44 General Code G-T.1. and LMD Code paragraph N.4.2.2. and Table T2 as follows:

G-T.1. Acceptance Tolerances. - Acceptance tolerances shall apply to:

(a) **equipment to be put into commercial use for the first time;**

(b) **equipment that has been placed in commercial service within the preceding 30 days and is being officially tested for the first time;**

(c) **equipment that has been returned to commercial service following official rejection for failure to conform to performance requirements and is being officially tested for the first time within 30 days after corrective service;**

(d) **equipment that is being officially tested for the first time within 30 days after major reconditioning or overhaul; and**

(e) **equipment undergoing type evaluation** ~~(special test tolerances are not applicable)~~.

N.4.2.2. Retail Motor-Fuel Devices.

(a) Devices with a flow-rate capacity less than 100 L (25 gal) per minute shall have a "special" test performed at the slower of the following rates:

(1) **19 L (5 gal) per minute, or**

(2) **the minimum discharge rate marked on the device, or**

(3) **the minimum discharge rate at which the device will deliver when equipped with an automatic discharge nozzle set at its slowest setting** ~~provided it is not less than the marked minimum flow rate.~~

(b) Devices marked with a flow-rate capacity 100 L (25 gal) or more per minute shall have a "special" test performed at the slowest of the following rates:

   (1) **the minimum discharge rate marked on the device, or**

   (2) **the minimum discharge rate at which the device will deliver when equipped with an automatic discharge nozzle set at its slowest setting** ~~provided it is not less than the marked minimum flow rate.~~

Table T.2. Accuracy Classes for Liquid Measuring Devices Covered in NIST Handbook 44 Section 3.30					
Accuracy Class	Application	Acceptance Tolerance	Maintenance Tolerance	Special Test Tolerance
0.3	**Petroleum products delivered from large-capacity motor-fuel devices (**~~with marked maximum~~**) flow rates over 115 L/min (30 gpm))**, heated products at or greater than 50 °C, asphalt at or below temperatures 50 °C, all other liquids not shown where the typical delivery is over 200 L (50 gal).**	0.2 %	0.3 %	0.5 %
0.3A	Asphalt at temperatures greater than 50 °C	0.3 %	0.3 %	0.5 %
0.5*	**Petroleum products delivered from small-capacity (**~~at~~ **designed maximum flow rates of 4 L/min (1 gpm) through 115 L/min (30 gpm))** motor-fuel devices, agri-chemical liquids, and all other applications not shown where the typical delivery is** # **200 L (50 gal).**	0.3 %	0.5 %	0.5 %
1.1	**Petroleum products and other normal liquids from devices with flow rates** less than 1 gpm and devices designed to deliver less than one gallon.**	0.75 %	1.0 %	1.25 %
*For 5-gallon and 10-gallon test drafts, the tolerances specified for Accuracy Class 0.5 in the table above do not apply. For these test drafts, the maintenance tolerances on normal and special tests for 5-gallon and 10-gallon test drafts are 6 cubic inches and 11 cubic inches, respectively. Acceptance tolerances on normal and special tests are 3 cubic inches and 5.5 cubic inches. ** Flow rate refers to designed or marked maximum flow rate.				

(Added 2002)

Decision: The Sector modified the recommendation as shown below and agreed to forward it to the NCWM and Southern Weights and Measures Association S&T Committees for consideration.

Recommendation: Modify Handbook 44 Section 1.10 paragraph G-T.1. Acceptance Tolerances (e) and Section 3.30. paragraph N.4.2.2. Retail Motor-Fuel Devices as follows:

   G-T.1. Acceptance Tolerances. - Acceptance tolerances shall apply to:

   (a) **equipment to be put into commercial use for the first time;**

   (b) **equipment that has been placed in commercial service within the preceding 30 days and is being officially tested for the first time;**

(c) equipment that has been returned to commercial service following official rejection for failure to conform to performance requirements and is being officially tested for the first time within 30 days after corrective service;

(d) equipment that is being officially tested for the first time within 30 days after major reconditioning or overhaul; and

(e) equipment undergoing type evaluation ~~(special test tolerances are not applicable)~~.

N.4.2.2. **Retail Motor-Fuel Devices.**

(a) Devices with a flow-rate capacity less than ~~100~~ 115 L (~~25~~ 30 gal) per minute shall have a "special" test performed at the slower of the following rates:

(1) 19 L (5 gal) per minute, or

(2) the minimum discharge rate marked on the device, or

(3) the minimum discharge rate at which the device will deliver when equipped with an automatic discharge nozzle set at its slowest setting ~~provided it is not less than the marked minimum flow rate~~.

(b) Devices marked with a flow-rate capacity ~~100~~ 115 L (~~25~~ 30 gal) or more per minute shall have a "special" test performed at the slowest of the following rates:

(1) the minimum discharge rate marked on the device, or

(2) the minimum discharge rate at which the device will deliver when equipped with an automatic discharge nozzle set at its slowest setting ~~provided it is not less than the marked minimum flow rate~~.

10. Testing Required to Upgrade a RMFD from Audit Trail Category 2 to Category 3

Source: NTEP Director

Background/Discussion: Effective January 1, 2005, all devices with remote configuration capability must comply with the sealing requirements of Category 3. Several manufacturers have asked what level of testing is required to upgrade their Certificate of Conformance for a Category 2 device to cover a modification of their device to meet Category 3 requirements.

The Sector was asked to discuss the subject and provide input to the NTEP Committee regarding the amount of laboratory and/or field evaluation required to upgrade an existing certificate for a Category 2 device to cover an upgrade to Category 3.

Decision: The Sector agreed CC holders for liquid measuring devices with remote configuration capability that meet Category 2 sealing requirements must submit their device(s) for evaluation to verify the device meets Category 3 sealing requirements and have the CC upgraded. The Sector agreed to forward the following amended NCWM Publication Audit Trail Category Tables to the NTEP Committee for consideration.

Category 1 Devices (Devices with No Remote Configuration Capability):

The device is sealed with a physical seal or it has an audit trail with two event counters (one for calibration, the second for configuration).	Yes ☐ No ☐ N/A ☐
A physical seal must be applied without exposing electronics.	Yes ☐ No ☐ N/A ☐
Event counters are non-resettable and have a capacity of at least 000 to 999.	Yes ☐ No ☐ N/A ☐
Event counters increment appropriately.	Yes ☐ No ☐ N/A ☐
The audit trail information must be capable of being retained in memory for at least 30 days while the device is without power or must be retained in nonvolatile memory.	Yes ☐ No ☐ N/A ☐
Accessing the audit trail information for review shall be separate from the calibration mode.	Yes ☐ No ☐ N/A ☐
Accessing the audit trail information must not affect the normal operation of the device.	Yes ☐ No ☐ N/A ☐
Accessing the audit trail information shall not require removal of any additional parts other than normal requirements to inspect the integrity of a physical security seal. (e.g., a key to open a locked panel may be required).	Yes ☐ No ☐ N/A ☐

Category 2 Devices (Devices with Remote Configuration Capability but Controlled by Hardware):

Category 2 applies only to devices manufactured prior to January 1, 2005. Devices with remote configuration capability manufactured after that date must meet the sealing requirements outlined in Category 3. Devices without remote configuration capability manufactured after that date will be required to meet the minimum criteria outlined in Category 1.	~~Yes ☐ No ☐ N/A ☐~~
~~The physical hardware enabling access for remote communication must be on-site.~~	~~Yes ☐ No ☐ N/A ☐~~
~~The physical hardware must be sealable with a security seal or~~	~~Yes ☐ No ☐ N/A ☐~~
~~The device must be equipped with at least two event counters: one for calibration, the second for configuration parameters~~ ~~= calibration parameters event counter~~ ~~= configuration parameters event counter~~	~~Yes ☐ No ☐ N/A ☐~~
~~Adequate provision must be made to apply a physical seal without exposing electronics.~~	~~Yes ☐ No ☐ N/A ☐~~
~~Event counters are nonresettable and have a capacity of at least 000 to 999.~~	~~Yes ☐ No ☐ N/A ☐~~
~~Event counters increment appropriately.~~	~~Yes ☐ No ☐ N/A ☐~~
~~Event counters may be located either:~~ ~~= at the individual measuring device or~~ ~~= at the system controller~~	~~Yes ☐ No ☐ N/A ☐~~
~~If the counters are located at the system controller rather than at the individual device, means must be provided to generate a hard copy of the information through an on-site device.~~	~~Yes ☐ No ☐ N/A ☐~~
~~An adequate number (see table below) of event counters must be available to monitor the calibration and configuration parameters of each individual device.~~	~~Yes ☐ No ☐ N/A ☐~~
~~The device must either:~~ ~~= clearly indicate when it is in the remote configuration mode or~~ ~~= the device shall not operate while in the remote configuration mode.~~	~~Yes ☐ No ☐ N/A ☐~~

~~If capable of printing in the calibration mode, it must print a message that it is in the calibration mode.~~   Yes ☐ No ☐ N/A ☐

~~The audit trail information must be capable of being retained in memory for at least 30 days while the device is without power or must be retained in nonvolatile memory.~~   Yes ☐ No ☐ N/A ☐

~~The audit trail information must be readily accessible and easily read.~~   Yes ☐ No ☐ N/A ☐

~~Event counters located at the system controller must be provided with a means to generate a hard copy of the audit trail information.~~   Yes ☐ No ☐ N/A ☐

Category 3 Devices (Devices with Unlimited Remote Configuration Capability):

Category 3 devices have virtually unlimited access to sealable parameters or access is controlled though a password.

For devices manufactured after January 1, 2001, the device must either: - clearly indicate when it is in the remote configuration mode, or - the device shall not operate while in the remote configuration mode	Yes ☐ No ☐ N/A ☐
The device is equipped with an event logger	Yes ☐ No ☐ N/A ☐
The event logger automatically retains the identification of the parameter changed, the date and time of the change, and the new value of the parameter.	Yes ☐ No ☐ N/A ☐
Event counters are nonresettable and have a capacity of at least 000 to 999.	Yes ☐ No ☐ N/A ☐
The system is designed to attach a printer, which can print the contents of the audit trail.	Yes ☐ No ☐ N/A ☐
The audit trail information must be capable of being retained in memory for at least 30 days while the device is without power or must be retained in nonvolatile memory.	Yes ☐ No ☐ N/A ☐
The event logger must have a capacity to retain records equal to ten times the number of sealable parameters in the device, but not more than 1000 records are required.	Yes ☐ No ☐ N/A ☐
The event logger drops the oldest event when the memory capacity is full and a new entry is saved.	Yes ☐ No ☐ N/A ☐

Describe the method used to seal the device or access the audit trail information.

[NOTE: All devices with remote communication that are manufactured after January 1, 2005, must meet the requirements outlined for Category 3.]

Minimum Number of Counters Required		
	Minimum Counters Required for Devices Equipped with Event Counters	Minimum Event Counter(s) at System Controller
Only one type of parameter accessible (calibration or configuration)	One (1) event counter	One (1) event counter for each separately controlled device, or one (1) event counter, if changes are made simultaneously.
Both calibration and configuration parameters accessible	Two (2) event counters	Two (2) event counters for each separately controlled device, or two (2) or more event counters if changes are made to all controlled devices simultaneously.

11. Specific Gravity Range to be Covered on a Certificate of Conformance Based on Products Tested

Source: Invensys/Foxboro

Background: NCWM Publication 14 Section D. Product Family for Mass Flow Meters allows a Certificate of Conformance to cover only a range of specific gravities based on the products with the highest and lowest specific gravities tested. The specific gravity covered by a certificate can only be expanded by testing with additional products having a higher and/or lower specific gravity. The submitter believes the current limit on specific gravity range listed on a certificate is too restrictive and would like to have the range of specific gravities covered on a certificate within ± 25 % (or at least a minimum of 10 %) from the highest and lowest specific gravities for products evaluated.

Recommendation: The Sector will consider the proposal, and if there is sufficient support, a work group should be formed to collect data to support expanding the range of densities covered on a certificate based on the densities of products tested. If the data collected provides evidence that the range can be expanded, the work group should provide a specific proposal for expanding the range by an appropriate percentage for the Sector to consider at its next meeting.

Decision: The Sector agreed to combine agenda Item 11 with agenda Item 13 for discussion.

12. Computer Jump on RMFD

Source: Maryland NTEP Laboratory

Background: As price for motor fuel nears or exceeds $2.00 per gallon, the number of complaints regarding computer jump has also increased. WMD has received numerous calls from jurisdictions related to this problem. It appears that the actual amount of jump or meter creep occurring because of internal pressure related to changes in temperature has not changed. However, at the higher unit prices this relatively small meter creep creates a delivery indication of several cents.

Recommendation: The Sector and the manufacturers of RMFDs may want to take a proactive role and develop a proposal for Handbook 44 to require that the measurement of product begins only after the system has reached normal delivery pressure. The Sector will review the following recommendation, and if it agrees, the recommendation will be forwarded to the NCWM S&T Committee for consideration.

S.1.6. **Operating Requirements, Retail Devices (Except Slow Flow Meters).**

S.1.6.1. **Indication of Delivery.** - The device shall automatically show on its face the initial zero condition and the quantity delivered (up to the nominal capacity).

~~However, the first 0.03 L (or 0.009 gal) of a delivery and its associated total sales price need not be indicated.~~

~~S.1.6.1.1. - The indication of delivered quantity and total price on a digital device shall be inhibited until the entire fuel delivery system reaches normal operating pressure.~~
(Amended 1982 and 200X)

Decision: The Sector amended the recommendation as shown below and agreed to forward it to the NCWM and Southern Weights and Measures Association S&T Committees for consideration.

Amend Handbook 44 Sec. 3.30. paragraph S.1.6.1. Indication of Delivery and add new paragraph S.1.6.1.1. Inhibiting Measurement and Indication of Delivery as follows:

S.1.6. **Operating Requirements, Retail Devices (Except Slow Flow Meters).**

S.1.6.1. **Indication of Delivery.** - The device shall automatically show on its face the initial zero condition and the quantity delivered (up to the nominal capacity).

However, the first 0.03 L (or 0.009 gal) of a delivery and its associated total sales price need not be indicated.

~~S.1.6.1.1. - After the suppression of up to 0.03 L (or 0.009 gal) the measurement of delivered quantity and indication of total price on a digital device shall be inhibited until the fueling position reaches normal delivery pressure.~~
(Amended 1982 and 200X)

13. Section D Product Family for Mass Flow Meters – Specific Gravity Range 0.1 Above and 0.1 Below Products Tested

Source: Endress & Hauser Flowtec AG

Background: Once tested with two liquids within a product group, a mass flow meter should be covered for liquids with specific gravities of 0.1 above and 0.1 below the range of specific gravities for the liquid(s) tested.

Recommendation: Add additional language to Section D, Page LMD 4 of Publication 14, 2004 edition as follows:

D. **Product Families for Mass Flow Meters**

When submitting a direct mass flow meter for evaluation, the manufacturer must specify the product or product group for which the meter is being submitted. To cover a product group, NTEP tests must be conducted with two liquids within the product group. Upon test completion, a range of specific gravities between the specific gravities of the two liquids attained within the product group will be covered on the Certificate of Conformance (CC). ~~The mass flow meter will be covered for approved liquids with density 0.1 above the highest specific gravity tested and 0.1 below the lowest specific gravity tested.~~ The specific gravity range within the product group can be expanded by conducting an NTEP test with a liquid of higher or lower specific gravity than is covered on the existing CC.

The above does not apply to the following product groups: compressed gases, compressed liquids, and cryogenic liquids. In the case of these product groups, only one liquid within each group is required to undergo an NTEP evaluation, and, upon completion, the entire product group will be covered on the existing CC.

Multi-product applications (i.e., applications in which the meter will be used without a change to zero or calibration to dispense different products which vary in specific gravity by more than 0.1) must include a multi-product test. The multi-product initial test will be performed on the meter without a change to zero or calibration using multiple products having a difference in specific gravity of at least 0.2. For devices which will be used to dispense multiple products having a specific gravity range greater than 0.2, the multi-product testing must be performed over the anticipated range before multi-product applications will be included on the CC. For the multi-product testing, throughput testing will be performed on one or a combination of the products; testing for the subsequent test will be conducted on both products without a change to zero or calibration. Multi-product testing requirements do not apply to meters used to dispense a product such as propane in which the density varies in normal operation.

Decision: The Sector agreed to forward the following amended first paragraph Section D of NCWM Publication 14 for Liquid Measuring Devices to the NTEP Committee for consideration.

D. **Product Families for Mass Flow Meters**

When submitting a direct mass flow meter for evaluation, the manufacturer must specify the product or product group for which the meter is being submitted. To cover a product group, NTEP tests must be conducted with two liquids within the product group. ~~Upon test completion, a range of specific gravities between the specific gravities of the two liquids attained within the product group will be covered on the Certificate of Conformance (CC). When two liquids of different densities are tested the Certificate of Conformance (CC) for the mass flow meter will cover approved liquids with a specific gravity range from 0.1 above the highest specific gravity tested to 0.1 below the lowest specific gravity tested.~~ The specific gravity range within the product group can be expanded by conducting an NTEP test with a liquid of higher or lower specific gravity than is covered on the existing CC.

The above does not apply to the following product groups: compressed gases, compressed liquids, and cryogenic liquids. In the case of these product groups, only one liquid within each group is required to undergo an NTEP evaluation, and, upon completion, the entire product group will be covered on the existing CC.

Multi-product applications (i.e., applications in which the meter will be used without a change to zero or calibration to dispense different products which vary in specific gravity by more than 0.1) must include a multi-product test. The multi-product initial test will be performed on the meter without a change to zero or calibration using multiple products having a difference in specific gravity of at least 0.2. For devices which will be used to dispense multiple products having a specific gravity range greater than 0.2, the multi-product testing must be performed over the anticipated range before multi-product applications will be included on the CC. For the multi-product testing, throughput testing will be performed on one or a combination of the products; testing for the subsequent test will be conducted on both products without a change to zero or calibration. Multi-product testing requirements do not apply to meters used to dispense a product such as propane in which the density varies in normal operation.

14. Section D Product Family for Mass Flow Meters – Multi-product Applications

Source: Endress & Hauser Flowtec AG

Background: A mass flow meter submitted and approved for multi-product testing where product densities differ by greater than 0.2 has demonstrated ability to perform with major density changes. Therefore, the mass flow meter should be able to be used for products with differing densities throughout the range of the meter approval.

Recommendation: Add additional language to Section D, Page LMD 4 of Publication 14, 2004 edition as follows:

D. **Product Families for Mass Flow Meters**

When submitting a direct mass flow meter for evaluation, the manufacturer must specify the product or product group for which the meter is being submitted. To cover a product group, NTEP tests must be conducted with two liquids within the product group. Upon test completion, a range of specific gravities between the specific gravities of the two liquids attained within the product group will be covered on the Certificate of Conformance (CC). The specific gravity range within the product group can be expanded by conducting an NTEP test with a liquid of higher or lower specific gravity than is covered on the existing CC.

The above does not apply to the following product groups: compressed gases, compressed liquids, and cryogenic liquids. In the case of these product groups, only one liquid within each group is required to undergo an NTEP evaluation and, upon completion, the entire product group will be covered on the existing CC.

Multi-product applications (i.e., applications in which the meter will be used without a change to zero or calibration to dispense different products which vary in specific gravity by more than 0.1) must include a multi-product test. The multi-product initial test will be performed on the meter without a change to zero or calibration using multiple products having a difference in specific gravity of at least 0.2. For devices which will be used to dispense multiple products having a specific gravity range greater than 0.2, the multi-product testing must be performed over the anticipated range before multi-product applications will be included on the CC. For the multi-product testing, throughput testing will be performed on one or a combination of the products; testing for the subsequent test will be conducted on both products without a change to zero or calibration. ~~The mass flow meter will be approved for multi-product applications where the specific gravity of a single product, or multiple products, varies by the amount tested throughout the entire approved specific gravity range of the meter. Example: Where a meter has been tested and a certificate issued for multi-product applications with one liquid having a specific gravity of 0.7 and another liquid having a specific gravity of 1.0 and the meter is subsequently tested to expand the range with a liquid having a specific gravity of 1.6 the allowed variation of densities will be from 0.7 through 1.6.~~ Multi-product testing requirements do not apply to meters used to dispense a product such as propane in which the density varies in normal operation.

Decision: The Sector agreed to forward the following amended last paragraph of Section D in NCWM Publication 14 for Liquid Measuring Devices to the NTEP Committee for consideration.

D. **Product Families for Mass Flow Meters**

When submitting a direct mass flow meter for evaluation, the manufacturer must specify the product or product group for which the meter is being submitted. To cover a product group, NTEP tests must be conducted with two liquids within the product group. Upon test completion, a range of specific gravities between the specific gravities of the two liquids attained within the product group will be covered on the Certificate of Conformance (CC). The specific gravity range within the product group can be expanded by conducting an NTEP test with a liquid of higher or lower specific gravity than is covered on the existing CC.

The above does not apply to the following product groups: compressed gases, compressed liquids, and cryogenic liquids. In the case of these product groups, only one liquid within each group is required to undergo an NTEP evaluation and, upon completion, the entire product group will be covered on the existing CC.

Multi-product applications (i.e., applications in which the meter will be used without a change to zero or calibration to dispense different products which vary in specific gravity by more than 0.1) must include a multi-product test. The multi-product initial test will be performed on the meter without a change to zero or calibration using multiple products having a difference in specific gravity of at least 0.2. For devices which will be used to dispense multiple products having a specific gravity range greater than 0.2, the multi-product testing must be performed over the anticipated range before multi-product applications will be included on the CC. For the multi-product testing, throughput testing will be performed on one or a combination of the products; testing for the subsequent test will be conducted on both products without a change to zero or calibration. ~~The CC for a mass flow meter will cover multi-product applications where the specific gravity of a single product, or multiple products, varies by the amount tested throughout the entire approved specific gravity range of the meter. Example: Where a meter has been tested and a certificate issued for multi-product with one liquid having a specific gravity of 0.7 and another liquid having a specific gravity of 1.0 and the meter is subsequently tested to expand the range with a liquid having a specific gravity of 1.6 the allowed variation of densities covered by the CC will be from 0.7 through 1.6.~~ Multi-product testing requirements do not apply to meters used to dispense a product such as propane in which the density varies in normal operation.

15. Next Meeting

The Sector discussed the time and location for its next meeting.

Decision: The Sector agreed to recommend to the NCWM NTEP Committee that the 2005 Measuring Sector Meeting be held immediately prior to the 2005 meeting of the Southern Weights and Measures Association beginning at 8:00 am on Friday and continuing through 5:00 pm on Saturday. The ending time on Saturday will be dependent on the length of the agenda.

Additional Items

16. ECRs Approved for Dispensers from Multiple Manufacturers

Source/Background: The NTEP Laboratories want to know how many dispensers and features should be evaluated in the laboratory and/or field when evaluating an ECR for use with multiple dispensers.

Decision: The Sector agreed that, as a minimum, two dispensers from different manufacturers, each of which includes all of the features listed on the ECR CC, must be evaluated with the ECR in order to have the statement "equivalent and compatible equipment" appear on the CC. The Sector further agreed to forward to the NTEP Committee for consideration the following amendment to NCWM Publication 14 Section A of the Electronic Cash Register Interfaced with Retail Motor-Fuel Dispensers.

A. Introduction

This checklist is intended for use when conducting general evaluations of new electronic cash registers that are to interface with retail motor-fuel dispensers. It is assumed that the dispenser was previously evaluated, if not, the LMD checklist must be applied to the dispenser sale system. The ECR must interface with a dispenser to perform this evaluation. Specific criteria that apply to service station control consoles are in the checklist for retail motor-fuel dispensers and must be applied if the cash register also serves as the service station controller. As a ~~minimum, two dispensers from different manufacturers, each of which includes all of the features to be listed on the ECR CC, must be evaluated with the ECR in order to have the statement "equivalent and compatible equipment" appear on the CC.~~

This checklist is designed in a logical sequence for the user to determine and record the conformance of the device with the elements of NIST Handbook 44. The user should make copies of the checklist to serve as worksheets and preserve the original for reference. In most cases, the results of evaluation for each element can be recorded by checking the appropriate response to the following:

17. Zero Set-back Interlocks on Vehicle-tank Meters

Source/Background: The S&T Committee has requested input from the Sector on Carryover Item 331-3, a Handbook 44 requirement for Zero Set-back Interlocks on Vehicle-tank Meters.

Decision: The Sector agreed to forward the following new paragraph S.2.4. for Handbook 44 Section 3.31. Vehicle-Tank Meters to the SWMA and NCWM S&T Committees for consideration.

> S.2.4. Zero-Set-Back Interlock, Vehicle-Tank Meters. – Except for aircraft fueling, an electronic device shall be so constructed that after an individual or multiple deliveries at one location have been completed, an automatic interlock system shall engage to prevent a subsequent delivery until the indicating and, if equipped, recording elements have been returned to their zero position. For individual deliveries, if there is no product flow for 3 minutes the transaction must be completed before additional product flow is allowed. The 3 minute timeout may be a sealable feature on an indicator designed for commercial and non-commercial applications.
> [Nonretroactive as of January 1, 200X]

18. Wireless Communication Systems

Source/Background: The Maryland NTEP Laboratory has a fuel dealer that wants to install a wireless communication system for transferring billing information from the vehicle-tank meter to a central billing office. Does the communication equipment installed for this purpose require an NTEP CC?

Decision: The Sector agreed that the scenario as described, where wireless communication is used to transfer billing information, is not an NTEP issue at this time. The scenario is similar in some respects systems that use telephone communication to transfer billing information to a central billing office. NTEP currently evaluates systems to the point of the first final indication of quantity delivered.

19. Display of Unit Price on Vehicle-Tank Meters

Source/Background: Maryland NTEP Laboratory and FMC requested clarification of the intent of Handbook 44 Section 3.31., paragraph S.1.4.1. The paragraph states that a device of the computing type shall provide a means to display the unit price at which the device is set to compute on the outside of the device.

1. Can the unit price be on the display screen?
2. If it is on the display screen, is it required to be displayed full time?
3. Does a posted sign plaque meet the requirement?

Decision: The Sector agreed to forward the following amended paragraph S.1.4.1. to the SWMA and NCWM S&T Committees for consideration.

> **S.1.4.1. Display of Unit Price. - In a device of the computing type, means shall be provided for displaying** on the outside of the device, **in a manner clear to the operator and an observer, the unit price at which the device is set to compute.** The unit price is not required to be displayed continuously.

20. Evaluations Using Simulated Input Devices

Source/Background: FMC Measurement Solutions requested the Sector provide guidelines for evaluating electronic indicating devices when submitted separate from the measuring element. Will NTEP allow electronic indicators to be evaluated using simulated inputs, i.e., meter pulse, temperature, pressure density, etc.?

Decision: The Sector agreed to forward to the NTEP Committee for consideration the following new Section U for addition to the Technical Policy for Liquid-Measuring Devices in Publication 14.

> **U. Testing Electronic Indicators for Stationary Installations Using Simulated Inputs.**
>
> **When evaluating electronic indicators for stationary installations, submitted separate from a measuring element, indicators may be evaluated using simulated inputs (i.e., meter pulse, temperature, pressure, density, etc.).**

21. Modifications to Pre-NTEP Certificates:

Source/Background: FMC Measurement Solutions requested the Sector provide guidelines for allowing feature modifications to pre-NTEP certificates without the need for permanence testing for established metering technologies, i.e., PD meters, if the modification can be shown that the measurement basis has not been changed (no metrological significance).

Example of feature modification: Changing a PD meter with a conventional shaft output to a direct electronic output. Cyclic volume remains unchanged as the modification is (1) the replacement of the top cover to remove the gear train and packing glands and (2) the addition of a target gear and electronic sensor(s). The measurement chamber (cyclic volume) remains unchanged.

Decision: The Sector agreed that changing from a conventional shaft output to an electronic output with the removal of a gear train, the external shaft, and packing gland, along with the addition of a target gear and electronic sensor(s), is a modification of type that requires, as a minimum, an initial evaluation of the modified device. Permanence testing may be required at the discretion NTEP based on the results of the initial evaluation.

NTEP Committee 2005 Interim Report
Appendix C – NTETC - Measuring Sector

Attendance List

Name	Company/Agency	Address	Telephone #	E-Mail Address
Belue, Mike	Belue Associates	1319 Knight Dr Murfreesboro TN 37128	615 867 1010	bassoc@aol.com
Beyer, Joseph	Liquid Controls	105 Albrecht Drive Lake Bluff, IL 60044	847 283 8300	jbeyer@idexcorp.com
Butler, Jerry	North Carolina Dept of Agriculture	1050 Mail Service Center Raleigh, NC 27699-1050	919 733 3313	Jerry.butler@ncmail.net
Buxton, Joe	Daniel Measurement Control	19267 Hwy 301 N Statesboro, GA 30461	912 489 0253	Joe.buxton@emersonprocess.com
Castro, Gary	State of California Meas Stds	8500 Fruitridge Rd Sacramento CA 95826	916 229 3049	gcastro@cdfa.ca.gov
Cooper, Rodney	Actaris Neptune	1310 Emerald Rd Greenwood SC 29646	864 942 2226	rcooper@greenwood.actaris.com
Forkert, Maurice	Tuthill Transfer Systems	8825 Aviation Dr Ft Wayne IN 46809	260 747 7529	mforkert@Tuthill.com
Gallo, Mike	Clean Fuel Technologies	140 Market Street Georgetown, TX 78626	512 942-8304	Mike.gallo@cftdispensers.com
Glowacki, Paul	Murray Equipment, Inc.	2515 Charleston Place Fort Wayne, IN 46808	260 484 0382	pglowacki@murrayequipment.com
Hoffman, David	Toptech Systems	280 Hunt Park Cove Longwood FL 32750	407 332 1774	dhoffman@toptech.com
Johnson, Gordon	Marconi Commerce Systems Inc	7300 W Friendly Ave Greensboro NC 27420	336 547 5375	gordon.johnson@marconi.com
Kalevoda, Raymond	FMC Measurement Solutions	1602 Wagner Avenue Erie, PA 16510	814 898 5264	Ray.kalivoda@fmcti.com
Katalinic, Allen	North Carolina Dept of Agriculture	1050 Mail Service Center Raleigh, NC 27699-1050	919 733 3313	
Katselnik, Yefim	Dresser Wayne	3814 Jarrett Way Austin, TX 78728	512 388 8763	Phil.katselnik@wayne.com
Keilty, Mike	Endress & Hauser Flowtech AG	2350 Endress Place Greenwood, IN 46143	317 535 2745	Michael.keilty@us.endress.com
Kingbury, Ted	Measurement Canada	Stds Bldg #4 Tunney's Pasture Ottawa Ontario K1AOC9	613 941 8919	Kingsbury.ted@ic.gc.ca
Kretzler, Randal	Dresser Wayne/Dresser, Inc.	3814 Jarrett Way Austin, TX 78728-1212	512 388 8420	Randal.kretzler@wayne.com
Lachance, Christian	Measurement Canada	Stds Bldg #4 Tunney's Pasture Ottawa Ontario K1AOC9	613 952 3528	Lachance.Christian@ic.gc.ca
Long, Douglas	RDM Industrial Electronics	850 Harmony Grove Rd Nebo, NC 28761	828 652 8346	doug@wnclink.com
Mattar, Wade	Invensys/Foxboro	33 Commercial Street PO Box 10428 Erie, PA 16514	508 549 2067	wmattar@foxboro.com
Miller, Richard	FMC Measurement Solutions	1602 Wagner Ave, Box 10428 Erie, PA 16514	814 898 5214	rich.miller@fmcti.com
Onwiler, Don	Nebraska Div of Weights & Meas	301 Centennial Mall South PO Box 94757 Lincoln, NE 68509	402 471 4292	donlo@agr.state.ne.us
Parrish, Johnny	Brodie Meter Co., LLC	19267 Highway 301 North Statesboro, GA 30461	912 489 0203	Johnny.parrish@brodiemeter.com
Patoray, Steve	NTEP/NCWM	1239 Carolina Dr Tryon NC 28782	828 859 6178	spatoray@mgmtsol.com
Rajala, David	Veder-Root Company	P.O. Box 1673 Altoona, PA 19906-1673	814 696 8125	drajala@veeder.com
Suiter, Richard	NIST/OWM	Stop 2600 100 Bureau Dr Gaithersburg MD 20878	301 975 4406	rsuiter@nist.gov
Wotthlie, Richard	State of Maryland	50 Harry S. Truman Parkway Annapolis MD 21771	410 841 5790	wotthlrw@mda.state.md.us

THIS PAGE LEFT INTENTIONALLY BLANK.

Appendix D

National Type Evaluation Technical Committee
Weighing Sector Annual Meeting

August 29-31 2004, Ottawa, Canada
Summary of Decisions

Carry-Over Items..2
1. Recommended Changes to Publication 14 Based on Actions at the 2004 NCWM Annual Meeting...................2
   (a). Manual Gross Weight Entries..2
   (b). Section Capacity Prefix...3
   (c). Field Standard Weight Cart...3
   (d). Discrimination Test...3
   (e). Automatic Weighing Systems..3
2. Identification: Built-for-Purpose Software-based Devices...4
3. Ad Hoc Procedures for Class I and II Scales used in Prescription Filling Applications..................................8
4. S.1.1.c. Zero Indication (Marking Requirements)...9
New Items..9
5. Bench/Counter Scale Shift Test and Definitions..9
6. Automatic Zero-Setting Mechanism (Zero-Tracking)..11
7. Prescription Scale with an Operational Counting Feature...12
8. "#" Symbol..14
9. Elimination of Temperature Testing for Separable Weighing/load-receiving Elements...............................14
10. Time Dependence Tolerances..17
11. Publication 14 Force Transducer (Load Cell) Family and Selection Criteria...19
12. Compatibility of Indicators Interfaced with Weighing and Measuring Elements.......................................20
13. Handbook 44 Computing Scales Interfaced with an Electronic Cash Register..21
14. Publication 14 Requirements for Computing Scales Interfaced with an Electronic Cash Register..............22
15. Publication 14 - Computing Scale Section...23
16. Publication 14 - New Items in Computing Scale Section..23
17. Handbook 44 - Location of Marking for "Capacity x d" on Scales...25
18. CLC Type Evaluation Tests on Railway Track/Vehicle Scales – Technical Policy....................................27
19. Display of a Negative Balance Condition and Required Markings..28
20. Dropping the 4th Step in Class III and IIII Tolerances..28
21. Cash Acceptors or Card-activated Systems..30
22. Tare on a Multiple Range Scales...30
23. Performance and Permanence Tests for Railway Track Scales Used to Weigh Statically.........................33
24. Next Sector Meeting...34
Appendix A - Recommendations for Amendments to Publication 14..35
Agenda Item 1 (a)..35
Agenda Item 1 (b)..36
Agenda Item 1 (d)..36
Agenda Item 1 (e)..38
Agenda Item 3...41
Agenda Item 14...44
Agenda Item 15...45
Agenda Item 19...47
Agenda Item 21...49
Appendix B – NTETC Weighing Sector Attendance List..52

NTEP Committee 2005 Final Report
Appendix D – NTETC - Weighing Sector

Details of All Items
(In Order by Reference Key Number)

Carry-Over Items:

1. Recommended Changes to Publication 14 Based on Actions at the 2004 NCWM Annual Meeting

The NTEP technical advisor provided the Sector with specific recommendations for incorporating into Publication 14 test procedures and checklist language based upon actions of the previous Annual Meeting of the NCWM. The Sector was asked to briefly discuss each item and provide general input on the technical aspects of the issues.

(a). Manual Gross Weight Entries

Background: See the Report of the 89th National Conference on Weights and Measures, Specifications and Tolerances Committee Agenda Item 320-1 for additional background information. During its 2004 Annual Meeting, the NCWM agreed to amend NIST Handbook 44 2.20. Scales Code paragraph S.1.12. Manual Gross Weights to allow the manual entry of net weights for prepackage applications and for pre-weighed items from other legal-for-trade scales.

Discussion: The Weighing Sector considered a proposal from the NIST technical advisor to amend NCWM Publication 14 Weighing Devices Technical Policy, Checklists, Test Procedures Digital Electronic Scales Section 17 Manual Weight Entries.

During the discussion, confusion arose regarding identifying preset tare weights (i.e., keyboard tare entry or tare stored in memory) as manual weight entries, and this confusion may be attributed to the adopted amended title of the amended paragraph S.1.12. "Manual Weights." One commenter was concerned that two manual weights may have to be entered for weigh-in/weigh-out transactions when there is a loss of communication between separate weighing locations and that the manual tare weight entries should be identified. Another commenter suggested additional language for paragraph S.1.12. that would state that preset tares do not have to be identified. The NIST technical advisor reported the intent of the proposed amendment to S.1.12. did not apply to preset tare weights and that amending the title of paragraph S.1.12. to Manual Gross or Net Weight Entries (did what--solved the problem?).

Additionally, the Sector made some editorial suggestions to the proposed amendment to Publication 14 Section 17.

Recommendation: The Sector recommends that amendments proposed in Appendix A agenda Item 1(a) be incorporated into Publication 14 Section 17. Manual Weights.

Additionally, the Weighing Sector suggested that the S&T technical advisors make the following editorial changes to paragraph S.1.12. of NIST Handbook 44, indicated in underlined text, to clarify that the amended paragraphs do not apply to manually entered tare weights, and that manual net weight entries are non-retroactive as of January 1, 2005:

> **S.1.12. Manual Gross or Net Weight Entries.** - *A device when being used for direct sale shall accept an entry of a manual gross or net weight value only when the scale gross or net weight indication is at zero. Recorded manual weight entries, except those on labels generated for packages of standard weights, shall identify the weight value as a manual weight entry by one of the following terms: "Manual Weight," "Manual Wt," or "MAN WT." The use of a symbol to identify multiple manual weight entries on a single document is permitted, provided that the symbol is defined on the same page on which the manual weight entries appear and the definition of the symbol is automatically printed by the recording element as part of the document. [Nonretroactive as of January 1, 1993] [Nonretroactive as of January 1, 2005]*
> *(Added 1992) (Amended 2004)*

² *The term "net" was added in 2004 to include net weights entered from items pre-weighed on a legal-for-trade scale.*

(b). Section Capacity Prefix

Background: See the Report of the 89th National Conference on Weights and Measures, Specifications and Tolerances Committee Agenda Item 320-3 for additional background information. During its 2004 Annual Meeting, the NCWM agreed to amend NIST Handbook 44 2.20. Scales Code paragraph S.6.4.3. Section Capacity Prefix and Table S.6.3.a. Marking Requirements. During its 2004 Annual Meeting, the NCWM agreed to additional language for the 2005 Edition of NIST Handbook 44 regarding the use of abbreviations for the marking of section capacity.

Discussion/Recommendation: The Weighing Sector considered a proposal from the NIST technical advisor to amend NCWM Publication 14 Weighing Devices Technical Policy, Checklists, Test Procedures Digital Electronic Scales Section 5. Marking – Livestock, Vehicle, and Railway Track Scales paragraph 5.1. and agreed to recommend that amendments proposed in Appendix A, agenda Item 1(b) be incorporated into Publication 14 Section 5.

(c). Field Standard Weight Cart

Background: See the Report of the 89th National Conference on Weights and Measures, Specifications and Tolerances Committee Agenda Item 320-4 for additional background information to amend NIST Handbook 44 2.20. Scales Code paragraph Item 320-4 N.3.2. Field Standard Weight Carts. During its 2004 Annual Meeting, the NCWM agreed to add language in the 2005 Edition of NIST Handbook 44 recognizing field standard weight carts for use as a certified test load.

Discussion/Recommendation: The Weighing Sector recommends no further action on this item.

(d). Discrimination Test

Background: See the Report of the 89th National Conference on Weights and Measures, Specifications and Tolerances Committee Agenda Item 320-5 for additional background information. During its 2004 Annual Meeting, the NCWM agreed to amend NIST Handbook 44 2.20. Scales Code paragraph N.1.5 Discrimination Test to add language to the 2005 Edition of NIST Handbook 44 to clarify discrimination test procedures for testing scales with an operational automatic zero-setting mechanism.

Discussion: NCWM Publication 14 already includes procedures to conduct discrimination tests near zero and near capacity. The Sector considered a proposal by the NIST technical advisor to amend Publication 14, Digital Electronic Scales Sections 63 "Performance and Permanence Test for Floor Scales" and 69 "Performance and Permanence Test for Dynamic Monorail Scales." The Sector discussed that Publication 14 Section 43 "Zone of Uncertainty" should also include test procedures for determining compliance with discrimination test requirements that are similar to requirements and tests recommended by Measurement Canada and OIML R76 for Non-automatic Weighing instruments.

Recommendation: The Weighing Sector recommends that NCWM Publication 14 Sections 43 Zone of Uncertainty, 63 Performance and Permanence Test for Floor Scales, and 69 Performance and Permanence Test for Dynamic Monorail Scales" be amended to clarify discrimination test requirements and procedures as shown in Appendix A, agenda Item 1 (d).

(e). Automatic Weighing Systems

Background: See the Report of the 89th National Conference on Weights and Measures, Specifications and Tolerances Committee Agenda Item 324-1 for additional background information. During its 2004 Annual Meeting, the NCWM agreed to change the status of Handbook 44, Section 2.24. Automatic Weighing Systems (AWS) from a tentative code to a permanent code. One of the changes to the tentative code was to remove the type evaluation test procedures and incorporate them into NCWM Publication 14.

NTEP Committee 2005 Final Report
Appendix D – NTETC - Weighing Sector

Discussion/Recommendation: The Weighing Sector reviewed the proposed language, as shown in Appendix A agenda Item 1(e), which was developed by Andrea Buie of the Maryland NTEP laboratory, and recommended that such language be added to Publication 14 Automatic Weighing Systems checklist. The Sector also recommended that a meeting should be planned to develop additional changes to Publication 14 that were identified during the 2002 meeting of the AWS NCWM Work Group. The Sector further believes that much of the work can be accomplished electronically among the participants following the next meeting.

2. Identification: Built-for-Purpose Software-based Devices

Background: See the Report of the 89th National Conference on Weights and Measures, Specifications and Tolerances Committee Agenda Item 320-1 for additional background information and the proposed language considered by the S&T Committee.

At the 2004 NCWM Interim Meeting, the S&T Committee requested that prior to the NCWM Annual Meeting in July 2004 the technical advisor to the NTETC Weighing Sector distribute to its members the proposal for the S&T Committee's Agenda Item 310-1 along with a ballot requesting support for the proposal. Although there were 15 responses to the ballot and the majority of the members of the Weighing Sector voted affirmatively, there was no clear consensus.

At the 2004 NCWM Annual Meeting, the Scale Manufacturers Association (SMA) stated that Item 310-1 should not go forward for a vote because the ballot of the NTETC Weighing Sector failed to provide clear support for the item. A manufacturer stated that the term "microprocessor" was not appropriate because their devices contain numerous microprocessors. Another manufacturer stated that the requirement for marking the current software version number would place an unrealistic burden on their company. The Committee agreed that sufficient opposition and questions were raised during the open hearing to demonstrate that the item is not sufficiently developed to be a voting item at this meeting. The Committee agreed to make Item 310-1 an information item to be returned to the NTETC Weighing and Measuring Sectors for further development.

Discussion: The Weighing Sector reviewed the background information from the NCWM S&T Committee, previous Sector recommendations, and information regarding international activities. The Sector also reviewed an updated proposal for S&T agenda Item 310-1 from NIST WMD. The updated proposal included new and amended definitions and attempted to address concerns raised during the NCWM S&T Committee and open hearing deliberations on this item. The definition for "not-built-for-purpose" devices was amended to clarify their use as auxiliary or peripheral equipment for weighing and measuring devices and systems.

Some of the private Sector members repeated their comments that current electronic weighing and measuring equipment technology easily permits the display of required identification information and that there was no technical justification for treating these devices differently than not-built-for-purpose devices.

Additionally, the proposed definitions would reclassify most measuring devices according to the physical property being measured (e.g., liquid, length, vapor, cryogenic, etc.). Since the proposed new definition for measuring devices applies to all types of Handbook 44 devices, there was some concern that laws and regulations would need changing because many states' statutes are written using the "weighing and measuring" device terminology.

Recommendation: The Sector recommended the following updated proposal submitted by NIST WMD with suggestions from the Weighing Sector be forwarded to the NTETC Measuring Sector for its review and comments.

Add new Terms and definitions as follows:

measuring device (general) – A device (instrument) intended to be used to make measurements, alone or in conjunction with supplementary devices. (VIM)

measuring system (general) - An instrument or group of instruments that serves to make measurements, alone or in conjunction with supplementary devices. (VIM)

electronic devices – A device operating by the principles of electronics, which may consist of one or more subassemblies and performs a specific function(s). (ASTM)

not-built-for-purpose device -- Any electronic peripheral or auxiliary device or element which was not originally manufactured with the intent that it be used as, or part of, a weighing or measuring device or system.

metrological software version (revision) – A designation that specifically defines the metrological software version used in a measuring instrument, system, or peripheral/auxiliary device with field programmable or downloadable metrological software).

weighing device (instrument) -- A measuring instrument that serves to determine the mass of a body by using the action of gravity on said body. The instrument may also be used to determine other quantities, magnitudes, parameters or characteristics related to the determined mass. According to its method of operation, a weighing instrument is classified as an automatic or non-automatic instrument. (OIML R76)

Amend the definition for built-for-purpose device as follows:

built-for-purpose device – Any main, ~~peripheral, or auxiliary~~ device or element which was manufactured with the intent that it be used as, or part of, a ~~weighing or~~ measuring device or system.

Amend General Code paragraph G-A.1. Commercial and Law Enforcement Equipment as follows:

G-A.1. **Commercial and Law Enforcement Equipment.** - These specifications, tolerances, and other technical requirements apply as follows:

(a) To commercial ~~weighing and measuring~~ devices or systems equipment; that is, to weights, and measures, and ~~weighing and measuring~~ devices or systems commercially used or employed in establishing the ~~size,~~ quantity, ~~extent, area,~~ or measurement of quantities, ~~things, produce, or articles for~~ distributed or consumed, purchased, offered, or submitted for sale, hire, or award, or in computing any basic charge or payment for services rendered on the basis of quantity determination ~~weight or measure~~.

(b) To any accessory attached to or used in connection with a commercial weighing or measuring device when such accessory is so designed that its operation affects the accuracy of the device.

~~(c) To weighing and measuring devices or systems equipment in official use for the enforcement of law or for the collection of statistical information by government agencies.~~

(These requirements should be used as a guide by the weights and measures official when, upon request, courtesy examinations of noncommercial equipment are made.)

Amend General Code paragraph G-S.1. Identification as follows:

G-S.1. **Identification.** - All equipment, except weights and separate parts necessary to the measurement process, but not having any metrological effect, shall be clearly marked in accordance with Table G-S.1 for the purposes of identification, with the following information:

(a) the name, initials, or trademark of the manufacturer or distributor;

(b) a model designation that positively identifies the pattern, ~~or~~ design, or metrological version or revision of the device in accordance with Table G-S.1;

(c) the model designation shall be prefaced by the term "Model," "Type," or "Pattern." These terms may be followed by the term "Number" or an abbreviation of that word. The abbreviation for the word "Number" shall, as a minimum, begin with the letter "N" (e.g., No or No.). The abbreviation for the word "Model" shall be "Mod" or "Mod."
[Nonretroactive January 1, 2003]
(Added 2000) (Amended 2001)

[Note: Prefix lettering may be initial capitals, all capitals or all lower case.]

(d) except for equipment with no moving or electronic component parts and not-built-for-purpose, ~~software-based electronic~~ devices, a nonrepetitive serial number;
[Nonretroactive as of January 1, 1968]

~~(e) for not-built-for-purpose, software-microprocessor-based devices the current software version designation or revision number;~~
~~(Added 2003)~~

(~~e~~f) the serial number shall be prefaced by words, an abbreviation, or a symbol that clearly identifies the number as the required serial number; and
[Nonretroactive as of January 1, 1986]

(~~f~~g) the serial number shall be prefaced by the words "Serial Number" or an abbreviation of that term. Abbreviations for the word "Serial" shall, as a minimum, begin with the letter "S," and abbreviations for the word "Number" shall, as a minimum, begin with the letter "N" (e.g., S/N, SN, Ser. No, and S No.).
[Nonretroactive as of January 1, 2001]

(~~g~~h) ~~F~~for devices that have an NTEP Certificate of Conformance (CC), the CC Number or a corresponding CC addendum number ~~shall be~~ prefaced by the terms "NTEP CC," "CC," or "Approval." These terms may be followed by the term "Number" or an abbreviation of that word. The abbreviation for the word "Number" shall, as a minimum, begin with the letter "N" (e.g., No or No.).
[Nonretroactive as of January 1, 2003]

The required information shall be so located that it is readily observable without the necessity of the disassembly of a part requiring the use of any means separate from the device.
(Amended 1985, 1991, 1999, 2000, 2001 and 2003)

Delete General Code paragraph G-S.1.1. Location of Marking Information for Not-Built-for-Purpose, Software-based Devices and renumber G-S.1.2. Remanufactured Devices and Remanufactured Main Elements as follows:

G-S.1.1. Location of Marking Information for Not-Built-for-Purpose, Software-based Devices. - For not-built-for-purpose, software-based devices, the following shall apply:

~~(a) the manufacturer or distributor and the model designation shall be continuously displayed or marked on the device (see note below), or~~

~~(b) the Certificate of Conformance (CC) Number shall be continuously displayed or marked on the device (see note below), or~~

~~(c) all required information in G-S.1. Identification. (a), (b), (c), (e), and (h) shall be continuously displayed. Alternatively, a clearly identified "view only" System Identification, G-S.1. Identification, or Weights and Measures Identification shall be accessible through the "Help" menu. Required~~

~~information includes that information necessary to identify that the software in the device is the same type that was evaluated.~~

~~Note: Clear instructions for accessing the remaining required G-S.1. information shall be listed on the CC. Required information includes that information necessary to identify that the software in the device is the same type that was evaluated.~~
~~[Nonretroactive as of January 1, 2004]~~
~~(Added 2003)~~

G-S.1.1~~2~~. **Remanufactured Devices and Remanufactured Main Elements. -** All remanufactured devices and remanufactured main elements shall be clearly and permanently marked for the purposes of identification with the following information:

(a) The name, initials, or trademark of the last remanufacturer or distributor;

(b) The remanufacturer's or distributor's model designation if different than the original model ~~designation~~
[Nonretroactive as of January 1, 2002]
(Added 2001)

Note: Definitions for "manufactured device," "repaired device," and "repaired element" are also included (along with definitions for "remanufactured device" and "remanufactured element") in Appendix D, Definitions.

Add new Table G-S.1. Identification as follows:

	Built-for-Purpose Instruments, Elements, or Systems	Not-Built-for-Purpose Devices or Elements
Name, initials, or trademark of the manufacture or distributor	~~M~~ D	[2]
Model designation ~~M~~	[1]	D[2]
Specific model designation[3]	~~M[1] or~~ D	
Serial number ~~M~~	—	Not required
Metrological version or revision designation[3]	~~M or D~~ NA D	—
Certificate of Conformance (CC) number	~~M or D~~ D	[2]
~~M:~~ Physically and permanently marked		
~~D:~~ Either: (1) displayed by accessing a clearly identified view only System Identification, G-S.1 Identification, or Weights and Measures Identification accessible through the "Help" menu. Required information includes that information necessary to identify the software in the device is the same type that was evaluated, or (2) continuously displayed. Note: For revision or software version number, clear instructions for accessing this information shall be listed on the CC in lieu of the "Help" menu. Required information includes that information necessary to identify the software in the device is the same or subsequent type that was evaluated. (Nonretroactive as of January 2004)		

Note 1:	As a minimum, the model designation (positively identifying the pattern, design, type, seriegeneric, or trademark designation) must be marked on the device. If the model designation changes with differing parameters such as size, features, options, intended application, not Handbook 44 compliant construction, etc., the specific model designation shall be physically marked or continuously displayed or be capable of being displayed. (Nonretroactive as of January 200X)
Note 2:	As a minimum, either the manufacturer or distributor and the model designation, or the CC Number shall be continuously displayed. Clear instructions for accessing the remaining required C.S.1 information shall be listed on the CC, which may be available as an unaltered copy of the CC or printed by the device or through another on-site device. (Nonretroactive as of January 200X)
Note 3:	Metrological version or revision designation for devices with downloadable or field programmable software

3. Ad Hoc Procedures for Class I and II Scales used in Prescription Filling Applications

Source: 2003 NTETC Weighing Sector Agenda Item 14 b.

Background: See the 2003 S&T Committee Annual Report Item 320-2 for additional background information. During its 2003 Annual Meeting, the NCWM agreed to modify paragraph S.1.2.3. of NIST Handbook 44. The approved language was incorporated in the 2004 Edition of NIST Handbook 44.

At its 2003 meeting, the Weighing Sector reviewed the language adopted by the 88th NCWM at its annual meeting and discussed a draft checklist developed by Brian Christopher (McKesson) that was distributed to the Sector. The Sector discussed the need to verify that minimum piece weight and piece count limits required by the new language in Handbook 44 are effective. Additionally, NTEP tests should be conducted with counts and loads that are less than the minimums in new paragraph S.1.2.3. that verify the scale is prevented from displaying a total piece count (e.g., 29 e and/or 9 pieces for samples to determine piece weights). There was a discussion that the scale cannot be recalibrated while evaluating the counting feature. The manufacturers explained that it is possible to have inaccurate weight measurements and still have correct count indications. Additionally, the recommended checklist should include verification of new marking requirements.

At the request of the Sector, the Publication 14 evaluation checklist submitted by Brian Christopher was further developed with the assistance of the participating laboratories, the NTEP director, and the NIST technical advisor and was used on an *ad hoc* basis until the procedure could be fully evaluated and accepted by the Sector.

The NTEP participating laboratories have used the *ad hoc* procedures on several evaluations this past year. Neither the applicants nor the laboratories identified any procedural issues.

Discussion: The Weighing Sector discussed the *ad hoc* procedures and noted that they did not include a reference to Handbook 44 specification paragraph S.2.5.3. Class I and II Prescription Scales with a Counting Feature and recommended an amendment to the procedures to correct the omission.

During the review of paragraph S.2.5.3., there was a discussion regarding motion detection requirements for recording elements that can print the number of pills when there is no display of weight in the counting mode. Currently, there is no language in the Scales Code that requires an effective means to permit the recording of count values when the count indication is stable. The Sector discussed the possibility of adding a motion detection requirement for the printing or recording of count. There was also a discussion questioning which "quantity" was required to have a stable indication. The Sector believes that the paragraph could be editorially amended to provide clarification that the term "quantity" is intended to be the sample quantity.

The Sector also discussed the *ad hoc* procedure abbreviations for minimum sample size (MSS), minimum piece weight (MPW), and minimum sample size in weight (MSSW) and agreed to recommend the abbreviations be listed in Publication 14 Section 75 List of Acceptable Abbreviations/Symbols.

Recommendation: The Weighing Sector recommends the ad hoc procedures, as amended by the Sector, be added to Publication 14 as shown in Appendix A agenda Item 3.

The Sector also recommends that paragraph S.2.5.3. be editorially amended to clarify that the quantity placed on the load-receiving element is for sample piece weight determination as follows:

> S.2.5.3. Class I and Class II Prescription Scales with a Counting Feature. - A Class I or Class II prescription scale shall indicate to the operator when the piece weight computation is complete by a stable display of the sample quantity placed on the load-receiving element.

Additionally, the Sector recommends amending paragraph S.2.5.1. Digital Indication Elements to clarify that the recording of indicated count values must be stable.

> S.2.5.3. Class I and Class II Prescription Scales with a Counting Feature. - A Class I or Class II prescription scale shall indicate to the operator when the piece weight computation is complete by a stable display of the sample quantity placed on the load-receiving element. ~~Prescription scales with a counting feature and recording element shall be equipped with effective means to permit the recording of count values only when the indication is stable within plus or minus 1 piece.~~

4. S.1.1.c. Zero Indication (Marking Requirements)

Source: 2003 Weighing Sector Agenda Item 19 - Screen Savers on Electronic Cash Registers and Point-of-Sale Systems.

Background: See the Report of the 89th National Conference on Weights and Measures, NTEP Committee Report 2003 NTETC Weighing Sector Meeting Summary agenda Item 19, and the S&T Committee Report agenda Item 320-8 for additional background information.

Discussion/Recommendation: The Sector reviewed the background information and accepted the 2004 S&T Committee interpretation of the intent of the 78th NCWM. However, the majority members of the Sector stated that no additional wording was needed since changes had already been added to Publication 14 that clarified that additional marking is required for weighing devices that use indications other than a digital zero to indicate the scale is operational and at a zero-balance condition.

During the discussion, some of the Sector members stated that is not appropriate for the Sector to further develop the proposal when the S&T Committee interpretation answered the Sector's questions. Additionally, the Sector stated that commenting on S&T Committee agenda items that have no impact on type evaluation and Publication 14 have a low priority and are typically discussed at the end of the Sector meeting if time permits.

The Sector recommends that no changes be made to the existing language in Handbook 44 Scales Code paragraph S.1.1. (c) Zero Indication. Additionally, the Sector did not have time at the end of its meeting to further discuss this item.

New Items:

5. Bench/Counter Scale Shift Test and Definitions

Source: NIST WMD

Background: During the 2002 meeting of the Weighing Sector, the NTEP director reported some confusion in the classification of bench/counter scales and other platforms and the location of test load while performing a shift test. Bench/counter and other platforms have different shift test positions depending if a scale is located on a counter or on the floor. The problem is compounded when a family of scales covers both bench/counter and other platform applications. **Bench and counter scale** shift tests are conducted with a one-half capacity test load centered successively at four points equidistant between the center and the front, left, back and the right edges of the load-receiving element (N.1.3.1.). **Other platform scale** shift tests are conducted with a one-half capacity test load centered, as nearly as possible, successively at the center of each quadrant.

The Weighing Sector proposal to amend Handbook 44 was intended to align the U.S. and Measurement Canada's shift test procedures that are based on the number of load supports in the scale. During the 2003 NCWM Annual Meeting, the Specifications and Tolerance Committee (S&T) agreed with comments from industry and weights and measures officials that paragraphs N.1.3.1. and N.1.3.8. already adequately address shift test procedures and any change would create confusion. The Committee agreed that the proposal to modify the definition of counter scale, as written, does not provide weights and measures officials with a means to determine the shift test procedure that is appropriate for a scale design (single or four load supports). The Committee recognized the difficulty or reluctance of field officials to dismantle a scale to determine its design. Consequently, the Committee changed this item's status to an information item and recommended the Weighing Sector consider the practice of including scale design information on all NTEP Certificates of Conformance to assist officials in performing shift tests.

The NIST technical advisor revised the 2002 Sector proposal to remove the reference to the number of load supports, align Handbook 44 shift test procedures for scales with OIML R76, and delete the definition for bench and counter scales. The NTEP participating laboratories have been requested to conduct a series of tests on instruments currently under NTEP evaluation comparing shift test results between the current Handbook 44 procedures and the shift test procedures in the following proposal. Note: The proposal does not permit corner testing for scales less than or equal to 150 kg. This limit was selected since corner testing is allowed if there are not enough test weights to perform the shift test or if the scale has four load supports, and Table 4 Minimum Test Weights requires that scales with a capacity of 150 kg or less have test weights up to 100 % of the scale capacity.

Proposal: Delete the definition of Bench and Counter Scale:

~~bench scale. See "counter scale." [2.20]~~

~~counter scale. One that, by reason of its size, arrangement of parts, and moderate nominal capacity, is adapted for use on a counter or bench. Sometimes called "bench scale." [2.20]~~

Delete Scales Code paragraph N.1.3.1. Bench and Counter Scales:

~~N.1.3.1. Bench or Counter Scales. - A shift test shall be conducted with a half-capacity test load centered successively at four points equidistant between the center and the front, left, back, and right edges of the load-receiving element.~~

Renumber remaining N.1.3.X paragraphs and amend paragraph N.1.3.8 as follows:

N.1.3.~~8~~. All Other Scales Except Crane Scales, Hanging Scales, Hopper Scales, Wheel-Load Weighers, and Portable Axle-Load Weighers. - A shift test shall be conducted using the following prescribed test loads and test patterns. ~~For livestock scales, the shift test load shall not exceed one-half the rated section capacity or one-half the rated concentrated load capacity, whichever is applicable. A shift test shall be conducted using either:~~

~~(a) A one-quarter nominal capacity test load centered as nearly as possible, successively over each main load support as shown in the diagram below; or~~
~~(Added 2003)~~
~~(b) A one-half nominal capacity test load centered as nearly as possible, successively at the center of each quarter of the load-receiving element as shown in the diagram below.~~

(a) **For scales greater than 150 kg (300 lb) a shift test load may be conducted by either using one-third nominal capacity test load centered as nearly as possible at the center of each quarter of the load receiving element as shown in Figure 1 below, or by using a one-quarter nominal capacity test load** centered as nearly as possible, successively over each corner of the weighing/load receiving element as shown in Figure 2 below.

(b) For scales with a nominal capacity of 150 kg (300 lb) or less, a shift test load shall be conducted using a one-third nominal capacity test. The load shall be applied centrally in the segment if a single weight is used, or applied uniformly over the segment, if several small weights are used.

(c) For livestock scales, the shift test load shall not exceed one-half the rated section or concentrated load capacity using the prescribed test pattern as shown in Figure 1, or one-quarter the section or concentrated load capacity as shown in Figure 2 below.

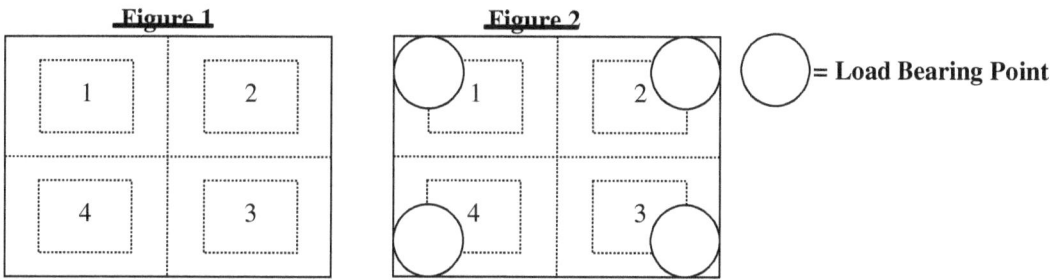

(Amended 1987, and 2003, and 200X)

Discussion/Recommendation: The NIST technical advisor reported that no data had been received by the time of the Sector meeting. The Weighing Sector continues to support aligning the shift test requirements in Handbook 44 with the equivalent requirements in OIML R76 Non-automatic Weighing Instrument to the fullest extent possible.

The Sector agreed with the proposal and commented that the exact test load of one-third capacity is not required or necessary. They also agreed that the test load of one-third capacity in the recommended test positions is roughly equivalent to one-half capacity in the current test load position for bench and counter scales. Since the test positions for other platform scales are not changed in this proposal and are tested at one-third instead of one-half capacity, the Sector believes that data should be collected to verify that the proposed test load would not pass scales that would have failed under the current test load requirements.

The Sector agreed to forward the above proposal as an information or developmental item to the regional weights and measures associations and the NCWM S&T Committee. The Sector further requests data demonstrating the performance differences or similarities between the current and proposed test procedures from the NTEP labs and other jurisdictions.

6. Automatic Zero-Setting Mechanism (Zero-Tracking)

Source: NIST WMD

Background: During the 2002 meeting of the Weighing Sector discussion on shift test positions, the NTEP director reported some confusion in the classification of bench/counter scales and other platforms and the range of the automatic zero-setting mechanism (AZSM). Bench/counter and other platforms have different zero-tracking requirements depending if a scale is located on a counter or on the floor. The problem is compounded when a family of scales covers both bench/counter and other platform applications. **Bench and counter scale** limit for AZSM is 0.6 e (S.2.1.3.a). **Other platform scales** limit AZSM to 1.0 e (S.2.1.3.c).

The NIST technical advisor and the participating NTEP laboratories recommended the following proposal to amend Handbook 44, Scales Code paragraph S.2.1.3. Scales Equipped with an Automatic Zero-Setting Mechanism to remedy the problem and partially align AZSM requirements with Measurement Canada and OIML R76 recommendations. The following proposal retains AZSM requirements for Class III L weighing instruments.

S.2.1.3. Scales Equipped with an Automatic Zero-Setting Mechanism (~~Zero Tracking~~) - ~~Under normal operating conditions the maximum load that can be "rezeroed," when either placed on or removed from the platform all at once, shall be:~~

S.2.1.3.1. - For scales manufactured before January 1, 200X, the maximum load that can be "rezeroed," when either placed on or removed from the platform all at once under normal operating conditions, shall be:

(a) for bench, counter, and livestock scales: 0.6 scale division;

(b) for vehicle, axle-load, and railway track scales: 3.0 scale divisions; and

(c) for all other scales: 1.0 scale division.
[Nonretroactive and enforceable as of January 1, 1981]

S.2.1.3.2. - For scales manufactured after January 1, 200X, the maximum load that can be "rezeroed," when either placed on or removed from the platform all at once under normal operating conditions, shall be:

~~*(a) for vehicle, axle-load, and railway track scales: 3.0 scale divisions; and*~~

~~*(b) for all other scales: 0.5 scale division.*~~
~~*[Nonretroactive and enforceable as of January 1, 200X]*~~

S.2.1.3.3~~1~~. Automatic Zero-Setting Mechanism (~~Zero Tracking~~) on Class III L Devices - *Class III L devices equipped with automatic zero-setting mechanisms shall be designed with a sealable means to allow the automatic zero setting to be disabled during the inspection and test of the device.*
[Nonretroactive as of January 1, 2001]
(Added 1999) (Renumbered 200X)

Discussion/Recommendation: The Sector agrees with the concept of the proposal and the alignment of Handbook 44 with OIML R76. The public Sector members discussed the implication the proposal may have on field officials in determining the date of manufacture of other platform scales (i.e., floor scales) when verifying compliance with AZSM (zero-tracking) requirements. Since other platform scales currently have a zero tracking requirement of 1 e, some of the public members were concerned about the ability of field officials to determine the date of manufacture of these scales to verify if it complied with 1 e or 0.5 e.

The private Sector members were concerned with the effective date of the proposed requirements and suggested a delay of several years in the effective date. This would allow manufacturers to avoid costly changes to their products that are nearing the end of their production cycle. This may also allow time for field officials to become trained in the requirements before the requirement becomes effective.

The Sector recommended this item be forwarded to the regional weights and measures association and the NCWM S&T Committee as a developmental item in order to gather information on the impact on field evaluations.

7. Prescription Scale with an Operational Counting Feature

Source: Mettler Toledo

Background: Handbook 44, paragraph S.6.6. Counting Feature, Minimum Individual Piece Weight and Minimum Sample Piece Count states:

S.6.6. Counting Feature, Minimum Individual Piece Weight and Minimum Sample Piece Count – A Class I or Class II prescription scale with an operational counting feature shall be marked with the minimum individual piece weight and minimum number of pieces used in the sample to establish an individual piece weight.

This marking is unnecessary if proper operation is confirmed during the NTEP evaluation using the defined minimum values since paragraph S.1.2.3. states:

S.1.2.3. *A Class I or Class II prescription scale with an operational counting feature shall not calculate a piece weight or total count unless the sample used to determine the individual piece weight meets the conditions:*

minimum individual piece weight is greater than or equal to 3 e; and
minimum sample piece count is greater than or equal to 10 pieces.
(Added 2003)

During the NTEP evaluation, a series of tests are conducted to determine these values as a minimum operation requirement. These tests could also be conducted in the field to confirm continued compliance with this requirement.

For example:

- A test weight equal to 30 e or more is placed on the platter; a sample size of less then 10 is entered or selected. If the device displays a total count, the instrument fails the test.

- A test weight of less than 30 e is placed on the platter; a sample size of 10 or more is entered or selected. If the device displays a total count, the instrument fails the test.

- A test weight of less than 30 e is placed on the platter; a sample size of less than 10 is entered or selected. If the device displays a total count, the instrument fails the test.

- A test weight equal to 30 e is placed on the platter; a sample size of 10 is entered or selected. If the device displays the proper count, the instrument passes and the marking requirements are waived. If the evaluation shows that the minimum sample weight must be greater than 30 e or the sample size must be greater than 10 for the instrument to perform an accurate count, the marking requirements are mandatory.

It is certainly within a scale's ability to compare the operator entered or selected, the sample size to ensure that the number is 10 or greater, and then to divide the weight on the platter to ensure that the sample weight is equal to or greater than 30 increments. The above test examples would confirm compliance to this requirement and remove the need to have this information marked on the scale.

The submitter of this item recommended amending Handbook 44, Scales Code, S.6.6. to remove the marking requirements for the minimum individual piece weight and minimum number of pieces providing the instrument conforms to both individual minimum values as stated in paragraph S.1.2.3. as follows:

S.6.6. Counting Feature, Minimum Individual Piece Weight and Minimum Sample Piece Count – A Class I or Class II prescription scale with an operational counting feature shall be marked with the minimum individual piece weight and minimum number of pieces used in the sample to establish an individual piece weight if the minimum individual piece weight or the minimum number of pieces used to establish an individual piece weight is different from that specified in S.1.2.3. a and b.

NOTE: The NIST technical advisor suggests the Sector consider the potential confusion created or implications involved if an applicant submits a scale with minimums smaller than specified in S.1.2.3. a and b.

Discussion/Recommendation: Mettler Toledo withdrew this item from the Weighing Sector agenda since the proposal did not relate to problems encountered with Publication 14 type evaluation procedures. Additionally, there was no additional time at the end of the meeting to further discuss this item.

NTEP Committee 2005 Final Report
Appendix D – NTETC - Weighing Sector

8. "#" Symbol

Source: Rice Lake Weighing Systems (RLWS)

Background: NCWM Publication 14 Section 75 List of Acceptable Abbreviations/Symbols lists "#" as an acceptable (but discouraged) symbol for recorded representations for electronic cash registers (ECR) and point-of-sale systems. RLWS reasons that if the symbol is suitable for recorded representations for ECRs, there is no justification for its prohibition for other recorded representations or markings. It should either be Acceptable or Not Acceptable.

According to the 61st NCWM Annual Report, the "#" was originally allowed in 1976 because of space limitations on recording elements. The "#" only took up one column where "lb" took two columns. The "#" was also allowed since it was reported that it is used in the dictionary.

The NIST technical advisor also noted the symbol is known by many names such as the octothorp, dry pound, avoirdupois pound, number, hash, sharp, crunch, hex, grid, crosshatch, square, pig-pen, ticktacktoe, scratch mark, thud, thump, and splat. In cartography, it is the symbol for a village (eight fields around a central square). The U.S. usage is derived from an old-fashioned commercial practice of using a "#" suffix to tag pound weights on bills of lading. Outside the U.S., the symbol is usually pronounced "hash" (the British symbol for pound is "£").

The submitter recommends the "#" symbol be removed from Publication 14 as an acceptable symbol and be reclassified as no longer acceptable based upon the changes in printer technology over the past 30 years and multiple definitions of the "#" mark. Additionally, Handbook 44 Scales Code footnote for paragraph S.1.8.4. Recorded Representations, Point-of-Sale Systems should be amended to eliminate the use of the "#" symbol as follows:

> [1]Weight values shall be identified by kilogram, kg, grams, g, ounces, oz, pound, or lb, ~~or the sign "#." For~~ devices interfaced with scales indicating in metric units, the unit price may be expressed in price per 100 grams.
> (Amended 200X)

Discussion/Recommendation: The Weighing Sector agreed that the "#" symbol should be removed from Publication 14 as an acceptable symbol and be reclassified as no longer acceptable based upon the changes in printer technology over the past 30 years and multiple definitions of the "#" mark. Additionally, Handbook 44 Scales Code footnote for paragraph S.1.8.4. Recorded Representations, Point-of-Sale Systems should be amended to eliminate the use of the "#" symbol as follows:

> [1] Weight values shall be identified by kilogram, kg, grams, g, ounces, oz, pound, or lb, ~~or the sign "#."~~ For devices interfaced with scales indicating in metric units, the unit price may be expressed in price per 100 grams.
> (Amended 200X)

9. Elimination of Temperature Testing for Separable Weighing/load-receiving Elements

Source: Rice Lake Weighing Systems (RLWS)

Background: RLWS reported temperature testing (influence factor) failures of separable weighing/load-receiving elements that incorporate load cells that have an NTEP Certificate of Conformance (CC). RLWS builds the instrument to be submitted for tests using load cells from their inventory, installs them into a weighing/load-receiving element, and performs the room temperature testing before submitting the instrument to the NTEP laboratory for evaluation. The instrument passes all applicable tests performed at room temperature but fails the temperature test. RLWS reported that the load cells are from a well-known and respected load cell manufacturer.

When RLWS contacted the load cell manufacturer, they responded by stating, "You should have told us these load cells were for NTEP testing." RLWS stated that the load cell manufacturer will send them four "GOLDEN" load cells that have been separately temperature tested to enable the weighing/load receiving element to pass temperature testing. RLWS further stated that it takes between 4 to 6 weeks or longer to receive load cells if they are requested for a weighing/load-receiving element to be submitted for NTEP evaluation.

An NTEP laboratory reported to RLWS that load cell manufacturers told other weighing/load-receiving element NTEP applicants the same thing after their weighing/load-receiving element failed the NTEP temperature testing.

RLWS does not believe that separable weighing/load-receiving elements using load cells that have an NTEP CC should be subject to additional temperature testing for the following reasons:

- Weighing/load receiving elements over 2000 lb are not subject temperature testing by NTEP;
- The NCWM Conformity Assessment program will help assure that production load cells comply with temperature and other influence factor requirements; and
- The costs associated with the temperature test for the weighing/load-receiving element can become excessive when the load cells already comply with temperature tests, especially if there is a failure. RLWS has provided a breakdown of NTEP costs associated with the temperature test using the Ohio NTEP laboratory rate schedule.

RLWS acknowledged that Measurement Canada does not approve load cells and that temperature testing may still be required for an evaluation approval under the Mutual Recognition Agreement.

The NIST technical advisor has contacted two load cell manufacturers and inquired what they did to provide a scale applicant with "golden" load cells. They reported that they retest and select the load cells that are well within the error requirements. They also acknowledged that load cells are NTEP evaluated in ideal loading conditions. There are no load cell tests that simulate off-center loading caused by deflection of the load-receiving element and changes to the mechanical interface at different temperatures between the load cell mount and the load-receiving element.

RLWS recommended amending Publication 14 by removing the temperature testing of separable bench and other platform weighing/load receiving elements and establishing a new tolerance for these devices while tested at room temperature.

Time	Cost	Description
1 hour	$110	Set-up of weighing/load-receiving element
2 hours	$220	Full test (increasing/decreasing, shift, corner)
1 hour	$110	Increasing/decreasing at temperature. $-10°$ (FAIL)
Chamber	$200	Billed for a half cycle of the temperature chamber
1 hour	$110	Ship weighing/load-receiving element back to manufacturer
*	Ship	weighing/load-receiving element back to manufacturer
*		Order "GOLDEN" load cells to pass temperature tests
*		Remove original load cells, install new load cells, and re-test at room temp
*		Ship weighing/load receiving element back to lab
1 hour	$110	Setup of weighing/load receiving element
2 hours	$220	Full test (increasing/decreasing, shift, corner)
1 hour	$110	Increasing/decreasing at temperature.
Total	**$1190**	**Costs to the point where the failure occurred**
* Additional time to complete an evaluation and applicant costs		

Divisions	Acceptance Tolerances Complete Weighing Device	Acceptance Tolerances Weighing/load-receiving Element with Temp Testing	Acceptance Tolerances Weighing/load-receiving Element only room Temp Testing
0 to 500	0.5 e	0.35 e	0.30 e **(proposed)**
501 to 2000	1.0 e	0.70 e	0.60 e **(proposed)**
2001 to 4000	1.5 e	1.05 e	0.70 e **(proposed)**
4001 to 10 000	2.0 e	1.40 e	0.80 e **(proposed)**

This recommended new tolerance applies to weighing/load-receiving elements that meet the following criteria:

1. Weighing elements must have NTEP-approved load cells with an n_{max} of 5000 and must be approved for temperatures $-10\ °C$ to $+40\ °C$ ($14\ °F$ to $104\ °F$).

2. Weighing elements Certificate of Conformance (CC) will specify the load cell used during the evaluation and state that a similar NTEP-approved load cell could be used.

   NOTE: The replacement load cell must have an n_{max} of 5000 and be approved for temperatures $-10\ °C$ to $+40\ °C$ ($14\ °F$ to $104\ °F$).

The Weighing Sector should consider that the proposed change to amend Publication 14 tolerances for weighing/load-receiving elements tested at room temperature would likely require supporting language in NIST Handbook 44. Additionally, the proposal, as submitted, will continue to require temperature testing if the load cell does not have an NTEP CC or if the load cells have a temperature range other than $-10\ °C$ to $40°\ C$.

The technical advisor seeks input from manufacturers that are holders of OIML R76 test reports conducted by other international laboratories and information on the international policies regarding the testing of these devices that use OIML R60 load cells.

Discussion: During the discussion of this item, the NIST technical advisor reported that load cell manufacturers do not make special cells for weighing/load-receiving elements that are submitted for type evaluation. The load cell manufacturers reported that they select load cells with errors that are well within the maximum permissible errors if they know a weighing/load-receiving element is to be submitted for type evaluation.

Some of the NTEP participating laboratories reported that they continue to see problems with weighing/load-receiving elements during the influence factor tests that do not comply with tolerances. The NTEP applicants have stated that the materials used in the construction of weighing/load-receiving elements and components in load cell junction boxes that are affected by influence factors were the reason the device failed influence factor testing.

A manufacturer commented that weighing/load-receiving elements above 2000 lb are also required to comply with influence factor requirements and suggested that NTEP perform testing above the 2000 lb limit. Another manufacturer stated that international laboratories testing for compliance with OIML R76 for Non-automatic Weighing Instruments do not evaluate weighing/load-receiving elements above 1000 kg (2000 lb). Additionally, the manufacturer reported that R76 used a different apportion of errors for evaluation of elements (modules) that reduced the problems encountered by NTEP.

The NTEP director expressed concern with the current apportionment of errors for separable elements and load cells. The load cells used in weighing/load-receiving elements have an "M" (multiple load cell application) designation, which means that a 1.0 factor is applied to the applicable tolerance. This may present a problem with weighing/load-receiving elements since they are evaluated to a tighter tolerance (0.7 time the applicable tolerance) than the load cells.

Recommendation: Based upon the discussion and comments, the submitter withdrew its proposal.

10. Time Dependence Tolerances

Source: NIST WMD and NTEP Laboratories

Background: John Elengo, in his comparison of Handbook 44, OIML R76 – Non-automatic Weighing Instruments, and OIML R60 – Load Cells, provided the following background information on the development and evolution of Handbook 44 Scales Code T.N.4.5. Time Dependence.

> Prior to the establishment of Handbook 44 paragraph T.N.4.5., there was no such U.S. requirement for "creep" and, at the time of its consideration, the OIML requirement was based on a 4-hour period. This was considered excessive, especially since the error is primarily that of the load cells used in a scale. Generally, the greatest amount of load cell creep occurs during a short period (minutes) immediately following a step change in load. Thereafter, the output becomes more and more constant. Hence, Handbook 44 adopted a 1-hour requirement rather than a 4-hour requirement. Some years later and during the course of revising OIML R60, it became evident that most international evaluation laboratories were not conducting the 4-hour test but a shorter one, and the creep proved to stabilize sufficiently during this shorter test. The assumption was made that it would meet the 4-hour requirement. This assumption was verified by sample tests. Based on this experience and that gained in the international comparison of load cell evaluations, the international work group for R60 concluded that a 30-minute test is sufficient provided that, in addition to measuring the difference over a 30-minute period, the difference occurring in the last 10 minutes of this period be measured also. A more restrictive allowance than the total allowance for the 30-minute period is applied to the 10-minute period difference in order to assure the creep is becoming more and more constant and not increasing. OIML R76 adopted the R60 30-minute requirement. In so doing, the requirement now applies to the instrument as a whole and not only to the load cell. If main components other than the load cell are a source of creep, they can be accounted for using the principle of apportionment of errors (including the assignment of fractions *pi* to those various separate main components of an instrument that can be evaluated separately). [refer to R76-1, 3.5.4]

This item was further discussed at the 2004 meeting of the NTEP participating laboratories where they agreed to forward a proposal to align Handbook 44 with R76 and R60. However, there was some discussion about the accuracy class marking for load cells (A, B, C, and D). Steve Patoray indicated that OIML recommended load cells be marked with letter accuracy class designations so that load cells would not be confused with scales. This is consistent with the NTEP policy that a load cell by itself does not constitute a weighing/load-receiving element. The labs felt that there would be confusion by field inspectors if scales could have load cells marked with either an alpha or numeric accuracy class.

The NIST technical advisor recommended amending paragraph T.N.4.5. and adding new paragraphs T.N.4.5.1. and T.4.5.2. to include performance and zero return requirements that are aligned with OIML R76 and R60 as follows:

T.N.4.5. Time Dependence (Creep) for Non-automatic Weighing Instruments (Scales) during Type Evaluation. - At constant test conditions, the indication 20 seconds after the application of a load and the indication after 1 hour shall not differ by more than:

(a) one-half of the absolute value of the applicable tolerance for the applied load for class III L devices, and

(b) the absolute value of the applicable tolerance for the applied load for all other devices.
(Amended 1989)

T.N.4.5.1. A non-automatic weighing instrument of Class II, III, and IIII shall meet the following requirements at constant test conditions:

(a) When any load is kept on an instrument, the difference between the indication obtained immediately after placing a load and the indication observed during the following 30 minutes shall not exceed 0.5 e.

(b) However, the difference between the indication obtained at 15 minutes and that at 30 minutes shall not exceed 0.2 e. If these conditions are not met, the difference between the indication obtained

~~immediately after placing a load on the instrument and the indication observed during the following four hours shall not exceed the absolute value of the maximum permissible error at the load applied.~~

~~(c) The deviation on returning to zero as soon as the indication has stabilized, after the removal of any load which has remained on the instrument for one half hour, shall not exceed 0.5 e.~~

~~For a multi-interval instrument, the deviation shall not exceed 0.5 e_1 (first weighing segment).~~

~~On a multiple range instrument, the deviation on returning to zero from Max$_i$ (load in the applicable weighing range) shall not exceed 0.5 e_i (interval of the weighing segment). Furthermore, after returning to zero from any load greater than Max$_1$ (capacity of the first weighing range) and immediately after switching to the lowest weighing range, the indication near zero shall not vary by more than e_1 (interval of the first weighing range) during the following 5 minutes.~~

~~**T.N.4.5.2.** A weighing instrument of Class III L shall meet the following requirements:~~

~~(a) When any load is kept on an instrument, the difference between the indication obtained immediately after placing a load and the indication observed during the following 30 minutes shall not exceed 1.5 e.~~

~~(b) However, the difference between the indication obtained at 15 minutes and that at 30 minutes shall not exceed 0.6 e. If these conditions are not met, the difference between the indication obtained immediately after placing a load on the instrument and the indication observed during the following four hours shall not exceed the absolute value of the maximum permissible error at the load applied.~~

~~The deviation on returning to zero as soon as the indication has stabilized, after the removal of any load which has remained on the instrument for one-half hour, shall not exceed one-half of the absolute value of the applicable tolerance for the applied load for Class III L devices.~~

Add new paragraphs T.N.4.6. through T.N.4.6.3. and Table T.N.4.6.2. to include tolerances for load performance and zero repeatability that are aligned with OIML R60.

T.N.4.6. Time Dependence (Creep) for Load Cells during Type Evaluation. – A load cell (force transducer) marked with an accuracy class, shall meet the following requirements at constant test conditions:

T.N.4.6.1. - With a constant maximum load for the measuring range, D_{max}, between 90 % and 100 % of maximum capacity, E_{max}, applied to the load cell, the difference between the initial reading and any reading obtained during the next 30 minutes shall not exceed the absolute value of the maximum permissible error (mpe) for the applied load (see N.4.6.2.). The difference between the reading obtained at 20 minutes and the reading obtained at 30 minutes shall not exceed 0.15 times the absolute value of the mpe (see N.4.6.2.).

T.N.4.6.2. - The mpe for creep shall be determined from Table 5 using the following apportionment factors (pLC):

pLC = 0.7 for load cells marked with S (single load cell applications), and
pLC = 1.0 for load cells marked with M (multiple load cell applications).

Table T.N.4.6.2. Maximum Permissible Errors (mpe) on Type Evaluation				
Tolerance (mpe)	**Load (m)**			
	Class I	Class II	Class III	IIII
pLC x 0.5v	$0 \leq m \leq 50,000v$	$0 \leq m \leq 5000v$	$0 \leq m \leq 500v$	$0 \leq m \leq 50$
pLC x 1.0v	$50,001v \leq m \leq 200,000v$	$5001v \leq m \leq 20,000v$	$501v \leq m \leq 2000v$	$51v \leq m \leq 200v$
pLC x 1.5v	$200,001v \leq m$	$20,001v \leq m \leq 100,000v$	$2001v \leq m \leq 10,000v$	$201v \leq m \leq 1000v$
	Load m, Class III L			

| pLC x 0.5v | $0 \leq m \leq 500v$ | |
| pLC x 1.0v | $501 \leq m \leq 1000v$ * | |

* Add 0.7 to the tolerance for each 500 v of load or fraction thereof up to a maximum load of 10 000 v for load cells marked with S.
* Add 1.0 to the tolerance for each 500 v of load or fraction thereof up to a maximum load of 10 000 v for load cells marked with M.

The NIST technical advisor acknowledges that this proposal and the proposal in the following agenda item address the alignment issue in small steps. Another possible alternative for aligning Handbook 44 and Publication 14 with OIML R60 is to consider incorporating OIML R60 chapters 1 through 7 by reference into Handbook 44 and OIML R60 Annexes A through E into Publication 14. Handbook 44 and Publication 14 could further include paragraphs that state which requirements are not adopted, are different than, or are in addition to OIML R60.

Discussion/Recommendation: The Weighing Sector discussed the impact and implications of amending the marking requirements for load cells to align with the marking requirements in OIML R60 (see applicable extracts of OIML R60 marking requirements and selection guidelines in Appendix A). One of the Sector members noted that the proposal for time dependence testing did not include Class I scales (Note: OIML R76 does not require Class I scales comply with time dependence (creep) requirements). However, the current language in Handbook 44 paragraph TN.4.5. includes Class I scales.

The Sector withdrew this item from the Weighing Sector agenda since the proposal did not relate to problems encountered with Publication 14 type evaluation procedures. Additionally, there was no time at the end of the meeting to further discuss this item.

11. Publication 14 Force Transducer (Load Cell) Family and Selection Criteria

Source: NTEP Committee Technical Advisor

Background: The OIML Mutual Acceptance Agreement (MAA) was adopted at a recent International Committee on Legal Metrology (CIML) meeting in Kyoto, Japan, in November 2003. The agreement will likely allow NTEP to accept (and eventually exchange) reports and test data for load cells that have been evaluated to OIML R60 – Load Cells requirements. The data then can be evaluated to NCWM Publication 14 requirements in order to issue an NTEP Certificate of Conformance. Although the MAA does not require the U.S. and NTEP requirements to be fully harmonized and aligned with the requirements in R60, it does require that NTEP identify the differences **between the** requirements so that an OIML applicant is aware of additional testing and policies applicable to its load cells such as markings, Class III L tolerances, and family and selection guidelines.

Additionally, the original NTEP Publication 14 load cell family and selection guidelines were originally developed prior the adoption of similar guidelines in the 2000 revision of OIML R60. John Elengo and the U.S. National Work Group developed and submitted the guidelines that are currently in R60.

The NIST technical advisor recommended that the selection guidelines and definition of a load cell family in OIML R60 be incorporated in NCWM Publication 14 to the fullest extent possible. Additionally, it was suggested that the Sector consider making a recommendation to adopting the R60 marking requirements into Handbook 44. The primary difference between R60 and Handbook 44 are markings for humidity and accuracy classes. The R60 class markings for load cells are A, B, C, and D. Handbook 44 class markings for load cells are the same for scales and load cells (I, II, III, III L and IIII). It has been reported that the purpose of different class markings for R60 load cells was to ensure that a load cell and indicating element would not be considered a non-automatic weighing instrument. This is consistent with the NTEP policy stating that a load cell incorporated with a tank, hopper, hook or platform does not convey that the load cell (and indicating element) CC covers the complete weighing system.

Discussion: The NTEP director summarized the current NTEP load cell selection process as follows:

- One load cell would be selected if the family is small (e.g., 10:1).

- The capacity selected would be close to the middle of the family and within 4:1 of the highest and lowest capacity load cell in the family.

Using this process, NTEP typically selects a capacity that is not the most difficult to manufacture but is likely to be the most popular. The R60 selection process typically selects load cells of a lower capacity, which are more difficult to build and manufacture. The NTEP system is significantly different from international requirements.

Several of the load cell manufacturers present agreed that the lowest capacity load cell is the most difficult to manufacturer. One of the manufacturers further stated that he believes the OIML R60 selection process is more stringent. However, the OIML R60 family definition is broader than NTEP, and they have not seen an increase or decrease in the number of cells submitted for evaluation.

Recommendation: The Weighing Sector agreed to assign a work group (Stephen Patoray (NTEP), Steven Cook (NIST), the NIST Force Group, Joseph Antkowiak (Flintec), Frank Rusk (Coti), and the California NTEP laboratory) to:

1. **Develop the definition of a family, determine load cell selection criteria, and develop an example of a load cell selection for 2005 NCWM Interim Meeting.**
2. **Review and adapt OIML R60 language for incorporation into Publication 14 for the next meeting of the Weighing Sector.**

The NIST technical advisor will forward an electronic copy of OIML R60 to assist the work group members.

12. Compatibility of Indicators Interfaced with Weighing and Measuring Elements

Source: NTETC Measuring Sector and NCWM S&T Committee

Background: See the Report for the 89th National Conference on Weights and Measures, Specifications and Tolerances Committee Agenda Item 310-2 for additional background information.

During its 2003 meeting, the NTETC Measuring Sector agreed to forward a proposal to the NCWM S&T Committee through the SWMA to add a new paragraph G-N.3. Compatibility of Indicators and Weighing or Measuring Elements to Handbook 44. The proposal intended to clarify what requirements must be met to interface an indicating element and a weighing or measuring element, each of which has its own NTEP CC listing compatible communication specifications, but not previously evaluated together on a single NTEP CC.

At the 2004 NCWM Interim Meeting, the S&T Committee heard several comments indicating that this item is not sufficiently developed to move forward. The S&T Committee decided to **withdraw** Item 310-2 from the S&T Committee agenda until it is further developed and resubmitted by the NTETC Weighing and Measuring Sectors.

Discussion: The Weighing Sector reviewed the background information. The NIST technical advisor reported that an *ad hoc* meeting may be scheduled on Saturday, October 23, 2004, with the Measuring Sector members attending the Southern Weights and Measures Association meeting in Gulfport, Mississippi, to discuss this item.

The Weighing Sector agreed with the NTEP director that the policies used by the NTETC Measuring Sector are very restrictive. Members of the Measuring Sector want to have policies for measuring elements that are as flexible as existing Weighing Sector policies. Weighing device policies permit separate main elements (e.g., indicators, load cells, and weighing elements) with separate NTEP Certificates of Conformance to be combined—a practice referred to as "mixing and matching"—to create weighing systems which are recognized by NTEP.

The representatives from Canada reported that their liquid-measuring device type evaluation laboratory performs additional evaluations on the pulse output from the measuring element and the pulse input capability of the indicating element. NTEP essentially evaluates the performance of the combination of elements.

Some of the Weighing Sector members believed that the proposal belongs in the Liquid-Measuring Devices Code. They also were concerned that the terms "previously evaluated" and "Handbook 44 compliant ticket" are not clear and need further development. Another concern expressed by the Weighing Sector was that the proposed language in G-N.3. (a) could be interpreted to mean that all combinations of communication means between elements would have to be evaluated without adequate Handbook 44 standards and Publication 14 tests.

Other Weighing Sector members believed `there are no significant compatibility issues with weighing devices. Separable indicating and weighing/load receiving elements will either work correctly (if properly installed and configured) or not be operable. The NTEP director discussed the fact that NTEP does have an issue with the compatibility of separable indicating and weighing/load receiving elements, especially with vehicle scales with several load cells. OIML R76 evaluates the minimum voltage per scale verification division, which has not been adopted in Handbook 44 and Publication 14. The combination of separable indicating and weighing/load-receiving elements would not be a suitable combination if the signal from the weighing/load-receiving element were too small for the indicating element. The resultant combination will appear to perform correctly; however, it may no longer comply with influence factors and have a zone of uncertainty that would be too large to display a stable weight.

The Weighing Sector also stated that they do not fully understand liquid-measuring device technology compatibility issues (i.e., pulse counting compatibility, partially compatible digital communications, and applicable NTEP liquid-measuring device testing) to give additional input on the proposal.

Recommendation: The Sector believes that the proposal is not appropriate for weighing devices since the language could require all combinations of devices and communications be evaluated. The Weighing Sector agrees with the Measuring Sector that this is not the intent of the proposed language.

The Sector supports the joint meeting of the NTETC Weighing and Measuring Sector members who are attending the 2004 SWMA Technical Conference. If the Sectors agree on the issues and proposal, then the proposal can be placed in the General Code; otherwise, any proposals should remain in the specific codes. If there is no clear consensus of that meeting, the Measuring Sector could request a separate work group to develop a proposal to address the compatibility of multiple elements issue.

13. Handbook 44 Computing Scales Interfaced with an Electronic Cash Register

Source: NTEP Participating Laboratories

Background: Field inspectors have reported to one of the NTEP laboratories that they are finding computing scales interfaced with electronic cash registers (ECR) where an ECR will accept weighing results from the computing scale, use the ECR's price look-up (PLU) to retrieve tare and unit price information, and calculate the total price. The inspectors have reported that a different unit price, tare, and total price may already be entered and displayed on the computing scale. What the customer sees on the display of the computing scale (the net weight, unit price, and total price) may not be what the customer is actually charged and printed on the ECR receipt. The NTEP laboratories have reported that at least three companies have requested this method of operation for NTEP certification.

In one example, the scale manufacturer is marketing the computing scale as a point-of-sale scale for use with an ECR. The computing scale has push button tare, percent tare, PLUs, gross/net display, and memory recall. The company wants to amend its CC to allow the scale's use in general applications and for use with an ECR. The company notes that this is one of the most important selling features for its product line. It gives the operator the ability to quote the price of an item without having to "ring it up" on the ECR.

The operation is addressed in Sections 11.15. to 11.21. of the 2004 Publication 14 Electronic Cash Registers Interfaced with Scales (ECRS) checklist. If the ECR were setup to meet the requirements of those sections there wouldn't be a problem. The company does not want to burden the end user with using a compatible ECR designed to work with a computing scale. The company stated that the computing scale, interfaced with an ECR, is already approved by a weights and measures jurisdiction.

The NTEP laboratories believe NIST Handbook 44 needs clarification in this area and are proposing the following paragraph be added to the Scales Code to address those areas already noted in NCWM Publication 14:

~~**S.1.8.5. Computing Scale Interfaced to a Cash Register.** - A computing scale may interface with a cash register provided:~~

> ~~(a) The cash register only records (serves as a printer) the information received from the scale.~~
> ~~(b) The computing scale has tare capability.~~
> ~~(c) The computing scale is not equipped with PLU capability.~~
> ~~(d) The electronic cash register does not have any input to the computing scale in the process of determining the total price of a weighed item.~~

Discussion: The Sector reviewed the background information and proposed language for NIST Handbook 44. The Maryland participating laboratory added that in the example they encountered, a unit price that would be displayed on the scale would be different than the unit price associated with product look-up code in the electronic cash register. Tares can also be overridden. The device was subsequently submitted for NTEP evaluation and the identified problems were corrected. The participating laboratories believe there is no problem with the test performed in Publication 14; however, they stated that the field inspector does not have the information contained in Publication 14 and has not been trained to look for the problems identified in the background information.

Several Sector members stated that the Maryland field officials properly identified a problem with the agreement of indications, noted that the ECR and computing scale Certificates of Conformance did not list this combination of interfaces, and took appropriate corrective actions.

Recommendation: The Sector agreed not to recommend the proposed changes to NIST Handbook 44 since there are currently appropriate means in Handbook 44 (G-S.5. Indicating and Recording Elements and G-S.2. Facilitation of Fraud), and the examination procedure outlines address these issues during field evaluation.

14. Publication 14 Requirements for Computing Scales Interfaced with an Electronic Cash Register

Source: NTEP Participating Laboratories

Background: In addition to the background information in the above agenda item for computing scales interfaced with an electronic cash register (ECR), many computing scale manufacturers are not aware of the computing scale and ECR interface requirements in the ECRS checklist (electronic cash register interfaced with scales) in NCWM Publication 14. Also, there are no guidelines in the Digital Electronic Scales (DES) checklist to direct them to the appropriate language in the ECRS checklist.

The participating laboratories recommend that NCWM Publication 14 DES and ECRS be amended to:

1. Put a check box in the Publication 14 DES checklist that will state that the computing scale interfaced to an ECR meets the applicable requirements in the ECRS checklist, and

2. Add to the ECRS checklist: "If the scale has multiple sales accumulation capability, only weighed items are accumulated and the cash register only records the total accumulated price."

Discussion: The Sector discussed the proposal to amend Publication 14. The Sector agreed the addition to the DES checklist was appropriate. However, the Sector was concerned about the ability of a computing scale to have an operational accumulation capability while it was interfaced with an ECR because the receipt on an ECR itemizes purchases made by the customer, however the items that are accumulated on the computing scale would not be itemized in the ECR receipt.

NTEP Committee 2005 Final Report
Appendix D – NTETC - Weighing Sector

Recommendation: The Sector recommends that Publication 14 DES checklist be amended as proposed by the NTEP laboratories and that the proposal to amend the ECRS checklist be amended to require the computing scale accumulation capability be disabled if it can be interfaced with an ECR ("If the scale has multiple sales accumulation capability, only weighed items are accumulated and the cash register only records the total accumulated price, or the scale accumulation capability is disabled"). The NIST technical advisor further recommended an editorial change to the ECRS checklist by renumbering paragraphs 11.15. through 11.21. to 11.15.1. through 11.5.7. to clarify the requirements are for computing scales interfaced with an ECR. The proposed recommendation to amend Publication 14 is in Appendix A, agenda Item 14.

15. Publication 14 - Computing Scale Section

Source: NTEP Participating Laboratories

Background: The Weighing Sector discussed a Maryland NTEP laboratory proposal to clarify display identification, label formatting, and the use of other features (pre-pack, POS application, etc.) The NTEP laboratories agreed the computing scale section of the DES checklist lacks clarity in these areas.

The Maryland NTEP laboratory drafted amendments to NCWM Publication 14 DES Section 27 that clarifies checklist requirements for price computing scales.

Discussion: The Sector agreed with the proposal from the Maryland NTEP laboratory and reviewed the examples of correct and incorrect labels for compliance with applicable sections of NIST Handbook 130 Uniform Packaging and Labeling Regulation, including the use of "unit price" on the printed labels. The Sector suggested that the proposal be amended to correct the examples of correct labels that do no have a kg, lb, or count associated with the unit prices and add an additional example where the term "unit price" is correctly used on a label.

Recommendation: The Sector recommends the proposal to amend Publication 14, Section 27, as modified by the Sector, be incorporated into Publication 14, as shown in Appendix A agenda Item 15.

16. Publication 14 - New Items in Computing Scale Section

Source: Maryland Participating Laboratory

Background: This item is related to the computing scale proposal in agenda Item 15 and was included in the original discussion at the NTEP laboratory meeting. The Maryland NTEP laboratory believed the computing scale section of the DES checklist lacked clarity in the areas of multiple uses of displays, position of displays, and the use of other features (e.g., pre-pack)

Generally, manufacturers use the "unit price" or a separate display for indicating non-metrological information (e.g., PLU codes). If non-metrological numerical values are placed in the "weight" display or in the "total price" display, they could be misleading and interpreted as valid weight.

The Maryland NTEP laboratory recommended the following additional language for NCWM Publication 14, Section 27- Price Computing Scales:

27.X.	Dedicated displays (used only for the display of the specific information) are provided for the total price and the quantity information. (Values that could be interpreted as a weight shall not be displayed in the weight display window.)	Yes ☐ No ☐ N/A ☐
27.X.	The placement of displays shall be mathematically logical (net weight x unit price = total price) when reading from left to right (or top to bottom).	Yes ☐ No ☐ N/A ☐
27.X.	When a computing scale is setup in a mode for indirect sales to the customer, information that would not be available in the direct sales mode **is not** displayed on the customer side.	Yes ☐ No ☐ N/A ☐

NTEP Committee 2005 Final Report
Appendix D – NTETC - Weighing Sector

The following areas of R76-Non-automatic Weighing Instruments were used in developing the additional requirements.

OIML R76 states:

4.4.4. Multiple use of indicating devices

Indications other than primary indications may be displayed in the indicating device, provided that,

- the appropriate unit of measurement, or symbol thereof, or a special sign identifies quantities other than weight values,
- weight values that are not weighing results shall be clearly identified, or they may be displayed only temporarily on manual command and shall not be printed.

No restrictions apply if the weighing mode is made inoperative by a special command.

4.15.4. Special applications of a price-computing instrument

Only if all transactions performed by the instrument or by connected peripherals are printed on a ticket or label intended for the customer, a price-computing instrument may perform additional functions that facilitate trade and management. These functions shall not lead to confusion about the results of weighing and price computing.

Other operations or indications not covered by the following provisions may be performed, provided that no indication that could possibly be misunderstood as a primary indication is presented to the customer.

Discussion: The Maryland NTEP laboratory reported on a computing scale (see picture below) that used the "Total Price" display to indicate the product code prior to a load placed on the scale and a calculation of total price. If the product code was indicated in the "Total Price" display while a load was already on the scale, a customer may believe that the product code number is the total price to pay.

Many of the sector members did not believe the example provided by the Maryland laboratory was a problem since the product code did not use a decimal point similar to a representation of money.

Recommendation: The Sector believed the example provided by the Maryland NTEP laboratory did not demonstrate a problem. It also believed the proposed language could cause additional confusion. The submitter agreed to develop language to further its case and submit such to the Sector for discussion and ballot approval. If no consensus can be reached on the ballot, the item will be carried over to the next meeting of the Weighing Sector.

17. Handbook 44 - Location of Marking for "Capacity x d" on Scales

Source: NTEP Participating Laboratories

Background: NIST Handbook 44, Scales Code, Table S.6.3.b., Note 3 states:

The nominal capacity and the value of the scale division shall be shown together (e.g., 50 000 x 5 kg, 100 000 x 10 lb, 15 x 0.005 kg, or 30 x 0.01 lb) adjacent to the weight display when the nominal capacity and the value of the scale division are not readily apparent. Each scale division value or weight unit shall be marked on multiple range or multiple-interval scales.

There have been discussions with the NTEP labs on their interpretation of the location requirement for marking "capacity x d." Specifically, what is meant by the term "adjacent?" This item has been addressed several times in the past and the Weighing Sector and NCWM Executive Committee have been unable to develop a solution. The June 1990 NTETC Weighing Sector Report stated:

"The Committee was unable to be more definitive and maintained its opinion that the NTEP Laboratory's judgment remains the best solution. In cases of extreme disagreement, the appeal process (to the Board of Governors) is the avenue to resolve."

Attempts to interpret this requirement continue to cause conflict between NTEP labs and manufacturers. The NTEP labs maintain that the marking shall be next to the weight display on the face of a scale, but devices are being submitted with the marking located elsewhere on the face of the scale. (See the following examples.)

Example 1 - Correct

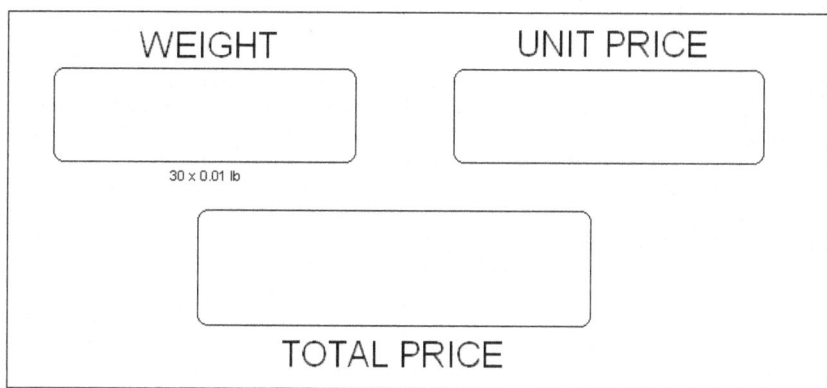

Example 2 - Incorrect

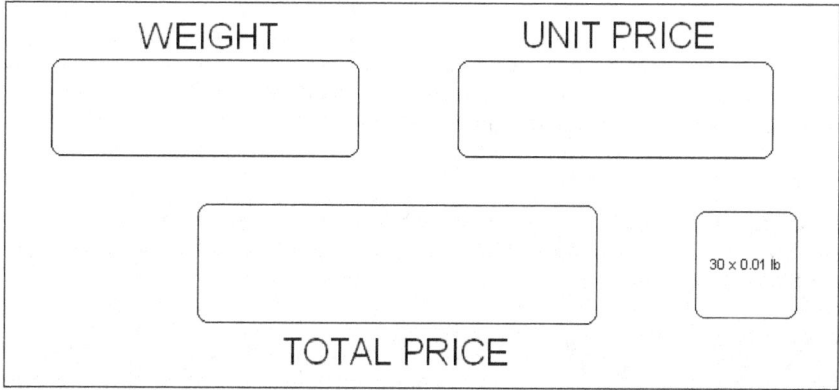

NOTE: By amending Handbook 44 as proposed, both examples would be acceptable.

The NTEP laboratories agree with the following premises:

- Example 2 is incorrect according to Handbook 44 because the marking does not appear *adjacent* to the weight display *(Tech Advisor comment: Additionally, the markings are not placed as close as practical to the weight indication as required in G-S.5.2.4. Values).*
- The operator is familiar with the device and does not rely heavily on the location of the marking for capacity x division.
- The customer rarely understands the marking or its significance.
- The marking in both examples is conspicuous enough for the inspector and service technician who rely most heavily on the information.
- Both examples in the attachment would be acceptable if the requirement could be amended to allow for the marking to simply be placed conspicuously on the face of the indicating portion of the scale. *(Tech advisor comment: The current Scales Code requirements are not in conflict with the General Code paragraph G-S.5.2.4. Values, however, the proposal submitted by the NTEP laboratories does create a conflict since the markings may not be placed as close as practical to the indications.)*

NCWM Publication 14 DES Section 2.13. states:

~~2.13. The nominal capacity by minimum scale division shall be clearly and conspicuously marked adjacent to the weight display. (Acceptable location depends on conspicuousness.)~~

This statement implies, and the NTEP laboratories concur, that "conspicuousness" should be the primary concern, not "adjacent." But until "adjacent" is removed from the requirement, NTEP is tied to that portion of the requirement as well.

The NIST technical advisor also included language in OIML R76 for Non-automatic Weighing Instruments paragraph 7.1.4 Presentation of descriptive markings. The NIST technical advisor believes the recommendations in R76 satisfy the intent of the participating laboratories' recommendations and does not require a third definition of "face" in NIST Handbook 44, Appendix D, as follows:

7.1.4. Presentation of descriptive markings
The descriptive markings shall be indelible and of a size, shape and clarity allowing easy reading. They shall be grouped together in a clearly visible place either on a descriptive plate fixed to an instrument or on a part of the instrument itself.
The markings:
Max …
Min …
e …
and d if d does not equal e
shall also be shown near the display of the result if they are not already located there *(Tech advisor note: The markings may need to be repeated near the result if they are on a plate or location that is not near the weight display, or if the markings are on separable elements).* It shall be possible to seal the plate bearing the descriptive markings unless its removal will result in its destruction. If the data plate is sealed, it shall be possible to apply a control mark to it.

The participating laboratories asked the Nebraska NTEP laboratory to develop a proposal to amend Scales Code Table S.6.3.b., Note 3 and add a new definition of "face" based upon discussions of this item during the 2004 meeting of the NTEP laboratories.

Discussion/Recommendation: The Weighing Sector reviewed the background information and the proposed amendments to Handbook 44 from the NTEP laboratories and the NIST technical advisor. The Sector agreed to forward to the regional and NCWM S&T Committees the following amended recommendation:

The nominal capacity and value of the scale division shall be shown together (e.g., ~~50 000 x 5 kg, 100 000 x 10 lb,~~ 15 x 0.005 k, or 30 x 0.01 lb) ~~adjacent to the weight display in a clear and conspicuous manner and be readily apparent when viewing the reading face of the scale indicator unless when the nominal capacity and the value of the scale division are not immediately~~ it is already apparent by the design of the device. **Each scale division value or weight unit shall be marked on multiple range or multi-interval scales.**
[Nonretroactive as of January 1, 1983]
(Amended January 1, 200X)

18. CLC Type Evaluation Tests on Railway Track/Vehicle Scales – Technical Policy

Source: Brechbuhler Scales Inc.

Background: During the 1998 NTETC Weighing Sector meeting, the Sector agreed the GIPSA (Grain Inspection Packers and Stockyards Administration) test car may be used to satisfy testing requirements for CLC and section capacity. However, there was no recommendation regarding the addition of vehicle weighing applications for existing Certificates of Conformance (CC) that were certified for only railway track applications. Brechbuhler Scales believes that vehicle weighing applications (e = 20 lb) can be added on a railway track scale NTEP CC without additional testing, and that the CLC rating can be established based upon previous section tests using the GIPSA test car (or other railroad test cars and additional test weights used for the evaluation). Brechbuhler Scales states that there is no benefit for performing additional CLC tests to include the vehicle weighing application to an existing railway track scale CC.

It should be noted that existing NTEP technical policy A. Models to be submitted for Evaluation, paragraph 8(a) Weighing Systems, Scales or Weighing/Load-receiving Elements Greater than 30 000 lb Capacity states that the scale division **e** will be limited to the value of **e** that was originally evaluated and listed on the CC.

Brechbuhler Scales requested that vehicle weighing applications (e = 20 lb) be added to existing railway track scale CCs (e = 50 lb) that have been designed to Cooper E-80 standards and tested using the GISPA test car (or other railroad test cars and additional test weights).

Discussion: The Sector reviewed the background information and discussed amending the appropriate NTEP Technical Policy. Brechbuhler Scales also provided additional history of the item. The railroad track scale in question was originally submitted as a combination vehicle/railroad track scale. However, the user changed the application such that vehicles could not drive onto the scale, therefore, the device was evaluated and a Certificate of Conformance was issued for railroad track applications only. On a later installation, a CLC test was performed. Brechbuhler Scales questions the value of the additional evaluation.

Some of the Sector members support additional testing to verify that a railroad track scale can accurately weigh at lower capacities used by highway vehicles. They report frequent problems when the scale is calibrated for railroad use and is inaccurate for vehicle weighing. Additionally, the traffic patterns are different between highway vehicles and railroad cars. Highway vehicles frequently travel along the side of the scale where railroad cars travel on the rails, which are typically located on the main girders of the weighbridge. These Sector members believed that a scale designed for railroad cars might not have been designed to adequately support highway vehicles along the sides of the scale.

The manufacturers stated that the calibration problems encountered during verifications are the result of improper use and maintenance of railway track scales.

Other Sector members believe that CLC testing can be eliminated on combination vehicle/railroad track scales because of the amount of weights placed on the scale. Dave Quinn reported that he is working on a white paper that will help clarify the CLC issue.

Recommendation: The Weighing Sector did not reach a consensus on this item. Brechbuhler Scales stated that they would develop and submit a proposal for testing for railroad track scales that will include procedures to include highway vehicle applications.

NTEP Committee 2005 Final Report
Appendix D – NTETC - Weighing Sector

This item will be carried over to the 2005 meeting of the Weighing Sector.

19. Display of a Negative Balance Condition and Required Markings

Source: NTEP Participating Laboratories

Background: One of the NTEP laboratories has reported that it has seen not-built-for-purpose primary weight displays in which blanking the weight display is used to indicate a behind zero condition. The problem occurs when all of the required G-S.1. Identification markings also blank. The scale is in an error condition, is still functioning in a normal operational mode as it was designed to operate (display an error code within specific parameters), and is not in a screen saver or sleep mode. Blanking the required markings is not necessary and would give the false impression that the weight display feature is not enabled. Primary indications must be clear and definite. G.S.1. information must be permanently marked.

The laboratories recommended adding the following statement to the end of Publication 14, Digital Electronic Scales, Section 18.2 –Blanking the Display:

> ~~When blanking a primary weight display with live on screen G-S.1. and/or S.6.3. markings, the required markings must not blank.~~

The laboratories also recommended:

- adding language to Section 5- Identification in the ECRS checklist Section 18. Zero Indication;
- similar wording be added to Section 5 of the ECRS checklist;
- group existing paragraphs 5.6. thru 5.9. under a new Section 5.7. to clarify that paragraphs above the phrase "For not-built-for-purpose, software-based devices, the following shall apply:" may be applicable to all ECRs (including not-built-for-purpose, software-based devices).

Discussion/Recommendation: The Weighing Sector reviewed and discussed the proposed changes to Publication 14. A question was asked if the use of "pop-up" displays or menus that temporarily blocked the required information was a problem. The Sector agreed there should be no issues with the "pop-up" feature since this is a temporary condition during normal operation; a transaction cannot be conducted while the temporary feature is operational, and the customer is able to review the entire transaction (zero-load, weight, and price calculations if applicable).

The Sector agreed to recommend that the proposed language, as shown in Appendix A - Agenda Item 19, be added to NCWM Publication 14.

20. Dropping the 4th Step in Class III and IIII Tolerances

Source: NIST Technical Advisor

Background: During the August 2003 meeting of the U.S. National Work Group (USNWG) for R76 Non-Automatic Weighing Instruments, the group discussed the difference in the tolerance for Class III and IIII weighing instruments. The USNWG confirmed that the original intent of the step tolerances was to provide a relationship between scale accuracy and resolution. They further recommended that Handbook 44 Class III and Class IIII tolerances be aligned with OIML R76. The manufacturers present during the meeting reported that they essentially build identically performing instruments and load cells for both national and international markets. Additional background information is presented in Appendix A.

Since the August 2004 meeting Nigel Mills and Gary Lameris of the Hobart Corporation provided the following additional "production data" comparing the different Class III tolerances:

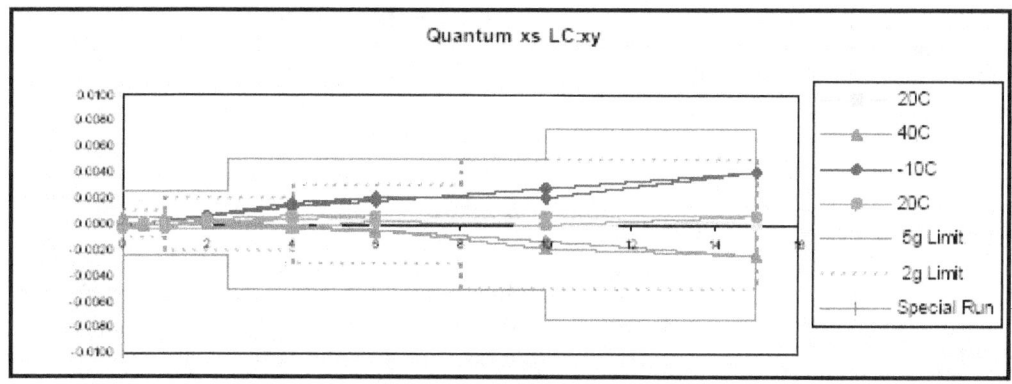

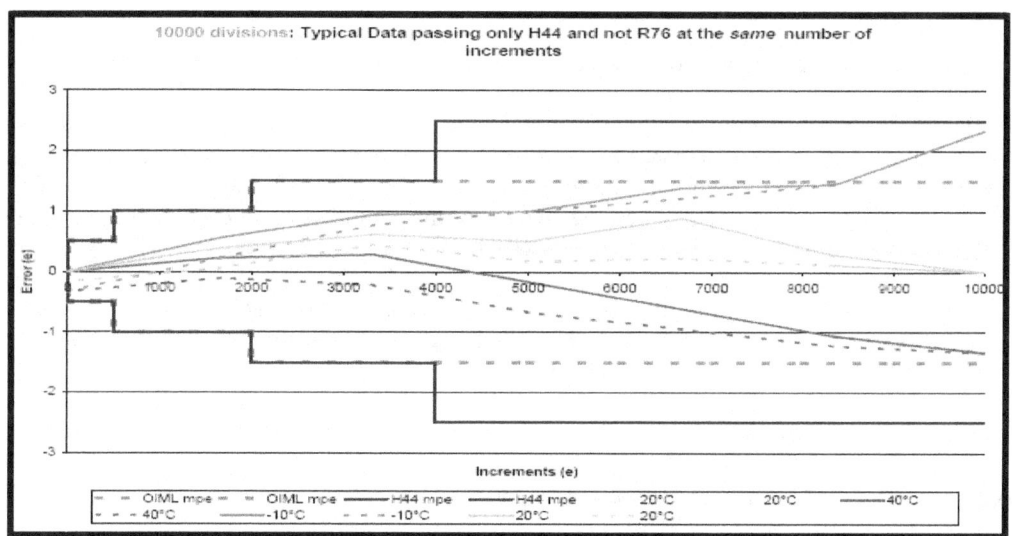

The charts indicate that the above production scales would comply with Handbook 44 linearity tolerances up to 10 000 e and OIML R76 tolerances up to approximately 7000 e. Hobart Corporation also reported that many scales and load cells would have difficulty complying with the temperature effect on zero with an n $_{max}$ greater than 5000 e in both Handbook 44 and OIML R76.

The Sector was requested to review the background information and discuss submitting the following proposal to amend Scales Code Table 6 Maintenance Tolerances as follows:

Table 6. Maintenance Tolerances (All values in this table are in ~~verification~~ scale divisions e)				
Tolerance in ~~verification~~ scale divisions e				
1 2 3 5				–
Class Test	Load			
I	0 - 50 000	50 001 - 200 000	200 001 +	
II	0 - 5 000	5 001 - 20 000	20 001 +	
III	0 - 500	501 - 2 000	2 001 ±	~~4 000~~ ~~4 001 +~~
IIII	0 - 50	51 - 200	201 ±	~~400~~ ~~401 +~~
III L	0 - 500	501 - 1 000	(Add 1d for each additional 500 d or fraction thereof)	

The NIST technical advisor requested that the Sector discuss Accuracy Class III L and offer a technical justification to retain the Handbook 44 Class III L tolerance and propose a similar tolerance be incorporated in OIML R76 or recommend that Class III L be removed from Handbook 44, and if so, should it be non-retroactive? The Class III L tolerance structure in Handbook 44 deviates from the intent step tolerances since there is little relation of the value of the scale division (e.g., e = 20 lb resolution) to the accuracy required (i.e., ± 8 e at 80 000 lb maintenance tolerance). The tolerance values, zero-tracking limit and motion detection requirements in Handbook 44 are roughly equivalent to an R76 instrument when e = 50 lb.

Discussion/Recommendation: The Weighing Sector withdrew this item from its agenda since the proposal did not relate to problems encountered with Publication 14 type evaluation procedures. The Sector recommended that the proposal submitted by NIST and the U.S. National Work Group be made an information/developmental item if it were submitted to the regional weights and measures associations and the NCWM S&T Committee.

Members of the Weighing Sector offered the following comments:

The elimination of the fourth step in Class III weighing devices may encourage the increased usage of multiple range scales. This by itself is desirable, however, NTEP should consider manufacturers' concerns with existing Publication 14 interpretations of Handbook 44 that require the range or interval in use be adequately identified. A problem arises when the change in minimum interval does not change the number of significant digits in the display (frequently used to adequately define which range is in use).

Additionally, the proposal may have an impact on Class III separable weighing/load-receiving elements and load cells and the maximum permissible errors allowed during type evaluation since the apportionment of errors in Handbook 44 is different than OIML R76 and R60.

There was no time available at the end of the meeting to discuss Class III L scales and load cells.

21. Cash Acceptors or Card-activated Systems

Source: NTEP Participating Laboratories

Background: During the 2001 Weighing Sector Meeting, the cash/coin acceptor capability for self-service ECR-POS systems was discussed.

The Sector concluded that the participating labs would use the draft procedure on a one-year trial basis and report back to the NIST technical advisor with their comments. Additionally, the NIST technical advisor would attempt to contact the affected manufacturers of self-service checkout systems interfaced with scales for their comments on the proposed checklist addition.

The NTEP laboratories reported no problems with the draft procedures and agreed to forward them to the Weighing Sector for review and comment. The Sector should also consider if the draft procedures are needed or suitable for Digital Electronic Scales checklist. The NIST technical advisor was requested to send the draft procedures to CC holders of self-checkout POS systems. Unfortunately, this has not been done yet.

Discussion/Recommendation: The Sector agreed to recommend the procedures, as shown in Appendix A, agenda Item 21, be added to Publication 14 ECRS.

22. Tare on a Multiple Range Scales

Source: **NTEP Participating Laboratories:**

Background: NCWM Publication 14, Section 33 is not clear on what is expected of tare on a multiple range scale when switching from a lower weighing range to a higher weighing range. Section 33 states: "On a multiple range instrument, a tare value may only be transferred from one weighing range to another one with a larger verification scale interval but shall then be rounded in the upward direction to the latter verification interval." It is not clear if this means the tare must ~~always~~ be rounded to a ~~higher value~~, or if tare can be rounded ~~to the resolution~~ of the higher range.

During the 2004 NTEP Laboratory meeting in Ottawa Canada, there was discussion about the rounding of tare to zero when the tare value was less than 0.5 e. The Ohio NTEP laboratory believes that rounding of tare should follow normal rounding rules, except that the scale can never round tare to zero and maintain the scale in Net mode, indicating that zero Tare is entered. Don Onwiler, Nebraska, stated that Nebraska's policy is to consider tare less than 0.5 e to be a product without tare material. Canada allows tare to round to the nearest division, including zero. The labs (except NE) agreed to submit the Ohio proposal as amended by the NTEP labs to the Sector with changes noted during the discussion. The tare value can round down to the nearest scale division except when the nearest scale division is zero. Then tare has to round up.

The NTEP laboratories submitted the following amendments to NCWM Publication 14 as indicated in the highlighted text.

33. Multiple Range Scales

A multiple range scale is an instrument having two or more weighing ranges with different maximum capacities and different scale intervals for the same load receptor, each range extending from zero to its maximum capacity. The weighing ranges may be either manually or automatically selected. Each weighing range is considered to be an individual scale and evaluated accordingly.

The capacity and verification scale division must be conspicuously marked near the weight display. The range in use must be clearly indicated. If a scale has a decimal point and a different number of decimal places in each weighing range, the position of the decimal point and the number of digits following is an adequate definition of the weighing range in use. If the weighing ranges do not utilize a decimal point and differing numbers of decimal places (e.g., scale divisions are 20 lb, 50 lb, and 100 lb), another method such as an external range indicator must be provided to indicate the weighing range in use.

Whenever gross and tare weights fall in different weighing ranges so that the scale divisions for the gross and tare weights differ, the net weight must agree mathematically with the gross and tare weights that are indicated or recorded (i.e., net = gross - tare).

On a multiple range instrument, a **tare value may only be transferred from one weighing range to another with a larger verification scale interval. When transferring a tare value from a lower range to a higher range, the tare value should be rounded appropriately to the latter verification interval with care taken to prevent a zero tare value, but** ~~shall then be rounded in the upward direction to the latter verification interval.~~

Examples: (Assuming an interval value for range 1 is 2 lbs and an interval value for range 2 is 5 lbs.)

- Tare value entered in range 1 is 8 lbs – when switching to range 2, the tare value would become 10 lbs.
- Tare value entered in range 1 is 6 lbs – when switching to range 2, the tare value would become 5 lbs.
- Tare value entered in range 1 is 2 lbs – when switching to range 2, the tare value would become 5 lbs ~~or the tare value may be cleared and the scale returned to the gross mode.~~ *(Strikeout was suggested at the spring meeting of the NTEP labs)*
- In examples 1 and 2 above, the tare value is rounded appropriately to realize the smallest error introduced by rounding. ~~In example 3, appropriate rounding could create a zero tare condition. In this example, the tare value would be rounded up or cleared.~~ *(Strikeout was suggested at the spring meeting of the NTEP labs)*

33.1. The range in use shall be conspicuously indicated. **Yes ☐ No ☐ N/A**

33.2. Ranges may be changed:

33.2.1. Manually **Yes ☐ No ☐ N/A**

33.2.1.1.	from a smaller to greater range at any load.	Yes ☐ No ☐ N/A
33.2.1.2.	from a greater to a smaller weighing range when there is no load on the load receptor and the indication is zero or at a negative net value; the tare operation shall either be canceled or revert to the original value and zero shall be set, both automatically.	Yes ☐ No ☐ N/A

33.2.2. Automatically

33.2.2.1.	from a smaller to the following greater weighing range when the load exceeds the maximum gross weight of the range being operative.	Yes ☐ No ☐ N/A
33.2.2.2.	only from a greater to the smallest weighing range when there is no load on the load receptor and the indication is zero or at a negative net value; the tare operation shall either be canceled or revert to the original value and zero shall be set, both automatically.	Yes ☐ No ☐ N/A

33.3. Devices with a tare capability must indicate and record values that satisfy the equation: net = gross − tare, and When automatically changing to a higher range from a lower range, the round the tare value shall be rounded up to the appropriate verification interval for the higher range. Care shall be taken to prevent a zero tare value. larger division size when entering the larger division. Example, 2 g changes to 5 g not 0 g.   Yes ☐ No ☐ N/A

33.4. Keyboard tare entries must be consistent with the displayed scale division.   Yes ☐ No ☐ N/A

33.5. For manual multiple range scales, the maximum weight value indicated in each range must not exceed:

33.5.1. 105 % of the rated capacity for the weighing range, or   Yes ☐ No ☐ N/A

33.5.2. maximum capacity plus 9 d.   Yes ☐ No ☐ N/A

33.6. For all weighing ranges, e must equal d.   Yes ☐ No ☐ N/A

33.7. On a multiple range instrument, the deviation on returning to zero from Max shall not exceed 0.5 e. Furthermore, for automatic range changing devices, after returning to zero from any load greater than Max and immediately after switching to the lowest weighing range, the indication near zero shall not vary by more than **e** during the following 5 minutes.   Yes ☐ No ☐ N/A

Discussion: Several Weighing Sector members stated that forcing a user to round tare up forces them to give away product. Other Sector members responded that they tell the users that items are to be sold on the basis of net weight, customers are not expected to pay for the package material (tare), and that costs associated with tare are part of the cost associated with doing business. Therefore, the unit price of the commodity should be adjusted accordingly. Another Sector member reported that actual quantities of products and tare often fall more or less randomly between indicated amounts and rounding to the nearer value and should balance out over a number of transactions.

It was also reported that Publication 14 allows for tare to be rounded to the nearest scale division for single range scales (DES 2004 paragraph 47.2.2.), but forces tare to be rounded to the next higher division for multiple range scales (DES 2004 paragraph 32.3.). Members of the Sector questioned why the rounding of tare is treated differently between the two types of scales and whether or not Handbook 44 supports the Publication 14 requirements in paragraph 32.3.

Some of the manufacturers stated that they recommend to their customers with pre-packaging scales that they round tare up to the next higher division to reduce the possibility of packages being rejected by weights and measures officials.

Recommendation: The Sector did not reach consensus on this item. This issue will be carried over to the next meetings of the NTEP laboratories and NTETC Weighing Sector.

23. Performance and Permanence Tests for Railway Track Scales Used to Weigh Statically

Source: NTEP Participating Laboratories

Background: The 2004 edition of NCWM Publication 14 states the following:

68. Performance and Permanence Tests for Railway Track Scales Used to Weigh Statically

68.7. Permanence Test

The permanence test shall be conducted from 20 to 30 days after successful completion of the initial performance test. It is recommended that the performance tests described above be repeated. However, if the original test car is not available, the test may be conducted to the extent possible with at least two railroad test weight cars. The results of this test must be within acceptance tolerance [13]. If the device does not meet these tolerance limits, the entire test must be repeated.

(footnote 13) If the subsequent performance test cannot be completed within 30 days because of the unavailability of test cars, maintenance tolerance will be applied.

The NTEP laboratories agreed the wording for this and all permanence testing should be changed to say a "minimum of 20 days" (not stating a maximum). Additionally, Footnote 13 should be removed and acceptance tolerances should be applied for all type evaluation testing, except where absolute values are to be used.

Discussion: The Weighing Sector reviewed the summary of the June 1992 meeting of the NTETC Weighing Sector that addressed the permanence test for railway track scales. The Sector recognized the language in Publication 14, Section 68, footnote 13 is not supported by Handbook 44 paragraph G-T.1. Acceptance Tolerances. However, manufacturers are concerned with eliminating the footnote since it is difficult to perform the subsequent permanence test within the 20- to 30-day time period. They are also concerned that the use (abuse) of these scales makes it difficult for them to maintain acceptance tolerances for periods significantly beyond the 30 days. Additionally, it is costly for the NTEP applicant if the scale fails the permanence test and they have to discontinue the evaluation until a GISPA type test car can return to the site or if they have to pay the railroads to deliver two railroad test cars to the test site.

Recommendation: The Sector agreed to recommend the requirement that the subsequent permanence test be "conducted 20 to 30 days after the successful completion of the initial permanence test" be changed to "after a minimum of 20 days…."

However, there was no consensus or recommendation for the minimum number of weighments between tests or the deletion of footnote 13.

The NIST technical advisor and Ed Luthy (Brechbuhler Scales) volunteered to submit this issue to the railroads during the October 2004 meeting of AREMA Committee 34-Scales (American Railway Engineering and Maintenance of Way Association).

This item will be carried over for the 2005 meeting of the NTETC Weighing Sector.

24. Next Sector Meeting

Discussion/Recommendation: The normal rotation of laboratories for the next Weighing Sector meeting is at the Ohio NTEP participating laboratory. However, the Sector recommends that the meeting be held in conjunction with the Western Weights and Measures Association regional meeting which will be held in Phoenix, AZ, in September 2005.

NTEP Committee 2005 Final Report
Appendix D – NTETC - Weighing Sector

Appendix A - Recommendations for Amendments to Publication 14

Agenda Item 1 (a)

17. Manual Weights

Code References: G-S.2. and S.1.12

The following requirements apply to scales being used for direct sales to the customer, unattended scales, or customer-operated scales and scales used in weighmaster applications. These requirements do not apply to scales and weighing systems used to generate labels for standard net content packages.

17.1. Manual entries of gross or net weights are permitted when being used for direct sales ~~for use~~ in the following applications only: Yes ☐ No ☐ N/A ☐

~~(1)~~POS systems interfaced with a scale when giving credit for a weighed item;
~~(2) when generating labels for standard weight packages;~~
(3̶) postal and package shipping scales when generating manifests for pick-up at a later time; ~~and~~
(4̶) on livestock scales and vehicle scales to correct erroneous tickets; and
(5̶) when an item is pre-weighed on a legal-for-trade scale and marked with the correct net weight.

17.2. The scale shall ~~must~~ be at gross-load or net zero and the scale indication shall ~~must~~ be at zero ~~in the gross weight display mode~~ before manual weight entries are permitted (except for scales being used not-for-direct sales to the customer) and; Yes ☐ No ☐ N/A ☐

17.3. Recorded weight values shall be identified as MAN WT, MANUAL WT, MAN WEIGHT, or similar statement. R recorded manual gross or net weight values must be adequately defined so it is clear that the ~~gross~~ weight values are manual gross or net weight entries. ~~Recorded weight values must be identified as MAN WT, MANUAL WT, MAN WEIGHT, or similar statement.~~ Yes ☐ No ☐ N/A ☐

The use of a symbol to identify multiple manual weight entries is permitted, provided the symbol is defined on the same page on which the manual weight entries appear and the definition of the symbol is automatically printed by the recording element as part of the document.

17.4. Scales that can be used for both direct and indirect scales to the customer by the use of an external button or switch to issue prepack random weights or standard pack labels, the manual weight capability shall only be operable in the prepack and unit price) or similar modes of operation that retain tare (and unit price) information for labeling multiple packages. Yes ☐ No ☐ N/A ☐

17.5. Manual tare entries shall not interact with a feature that compares one weight value to another to identify the larger weight as the gross weight. Yes ☐ No ☐ N/A ☐

17.6 Manual tickets may be entered from scales that are not interfaced (physically connected) to the system provided it is clearly stated on the ticket.
NOTE: *The use of a "hot key" or other means to selectively interrupt communication with the scale is not permitted.* Yes ☐ No ☐ N/A ☐

17.7. In the normal weighing mode, when scale to computer communications exists, manual gross and net weights cannot be entered for a new (not voided) ticket. Manual gross and tare weights can be entered for new tickets if scale communication is lost. Scales reading errors such as motion, below zero, over capacity, or wrong display units are not considered a loss of communication with the scale. Yes ☐ No ☐ N/A ☐

A conspicuous message must be printed on the ticket that this is a manually generated weigh-ticket.

Agenda Item 1 (b)

2.21. The section capacity of a railway track and livestock scale-indicating element shall be marked on or adjacent to the identification badge on the indicating element. The section capacity shall be prefaced by the words "Section Capacity" or an abbreviation of that term. Abbreviations shall be "Sec Cap" or "Sec C." All capital letters and periods may be used. Yes ☐ No ☐ N/A ☐

5.1. The section capacity of a railway track and livestock scale shall be marked on or adjacent to the identification badge on the indicating element. The section capacity shall be prefaced by the words "Section Capacity" or an abbreviatin of that term. Abbreviations shall be "Sec Cap" or "Sec C." All capital letters and periods may be used. Yes ☐ No ☐ N/A ☐

5.4. Combination vehicle/railway track and combination vehicle/livestock scales shall be marked with (1) the nominal capacity and CLC for vehicle weighing, and (2) the nominal capacity and section capacity for railway and livestock weighing. The e_{min} for both vehicle weighing, and railway, and livestock weighing shall also be marked. Yes ☐ No ☐ N/A ☐

NOTE: *Combination scales (vehicle/railway track and vehicle/Livestock) shall be marked with all required information.*

75. List of Acceptable Abbreviations/Symbols

Weighing and Indicating Elements:	Accuracy Class	I, II, III, III L, IIII or Symbols enclosed in an ellipse such as: ⓘ	1, ll, lll, lll L, llll, 1, 2, 3, 3 L, 4
	maximum number of scale divisions	n_{max}	
	Section Capacity	Sec C or Sec Cap	

Agenda Item 1 (d)

43. Discrimination and Zone of Uncertainty

Code Reference: T.N.7.1 and T.N.7.2.

The zone of uncertainty for digital indications must be <= 0.3 d. This test shall be conducted under controlled conditions in which environmental factors are reduced to the extent that they will not affect the results obtained.

43.1. Zone of Uncertainty Test for digital indications: Record the width of the zone of uncertainty as a decimal fraction of a scale division.

    43.1.1. Near Zero.   **Yes** ☐ **No** ☐ **N/A** ☐

    AVOIRDUPOIS_____d
    METRIC _____d
    OTHER UNITS (Identify units_____)_____ d

43.1.2.   Near Capacity.   **Yes** ☐ **No** ☐ **N/A** ☐

    AVOIRDUPOIS_____d
    METRIC _____d
    OTHER UNITS (Identify units_____)_____ d

43.2. Discrimination Test. The following tests shall be performed within 10 e of zero and at the maximum test load.

    43.2.1. Digital Indications – Decreasing-load Test

    Gently place the error weights in 1/10 e increments until the indication (I) increases by 1 displayed division (I + 1). Gently remove a test load equivalent to 1.4 e. This shall cause a decrease in the indicated or recorded value of 2 e.

43.2.1.1.   At or near zero (zero plus 10 e)   **Yes** ☐ **No** ☐ **N/A** ☐

43.2.1.2.   At maximum test load.   **Yes** ☐ **No** ☐ **N/A** ☐

    43.2.2 Digital Indications – Increasing-load Test

    Place error weights on the load receptor at least 10 times 1/10 e. Gently remove the error weights in 1/10 e increments until the indication (I) decreases by 1 displayed division (I-1). Gently add a test load equivalent to 1.4 e. This shall cause an increase in the indicated or recorded value of 2 e.

43.2.2.1.   At or near zero (zero plus 10 e)   **Yes** ☐ **No** ☐ **N/A** ☐

43.2.2.2.   At maximum test load.   **Yes** ☐ **No** ☐ **N/A** ☐

43.2.3.   Automatic Analog Indications

    A test load equivalent to 1.4 e placed gently on or removed from the load receptor while the instrument is at equilibrium shall cause the change in equilibrium in the indication of at least 1.0 e.

    43.2.3.1. At or near zero   **Yes** ☐ **No** ☐ **N/A** ☐

43.2.3.2.   At maximum test load.   **Yes** ☐ **No** ☐ **N/A** ☐

63.4. Subsequent Type Evaluation (Field) Permanence Test (Applicable for instruments above 2000 lb capacity, or instruments, because of their size, that can not be accommodated by the laboratory.)

A minimum of two increasing-load, two decreasing-load, and two shift (or a combination of shift and corner) tests, are to be conducted after a minimum of 20 days after the initial tests. The scales are to be tested to capacity using certified tests weights. If the test results are at or near acceptance tolerance limits, at least one more set of tests should be conducted immediately to verify the test results and determine device repeatability. If scale repeatability is not good (e.g., > 0.5d), conduct additional tests.

Repeat width-of-zero, zone of uncertainty, sensitivity, and discrimination tests near zero (outside the range of the AZSM) and at or near capacity on the subsequent tests.

69.1.1. Discrimination test at zero-load ~~or near zero outside the range of the AZSM,~~ and at scale capacity ~~or the maximum test load, whichever is less.~~

69.4.1. Discrimination test at zero-load or near zero outside the range of the AZSM, and at scale capacity or the maximum test load, whichever is less.

Agenda Item 1 (e)

50. Performance and Permanence Tests ~~for Counter (Bench) Scales (Including Computing Scales)~~

~~50.1. Increasing Load Test~~

~~Because of the ease of testing computing scales, it is recommended that the increasing load test for computing scales (approximately 30 lb capacity) consist of loads of 0.05, 0.45, and 0.95 lb, at 1 lb intervals thereafter to one-half capacity, and at 2 lb intervals from one-half capacity to capacity. Larger capacity scales should be tested at 1 lb intervals to 5 lb and in convenient steps to capacity, with a minimum of eight additional test loads. These are minimum tests.~~

~~50.2. Decreasing Load Test~~

~~The minimum decreasing load test is at a test load of one-half capacity after the scale has been loaded to capacity.~~

~~50.3. Shift Test~~

~~Test with test loads equal to one-half capacity as specified in N.1.3.1. and at test positions as illustrated below.~~

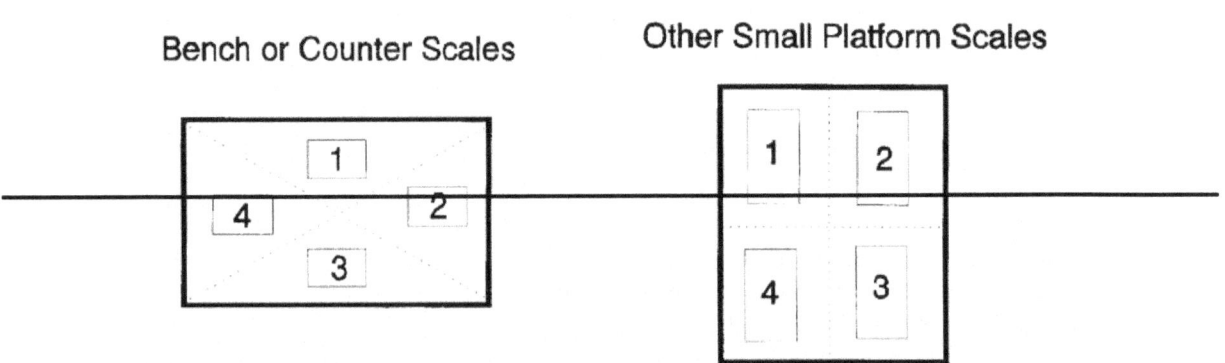

50.1. Performance Test (Weigh-Labelers)

Note:

- If the device is designed for use in static (non-automatic) weighing, it shall be tested statically using mass standards.

- If the device is designed for only automatic (dynamic or static) weighing, it shall only be tested in the automatic mode of operation.

50.1.1 Non-automatic (Static) Tests

50.1.1.1 Increasing-Load Test. - The increasing-load test shall be conducted with the test loads approximately centered on the load-receiving element of the scale.

50.1.1.2 Decreasing-Load Test. - The decreasing-load test shall be conducted with the test loads approximately centered on the load-receiving element of the scale.

50.1.1.3 Shift Test. - To determine the effect of off-center loading, a test load equal to one-half (½) maximum capacity shall be placed in the center of each of the four points equidistant between the center and front, left, back, and right edges of the load receiver.

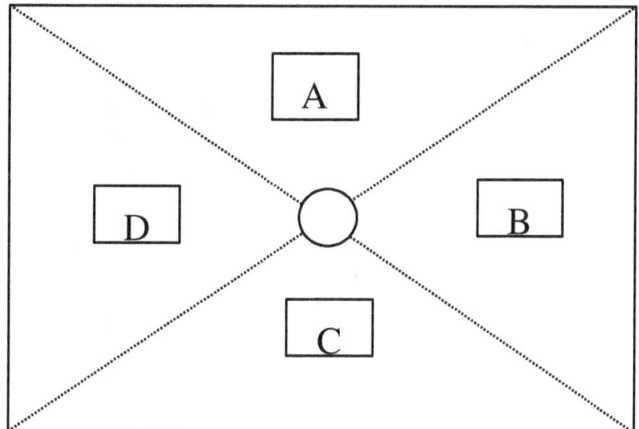

50.1.1.2 Discrimination Test. - A discrimination test shall be conducted with the weighing device in equilibrium at zero load and at maximum test load, and under controlled conditions in which environmental factors are reduced to the extent that they will not affect the results obtained. This test is conducted from just below the lower edge of the zone of uncertainty for increasing-load tests, or from just above the upper edge of the zone of uncertainty for decreasing-load tests.

50.1.1.5 Zero-Load Balance Change. - A zero-load balance change test shall be conducted on all automatic-weighing systems after the removal of any test load. The zero-load balance should not change by more than the minimum tolerance applicable. (Also see G-UR.4.2.)

50.1.1.6 Influence Factor Testing. - Influence factor testing shall be conducted.

50.1.2 Automatic (dynamic or static) Tests. - The device shall be tested at the highest speed for each weight range using standardized test pucks or packages. Test runs shall be conducted using four test loads as described in Table N.3.2. Each test load shall be run a minimum of 10 consecutive times.

Table N.3.2. Test Loads
At or near minimum capacity.
At or near maximum capacity.
At two (2) critical points between minimum and maximum capacity.
Test may be conducted at other loads if the device is intended for use at other specific capacities.

50.1.2.1 Shift Test. - To determine the effect of eccentric loading, for devices without a means to align packages, a test load equal to one-third (1/3) maximum capacity shall be passed over the load receiver or transport belt (1) halfway between the center and front edge, and (2) halfway between the center and back edge.

1)
(2)

50.2. Performance Test (Automatic Checkweighers)

50.2.1. Non-automatic (static) Tests - If the scale is designed to operate statically during normal user operation, it shall be tested statically using the applicable weigh-labeler requirements.

50.2.2. Automatic (dynamic or static) Tests - The device shall be tested at the highest speed in each weight range using standardized test pucks or packages. Test runs shall be conducted using four test loads. The number of consecutive test weighments shall be as described in Table N.4.2.

Table N.4.2. Number of Sample Weights per Test for Automatic Checkweighers	
Weighing Range m = mass of test load	**Number of sample weights per test**
20 divisions < m ≤ 10 kg 20 divisions < m ≤ 22 lb	60
10 kg < m ≤ 25 kg 22 lb < m ≤ 55 lb	32
25 kg < m ≤ 100 kg 55 lb < m ≤ 220 lb	20
100 kg (220 lb) < m	10

50.3. Out-of-Level Tests for Weigh-labelers and Checkweighers (If Applicable)

If the scale is not equipped with a level-indicating means, it must be tested in an out-of-level condition to determine compliance with paragraph S.4. Leveling-Indicating Means.

50.3.1. Place one side of the scale three degrees (or 5 %) out-of-level with respect to the width axis of the scale. The scale should then be zeroed. Conduct a shift test[1] and increasing and decreasing load tests.

50.3.2. Place the opposite side or the scale out-of-level, zero the scale, and repeat tests.

50.3.3. Place the front of the scale three degrees (or 5 %) out-of-level with respect to the length axis of the scale. Zero the scale and conduct the shift, increasing and decreasing load tests.

50.3.4. Place back of scale out-of-level, zero the scale, and repeat tests. All test results must be within acceptance tolerances. If the scale fails any of these tests, a level-indicating means is needed.

[1] The shift test is usually conducted first since this test frequently reveals accuracy problems.

Agenda Item 3

PROPOSED CHANGES TO PUB 14 TO INCLUDE COUNTING FEATURE
Page DES 17
UNDERLINED TEXT IS PROPOSED TO BE ADDED

Marking Nominal Capacity, Value of the Scale Division, Special Applications
Code References: S.6., S.6.6. Table S.6.3.a., and Table S.6.3.b.

This requirement applies to digital indicating elements and to both the operator and customer's indications on complete scales. The lettering must be permanent as described in section 1, but the attachment of any badge or decal is slightly less stringent than for the G-S.1. Information. In terms of attachment, any badge or decal must be "durable", that is, it must be difficult to remove (at all temperatures). Remote weight displays (except "scoreboard" displays), the customer's weight display provided for scales interfaced with electronic cash registers (ECRs), and weight displays that are built into ECRs must be marked with the scale capacity and scale division. The capacity by division statement may be part of the scale display or marked adjacent to the display. Large remote customer's ("scoreboard") displays have not been required to meet the marking requirements because the markings probably cannot be read from a customer's position. In those cases, the operator's weight display must be properly marked.

The marked nominal capacity on all vehicle, axle-load, and livestock scales shall not exceed the concentrated load capacity times the quantity of the number of sections in the scale minus 0.5. As a formula, this is stated as:

$$\text{Nominal Capacity} = \text{Concentrated Load Capacity} \times (N - 0.5)$$
where N = the number of sections in the scale.

Devices designed for special applications are to be so marked to prevent them from being used in an unsuitable application. Examples of special application scales are prepackaging scales, digital postal scales with simultaneous pound and ounce weight unit indications, weight classifying scales, and Class III scales with a small number of scale divisions and a verification scale division. When a scale is installed with an operational counting feature, the scale shall be marked on both the operator and customer side with the statement, "The counting feature is not legal for trade." Exception: When a prescription scale complies with paragraphs S.1.2.3., S.2.5.3., and S.6.6., it shall be marked, "Counting Feature for Prescription Filling Only."

The system must be clearly and permanently marked on an exterior surface, visible after installation, as follows:

1.1	The name, initials, or trademark of the manufacturer or distributor. A remote display is required to have the manufacturer's name or trademark and model designation. (Code Reference G-S.1.)	Yes ☐ No ☐ N/A ☐
1.2	A model designation that positively identifies the pattern or design of the device. The Model designation shall be prefaced by the word "Model," "Type," or "Pattern." These terms may be followed by the term "Number" or an abbreviation of that word. The abbreviation for the word "Number" shall, as a minimum, begin with the letter "N" (e.g., No or No.) The abbreviation for the word "Model" shall be "Mod" or "Mod." (Effective January 1, 2003) (Code Reference G-S.1.)	Yes ☐ No ☐ N/A ☐
1.3	Except for equipment with no moving or electronic component parts, a non-repetitive serial number. (Code Reference G-S.1.)	Yes ☐ No ☐ N/A ☐

DES-20

1.18.	If a scale has an operational counting feature, it must be marked on both the operator and customer side with the statement, "The counting feature is not legal for trade." Note: Not applicable to prescription scales meeting paragraph 1.19 below.	Yes ☐ No ☐ N/A ☐

NTEP Committee 2005 Final Report
Appendix D – NTETC - Weighing Sector

1.19.   If a Class I or Class II prescription scale complies with paragraphs S.1.2.3., S.2.5.3., and S.6.6., it shall be:

    1.19.1   marked, "Counting Feature for Prescription Filling Only" (see test procedure in Section 58);   **Yes** ☐ **No** ☐ **N/A** ☐

1.19.2   marked with the minimum piece weight and minimum number of pieces used to establish an individual piece count.   **Yes** ☐ **No** ☐ **N/A** ☐

1.~~19~~ 20   All markings must be clear and easily readable.   **Yes** ☐ **No** ☐ **N/A** ☐

1.~~20~~ 1.   The lettering for all markings must be permanent. Record the grade for the permanence of markings: _____   **Yes** ☐ **No** ☐ **N/A** ☐

1.~~21~~ 2.   If the markings for other than device identification required by G-S.1. are placed on badge or decal, then the badge or decal must be durable (difficult to remove at all temperatures).   **Yes** ☐ **No** ☐ **N/A** ☐

Proposed New Section to be inserted after Grain Test Scales, Section 38, Page DES 57

38. Counting Feature on Class I or II Scales Used in Prescription Filling Applications
Code References: S.1.2.3, S.2.5.3, N.1.10, T.N.3.10, and Table T.N.3.10

38.1   The scale's accuracy class is Class I or Class II
Note accuracy class: **Yes** ☐ **No** ☐ **N/A** ☐

38.2   The counting mode is clearly marked on the display or by an annunciator   **Yes** ☐ **No** ☐ **N/A** ☐

38.3   The scale display differentiates between count indications and weight indications.   **Yes** ☐ **No** ☐ **N/A** ☐

    38.3.1   If symbol "ct" is used to identify count, it is not used to identify carat in the weighing mode.   **Yes** ☐ **No** ☐ **N/A** ☐

38.4   Values must be identified with the word or symbol for pieces (pcs) or count (ct)   **Yes** ☐ **No** ☐ **N/A** ☐

38.5   Count values must be displayed as a whole integer, without a decimal point.   **Yes** ☐ **No** ☐ **N/A** ☐

38.6   The scale is capable of displaying zero count.   **Yes** ☐ **No** ☐ **N/A** ☐

Record the marked minimum piece weight (**MPW**):_____

Record the marked minimum sample size in pieces (**MSS**):_____

Calculate and record the minimum sample size in weight (**MSSW**) =MPW x MSS=_____

38.7   The counting feature shall not calculate a piece weight or total count unless the following conditions are met:

    38.7.1   Individual piece weight is equal to or greater than 3 e.   **Yes** ☐ **No** ☐ **N/A** ☐

    38.7.2   Sample size is equal to or greater than the marked minimum sample size in pieces.   **Yes** ☐ **No** ☐ **N/A** ☐

38.8   The marked minimum sample size must be equal to or greater than 10 pieces.   **Yes** ☐ **No** ☐ **N/A** ☐

38.9   Place a load of less than **MSSW** on the scale, and enter the **MSS**. The device   **Yes** ☐ **No** ☐ **N/A** ☐

shall reject the entry.

38.10 Place a load equal to the **MSSW** on the scale and enter a sample count less than the **MSS**. The device shall reject the entry. Yes ☐ No ☐ N/A ☐

In addition to Table 6 Maintenance Tolerances (for weight), the indicated piece count value computed by a Class I or Class II prescription scale counting feature shall comply with the tolerances in Table T.N.3.10. Maintenance and acceptance tolerances are the same.

Table T.N.3.10 Maintenance and Acceptance Tolerances In Excess and in Deficiency for Count	
Indication of Count	Tolerance (piece count)
0 – 100	0
101 to 200	1
201 or more	0.5 %

Notes on testing:

Conduct at least two increasing and decreasing load tests with at least four different test loads, including the maximum at each tolerance level. Do not recalibrate the scale during this test. Document any non-conformance results.

Example:
  Scale Capacity = 620g x 0.01 g
  (marked with a minimum piece weight of 0.03 g and a minimum piece count of 10)
  Piece weight = 0.03 g = 3 e
  Minimum sample size = 10 pieces = 30 e = 0.30 g
  100 pcs = 300 e = 3 g
  200 pcs = 600 e = 6 g

To achieve the highest possible count, divide the capacity (620 g) by the minimum weight of the piece count (0.03 g). Truncate the quotient (20666.666 counts) to the nearest whole integer (20666 counts).

To perform the test at near maximum, pick a whole number near this amount, such as 20500. Calculate the amount of weight that should cause the scale to indicate a count of 20500 by multiplying the desired count (20500) by the weight of the minimum piece weight (0.03 g). The result is 615 g. Place 615 g on the scale and it should indicate 20500 counts.

38.11 Calculate the loads required to cause the scale to indicate, respectively, a count of 10 100, 200, and maximum count capacity (based on scale capacity and minimum individual piece weight). The device indicates each of these loads within the tolerance specified in table T.N.3.10. Yes ☐ No ☐ N/A ☐

(If necessary, check several more loads to verify the count calculation at other loads and minimum sample counts.)

38.7 The counting feature shall not calculate a piece weight unless the following conditions are met:

  38.7.1 The individual piece weight is equal to or greater than 3 e. Yes ☐ No ☐ N/A ☐

NTEP Committee 2005 Final Report
Appendix D – NTETC - Weighing Sector

38.7.2 The sample size is at least 10 pieces or the marked minimum sample size in pieces, whichever is greater.   Yes ☐ No ☐ N/A ☐

38.7.3 The sample count indication is stable.   Yes ☐ No ☐ N/A ☐

75. List of Acceptable Abbreviations/Symbols

Device Application	Term Acceptable		<u>No</u>t Acceptable
Livestock & Animal Scales:	Head (sale by)	HB or H	
	Weight (sale by)	WT or W	
	Other symbols recognized by the Packers & Stockyards Administration		
~~**Prescription Filling Count Feature for Class I & II Scales:**~~	~~Minimum Piece Weight~~ MPW	—	
	~~Minimum Sample Size~~ MSS	—	
	~~Minimum Sample Size in Weight~~	MSSW	
Belt Conveyor Scales:	U.S. short ton (note: different from "General" application)	T	

Agenda Item 14

Add a check box in the Publication 14 DES checklist that states the computing scale interfaced to an ECR meets the applicable requirements in the ECRS checklist as follows:

27.4 If the computing scale is interfaced with a electronic cash register (ECR), the ECRS checklist must also be completed. The operation of the computing scale with the ECR meets the ECRS checklist.   Yes ☐ No ☐ N/A ☐

and

Amend ECRS Sections 11.15 through 11.21 as follows:

11.15. A computing scale may interface with a cash register, and the cash register need only record the total price, that is, serve merely as a printer, provided:

~~11.15.~~	11.15.1.	The computing scale displays the net weight, unit price, and total price on both the operator and customer sides of the scale.		Yes ☐ No ☐ N/A ☐
~~11.16.~~	11.15.2	The computing scale has a tare capability.		Yes ☐ No ☐ N/A ☐
~~11.17.~~	11.15.3	The scale is positioned so the customer can accurately read the indications and observe the weighing operation.		Yes ☐ No ☐ N/A ☐
~~11.18.~~	11.15.4	The scale must be equipped with motion detection that complies with Handbook 44 requirement S.2.4.1.		Yes ☐ No ☐ N/A ☐
~~11.19.~~	11.15.5	The scale is not equipped with a price-look-up capability. The unit price must be manually entered into the computing scale to give the customer adequate time (equivalent to a transaction in the delicatessen department) to assimilate the display information.		Yes ☐ No ☐ N/A ☐

NTEP Committee 2005 Final Report
Appendix D – NTETC - Weighing Sector

~~11.20.~~	11.15.6	The electronic cash register must not have any input to the computing scale in the process of determining the total price of a weighed item.	Yes ☐ No ☐ N/A ☐
~~11.21.~~	11.15.7	If the ECR is equipped with a computing scale, it shall meet the criteria given above.	Yes ☐ No ☐ N/A ☐
	11.15.8.	If the scale has multiple sales accumulation capability, the scale accumulation capability is disabled.	Yes ☐ No ☐ N/A ☐
	11.15.9.	If the ECR is equipped with a computing scale, it shall meet the criteria given above.	Yes ☐ No ☐ N/A ☐

Agenda Item 15

27. Computing Scales – General ~~Without Multiple Sales Accumulation Capability~~

Code Reference: S.1.8.3, G-S.2, G-S.5.1, G-S.6, S.1.9.2

27.1   The net weight, unit price, and total price are clearly displayed and identified on both the operator and customer sides of the scale.   **Yes ☐ No ☐ N/A ☐**

      27.1.1   The unit price is clearly defined.   **Yes ☐ No ☐ N/A ☐**

           The symbols "$/" with a unit symbol (i.e., lb, kg, g) may be used, provided:

           27.1.1.1   -the scale is capable of only displaying net weight in that weight unit, or   **Yes ☐ No ☐ N/A ☐**

           27.1.1.2   -the scale has an internal units selection switch that can be sealed in the unit used for both the unit price and the net weight display, or   **Yes ☐ No ☐ N/A ☐**

           27.1.1.3   -the scale has an external unit conversion key, and the unit of mass marked in the unit price display and the unit of mass marked in the weight display are the same.   **Yes ☐ No ☐ N/A ☐**

Examples of scale display

Correct

WEIGHT	$ / lb	TOTAL PRICE $
1.00 lb	2.00	2.00

Capacity 30 x 0.01 lb / 15 x 0.005 kg

Correct

WEIGHT	UNIT PRICE	TOTAL PRICE $
1.00 lb	2.00	2.00

Capacity 30 x 0.01 lb / 15 x 0.005 kg

Incorrect

WEIGHT	$ / lb	TOTAL PRICE $
1.00 kg	2.00	2.00

Capacity 30 x 0.01 lb / 15 x 0.005 kg

27.2   The computing scale has tare capability.   **Yes ☐ No ☐ N/A ☐**

27.3   Computing Scales with Printers

In the case of printers that issue labels for packages, requirements of the Fair Packaging and Labeling Act and the Uniform Packaging and Labeling Regulation apply.

Preprinted labels stating the unit of measure (i.e., lb, kg) acceptable for scales capable of displaying one weight unit or which have an internal lb/kg conversion switch.

      27.3.1   The unit price is clearly defined.   **Yes ☐ No ☐ N/A ☐**

The symbols "$/" with a unit symbol (i.e., lb, kg, g) may be used, provided:

27.3.1.1	-the scale is only capable of printing the net weight in that weight unit, or		Yes ☐ No ☐ N/A ☐
27.3.1.2	-the scale has an internal units selection switch that can be sealed in the unit used for both the unit price and the net weight, or		Yes ☐ No ☐ N/A ☐
27.3.1.3	-the scale has an external unit conversion key, and the unit of mass printed in the unit price and the unit of mass printed with the weight are the same.		Yes ☐ No ☐ N/A ☐
27.3.2	The symbol "$" or the word "dollars" is printed with the total price and must be printed by the device or pre-printed on the label.		Yes ☐ No ☐ N/A ☐
27.3.3	The quantity block must be headed with the words "Net Weight/Count". (The term "Net Weight" is optional.) If the printer does not print the specific weight unit, the pre-printed label must include this information; for example, pound, lb, or kg.		Yes ☐ No ☐ N/A ☐
27.3.4	For items sold by count, the count is printed in the quantity block. **NOTE:** If there are no individual blocks for the printed information, and the printer prints a qualifying term such as "pieces" or a symbol such as "pcs" in a horizontal manner reading from left to right, and if there is little doubt as to the meaning of the label, then it is considered appropriate.		Yes ☐ No ☐ N/A ☐
27.3.5	The count must be printed as an integer without a decimal point and must be modified with the word or symbol for pieces (pcs) or count (ct) either in the heading or next to the number.		Yes ☐ No ☐ N/A ☐
27.3.6	Printing of non-weighed items by count shall either *(27.1 in 2004 edition)*		
27.3.6.1		operate only under no load condition or *(27.1.1 in 2004 edition)*	Yes ☐ No ☐ N/A ☐
27.3.6.2		cause the display to blank. *(27.1.2 in 2004 edition)*	Yes ☐ No ☐ N/A ☐

Incorrect Label		
Net Weight	Unit Price	Total Price
1.00 kg	$2.00	**$2.00**

(unit price not identified with unit)

Correct Label		
Net Weight	Price	Total Price
1.00	kg $2.00/kg	**$2.00**

Incorrect Label		
Net Weight	Unit Price	Total Price
1.00 lb	$2.00	**$2.00**

(unit price not identified with unit)

Correct Label		
Net Weight	Unit Price	Total Price
1.00	lb $2.00/lb	**$2.00**

Incorrect Label		
Net Weight	Price/lb	Total Price
1.00 kg	$2.00	**$2.00**

(different units of net weight and unit price)

Correct Label		
Net Weight	Price/kg	Total Price
1.00 kg	$2.00	**$2.00**

Correct Label		
Net Weight/CT	Unit Price	Total Price
10	$2.00	**$20.00**

Correct Label		
Net	Weight $/lb	Total Price
1.00	lb $2.00	**$2.00**

| 27.4 | If the computing scale is interfaced with a electronic cash register (ECR), the ECRS checklist must also be completed. The operation of the scale with the ECR meets the ECRS checklist. *(from previous agenda item)* | Yes ☐ No ☐ N/A ☐ |

Agenda Item 19

The Sector recommends that following amendments to Publication 14 DES Section 18 indicated in underlined text be included in Publication 14.

18. Zero Indication - General

Code Reference: G.S.5.1., G.S.1, S.6.3

Any of the following methods may be used to indicate a negative balance condition.

18.1.	Display of negative values.	Yes ☐ No ☐ N/A ☐
	A display of negative weight values is required in the net display mode when the gross weight is less than the tare value. This assumes that the gross weight is zero or positive. If the gross weight is negative (behind zero-balance condition), and if blanking the display is used to indicate a behind-zero-balance condition, the gross and net display may blank.	
18.2.	Blanking the display	Yes ☐ No ☐ N/A ☐
	This method cannot be used to indicate a negative balance condition if the device also: (1) blanks the display to indicate over-capacity and (2) the load condition of the weighing/load receiving element is not evident to the operator, (e.g., a hopper scale where the operator cannot see the load condition, empty or full, of the hopper).	
	If blanking is used, it is recommended that the indicator also have an annunciator to indicate "power on" so the operator does not think that power has been lost when the display is blank.	
18.2.1	When blanking a primary weight display with live on screen G-S.1 and/or S.6.3 markings, the required markings must **not** blank.	Yes ☐ No ☐ N/A ☐
18.3.	Display of a symbol which cannot be interpreted as a quantity value, (e.g., -, ---, EEEE, E S-1) is acceptable; however, the display of complements are not acceptable, and flashing zeros or a minus sign preceding a zero or zeros cannot be used.	Yes ☐ No ☐ N/A ☐

The Sector recommends that following amendments to Publication 14 ECRS Section 5 indicated in underlined text be included in Publication 14. Language to be removed is indicated strikeout text.

5. Identification

Code Reference: G.S.5.1., G.S.1, S.6.3

.... **No changes in this area**
.... **No changes in this area**
.... **No changes in this area**

NTEP Committee 2005 Final Report
Appendix D – NTETC - Weighing Sector

5.1. The cash register shall be clearly and permanently marked for the purposes of identification with the following information:

    5.1.1. The name, initials, or trademark of the manufacturer or distributor.   Yes ☐ No ☐ N/A ☐

    5.1.2. A model designation that positively identifies the pattern or design of the device. The Model designation shall be prefaced by the word "Model", "Type", or "Pattern". These terms may be followed by the term "Number" or an abbreviation of that word. The abbreviation for the word "Number" shall, as a minimum, begin with the letter "N" (e.g., No or No.) The abbreviation for the word "Model" shall be "Mod" or "Mod.". (Effective January 1, 2003).   Yes ☐ No ☐ N/A ☐

    5.1.3. Except for equipment with no moving or electronic component parts and not-built-for-purpose, software-based devices, a nonrepetitive serial number.   Yes ☐ No ☐ N/A ☐

    5.1.4. For not-built-for-purpose, software-based devices, the current software version designation.   Yes ☐ No ☐ N/A ☐

    5.1.5. The serial number shall be prefaced by the words "Serial Number" or an abbreviation of that term. Abbreviations for the word "Serial" shall, as a minimum, begin with the letter "S," and abbreviations for the word "Number" shall, as a minimum, begin with the letter "N" (e.g., S/N, SN, Ser. No, and S No.).   Yes ☐ No ☐ N/A ☐

    Location of the information: _____

~~Code Reference G-S.1. (g). Effective January 1, 2003~~

    5.1.6. The NTEP Certificate of Conformance (CC) Number or a corresponding CC addendum number for devices that have a CC. The number shall be prefaced by the terms "NTEP CC", "CC", or "Approval." These terms may be followed by the word "Number" or an abbreviation for the word "Number." The abbreviation shall, as a minimum, begin with the letter "N" (e.g., No or No.).   Yes ☐ No ☐ N/A ☐

    The device must have an area, either on the identification plate or on the device itself, suitable for the application of the Certificate of Conformance Number. If the area for the CC Number is not part of an identification plate, note its intended location and how it will be applied.   Yes ☐ No ☐ N/A ☐

    Location of CC Number if not located with the identification
_____
_____

5.2. The other components of the system are marked consistent with the above description.   Yes ☐ No ☐ N/A ☐

5.3. Identifying information shall be:

    5.3.1. Located so that it is readily observable without the necessity of disassembling a part requiring the use of any means separate from the device. If the required information is located on the back of a device, the same information must also appear on the side, front, or top. The bottom of a device is not an acceptable surface. If required markings are behind a door or panel, the manufacturer is encouraged to put a label on the outside of the device that explains where the identification information is located   Yes ☐ No ☐ N/A ☐

    5.3.2. Marked on a surface that is an integral part of the chassis.   Yes ☐ No ☐ N/A ☐

5.4. If the required marking is on a plate or badge, the plate must be permanent. (See criteria above for Permanence of Attachment of Badge.)   Yes ☐ No ☐ N/A ☐

5.5.	The lettering for all markings must be permanent.		Yes ☐ No ☐ N/A ☐
	Record the grade for the markings: _____		

~~Code Reference: G-S.1.1. Location of Marking Information for Not Built-for-Purpose, Software-Based Devices. Effective January 1, 2004~~

5.6	When blanking a primary weight display, with live on screen G-S.1 and/or S.6.3 markings, the required markings must **not** blank.		Yes ☐ No ☐ N/A ☐
5.~~6.~~7	For not-built-for-purpose, software-based devices, the following shall apply:		
	5.7.1	The manufacturer or distributor and the model designation shall be continuously displayed or marked on the device; or	Yes ☐ No ☐ N/A ☐
~~5.7.~~	5.7.2	The Certificate of Conformance (CC) Number shall be continuously displayed or marked on the device, or	Yes ☐ No ☐ N/A ☐
~~5.8.~~	5.7.3	All required information in G-S.1. Identification. (a), (b), (c), (e), and (h) shall be continuously displayed. Alternatively, a clearly identified "view only" System Identification, G-S.1. Identification, or Weights and Measures identification shall be accessible through the "Help" menu. Required information includes that information necessary to identify that the software in the device is the same type that was evaluated.	Yes ☐ No ☐ N/A ☐
~~5.9.~~	5.7.4	Clear instructions for accessing the remaining required G-S.1. information shall be listed on the CC. Required information includes that information necessary to identify the software in the device is the same type that was evaluated.	Yes ☐ No ☐ N/A ☐

Agenda Item 21

X. Cash Acceptors or Card-activated Systems
Code Reference: G-S.2., G-S.5.1., G-S.6

Accidental or intentional fraud causes great concern when customers use cash acceptors or card-activated systems.

Because systems may be installed with separate power lines to the controller, card reader, and scale, tests should be run with power failures to different parts of the system to evaluate the potential for accidental or intentional errors. The appropriate device response depends upon when the power loss occurs during the transaction.

Tests using various denominations of bills accepted by the cash acceptor should be performed.

Certificates of Conformance will cover the use of the cash acceptor option at both attended and unattended systems. Cash acceptors, which are used at unattended locations, must meet the marking requirements of paragraph G-UR.3.4. Responsibility, Money-Operated Devices shall be clearly and conspicuously displayed on the device or immediately adjacent to the device information detailing the return of monies paid when the product cannot be obtained.

Note: For bills that have not yet been drawn into the cash acceptor to the point that the bill is no longer visible, it is assumed that the information on the bill denomination can be obtained from visual examination.

Various methods may be used to recall specific portions of the transaction depending on how the basic system operates. For example, systems that can print a record of the amount fed into the machine as each bill is fed into the device maintain an ongoing record of bills recognized by the system. Other systems may not print a receipt until the end of the transaction, so the information is recalled on a journal printer accessible to the customer or can be recalled on the cash acceptor display

1.1 Systems with Battery Back-up or Uninterruptible Power Supply or Equivalent - **Yes ☐ No ☐ N/A ☐**
Some systems are equipped with a battery back-up or an uninterruptible power supply (or equivalent) which allows a transaction to continue in the event of a power loss. For such systems, the transaction in progress at the time of a power interruption must continue as if no power interruption had occurred (or comply with the requirements for systems not equipped with a battery back-up). That is, all bills (including bills being fed into the device at the time of the power loss) must be correctly accounted for, and the total sale amount must be mathematically correct. Check these systems by interrupting power at several points in the transaction to ensure that all information (total price, mathematical agreement, and total dollar amount inserted by the customer) is accounted for correctly.

1.2. All Other Systems - To check the operation of systems not equipped with a battery **Yes ☐ No ☐ N/A ☐**
back-up, uninterruptible power supply, or equivalent, interrupt power as described below. As noted earlier, if separate power lines supply different components in the system, interrupt power to different parts of the system.

When one or more bills have been accepted and registered by the device, at least one of the following criteria must be met to ensure that this information can be recalled in the event of a power interruption:

    1.2.1. The printer on the device must print the denomination of the bill as the **Yes ☐ No ☐ N/A ☐**
device recognizes the bill. (The printed receipt must be available to the customer.)

    1.2.2. A journal or other printer accessible to the customer must print the **Yes ☐ No ☐ N/A ☐**
denomination of each bill as the device recognizes each bill.

    1.2.3. The total display must be capable of being recalled for at least 15 **Yes ☐ No ☐ N/A ☐**
minutes.

    1.2.4. Means are provided to enable the customer to retrieve the money inserted **Yes ☐ No ☐ N/A ☐**
into the device (e.g., a button which can be used during a power interruption to eject the money inserted by the customer).

    1.2.5. Other means is used to provide a visual or printed record of the total **Yes ☐ No ☐ N/A ☐**
amount of money accepted by the device.

1.3. There is a brief period of time during which a bill has been accepted by the cash **Yes ☐ No ☐ N/A ☐**
acceptor but has not yet been recognized by the device. The following criteria must be met to ensure completion of that this information can be recalled in the event of a power failure.

    1.3.1. Means is provided to enable the attendant or customer to retrieve the bill **Yes ☐ No ☐ N/A ☐**
(for example, a button which can be used during a power interruption to eject the bill or if the cash acceptor box can be removed by the attendant and the bill retrieved).

Note: There may be a space of time in which a bill can be caught partially in and out of the cash acceptor during a power interruption. In such a case, if the denomination of the bill is visible to the customer and attendant, this is sufficient to provideinformation about the bill being fed into the device at the time of the power interruption. The cash acceptor must comply with the other applicable items noted above.

NTEP Committee 2005 Final Report
Appendix D – NTETC - Weighing Sector

1.4. Power should be interrupted at different points in the transaction to determine that all transaction information can be recalled in the event of a power interruption including combinations of the following:

    1.4.1. after one bill has been inserted.   Yes ☐ No ☐ N/A ☐

    1.4.2. after several bills have been inserted.   Yes ☐ No ☐ N/A ☐

    1.4.3. while a bill is being inserted.   Yes ☐ No ☐ N/A ☐

    1.4.4. after a bill has been inserted but not yet recognized.   Yes ☐ No ☐ N/A ☐

    1.4.5. after a bill(s) has been inserted and recognized.   Yes ☐ No ☐ N/A ☐

1.5. Total Money Display - A running display showing the amount of money fed into the machine must be provided.   Yes ☐ No ☐ N/A ☐

1.6. Printed Receipt - A printed receipt must be available to the customer from the device at the completion of the transaction.   Yes ☐ No ☐ N/A ☐

Because the customer must be provided with a receipt, the system must not accept cash if sufficient paper is not available to complete the transaction.

    The cash acceptor must not initiate a cash transaction if either of the following conditions are true:

    • no paper is in the receipt printer of the cash acceptor;   Yes ☐ No ☐ N/A ☐

    • insufficient paper is available to complete a transaction.   Yes ☐ No ☐ N/A ☐

1.7. Instructions must be marked on the device to inform the customer how to operate the cash acceptor.   Yes ☐ No ☐ N/A ☐

1.8. Means must be provided for the customer to cancel the transaction at any point.   Yes ☐ No ☐ N/A ☐

    1.8.1. The customer has inserted cash. If the customer cancels the transaction by pressing the cancel key (or equivalent key(s)), the device must either: Yes ☐ No ☐ N/A ☐

1.8.1.1. be equipped with means for the customer to retrieve the cash inserted from the device, AND   Yes ☐ No ☐ N/A ☐

    automatically issue a printed receipt indicating the amount tendered and the amount returned, OR

1.8.1.2. display instructions (such as "sale terminated, see attendant," "sale terminated, get receipt" or similar wording) for the customer to see the attendant, AND   Yes ☐ No ☐ N/A ☐

    automatically issue a printed receipt showing the amount of cash inserted by the customer, a statement indicating that the sale was terminated, and instructions for the customer to see the attendant.   Yes ☐ No ☐ N/A ☐

Note: It is acceptable for different messages to be used. This depends upon whether the transaction is terminated by use of the cancel key (e.g., "sale terminated, get receipt" or "sale terminated, see cashier", "change due, see cashier").

Appendix B – NTETC Weighing Sector Attendance List

First Name	Last Name	Organization	E-Mail
Cary	Ainsworth	c/o USDA GIPSA	L.Cary.Ainsworth@usda.gov
Joseph	Antkowiak	Flintec, Inc.	jantkowiak@flintec-us.com
William E.	Bates	USDA, GIPSA, FMD, PPB	william.e.bates@usda.gov
Andrea P.	Buie	Maryland Dept. of Agriculture	buieap@mda.state.md.us
Luciano	Burtini	Measurement Canada	burtini.luciano@ic.gc.ca
Ken	Chin	Measurement Canada	chin.ken@ic.gc.ca
Brian	Christopher	McKesson Automated Prescription Systems	brian.christopher@mckessonaps.com
Steven E.	Cook	NIST, Weights & Measures Division	steven.cook@nist.gov
Scott	Davidson	Mettler-Toledo, Inc.	scott.davidson@mt.com
Terry	Davis	Kansas Dept. of Agriculture	tdavis@kda.state.ks.us
William	Fishman	New York Bureau of Weights & Measures	bill.fishman@agmkt.state.ny.us
Darrell E.	Flocken	Mettler-Toledo, Inc.	darrell.flocken@mt.com
Gary	Lameris	Hobart Corporation	gary.lameris@hobartcorp.com
Stephen	Langford	Cardinal Scale Manufacturing Co.	slangford@cardet.com
Jean	Lemay	Measurement Canada	lemay.jean@ic.gc.ca
Paul A.	Lewis, Sr.	Rice Lake Weighing Systems	paulew@rlws.com
Todd R.	Lucas	Ohio Dept. of Agriculture	lucas@mail.agri.state.oh.us
L. Edward	Luthy	Brechbuhler Scales Inc	eluthy@brechbuhler.com
Michel	Maranda	Measurement Canada	maranda.michel@ic.gc.ca
Don	Onwiler	Nebraska Division of Weights & Measures	donlo@agr.state.ne.us
Stephen	Patoray	National Conference on Weights & Measures	spatoray@mgmtsol.com
Ron	Peasley	Measurement Canada	
David W.	Quinn	Fairbanks Scales	dave.w.quinn@mindspring.com
Frank	Rusk	Coti, Inc.	frankjrusk50@hotmail.com
Milton	Smith	Measurement Canada	smith.milton@ic.gc.ca
Russ	Wyckoff	Oregon Dept. of Agriculture	rwyckoff@oda.state.or.us
Jesus P.	Zapien	A&D Engineering Inc	jzapien@andweighing.com

Appendix E

Provisional Committee on Participation Review (CPR) Meeting Summary

The following is a general summary of information from Provisional Committee on Participation Review (CPR) meeting in Lyon, France in June 2005.

Both BIML and a majority of the CPR participants expressed interest in NCWM/NTEP participation in the MAA and the future Declaration of Mutual Confidence (DoMC) for R 60 and R 76.

1. The CPR agreed to include Class III L and Class III HD in the DoMC as additional requirements for devices covered by OIML R 76 and R 60 Recommendations
   a. Under this, the United States and Canada will attempt to agree on which requirement is stricter so that only one additional requirement will be needed for either Class III L or Class III HD.
   b. The United States and Canada will present information and test report forms for the required test points and other information for these devices.
   c. Note: If United States chooses not to participate, Class III L will not be included in the DoMC.

2. The CPR agreed to include endurance testing per NCWM Publication 14 for devices covered under OIML R 76.
   a. United States and Canada will provide information on the laboratory and field-testing requirements (currently OIML lab testing stops at 100 kg, field endurance testing is not performed by OIML testing laboratories).
   b. United States and Canada will also provide information on the test equipment used by the NTEP labs to show the design and that it is safe to conduct such a test.

NOTE: for both of the above items the TC was instructed to review this information and discuss among the full Committee as to the merits of both the additional class and the endurance testing.

3. The CPR agreed to include marking information (if not harmonized) as an additional requirement for devices covered under OIML R 60 and R 76.

4. The United States needs to clarify eccentric (shift test) loads for large capacity devices.

5. The United States needs to clarify the test and use of concentrated load capacities (CLC).

6. The United States reported on the following items that are currently being reviewed by NCWM for harmonization between NIST Handbook 44 and OIML R 76:
   a. Eccentric load testing (Canada stated that R 76 testing is sufficient for them.)
   b. Accuracy Class III Tolerances
   c. Auto-zero tracking (except for Class III L)
   d. Time Dependence (Creep)

7. Items excluded from the agreement include (based on potentially ambiguous examinations and national requirements):
   a. Securing and Sealing of Components (OIML R 76 section 4.1.2.4).
   b. Examination (OIML R 76 section 8.2.2).
   c. Reading OIML R 76 section 4.2.1.
   d. Detection of significant fault (OIML R 76 section 4.14.9).
   e. Disturbances (OIML R 76 section 5.2).
   f. External Equipment (OIML R 76 section 5.3.6).

8. It was discussed and supported by several countries that manufactures data would not be used in the CPR at this time.

Impartiality and "conflict of interest" was discussed by the CPR and will also be addressed in the peer assessment training. It is already part of ILAC. Also, there are provisions in OIML to appeal the make-up of the peer review team.

9. On both peer review and ILAC audits, and a metrological expert will be part of the evaluation team along with the quality system expert(s).

10. Australia reported problems with their bi lateral agreements are caused by lack of clarification on functionality tests.

11. Extra tests performed by the Issuing Authority are listed on the OIML Test Report, not the OIML Certificate.

12. There was a distinction between "tests" and "examinations." In all cases of the MAA, an instrument will have to be submitted to the accepting country for "evaluation" (sealing, ID, tare performance as opposed to tare tests, additional equipment, etc.).

13. There appears to be no concerns about SI and inch-pound units.

14. Some OIML testing labs will not test to Class III L/III HD

15. Regarding peer assessments, a question was asked if the United States could evaluate the NTEP lab(s)? The response from BIML was yes, with the use of 17025 or equivalent criteria and consultation with the CPR.

16. How may the U.S./Canada mutual recognition be affected if the United States chooses not to participate while Canada does?

MORE INFORMATION ABOUT International Laboratory Accreditation Cooperation (ILAC)

ILAC is the peak international authority on laboratory accreditation, with a membership consisting of accreditation bodies and affiliated organizations throughout the world. It is involved with the development of laboratory accreditation practices and procedures, the promotion of laboratory accreditation as a trade facilitation tool, the assistance of developing accreditation systems, and the recognition of competent test and calibration facilities around the globe. ILAC actively cooperates with other relevant international bodies in pursuing these aims.

Currently, 47 laboratory accreditation bodies of ILAC have signed the multi-lateral, mutual recognition arrangement (the "ILAC Arrangement") to promote the acceptance of accredited test and calibration data. (A list of these signatories is printed at the end of this brochure and can also be found on the ILAC website at www.ilac.org).

The United States is a "member" of ILAC. The following U.S. accreditation bodies are recognized by ILAC.

- American Association for Laboratory Accreditation (A2LA)
  SCOPE: Testing and Calibration

- National Voluntary Laboratory Accreditation program (NVLAP)
  SCOPE: Testing and Calibration

- International Accreditation Service, Inc (IAS)
  SCOPE: Testing and Calibration

NCWM 90th Annual Meeting
July 10-14, 2005 – Orlando, FL

Attendee List

Cary Ainsworth
c/o USDA GIPSA
75 Spring Street, #230
Atlanta, GA 30303-3309
(404)562-5840, FAX: (404)562-5848
Email: L.Cary.Ainsworth@usda.gov

Mahesh Albuquerque
Division of Oil and Public Safety
633 17th Street, Suite 500
Denver, CO 80202-3660
(303)318-8533, FAX: (303)318-8518
Email: mehesh.albuquerque@state.co.us

Ross Andersen
New York Bureau of Weights & Measures
10B Airline Drive
Albany, NY 12235
(518)457-3146, FAX: (518)457-5693
Email: ross.andersen@agmkt.state.ny.us

Lanny Arnold
Kentucky Department of Agriculture
107 Corporate Drive
Frankfort, KY 40601
(502)573-0282, FAX: (502)573-0303
Email: lanny.arnold@kyagr.com

F. Michael Belue
Belue Associates Court View Towers
201 North Pine, Suite 111A
Florence, AL 35630
(256)768-9917, FAX: (256)768-9912
Email: Bassoc@aol.com

Joe Benavides
Texas Department of Agriculture
1700 North Congress Avenue, Stephen F. Austin Building, 11th Floor
Austin, TX 78711
(512)463-7401, FAX: (512)463-8225
Email: joe.benavides@agr.state.tx.us

Celeste Bennett
Michigan Department of Agriculture
940 Venture Lane
Williamston, MI 48895
(517)655-8202, FAX: (517)655-8303
Email: bennettc9@michigan.gov

Linda Bernetich
NCWM
15245 Shady Grove Road, Suite 130
Rockville, MD 20850
(240)632-9454, FAX: (301)990-9771
Email: lbernetich@mgmtsol.com

Tom Bloemer
Kentucky Department of Agriculture
107 Corporate Drive
Frankfort, KY 40601
(502)573-0282, FAX: (502)573-0303
Email: tom.bloemer@kyagr.com

Greg Boers
California Division of Measurement Standards
6790 Florin Perkins Road, Suite 100
Sacramento, CA 95828
(916)229-3018, FAX: (916)229-3015
Email: gboers@cdfa.ca.gov

Dennis F. Bray
Alameda County
224 West Winton Avenue, Room 184
Hayward, CA 94544
(510)670-5232, FAX: (510)783-3928
Email: dennis.bray@acgov.org

Norman R. Brucker
Precision Measurement Standards, Inc.
1665 135th Street West
Rosemount, MN 55068
(651)423-3241, FAX: (651)322-7938
Email: sharnoma@mninter.net

Mark Buccelli
State of Minnesota, Weights and Measures
2277 Highway 36
Roseville, MN 55113
(651)628-6850, FAX: (651)639-4014
Email: mark.buccelli@state.mn.us

Gerald A. Buendel
Washington Department of Agriculture
PO Box 42560
Olympia, WA 98504-2560
(360)902-1856, FAX: (360)902-2086
Email: jbuendel@agr.wa.gov

Tina G. Butcher
NIST Building 820,
100 Bureau Drive MS 2600
Gaithersburg, MD 20899-2600
(301)975-2196, FAX: (301)926-0647
Email: tina.butcher@nist.gov

Jerry W. Butler
North Carolina Department of Agriculture
1050 Mail Service Center
Raleigh, NC 27699-1050
(919)733-3313, FAX: (919)715-0524
Email: jerry.butler@ncmail.net

Joe Buxton
Daniel Measurement & Control
19267 Hwy 301
North Statesboro, GA 30461
(912)489-0253, FAX: (912)489-0264
Email: joe.buxton@emersonprocess.com

Judy Cardin
Wisconsin Dept. of Agri. & Consumer Protect.
PO Box 8911,
2811 Agriculture Drive
Madison, WI 53708-8911
(608)224-4945, FAX: (608)224 4939
Email: judy.cardin@datcp.state.wi.us

Loretta Carey
U.S. Food and Drug Administration
5100 Paint Branch Parkway
College Park, MD 20740
(301)436-1799, FAX: (301)436-2639
Email: lcarey@cfsan.fda.gov

Stacy K. Carlsen
Marin County Weights & Measures
1682 Novato Boulevard, Ste 150-A
Novato, CA 94947-7021
(415)499-6700, FAX: (415)499-7543
Email: scarlsen@co.marin.ca.us

Charles H. Carroll
Massachusetts Division of Standards
One Ashburton Place, Room 1115
Boston, MA 02108
(617)727-3480, FAX: (617)727-5705
Email: Charles.Carroll@state.ma.us

NCWM 90th Annual Meeting
July 10-14, 2005 – Orlando, FL

Attendee List

James P. Cassidy, Jr.
Cambridge Weights & Measures
831 Massachusetts Ave
Cambridge, MA 02139
(617)349-6133, FAX: (617)349-6134
Email: jcassidy@CambridgeMA.gov

Mike Cleary
California Division of Measurement
 Standards
6790 Florin Perkins Road, Suite 100
Sacramento, CA 95828
(916)229-3000, FAX: (916)229-3026
Email: mcleary@cdfa.ca.gov

Belinda Collins
NIST
100 Bureau Drive
Gaithersburg, MD 20899-2000
(301)975-4500, FAX: (301)975-2183
Email: belinda.collins@nist.gov

Rodney Cooper
Actaris Neptune
1310 Emerald Road
Greenwood, SC 29646
(864)942-2226, FAX: (864)223-0341
Email: rcooper@greenwood.actaris.com

Kenneth Deitzler
Bureau of Ride & Measurement
 Standards
2301 North Cameron Street
Harrisburg, PA 17110-9408
(717)787-9089, FAX: (717)783-4158
Email: kdeitzler@state.pa.us

James Dudash
Bureau of Ride & Measurement
 Standards
2301 North Cameron Street
Harrisburg, PA 17110
(570)433-2640, FAX: (570)433-4770
Email: jdudash@state.pa.us

Jerry Flanders
Georgia Department of Agriculture
Agriculture Bldg.,
19 MLK Drive, Rm 321
Atlanta, GA 30334
(404)656-3605, FAX: (404)656-9648
Email: jflander@agr.state.ga.us

Stephen Casto
West Virginia Weights & Measures,
 Division of Labor
570 McCorkle Avenue West
St. Albans, WV 25177
(304)722-0602, FAX: (304)722-0605
Email: scasto@labor.state.wv.us

William Cobb
West Virginia Weights & Measures,
 Division of Labor
570 McCorkle Avenue West
St. Albans, WV 25177
(304)722-0602, FAX: (304)722-0605
Email: wcobb@labor.state.wv.us

Steven E. Cook
NIST, Weights & Measures Division
100 Bureau Drive
MS 2600 Building 820/Rm 223
Gaithersburg, MD 20899-2600
(301)975-4003, FAX: (301)926-0647
Email: steven.cook@nist.gov

Mark P. Coyne
Brockton Weights & Measures
45 School Street, City Hall
Brockton, MA 02301-9927
(508)580-7120, FAX: (508)580-7173
Email: mcoyne@ci.brockton.ma.us

Vicky Dempsey
Montgomery County Weights &
 Measures
451 West Third Street
P.O. Box 972
Dayton, OH 45422-1027
(937)225-6309, FAX: (937)224-3927
Email: dempseyv@mcohio.org

David Edsall
County of Sussex
150 Morris Turnpike
Newton, NJ 07860
(973)579-0360, FAX: Email:
Email:

Darrell E. Flocken
Mettler-Toledo, Inc.
1150 Dearborn Drive
Worthington, OH 43085
(614)438-4393, FAX: (614)438-4355
Email: darrell.flocken@mt.com

Samuel Chang
ZEMIC
(USA) Inc.
830 Commercial Avenue
San Gabriel, CA 91776
(562)464-9416, FAX: (562)464-9415
Email: SEDJC@aol.com

Thomas Coleman
NIST
100 Bureau Drive
MS 2600 Building 820
Gaithersburg, MD 20899-2600
(301)975-4868, FAX: (301)926-0647
Email: t.coleman@nist.gov

Clark Cooney
Oregon Measurement Standards
635 Capitol Street, N.E.
Salem, OR 97301-2532
(503)986-4677, FAX: (503)986-4784
Email: ccooney@oda.state.or.us

Richard L. Davis
Georgia-Pacific
1915 Marathon Avenue
Neenah, WI 54957-0899
(920)729-8174, FAX: (920)729-8089
Email: richard.davis@gapac.com

G.W. (Wes) Diggs
Virginia Product & Industry Standards
PO Box 1163 Rm 402
Richmond, VA 23218
(804)786-2476, FAX: (804)786-1571
Email: Wes.Diggs@vdacs.virginia.gov

Chuck Ehrlich
NIST
100 Bureau Drive
MS 2600 Building 820
Gaithersburg, MD 20899-2600
(301)975-4834, FAX: (301)926-0647
Email: charles.ehrlich@nist.gov

Kurt Floren
Agricultural Commissioner/Director of
 Weights & Measures
12300 Lower Azusa Road
Arcadia, CA 91006
(626)575-5451, FAX: (626)350-3243
Email: KurtF@acwm.co.la.ca.us

NCWM 90th Annual Meeting
July 10-14, 2005 – Orlando, FL

Attendee List

Maurice J. Forkert
Tuthill Transfer Systems
8825 Aviation Drive
Fort Wayne, IN 46809
(260)747-7529, FAX: (260)747-7064
Email: Mforkert@tuthill.com

Carol P. Fulmer
South Carolina Department of
   Agriculture
PO Box 11280
Columbia, SC 29211
(803)737-9690, FAX: (803)737-9703
Email: cfulmer@scda.sc.gov

Thomas Geiler
Town of Barnstable
200 Main Street
Hyannis, MA 02601
(508)862-4670, FAX: (508)778-2412
Email:
   Tom.Geiler@town.barnstable.ma.us

Steve P. Gill
Missouri Department of Agriculture
P.O. Box 630
Jefferson City, MO 65102-0630
(573)751-4278, FAX: (573)751-0281
Email: steve.gill@mda.mo.gov

Steven T. Grabski
Bureau of W & M, Div. of Measurement
   Standards
2150 Frazer Avenue
Sparks, NV 89431
(775)688-1166, FAX: (775)688-2533
Email: sgrabski@govmail.state.nv.us

Christopher B. Guay
Procter & Gamble Co
2 Procter & Gamble Plaza
Cincinnati, OH 45202
(513)983-0530, FAX: (513)983-8984
Email: guay.cb@pg.com

Charles Hackett
City of Kokomo Weights and Measures
100 South Union Street
Kokomo, IN 46901
(765)456-7466, FAX: (765)456-7571
Email: chackett@cityofkokomo.org

Ken L. Fraley
Oklahoma Bureau of Standards
2800 N. Lincoln Blvd.
Oklahoma City, OK 73105
(405)522-5459, FAX: (405)521-4912
Email: kfraley@oda.state.ok.us

John Gaccione
Westchester County Weights &
   Measures
112 East Post Road, 4th Floor
White Plains, NY 10601
(914)995-2160, FAX: (914)995-3115
Email: jpg4@westchestergov.com

William GeMeiner
Union Pacific Railroad
1400 Douglas, Stop 0910
Omaha, NE 68179
(402)544-6248, FAX:
Email: wgemeiner@up.com

Paul Glowacki
Murray Equipment, Inc.
2515 Charleston Place
Fort Wayne, IN 46808
(260)484-0382, FAX: (260)484-9230
Email:
   pglowacki@murrayequipment.com

Maxwell Gray
Florida Dept. of Agriculture &
   Consumer Services
3125 Conner Boulevard, Lab 2
Tallahassee, FL 32399-1650
(850)488-9140, FAX: (850)922-6064
Email: graym@doacs.state.fl.us

John T. Gurkin, Jr.
North Carolina Department of
   Agriculture
1050 Mail Service Center
Raleigh, NC 27699-1050
(919)733-3313, FAX: Email:

Carolyn Hall
Foster Farms
P.O. Box 457
Livingston, CA 95334
(209)394-7901 x4348
FAX: (209)852-0300
Email: hallcd@fosterfarms.com

Roger Frazier
Area Investigator Supervisor
800 Kenwood
Benton, AR 72015
(501)570-1159, FAX: (501)562-7605
Email: roger.frazier@aspb.state.ar.us

Mark Galletta
Nestle USA
800 North Brand Blvd
Glendale, CA 91203
(818)549-6089, FAX: (818)637-3348
Email: mark.galletta@us.nestle.com

Steve Giguere
Maine Quality Assurance & Regulations
28 State House Station
Augusta, ME 04333
(207)287-3841, FAX: (207)287-5576
Email: steve.giguere@state.me.us

Joe Gomez
New Mexico Department of Agriculture
MSC 3170, PO Box 30005
Las Cruces, NM 88003-8005
(505)646-1616, FAX: (505)646-2361
Email: jgomez@nmda.nmsu.edu

Michael F. Grenier
New Hampshire Department of
   Agriculture Markets & Food
PO Box 2042
Concord, NH 03302-2042
(603)271-3709, FAX: (603)271-1109
Email: mgrenier@agr.state.nh.us

Brett Gurney
Utah Department of Agriculture & Food
P.O. Box 146500
Salt Lake City, UT 84114-6500
(801)538-7158, FAX: (801)538-4949
Email: bgurney@utah.gov

Jonathan Handy
Colorado Department of Agriculture
3125 Wyandot Street
Denver, CO 80211
(303)477-4220, FAX: (303)477-4248
Email: Jonathan.Handy@ag.state.co.us

NCWM 90th Annual Meeting
July 10-14, 2005 – Orlando, FL

Attendee List

Krister K. Hard af Segerstad
IKEA Wholesale Inc.
496 West Germantown Pike
Plymouth Meeting, PA 19462
(610)834-0180, FAX: (610)834-0872
Email: krister@memo.IKEA.com

Scott Henry
NCR Corporation
2651 Satellite Blvd
Duluth, GA
(770)623-7543, FAX: (770)479-1174
Email: scott.henry@ncr.com

Stephen Hill
Orange County Weights & Measures
1750 S. Douglass Rd, BldgD
Anaheim, CA 92806-6031
(714)447-7100, FAX: (714)567-6203
Email: steve.hill@pfrd.ocgov.com

Abram Huey
Micro Motion, Inc.
192 Montvale Drive
Hoschton, GA 30548
(706)654-0009, FAX: (706)654-0010
Email:
    chuck.huey@emersonprocess.com

Grace Jan, CMP
NCWM
15245 Shady Grove Road, Suite 130
Rockville, MD 20850
(240)632-9454, FAX: (301)990-9771
Email: gjan@mgmtsol.com

Dennis Johannes
California Division of Measurement
    Standards
6790 Florin Perkins Road, Suite 100
Sacramento, CA 95828
(916)229-3000, FAX: (916)229-3026
Email: DJohannes@cdfa.ca.gov

Alan Johnston
Measurement Canada Main Bldg No. 3,
    Tunney's Pasture
Ottawa, Ontario K1A0C9 Canada
(613)952-0655, FAX: (613)957-1265
Email: johnston.alan@ic.gc.ca

Georgia Harris
NIST
100 Bureau Drive
Building 820, MS 2600
Gaithersburg, MD 20899-2600
(301)975-4014, FAX: (301)926-0647
Email: gharris@nist.gov

Maureen Henzler
Kansas Department of Agriculture
2510 S.W. Gainsboro Rd
Topeka, KS 66614
(785)862-2415, FAX: (785)862-2460
Email: mhenzler@kda.state.ks.us

Dean Hill
Agri-Products, Inc.
P.O. Box 12728
Tallehassee, FL 32309
(850)668-0006, FAX: (850)668-9800
Email: dhill@suncoastbedding.com

Jeff Humphreys
Los Angeles County Weights &
    Measures
11012 Garfield Avenue, Building A
South Gate, CA 90280
(562)940-8922, FAX: (562)861-0278
Email: jeffh@acwm.co.la.ca.us

Randy Jennings
State of Tennessee
Box 40627, Melrose Station
Nashville, TN 37204
(615)837-5147, FAX: (615)837-5335
Email: randy.jennings@state.tn.us

Gordon W. Johnson
Gilbarco, Inc.
7300 West Friendly Avenue
Greensboro, NC 27420
(336)547-5375, FAX: (336)547-5079
Email: Gordon.Johnson@gilbarco.com

Zina Juroch
Pier 1 Imports
100 Pier 1 Place
Fort Worth, TX 76102
(817)252-8348, FAX: (817)252-6220
Email: zmjuroch@pier1.com

Ronald G. Hayes
Missouri Department of Agriculture
P.O. Box 630
Jefferson City, MO 65102
(573)751-2922, FAX: (573)751-8307
Email: Ron.Hayes@mda.mo.gov

Tyler Hicks
Oklahoma Dept. of Agriculture
P.O. Box 528804
Oklahoma City, OK 73152
(405)205-2697, FAX: (405)522-5885
Email: thicks@oda.state.ok.us

Carol T. Hockert
State of Minnesota, Weights and
    Measures
2277 Highway 36
Roseville, MN 55113
(651)215-5823, FAX: (651)639-4014
Email: carol.hockert@state.mn.us

Normand Jacques
Kilotech
3245 J.B. Deschamps
Montreal, Quebec H8T3E4 CANADA
(877)328-5988, FAX: (877)485-9210
Email: njacques@kilotech.com

Rafael Jimenez
Association of American Railroads
P.O. Box 11130, 55500 D.O.T. Road
Pueblo, CO 81001
(719)584-0691, FAX: (719)584-0770
Email: rafael_jimenez@ttci.aar.com

Raymond Johnson
New Mexico Department of Agriculture
MSC 3170, PO Box 30005
Las Cruces, NM 88003-8005
(505)646-1616, FAX: (505)646-2361
Email: rjohnson@nmda.nmsu.edu

Jack Kane
Montana Bureau of Weights & Measures
P.O. Box 200516
Helena, MT 59620-0516
(406)841-2240, FAX: (406)841-2060
Email: jkane@state.mt.us

NCWM 90th Annual Meeting
July 10-14, 2005 – Orlando, FL

Attendee List

Michael J. Keilty
Endress & Hauser Flowtec AG
2350 Endress Place
Greenwood, IN 46143
(317)535-2745, FAX: (317)535-1341
Email: michael.keilty@us.endress.com

Mark Knowles
HBM Inc.
19 Bartlett Street
Marlboro, MA 01752
(508)624-4500, FAX: (508)485-7480
Email: mark.knowles@hbm.com

Leon Lammers
Avery Weigh-Tronix
1000 Armstrong Drive
Fairmont, MN 56031-1439
(800)533-0456, FAX: (507)238-8255
Email: leon.lammers@weigh-tronix.com

Brian Lemon
Competition Bureau Canada 400 St
  Mary Avenue, 4th Floor
Winnipeg, Manitoba R3C 4K5 Canada
(204)983-8911, FAX: (204)984-2658
Email: lemon.brian@cb-bc.gc.ca

Harvey Lodge
Dunbar Manufacturing
2400 Egg Harbor Road
Lindenwold, NJ 08021
(609)714-2222, FAX: (609)714-1313
Email: pstrobl@espkits.com

J. Arturo Macias, Jr.
Arizona Dept. of Weights & Measures
4425 West Olive Avenue, Suite 134
Glendale, AZ 85302
(623)463-9935, FAX: (602)255-1950
Email: amacias@azdwm.gov

Judy Markoe
NCWM
15245 Shady Grove Road, Suite 130
Rockville, MD 20850
(240)632-9454, FAX: (301)990-9771
Email: jmarkoe@mgmtsol.com

Michael Kelley
Wal-Mart Stores, Inc.
6 Chelsea Lane
Bellavista, AR 72714
(479)644-4833, FAX:
Email: mkelly1@wal-mart.com

Dan Kushnir
Seraphin Test Measure
30 Indel Avenue
Rancocas, NJ 08073
(609)267-0922, FAX:
Email:

Robert L. Land
Anderson Weights & Measures
120 East 8th Street
Anderson, IN 46016
(765)648-6186, FAX: (765)648-5917
Email: rland@cityofanderson.com

Paul A. Lewis, Sr.
Rice Lake Weighing Systems
230 West Coleman Street PO Box 272
Rice Lake, WI 54868-2404
(715)234-3494 x5322
 FAX: (715)234-6967
Email: paulew@rlws.com

Todd R. Lucas
Ohio Department of Agriculture
8995 East Main Street, Building 5
Reynoldsburg, OH 43068
(614)995-0641, FAX: (614)728-6424
Email: lucas@mail.agri.state.oh.us

Keith L. Mahan
Merced County Weights and Measures
2139 Wardrobe Avenue
Merced, CA 95340-6495
(209)385-7431, FAX: (209)725-3961
Email: kmahan@co.merced.ca.us

Jeffrey X. Mason
DC Government Weights & Measures
1110 U Street SE
Washington, DC 20020
(202)698-2130, FAX: (202)698-2148
Email: jeffrey.mason@dc.gov

Ted Kingsbury
Measurement Canada
Standards Bldg #4, Tunney's Pasture,
  Holland Ave.
Ottawa, Ontario K1A0C9 CANADA
(613)941-8919, FAX: (613)952-1736
Email: kingsbury.ted@ic.gc.ca

Gary Lameris
Hobart Corporation
701 South Ridge Avenue
Troy, OH 45374
(937)332-3053, FAX: (937)332-3007
Email: gary.lameris@hobartcorp.com

Stephen Langford
Cardinal Scale Manufacturing Co.
203 East Daugherty, P.O. Box 151
Webb City, MO 64870
(417)673-4631, FAX: (417)673-5001
Email: slangford@cardet.com

Boon Lim
Virtual Measurement & Control
3196 Coffey Lane, Suite 604
Santa Rosa, CA 95403
(707)573-3111, FAX: (707)573-3113
Email: boon@virtualmc.com

L. Edward Luthy
Brechbuhler Scales Inc
1424 Scale Street SW
Canton, OH 44706
(330)453-2424, FAX: (330)453-5322
Email: eluthy@brechbuhler.com

Steven Malone
Nebraska Division of Weights &
  Measures
301 Centennial Mall South, Box 94757
Lincoln, NE 68509-4757
(402)471-4292, FAX: (402)471-2759
Email: stevenam@agr.state.ne.us

Gale Mason
U.S. Dept. of Agriculture, Grain
  Inspection Packers and Stockyards
  Administration
Stop 3646, 1400 Independence Ave.,
  S.W., Room 2430
Washington, DC 20250-3646
(202)690-2215, FAX: (202)690-3207
Email: gale.l.mason@usda.gov

NCWM 90th Annual Meeting
July 10-14, 2005 – Orlando, FL

Attendee List

Vernon Lee Massey
Shelby County Weights & Measures
157 Poplar Suite 402
Memphis, TN 38103
(901)545-3920, FAX: (901)545-3906
Email: vmassey@co.shelby.tn.us

Ashok Mehrotra
SGS North America
5209 Linbar Drive
Nashville, TN 37211
(615)831-1044, FAX: (615)831-1236
Email: ashok_mehrotra@sgs.com

Charlie Mitchell
Total Petrochemicals, Inc.
P.O. Box 849
Port Arthur, TX 77641-0849
(409)963-6885, FAX: (409)962-3458
Email: charlie.mitchell@total.com

Karl Newell
1415 Sykes Creek Drive
Merritt Island, FL 32953
(407)453-1492, FAX: (407)453-1492
Email: kgnewell@worldnet.att.net

O.R. "Pete" O'Bryan
Foster Farms
P.O. Box 457
Livingston, CA 95334-9900
(209)656-5049, FAX: (209)656-5055
Email: obryanp@fosterfarms.com

Don Onwiler
Nebraska Division of Weights & Measures
301 Centennial Mall South, Box 94757
Lincoln, NE 68509
(402)471-4292, FAX: (402)471-2759
Email: donwiler@agr.ne.gov

Terence McBride
Memphis Weights & Measures 590 Washington St
Memphis, TN 38105
(901)528-2905, FAX: (901)528-2948
Email: terence.mcbride@cityofmemphis.org

Yukinobu Miki
Advanced Industrial Science and Technology (AIST)
Tsukuba Central 3-9, 1-1-1
Umezono Tsukuba, JAPAN
305-8563 81-298-4266
FAX: 81-298-4334
Email: y.miki@aist.go.jp

Robert Murnane, Jr.
Seraphin Test Measure/Pemberton
PO Box 227 30 Indel Avenue
Rancocas, NJ 08073-0227
(609)267-0922, FAX: (609)261-2546
Email: rmurnane@seraphinusa.com

Tara Nordlander
NCWM
15245 Shady Grove Road, Suite 130
Rockville, MD 20850
(240)632-9454, FAX: (301)990-9771
Email: tnordlander@mgmtsol.com

Lucila Ohno-Machado
Harvard University 19 Southwood
Southborough, MA 01772
(508)485-7057, FAX: (617)739-3672
Email: machado@dsg.harvard.edu

Henry Oppermann
NIST Building 820, 100 Bureau Drive MS 2600
Gaithersburg, MD 20899-2600
(301)975-5507, FAX: (301)926-0647
Email: wmconsulting@cox.net

Robert McGrath
Boston ISD Weights & Measures
1010 Massachusetts Ave
Boston, MA 02118-2606
(617)961-3376, FAX: (617)635-5383
Email: robert.mcrath.isd@ci.boston.ma.us

Richard Miller
FMC Measurement Solutions
1602 Wagner Avenue, P.O. Box 10428
Erie, PA 16514
(814)898-5286, FAX: (814)899-3414
Email: rich.miller@fmcti.com

Kazuo Neda
Advanced Industrial Science & Technology
2-6-20, Ogimachi, Kita-ku ,
Osaka 530-0025 Japan
+81-6-6312-3173
FAX: +81-6-6312-0524
Email: kt@neda@aist.go.jp

Neal J. Nover
Nover Engelstein & Assoc., Inc./ WinWam Software AtriumExec. Sts
3000 Atrium Way, Ste 2203
Mt. Laurel, NJ 08054-3910
(856)273-6988, FAX: (856)751-0559
Email: sales@winwam.com

Arlyn Oman
IA Dept. of Agriculture
P.O. Box 73
Kirkman, IA 51447
(712)766-3331, FAX: (515)725-1459
Email: arlyn.oman@idals.state.ia.us

Vincent R. Orr
ConAgra Foods Six ConAgra Drive, PDL-405
Omaha, NE 68102
(402)595-6248, FAX: (402)595-7660
Email: vince.orr@conagrafoods.com

NCWM 90th Annual Meeting
July 10-14, 2005 – Orlando, FL

Attendee List

Nicholas J. Owens
Stark County Weights & Measures
110 Central Plaza South, Ste 220
Canton, OH 44702
(330)451-7356, FAX: (330)451-7630
Email: mowens412@aol.com

Johnny Parrish
Brodie Meter Co., LLC
P.O. Box 450
Statesboro, GA 30459
(912)489-0203, FAX: (912)489-0298
Email: johnny.parrish@brodiemeter.com

Edward A. Payne, Jr.
Maryland Department of Agriculture
50 Harry S Truman Parkway
Annapolis, MD 21401
(410)841-5790, FAX: (410)841-2765
Email: payneea@mda.state.md.us

Edd Price
AAA Tank Testers
5655 Golf Club Drive
Brazelton, GA 30517
(706)654-1580, FAX: (706)654-1509
Email:

David Quinn
ISWM 4153 Telfair Lane SE
Southport, NC 28461
(910)253-1424, FAX: (910)253-1424
Email: dave.w.quinn@mindspring.com

Robert A. Reinfried
Scale Manufacturers Association
6724 Lone Oak Boulevard
Naples, FL 34109
(239)514-3441, FAX: (239)514-3470
Email: bob@scalemanufacturers.org

Bill Ripka
Thermo Electron
501 90th Ave NW
Minneapolis, MN 55433
(763)783-2664, FAX: (763)780-1537
Email: bill.ripka@thermo.com

Stephen Pahl
Texas Department of Agriculture
1700 North Congress Avenue, Stephen
    F. Austin Building, 11th Floor
Austin, TX 78701
(512)463-7483, FAX: (512)463-8225
Email: stephen.pahl@agr.state.tx.us

Stephen Patoray
NCWM
15245 Shady Grove Road, Suite 130
Rockville, MD 20850
(240)632-9454, FAX: (301)990-9771
Email: spatoray@mgmtsol.com

Michael S. Pinagel
Michigan Department of Agriculture
940 Venture Lane
Williamston, MI 48895
(517)655-8202 ext 301
FAX: (517)655-8303
Email: PinagelM@michigan.gov

Gale Prince
Kroger Company
1014 Vine Street
Cincinnati, OH 45202-1100
(513)762-4209, FAX: (513)762-4372
Email: gale.prince@kroger.com

Mark Quisenberry
Sutter Co Weights & Measures
142 Garden Highway
Yuba City, CA 95991
(530)822-7500, FAX: (530)822-7510
Email: sutterag@co.sutter.ca.us

Robert E. Reynolds
Downstream Alternatives Inc
2259 Harwood Street
South Bend, IN 46614
(574)250-2811, FAX: (574)231-8975
Email: rreynolds-dai@earthlink.net

Alfonso Salinas
Lake County Weights & Measures
2293 North Main Street
Crown Point, IN 46307
(219)755-3680, FAX: (219)755-3064
Email: weightsandmeasures@yahoo.com

Beth W. Palys, CAE
NCWM
15245 Shady Grove Road, Suite 130
Rockville, MD 20850
(240)632-9454, FAX: (301)990-9771
Email: bpalys@mgmtsol.com

Larry Patton
Lake County Weights & Measures
2900 West 93rd Avenue
Crown Point, IN 46307
(219)755-3680, FAX: (219)755-3739
Email: weightsandmeasures@yahoo.com

Marvin Pound
Georgia Department of Agriculture
815 Milledeville Hwy
Devereux, GA 31087
(404)656-3605, FAX: (404)656-9648
Email: mpound@agr.state.ga.us

Kevin E. Pyle
Hamilton County Auditor's Office
138 East Court Street Room 501
Cincinnati, OH 45202
(513)946-4100, FAX: (513)946-4124
Email:
    kevin.pyle@auditor.hamilton-co.org

David Rajala
Veeder-Root Company
P.O. Box 1673
Altoona, PA 16603-1673
(814)696-8125, FAX: (814)695-7605
Email: drajala@veeder.com

Ralph A. Richter
NIST Building 820, 100 Bureau Drive
    MS 2600
Gaithersburg, MD 20899-2600
(301)975-4025, FAX: (301)926-0647
Email: ralph.richter@nist.gov

Jeffrey Santarpio
Dunbar Manufacturing, LLC
2400 Egg Harbor Road
Lindenwold, NJ 08021
(856)346-0666, FAX: (856)346-0016
Email: jeff.santarpio@dunbarusa.com

NCWM 90th Annual Meeting
July 10-14, 2005 – Orlando, FL

Attendee List

Ronen Schneiderovitch
Kilotech Inc.
3245 J.B. Deschamps
Lachine, QC H8T3E4 Canada
877-328-5988, FAX: 877-485-9210
Email: rschneider@kilotech.com

David Sefcik
Whole Foods Market
6015 Executive Boulevard
Rockville, MD 20852
(301)984-2093, FAX: (301)984-2068
Email: david.sefcik@wholefoods.com

Michael J. Sikula
New York Bureau of Weights &
 Measures Building 7A State Campus
Albany, NY 12235
(518)457-3452, FAX: (518)457-2552
Email: mike.sikula@agmkt.state.ny.us

Steven B. Steinborn
Hogan & Hartson
555 13th Street, NW
Washington, DC 20004
(202)637-5969, FAX: (202)637-5910
Email: sbsteinborn@hhlaw.com

William Strelioff
Norac
803 46th Street
East Saskatoon, SK S7K 0X1 Canada
(306)664-6711, FAX:
Email: bill@norac.ca

William H. Sveum
Kraft Foods North America, Inc.
910 Mayer Avenue
Madison, WI 53704
(608)285-4280, FAX: (608)285-6288
Email: wsveum@kraft.com

Michael P. Tracchia
City of Beverly 32 Essex Street
Beverly, MA 01915
(978)921-6062 ext.114,
FAX: (978)922-8329
Email: mtracchia@beverlyma.gov

Byron C. School
USDA, GIPSA, FMD, PPB
1400 Independence Ave. S.W. STOP
 3630
Washington, DC 20250-3630
(202)720-0280, FAX: (202)720-1015
Email: Byron.C.School@.usda.gov

Hratch Semerjian
NIST
100 Bureau Drive, MS 1000
Gaithersburg, MD 20899
(301)975-2300, FAX: (301)869-8972
Email: hratch@nist.gov

Chet Siwik
RdF Corporation
23 Elm Avenue
Hudson, NH 03051
(603)882-5195, FAX: (603)882-6925
Email: csiwik@rdfcorp.com

Randy Stevens
Norac, Inc.
2216 Post Oak Drive
Sherman, TX 75092
(903)814-9173, FAX:
Email: randy.stevens@digi.star.com

Lawrence J. Stump
Indiana Weights & Measures
PO Box 748
Upland, IN 46989
(317)356-7078, FAX: (317)351-2877
Email: lstump@isdh.state.in.us

Steven D. Sveum
Norac, Inc.
13915 Lake Drive Forest
Lake, MN 55025
(651)982-0641, FAX: (651)982-0642
Email: steve@norac.ca

James C. Truex
Ohio Department of Agriculture
8995 East Main Street, Building 5
Reynoldsburg, OH 43068-3399
(614)728-6290, FAX: (614)728-6424
Email: truex@mail.agri.state.oh.us

Alex Schuettenberg
ConocoPhillips Petroleum 148 AL,
 Phillips Research Center
Bartlesville, OK 74004
(918)661-3563, FAX: (918)661-8060
Email:
alex.schuettenberg@conocophillips.com

Agatha Shields
Franklin County Weights & Measures
373 S. High Street, 21st Floor
Columbus, OH 43215
(614)462-7380, FAX: (614)462-3111
Email: aashield@franklincountyohio.gov

Sean Sproul
SAS Consulting Inc.
6501 S. Douglas Hwy., Lot #8
Gillette, WY 82718
(307)686-0324, FAX: (307)686-0324
Email:

Louis E. Straub
Fairbanks Scales, Inc.
3056 Irwin Drive
Southport, NC 28461
(910)253-3250, FAX:
Email: strauble@yahoo.com

Richard C. Suiter
NIST, Weights & Measures Division
Building 820, 100 Bureau Drive MS
2600 Gaithersburg, MD 20899-2600
(301)975-4406, FAX: (301)926-0647
Email: rsuiter@nist.gov

Aves D. Thompson
Alaska Div of Measurement
 Standards/CVE
12050 Industry Way Bldg O, Ste. 6
Anchorage, AK 99515
(907)341-3210, FAX: (907)341-3220
Email: Aves_Thompson@dot.state.ak.us

Larry Turberville
1150 Riverton RoseTrail
Cherokee, AL 35616
(256)360-2609, FAX: (256)360-2609
Email: larryturberville@cherokeetel.net

NCWM 90th Annual Meeting
July 10-14, 2005 – Orlando, FL

Attendee List

Manuel Villicana
Kern County Dept. of Ag&
  Measurement Standards
1001 South Mount Vernon Ave.
Bakersfield, CA 93307
(661)868-6300, FAX: (661)868-6301
Email: william@co.kern.ca.us

John Walsh
Framingham Weights & Measures
150 Concord Street
Framingham, MA 01702
(508)626-9113, FAX: (508)626-8991
Email: jbw@framinghamma.org

JoAnn Waterfield
USDA
1400 Independence Ave, Ste 2055
Washington, DC 20250
(202)720-7051, FAX: (202)205-9237
Email: joann.waterfield@usda.gov

Juana Williams
NIST
Building 820, 100 Bureau Drive MS
2600 Gaithersburg, MD 20899-2600
(301)975-3989, FAX: (301)926-0647
Email: juana.williams@nist.gov

Steve Wrigley
Brodie Meter LLC
19 Somerset
Statesboro, GA 30458
(912)489-0170, FAX:
Email: steven.wrigley@brodiemeter.com

Kristin Young
Colorado Department of Agriculture
3125 Wyandot Street
Denver, CO 80211
(303)477-4220, FAX: (303)477-4248
Email: kristin.young@ag.state.co.us

Gilles Vinet
Measurement Canada Standards Bldg
#4, Tunney's Pasture, Holland Ave.
Ottawa, Ontario K1A0C9 CANADA
(613)952-0657, FAX: (613)952-1736
Email: vinet.gilles@ic.gc.ca

Otto K. Warnlof
9705 Inaugural Way
Gaithersburg, MD 20886
(301)926-8155, FAX: (301)963-2871
Email: warnlof@aol.com

Steve Wildberger
Shimadzu Scientific Instruments
7102 Riverwood Drive
Columbia, MD 21046
(410)381-1227, FAX: (410)381-1222
Email: stwildberger@shimadzu.com

Cary Woodward
Hamilton County Weights & Measures
One Hamilton County Square
Noblesville, IN 46060
(317)403-0639, FAX: (317)776-8525
Email: ceewoody@msn.com

Russ Wyckoff
Oregon Measurement Standards
635 Capitol Street, N.E.
Salem, OR 97301-2532
(503)986-4767, FAX: (503)986-4784
Email: rwyckoff@oda.state.or.us

Thomas Vormittag
SGS - Minerals Services
PO Box 474
Kayenta, AZ 86033
(928)677-5006, FAX: (928)677-3273
Email: tvormittag@peabodyenergy.com

Irene B. Warnlof
9705 Inaugural Way
Gaithersburg, MD 20886
(301)926-8155, FAX:
 Email:

Robert G. Williams
Tennessee Dept. of Agriculture W&M
PO Box 40627 Melrose Station
Nashville, TN 37204-0627
(615)837-5109, FAX: (615)837-5015
Email: robert.g.williams@state.tn.us

Richard W. Wotthlie
Maryland Department of Agriculture
50 Harry S Truman Parkway
Annapolis, MD 21401
(410)841-5790, FAX: (410)841-2765
Email: wotthlrw@mda.state.md.us

Jennifer Yezak
National Association of State
  Department of Agriculture
1156 15th Street NW, Suite 1020
Washington, DC 20005
(202)296-9680, FAX: (202)296-9686
Email: Jennifer@nasda.org

NCWM 90th Annual Meeting
July 10-15, 2005 – Orlando, FL

Annual Meeting Guest Attendees

Carole Andersen	Sharon Oman
Dawn Beitzel	Peggy Onwiler
Marlene Belue	Phil Onwiler
Julie Anna Bonfield	Mark Onwiler
Carrie Beth Bonfield	Tim Onwiler
Sharon Brucker	Janessa Onwiler
Vicki Coleman	Jenny Owens
Cindy Deitzler	Austin Owens
G.W. Diggs	Jan Quisenberry
Lynn Dudash	Megan Quisenberry
Linda Forkert	Molly Quisenberry
Jean Fraley	Kathy Ripka
Linda Galletta	Peter Ripka
Karen Gill	Tim Ripka
Jose Gomez	Chuan San Sim
Diane Gomez	Debbie Straub
Anabel Hackett	Carol Suiter
Ryne Hackett	Phyllis Thompson
Joel Hackett	Aaron Thompson
Isaac Hayes	Barbara Tracchia
Marielle Jacques	Gillian Vormittag
Deana Johnson	Chris Vormittag
Joe Juroch	George Vormittag
Kristen Juroch	Ellen Walsh
Katherine Juroch	Suzanne Woodward
Rose Marie Lammers	Julie Woodward
Judy Mahan	Bonnie Wotthlie
Marcia Malone	Barb Wyckoff
Donnie Massey	Lauren Young
Loretta McBride